Engaging the Next Generation of Aviation Professionals

Engaging the Next Generation of Aviation Professionals is an edited volume that brings together a diverse set of academic and professional perspectives within the three themes of attracting, educating, and retaining the next generation of aviation professionals (NGAP). This compilation is the first academic work specifically targeting this critical issue.

The book presents a rich variety of perspectives, academic philosophies, and real-world examples. Submissions include brief case studies, longer scholarly works from respected academics, and professional reflections from individuals who have made important contributions to their field. The book includes academic chapters that explore the topic from a more theoretical standpoint yet are accessible and understandable to a professional audience. These are complemented by both broad and specific practice examples that describe initiatives and applications occurring in the industry around the three themes. All submissions include descriptive insights, experiences, and first-hand accounts of accomplishments, intended to support the work of other professionals managing NGAP issues.

This work will be valuable to anyone involved in attracting, educating, or retaining NGAP, including academics, operators, national and international regulators, and outreach coordinators, among many others.

Suzanne K. Kearns is an Associate Professor of Aviation at the University of Waterloo in Canada. She is a former aeroplane and helicopter pilot.

Timothy J. Mavin is an Associate Professor at Griffith University's School of Education and Professional Studies. He is a member of the Griffith Institute for Educational Research.

Steven Hodge is a Senior Lecturer at Griffith University's School of Education and Professional Studies and a member of the Griffith Institute for Educational Research.

Engaging the Next Generation of Aviation Professionals

Edited by Suzanne K. Kearns, Timothy J. Mavin and Steven Hodge

LONDON AND NEW YORK

First published 2020 by Routledge

2 Park Square, Milton Park, Abingdon, Oxon OX14 4RN

605 Third Avenue, New York, NY 10017

Routledge is an imprint of the Taylor & Francis Group, an informa business

First issued in paperback 2021

Copyright © 2020 selection and editorial matter, Suzanne K. Kearns, Timothy J. Mavin and Steven Hodge; individual chapters, the contributors

The right of Suzanne K. Kearns, Timothy J. Mavin and Steven Hodge to be identified as the authors of the editorial material, and of the authors for their individual chapters, has been asserted in accordance with sections 77 and 78 of the Copyright, Designs and Patents Act 1988.

All rights reserved. No part of this book may be reprinted or reproduced or utilised in any form or by any electronic, mechanical, or other means, now known or hereafter invented, including photocopying and recording, or in any information storage or retrieval system, without permission in writing from the publishers.

Notice:
Product or corporate names may be trademarks or registered trademarks, and are used only for identification and explanation without intent to infringe.

Publisher's Note

The publisher has gone to great lengths to ensure the quality of this reprint but points out that some imperfections in the original copies may be apparent.

British Library Cataloguing-in-Publication Data
A catalogue record for this book is available from the British Library

Library of Congress Cataloging-in-Publication Data
A catalog record has been requested for this book

ISBN: 978-0-367-25427-8 (hbk)
ISBN: 978-1-03-217551-5 (pbk)
DOI: 10.4324/9780429287732

Typeset in Bembo
by Swales & Willis, Exeter, Devon, UK

This book is dedicated to the many passionate professionals who work within the international air transport sector, paving the way for the next generation of aviation leaders.

Contents

List of figures		xi
List of tables		xiii
Editor biographies		xiv
Contributor biographies		xv

Engaging the next generation of aviation professionals: introduction 1
SUZANNE K. KEARNS

1 Attracting the next generation of aviation professionals: section introduction 5
SUZANNE K. KEARNS

1.1 **Case study** – Local governments as enablers of the aviation workforce: a case in Portugal 7
MIGUEL C. MOREIRA

1.2 **Case study** – Nurturing the future aviation professional in Africa 11
SHEKOYECENU GLADYS NGBAKO

1.3 **Case study** – A sustainability perspective on the pilot shortage in Canada 15
ADEM OKAL, ANGELINE RAM, AND SUZANNE K. KEARNS

1.4 **Case study** – Introducing ALICANTO, the International Association of Aviation and Aerospace Education 20
ANGELA C. ALBRITTON, PASCAL REVEL, AND ROBERT REID

1.5	**Chapter** – Aviation outreach: reaching the next generation of aviation professionals REBECCA K. LUTTE AND CHENYU HUANG	24
1.6	**Chapter** – STEM and sustainability: creating aviation professional change agents PATTI J. CLARK, LAURA ZIZKA, AND DOREEN M. MCGUNAGLE	36
1.7	**Professional reflection** – The case of Cambodia: challenges in training the next generation of aviation professionals JENNIFER A. MESZAROS	49
1.8	**Professional reflection** – A Great Britain perspective on aviation skills SIMON WITTS	69
2	Educating the next generation of aviation professionals: section introduction SUZANNE K. KEARNS	81
2.1	**Case study** – Higher education in aviation for Portuguese speaking countries: Portugal's perspective RUI CASTRO E QUADROS	84
2.2	**Case study** – Industry–pilot training partnerships REBECCA K. LUTTE AND RUSSELL W. MILLS	89
2.3	**Case study** – How work influences cabin crew learning: a situated learning perspective MARIA F. LARREA, STEVEN HODGE, YORIKO KIKKAWA, AND TIMOTHY J. MAVIN	93
2.4	**Chapter** – Multi-piloted operations ALAN MARTINEZ, R. JOSEPH CHILDS, AND DAN SUTLIFF	100
2.5	**Chapter** – Ensuring success by using the 4 As of learning MARY NIEMCZYK	119

2.6	**Chapter** – Engaging practices for training the new generation of aircraft maintenance technicians KAREN JO JOHNSON AND DENIS MANSON	133
2.7	**Chapter** – Language education for ab initio flight training: a plan going forward JENNIFER ROBERTS AND ALAN ORR	149
2.8	**Professional reflection** – Mixed reality to augment the next generation of aviation professionals LORI J. BROWN	163
2.9	**Professional reflection** – The solution of customized Aviation English: training the aviation maintenance technician ANNE E. LOMPERIS	181
2.10	**Professional reflection** – Evidence-Based Training: the story MICHAEL VARNEY AND JOHN SCULLY	201
3	Retaining the next generation of aviation professionals: section introduction SUZANNE K. KEARNS	225
3.1	**Chapter** – Collegiate flight programs: how student experiences impact student retention and successful completions ANDREW LEONARD AND ELIZABETH BJERKE	227
3.2	**Chapter** – Executive education in aviation: addressing the managerial aspects of the fastest growing industry NADINE ITANI	239
3.3	**Chapter** – Entrepreneurial mindset development: a cog in the wheel of talent management in the aviation sector RAIHAN TAQUI SYED, MANISH YADAV, AND HESHAM MAGD	252

3.4	**Chapter** – The regulation of the airline industry: why it matters to you P. PAUL FITZGERALD	261
3.5	**Professional reflection** – Managing the paradox: asking for more qualified people in a shortage situation JOSÉ SÁNCHEZ-ALARCOS BALLESTEROS	277
	Index	294

Figures

1.3.1	Venn diagram representation of sustainability	16
1.3.2	Model of traditional pilot career progression in Canada	16
1.5.1	Aviation outreach model	25
1.5.2	Aviation outreach model checklist	27
1.5.3	Jodie Gawthrop, age 16, of Westchester, Illinois (left) represents 2 million young people flown in EAA's Young Eagles program with a flight with actor Harrison Ford on July 28 2016 at EAA Airventure Oshkosh in Oshkosh, Wisconsin (EAA photo/Michael Steineke)	29
1.5.4	WAI India chapter 2018 girls in aviation day	32
1.5.5	Girls Fly programme in Africa Fly for STEM event	33
1.6.1	Methods of including sustainability in STEM education	39
1.6.2	Lockheed L-188 Electra sustainability	43
1.7.1	Pochentong International Airport inaugural, 1964	53
1.7.2	Image of So Sokna	57
1.7.3	Pochentong International Airport, 1979	62
1.7.4	An Antonov An-24RV – Kampuchea Airlines, 1989	63
S2.1	The overlapping NGAP themes: attract, educate, and retain.	81
2.3.1	Research findings on the relationship between formal training and cabin crew work	96
2.5.1	The 4 A's Model of Learning	126
2.6.1	Pantelidis Model. Copyright 1997, 2009 by Veronica S. Pantelidis, Ph.D., East Carolina University, USA	141
2.6.2	Developmental Rating Spreadsheet, (unpublished) Copyright 2018 by Senseability Studios Pty Ltd	143
2.8.1	Virtual jet engine laboratory example	166
2.8.2	Classroom assessment with holographic jet engine viewed through the Microsoft HoloLens	167
2.8.3	Feedback loop example	170
2.8.4	CRJ-200 Mixed Reality JetXplore 3D application example	172
2.8.5	New aviation textbook with augmented reality	174
2.8.6	'Layer Aloft Ceiling vs. Indefinite Ceiling' (from Federal Aviation Administration, 2018b, pp. 16–19)	176

2.8.7	Estimating visibility trigger images for Experiential Education training module	177
2.9.1	Language, communication, and the workplace	193
2.10.1	Pilot competencies and performance indicators	207
2.10.2	EBT working group 2008–2012 participants	209
2.10.3	Letter from ICAO	211
2.10.4	Go-around events per flights with go-around	213
2.10.5	Events per flight (not related to approach and landing)	213
2.10.6	High training effect – Jet generations	214
2.10.7	LOSA – 10 characteristics	216
2.10.8	LOSA collaborative – destinations to January 2019	217
2.10.9	VENN system for pilot assessment	220
2.10.10	Was the debrief led by you or was it like a traditional debrief?	223
2.10.11	Overall, how would you rate the quality of the EBT sessions?	223
2.10.12	How well do you think your instructor embraced the facilitative style of instruction?	223
3.2.1	The pedagogical triangle	245
3.3.1	Employee competency life cycle (ECLC)	255
3.3.2	Decision-making sub-processes of an entrepreneurial mind	256
3.3.3	Conceptual illustration developed by the authors	257

Tables

2.4.1	MPL training stages	104
2.5.1	Bloom's Revised Taxonomy with Appropriate Learning Strategies	130
2.8.1	Examples of aviation-related learning objectives, assessments and methodologies	171
2.9.1	New Employee Demand by World Region and Client Category, 2019–2038	183
2.9.2	Workplace contexts: key business activities or workplace factors and sample language-related tasks	190
2.9.3	Staff schedules at oil exploration and production worksite: 7-day increments	191
2.9.4	Language skills and systems	194
2.9.5	Analysis of key language patterns for AMT English training	195
2.9.6	Grammar presentation from a general English textbook	196
2.9.7	Language-related professional associations and web addresses	199
3.2.1	Key design elements for executive education programs	244
3.4.1	The various topics covered by domestic and/or international regulation	270

Editor biographies

Suzanne K. Kearns is an Associate Professor of Aviation at the University of Waterloo in Canada. She is a former aeroplane and helicopter pilot. Her research explores human factors and teaching methodologies, including e-learning and competency-based education. She is the author or co-author of four other books, including *Competency-Based Education in Aviation: Exploring Alternate Training Pathways* also with Tim Mavin and Steven Hodge and the leading textbook *Fundamentals of International Aviation*. She is also the Series Editor of the *Aviation Fundamentals* textbook series and an active member of the International Civil Aviation Organization's Next Generation of Aviation Professionals task force.

Timothy J. Mavin (Tim) is an Associate Professor at Griffith University's School of Education and Professional Studies. He is a member of the Griffith Institute for Educational Research. Dr Mavin has been flying since the age of 15 and has worked with numerous major airlines flying the Boeing 737. He left aviation in 2006 to pursue his love of education, becoming a mathematics teacher. He left teaching in 2008 to take up a senior lecture position at Griffith University where he earned his Doctor of Education in 2010. In 2011 to 2015 he worked both as a Boeing 737 simulator instructor and researcher. These parallel roles enabled him to be both an "insider" and "researcher". In 2016 Dr Mavin continued this parallel role by re-joining the Royal Australian Air Force as a Wing Commander. Here he takes research findings and implements them into defence. Today he works with defence, airlines and maternity emergency medicine.

Steven Hodge is a Senior Lecturer at Griffith University's School of Education and Professional Studies and a member of the Griffith Institute for Educational Research. His research combines a long-term interest in philosophy with questions in education and training systems design. He is currently engaged with the problem of representing complex expertise for the purpose of training and assessment, exploring alternative methodologies and theoretical frameworks in the process. He collaborated with Suzanne and Tim on the book *Competency-Based Education in Aviation: Exploring Alternate Training Pathways* and continues researching education and training in aviation with a view to developing robust systems that take into account the real complexity of work in this industry.

Contributor biographies

Angela C. Albritton is Director of Military Relations and Strategic Initiatives at Embry-Riddle Aeronautical University's Worldwide Campus. Her primary focus is to advance and support the university's strategic goals by identifying, evaluating, and championing opportunities for external collaboration.

Dr. Elizabeth Bjerke is an Associate Dean and Professor of Aviation within the John D. Odegard School of Aerospace Sciences at the University of North Dakota, USA. Her research areas focus on student success and how it translates to their career aspirations.

Lori J. Brown is a Professor at Western Michigan University, USA, an ATP, Fellow of the Royal Aeronautical Society, and served as the ICAO NGAP Outreach Chair. She researches the use of augmented reality for the FAA PEGASAS Center of Excellence.

Dr. R. Joseph Childs is the Chair of the School of Business and Aviation at Southeastern University, Florida, USA. His research spans many disciplines and recent experience focuses on competency-based education and direct assessment for earning college credit.

Patti J. Clark is an Associate Professor at Embry-Riddle Aeronautical University, Daytona Beach, Florida, USA. Her research interests are promotion of all three pillars of sustainability in the aviation/aerospace industry with a focus on workforce development, diversity, and programmatic efficiency.

Dr. P. Paul Fitzgerald is an Adjunct Professor at McGill University's Institute of Air & Space Law, Montreal, Canada. He has been published widely on aviation law topics and lectured and presented at conferences in 11 countries around the world.

Chenyu Huang is an Assistant Professor at the University of Nebraska Omaha. His primary research interests include statistical modeling of aviation operations, Unmanned Aircraft System operations, and solutions to flight safety enhancement. He is based in Omaha, Nebraska, USA.

Dr. Nadine Itani is the Director of Research at the Middle East Aviation Research Center. Her research explores aviation strategy and policy development. Her primary research interest is supporting government agencies in planning and executing sustainable aviation programs. She is based in Beirut, Lebanon.

Karen Jo Johnson is an Associate Professor of Aviation Technologies at Southern Illinois University, Carbondale, USA. Her research focuses on the designs of learning system technologies for use in aviation maintenance training.

Dr Yoriko Kikkawa is a research fellow at Griffith University, Queensland, Australia, where she is a qualitative research methodologist. Yoriko conducts cross-cultural, cross-sector, and cross-disciplinary research in areas of teaching, learning, and simulation-based training within aviation and health.

Maria F. Larrea is a candidate for a Master of Education and Professional Studies research. Maria holds a Masters degree in Service Business Management and has 12 years' experience in the aviation industry, as a cabin crew instructor and training manager.

Dr. Andrew Leonard is an Assistant Professor in the John D. Odegard School of Aerospace Sciences at the University of North Dakota, USA. His primary research focuses on flight education, and the success of training future aviators.

Anne E. Lomperis specializes in workplace language training in support of international economic development priorities. Through her consulting practice, Language Training Designs, in Greater Washington, DC, USA, she addresses customization to industry sectors, such as aviation maintenance, and teacher training.

Dr. Rebecca K. Lutte is an Associate Professor at the University of Nebraska at Omaha Aviation Institute, USA and pilot (CFII, MEI). Her research focuses on aviation workforce issues including pilot supply and outreach, recruitment, and retention of underrepresented groups.

Hesham Magd is Associate Dean – Quality Assurance & Accreditation and Associate Professor & Head – Faculty of Business & Economics at Modern College of Business & Science (MCBS), Muscat, Oman. His key interests are TQM, organizational excellence, and entrepreneurship.

Denis Manson specializes in aircraft maintenance and human factors instructional design at Aviation Australia in Brisbane, Australia. His professional interest lies in designing virtual and augmented reality assets and implementing gameplay techniques for technical and non-technical skill transfer.

Dr. Alan Martinez is a professional pilot, certified flight instructor, and Adjunct Professor of Aviation at Southeastern University in Lakeland, Florida, USA. His research interest utilizes his instructional systems and human capital education and experience to promote aviation competency-based solutions.

Dr. Doreen M. McGunagle is an Assistant Professor at Embry-Riddle Aeronautical University, Florida, USA. Her research explores sustainability and higher education. Her primary research interest is developing sustainable leaders, corporate social responsibility and workforce skills for sustainable growth.

Jennifer A. Meszaros is an Instructor at Cambodia's Civil Aviation Training Center as well as an advocate for affordable and accessible training programs. She regularly consults and writes about the civil aviation industry in Southeast Asia.

Russell W. Mills is a Research Fellow at the Center for Regional Development at Bowling Green State University, Ohio, USA. His research interests include the link between air service and economic development and aviation policy.

Dr. Miguel C. Moreira is an Associate Professor at Atlântica University in Oeiras, Lisbon, Portugal, a private pilot, and quality manager and senior consultant for the strategic development of the LPSO Municipal Aerodrome.

Shekoyecenu Gladys Ngbako is a graduate of Aviation Management from Coventry University, UK. The founder of iConnect Aviators Ltd which is focused on promoting Aviation in Africa and supporting the next generation of aspiring aviation professionals. She is based in Nigeria.

Mary Niemczyk, PhD is an Associate Professor at Arizona State University, USA. Her research focuses on generational differences, instructional and learning strategies, and has developed a learning model – The 4 As of Learning (active, associate, anticipate, and awareness).

Adem Okal is a PhD student at the University of Waterloo, Ontario, Canada. His research explores sustainability in aviation, labor geography, and pilot supply.

Alan Orr is an Aviation English Specialist at Embry-Riddle Aeronautical University, Florida, USA. He specializes in online course delivery and assessment for international students enrolled in flight training.

Rui Castro e Quadros, Senior Lecturer (BSc Aviation Management Program Director) at ISEC Lisbon, Portugal. His industry experience spans more than 20 years: Iberia Airlines (Sales Executive), Portugalia Airlines (General Manager for Italy), Sata Air Azores and Azores Airlines (MD and CCO).

Angeline Ram is a Safety Management Systems and Audit Manager for the Chartright Air Group in Canada. With 17 years of international experience both professionally and academically, her interdisciplinary research explores the link between safety and sustainability.

Dr. Robert Reid is Associate Professor and Head of the School of Mechanical, Industrial and Aeronautical Engineering at the University of the Witwatersrand in Johannesburg, South Africa. He is a Fellow of the Royal Aeronautical Society. His fields of interest include aircraft structures, composite materials, and residual stresses.

Pascal Revel was the Dean for Research and International Relations and Vice-President for Strategy and Partnerships at ENAC, the French national civil aviation university in Toulouse. He also was a member of the ICAO NGAP Task Force. He has recently moved to Berlin, Germany, as Counselor for Science & Technology at the French embassy.

Jennifer Roberts works as an Aviation English Specialist at Embry-Riddle Aeronautical University, Florida, USA. She is interested in understanding and improving the many factors that affect the teaching and learning of English in aviation contexts, particularly ab initio flight training.

José Sanchez-Alarcos Ballesteros is Associate HR Professor at IE Business School. HF in Aviation researcher and consultant. Experienced in Aviation Design (MITAC) and HF teacher at major regulators and airlines. He is based in Madrid, Spain and his main research is related to side-effects of automation.

John Scully has been flying 36 years/22,000 hours. John flew for NWA and was an instructor developing initial AQP. With Airbus, he was a pilot/instructor, manager in Flight Ops/Training, and representative to the LOSA Collaborative. After Airbus he led/authored the EBT data-analysis published by IATA.

Dan Sutliff is an Assistant Professor in the School of Aviation Science at Utah Valley University, USA. His primary interest is aviation's role in a sustainable future. He currently lives in Salt Lake City, Utah.

Raihan Taqui Syed is Director of the Center for Entrepreneurship & Business Incubation (CEBI) and Lecturer in HRM and Entrepreneurship at the Modern College of Business and Science (MCBS), Muscat, Oman. His key research interests are entrepreneurial mindset, talent management and organizational development.

Capt. Michael Varney is an experienced airline pilot and instructor. He led the development of Evidence-Based Training worldwide, and currently supports the program as President of the EBT Foundation, Managing Director of EBT Solutions and a Director of the LOSA Collaborative.

Simon Witts founded Aviation Skills Partnership in 2013 to transform the approach to aviation skills. Based in London, UK, he is an experienced aviation and airline executive board member with forty years' experience, including twenty years at board, COO, and CEO level.

Manish Yadav is Coordinator of Airport & Aviation degree programs and Lecturer in Aviation Management at Modern College of Business & Science (MCBS), Muscat, Oman. He is an EU doctoral researcher and his key research interests are airline strategy and aviation education.

Dr. Laura Zizka is an Assistant Professor at Ecole hôtelière de Lausanne, HES-SO University of Applied Sciences and Arts Western Switzerland. Her research areas include communications, higher education (hospitality and STEM), and corporate social responsibility (CSR)/sustainability actions, initiatives, and reporting.

Engaging the next generation of aviation professionals

Introduction

Suzanne K. Kearns

In years past, it was common for student pilots to invest up to USD 100,000 in training costs and then accept a first job sweeping a hangar floor before gaining sufficient company seniority to pilot small aircraft. After such a large investment in training, young pilots would typically start their careers in small operators working for poverty-level wages – and sometimes on an unpaid volunteer basis. In most of the Western hemisphere, the attitude was that young professionals must pay their dues before earning the privilege of fair pay (with the average age for a newly hired airline First Officer being early-30s). A frequently used expression was that 'in aviation we eat our own young'. The industry has a long history of exploitative labour practices of its up-and-coming professionals.

Although this resulted in many young professionals choosing to quit aviation before reaching the desirable professional ranks, these practices continued for many decades as the number of people who wanted to work in the aviation industry was far greater than the number of professional positions available. That is no longer the case.

Boeing forecasts that between 2019 and 2038 the world demand for pilots will be 804,000. The greatest pilot demand will be within the Asian Pacific (266,000) followed by North America regions (212,000). Beyond pilots, a further 769,000 technicians and 914,000 cabin crew will be required to sustain the air transport sector through 2038.[1]

Growth in international aviation has resulted in new opportunities for young professionals. Airline cadet programs offered in some parts of Europe and Asia Pacific allow young adults with no previous training, after passing a rigorous selection process, to earn a salary throughout 18 months of training towards a multi-crew pilot license. After completing training, they fly as a First or Second Officer for a term of service with that airline. Although cadet programs offer an expedited path to a pilot's seat for a select few, most student pilots around the world still pay their own flight training costs via personal or government supported loans. However, the increased demand has resulted in many pilots being hired as First Officers on transport-category aircraft directly out of school (at 21 or 22 years of age).

By some accounts, the demand for new recruits in the coming decades will exceed the global training capacity to produce competent professionals. Although this growth presents tremendous opportunities for the next generation of aviation professionals, it imposes significant challenges upon traditional aviation training infrastructure and operational practices.

In today's industry, personnel shortages are already occurring. It is common to hear of cancelled flights resulting from: lack of available flight and cabin crew; difficulty hiring technicians to ensure aircraft airworthiness; and trouble hiring and retaining instructors. The hiring practices of the past are no longer sustainable within the current climate of the industry. If not managed properly, personnel shortages will have crippling and far-reaching implications throughout the global air transport sector.

To manage this issue, a new aviation academic sub-discipline is needed – best practices in attracting, educating, and retaining the next generation of aviation professionals (NGAP).

To understand how sub-disciplines emerge within aviation, consider the late 1970s when a series of high-profile airline accidents occurred that were caused by seemingly preventable human error. In 1979, the United States' National Aeronautics and Space Administration (NASA) held a workshop to explore this issue – which grew to become Crew Resource Management (CRM).[2] Academics, regulators, and industry professionals collaborated to draw together best practices from professional operations and academic research (such as psychology, physiology, ergonomics, and safety sciences). This work produced best practices in CRM training, teaching professionals about their limitations in an effort to prevent and manage human error. Regulations now require CRM training on an annual basis for many aviation professional groups.

In addition to practical training implications, this collaboration also stimulated academic studies into elements of CRM (such as situation awareness, workload management, decision making, fatigue, communication, and collaboration among many others). As a response to a recognized need, CRM emerged as a sub-discipline – producing academic work and operational best practices.

Today we are facing the dawn of a new aviation sub-discipline associated with the Next Generation of Aviation Professionals (NGAP). The origins of NGAP are traced back to 2009 when the International Civil Aviation Organization (ICAO) launched the NGAP initiative to ensure there were sufficient competent and qualified professionals to support the growing air transport sector. This initiative grew to become one of ICAO's global programs and is currently supported by a network of dedicated academics, professionals, and regulators from around the world.

The emerging NGAP sub-discipline will require experts to draw together guidance from a variety of sources: outreach techniques, human resources, education, safety science, national and organizational culture, language training, diversity and inclusion, scheduling practices, and professional development among many others.

Three main themes of the NGAP issue have been identified:

1. **Attract** – Encouraging youth, young adults, and transitioning professionals to choose an aviation profession. Themes include understanding the characteristics of younger generations, equalizing gender imbalance, sustainability, outreach concepts, youth engagement strategies, marketing and communications, outreach within emerging versus developed markets, and aviation education in primary and secondary school among others.
2. **Educate** – Globally, aviation education must evolve practices to meet the demand for professionals projected in the coming years. Training practices must advance and become more efficient and job-relevant. This may include the integration of competency-based and evidence-based training, new immersive training technologies, e-learning and simulations, and language training as many aviation professionals are required to be fluent in English.
3. **Retain** – Beyond attracting and training professionals, it is also critical that we foster working conditions, compensation, and benefits that are attractive to the NGAP. This will require measuring and managing human resources, retention initiatives such as innovative scheduling strategies, analyzing the role of immigration, analysis of compensation and retention rates in different regions, supporting mental health, and corporate social responsibility among others.

This volume was designed to bring together a diverse set of academic and professional perspectives within the three themes of attracting, educating, and retaining the NGAP. It is believed that this compilation is the first academic work on the NGAP topic – yet we expect this field to grow substantially in depth and breadth as the issue becomes increasingly critical in the coming years.

To best represent the scope of the issue we have invited a prestigious group of professionals and academics to author three types of contribution within this volume:

- Case studies – brief overviews of industry/practice/research-focused examples,
- Chapters – longer works from respected academics that explore topics in detail,
- Professional reflections – professionals who have made important contributions to the field here share their experiences, accomplishments, and insights to support the work of others.

The Editors would like to express our sincere appreciation for the talented and dedicated authors who contributed to this volume. Each brought diverse and interesting opinions that have enriched this work. A brief introduction to their work is included within the three section introductions in the volume.

Notes

1 Boeing. (2019). *Pilot and Technician Outlook*. Retrieved from *Boeing's Market Outlook*: www.boeing.com/resources/boeingdotcom/commercial/market/pilot-technician-services/assets/downloads/2019_pto_infographic.pdf.
2 Helmreich, R. L., Merritt, A. C., & Wilhelm, J. A. (1999). The evolution of Crew Resource Management training in commercial aviation. *International Journal of Aviation Psychology*, *9*(1), 19–32.

1 Attracting the next generation of aviation professionals
Section introduction

Suzanne K. Kearns

If you ask an aviation professional what it was that sparked their interest in the field, most can describe the moment that influenced them to pursue their career. They may share a story of being invited into a cockpit on an airline flight (before the security interventions of 9/11 prohibited this practice), seeing a Hollywood movie that glorified aviation careers, or of visiting a museum with interactive exhibits on flight.

The sector hasn't historically had to invest significant effort into attracting youth – as the inherent appeal of flight was enough to capture the interest of sufficient young people to support the need for professionals. However, attracting youth to aviation (which had long been taken for granted) is now a key pillar of NGAP strategy. Deliberate, strategic, and innovative efforts are now underway around the world to encourage youth to pursue careers in aviation.

The submissions within Section One highlight several key initiatives, considerations, strategies, and success stories related to attracting the next generation of aviation professional:

1.1 **Case study** – Local governments as enablers of the aviation workforce: a case in Portugal *by Miguel C. Moreira*
    A case study about how local governments can help youth discover their passion for aviation, by exploring the case of Ponte de Sor, a small town that transformed its aerodrome to become the fastest growing aerospace cluster in Portugal.
1.2 **Case study** – Nurturing the future aviation professional in Africa *by Shekoyecenu Gladys Ngbako*
    A roadmap to explore the skills gap of NGAP within Africa, examining the support provided by states, organizations, and industries. Key issues include the lack of female participation and financial obstacles in the profession. The Aviators Africa Academy (AAA) and iFly Academy are discussed.

1.3 **Case Study** – A sustainability perspective on the pilot shortage in Canada *by Adem Okal, Angeline Ram, and Suzanne K. Kearns*

A case study exploring how unsustainable recruitment practices are disrupting pilot career progression within Canada, particularly causing shortages of flight instructors and pilots to serve the remote northern regions.

1.4 **Case study** – Introducing ALICANTO, the International Association of Aviation and Aerospace Education *by Angela C. Albritton, Pascal Revel, and Robert Reid*

The authors introduce ALICANTO, the International Association of Aviation and Aerospace Education, which was developed to act as a coordinated voice of academia to international aerospace stakeholders.

1.5 **Chapter** – Aviation outreach: reaching the next generation of aviation professionals *by Rebecca K. Lutte and Chenyu Huang*

This chapter introduces a model of aviation outreach and explores existing outreach programs within the United States and internationally. A checklist is presented outlining essential elements of an outreach program.

1.6 **Chapter** – STEM and sustainability: creating aviation professional change agents *by Patti J. Clark, Laura Zizka, and Doreen M. McGunagle*

Sustainability is a critical element of aviation training. This chapter discusses sustainability and proposes a simple strategy for its integration into aviation science, technology, engineering, and math (STEM) programs to create authentic engagement in students.

1.7 **Professional reflection** – The case of Cambodia: challenges in training the next generation of aviation professionals *by Jennifer A. Meszaros*

This work explores the history of aviation within Cambodia, challenges being faced, and calls for an aviation workforce skills study to understand the training needs of Cambodia's air transport system.

1.8 **Professional reflection** – A Great Britain perspective on aviation skills *by Simon Witts*

A personal reflection of a professional's work building the Aviation Skills Partnership in the United Kingdom, including the drafting of an Aviation Skills Manifesto – a Charter for Aviation Skills and its supporting Aviation Skills Plan.

1.1 Case study – Local governments as enablers of the aviation workforce

A case in Portugal

Miguel C. Moreira

Introduction

In today's global economy, the aviation industry faces mounting challenges. Companies worldwide understand that talent is now a primary and critical source of competitive advantage. However, the aviation industry is gripped by an overwhelming shortage of skilled professionals, of which the global lack of airline pilots and aircraft maintenance technicians is just the most visible aspect. The answer to this problem must come from tightened partnerships between the industry and training and educational institutions, as education and career experience have been recognized as two of the highest-impact accelerators to global growth (Mercer, 2013).

While companies are making greater investments in talent, it is recognized that educational institutions are failing to generate the talent required across the industry. The new generation of aviation professionals must have the skills and knowledge necessary for the role (Lappas & Kourousis, 2016), as well as the broader creative and critical-thinking skills that can elevate organizational performance to its highest level. Despite high unemployment in many regions of the world, companies today face a shortfall of qualified talent to fill critical roles such as airline pilots, maintenance technicians, engineers, to name a few.

As the global economy faces this new paradigm, we compete regionally and globally for talent, investment, and entrepreneurs in technology-intensive industries such as the aviation industry. Yet we also compete against national and regional governments that are executing comprehensive strategies that seek to create innovation clusters in many of the same important, emerging industries. According to Paneo and Sasanelli (2016), there is clear evidence that universities and research institutions provide significant impetus to aerospace clusters, thanks to their ability to provide both support to R&D activities and highly skilled human capital, essential in high value-added industries and particularly in aerospace. We need to support these strategies with investment in universities, research collaborations, and skilled workforce training, in a modern science-park type of environment. With the acceleration of globalization, the decision on the location of clusters experienced a shift in its focus, moving from a mechanism for facilitating access to resources and workforce to a strategy for generating knowledge and developing skills to support global and sustainable competitive advantage (Silva, 2012).

Ponte de Sor

Ponte de Sor is a small town located 120 km north-east of Lisbon, Portugal with 17,000 inhabitants. Through the realization of substantial direct investments in the last decade, Ponte de Sor has made a systematic and consistent effort in the Aeronautics and Civil Aviation sector. In particular, the Ponte de Sor Municipal Aerodrome is being consolidated as an anchor infrastructure of the Aeronautical Cluster in Portugal, with a very positive effect on development for the region's economy. The project in question is the result of a territorially based strategy aimed at promoting the competitiveness, sustainable development, employment, and social cohesion and land use planning of the Ponte de Sor County.

The series of investments started in 2005 (expansion of the old small runway) in order to accommodate the main base of the Portuguese forest firefighting fleet and operations, in the wake of a state decision to base those activities in Ponte de Sor. The second phase of investment was induced by the need to monetize the first investment made, as the firefighting activities are seasonal and do not generate any real income to the municipality. Together with the opportunities that arose at the time the country was emerging from the debt crisis (2013), several airline pilot schools based in Lisbon were seeking to expand operations into a less occupied airspace, as the training efficiency near Lisbon International Airport is significantly limited.

As a result of the foresight of the municipality, its aerodrome was equipped with three state-of-the-art hangars, and a new 1,800 m runway, duly certified to be able to receive medium-haul commercial airplanes such as the Airbus A320 and Boeing B737. Such investments served the purpose to attract new companies and businesses to the region, as a means to tackle one of the higher (> 20 percent) unemployment rates in the country during the debt crisis years. Since 2013, companies such as L3 Airline Academy, TEKEVER (one of the largest producers of drones for maritime surveillance of the European Union), and the Rexiaa Group (producer of composite components and supplier of Airbus Helicopters and Dassault Aviation) were able to house their businesses in Ponte de Sor.

Following these initial investments, the municipality has been working hard since 2016 on an internationalization mission program to promote the local cluster and available facilities as a means of attracting both new national and international investors, but also young people to integrate the present and future workforce that is being developed there. This mission has included an EUR 11 million investment that will allow new hangars to be built, providing the opportunity for heavy aircraft maintenance activities and training of new young professionals.

However, the attraction of new talent to the industry in such a small region is a daunting challenge. The local government has sought to establish several partnerships with high schools and universities, so that aviation careers can be promoted among the young students of the region from an early age. As reported by Moreira (2015), the Ponte de Sor high school and the G Air flight academy created the first vocational training program in the country. This allowed a first group of 14 students, with no previous contact with aviation, to enter a four-month internship with G Air Maintenance (an EASA approved Part 145 organization). This first project was so successful, that it became imperative to allow these students to enter higher education degrees in aviation. However, the Ponte de Sor district, a large region covering 840 km^2, does not have a higher education institution (the nearest being located about 90 km away). To overcome this obstacle, we partnered with the Polytechnic Institute of Setúbal (located near Lisbon) in order to design a two-year degree that could be offered in Ponte de Sor. This has allowed a first generation of students to enrol in a higher education degree in aviation without having to leave the territory. This pilot project led to the development of additional partnerships with an increasing number of Portuguese leading universities, which now contribute to further the offer of training programs in Ponte de Sor, namely the degree in Aircraft Maintenance that is being developed under the EASA syllabus.

Portugal Air Summit

In recent years, the aviation industry has recognized that accelerating the rate of employment of the new generation of professionals can only be effective if aviation careers are widely promoted and understood by the younger generation. This means that there is a clear need to attract them to aviation and aerospace careers. This can only be achieved with a significant investment in the public awareness of the aeronautical and aerospace sciences. With this purpose in mind, in 2017 the Ponte de Sor local government launched the Portugal Air Summit initiative which is the largest aviation event in the Iberian Peninsula. The summit includes a four-day conference program which creates a unique occasion for the sector to discuss its challenges and opportunities, and for the young public to meet and learn from professionals. The summit has had a very significant impact on both the region and the country: as an example, the 2018 event generated a total of EUR 723,000 of net advertising value equivalence, and was exposed to 2.4 million individuals (which implies that on average each Portuguese citizen was impacted seven times by the event on online media).

For the 2019 edition, the Air Summit also welcomed the National Aeronautics and Space Administration and the European Space Agency (NASA and ESA) for their yearly "Partnership for Global Sustainability" event to attract the younger students for the new space era, in which the commercial exploration of space is becoming possible across the globe. It is of the utmost importance that the Ponte de Sor project helps in linking the higher education institutions to the local, national, and international business and scientific communities, as a way of enhancing the innovation capacity of our companies. This means that the aeronautical activities complex of the Ponte de Sor aerodrome, understood here as a regional cluster, should take innovation as a strategic driver. For this reason and bearing in mind the need to reinvent how students and employers communicate, a roadshow was conducted in 16 universities in Portugal to disseminate the new Huby smartphone application that is being created with local government funding. The aim is to link young students with the Portuguese leading aviation and aerospace companies (phase 1), and their counterparts in Brazil and Africa (phase 2), in order to foster employability throughout the Portuguese speaking countries. The aim is to establish the first competency and job offer dashboard, as a Portuguese contributing effort to the ICAO NGAP Index, a project that seeks to provide regional and state forecasts on the needs of the global aviation work force.

Conclusions

Ponte de Sor has ensured a continuous effort to create infrastructural conditions to support investment, gradually oriented toward hosting businesses, higher education activities and specialized R&D services. In the medium term, strategic and operational partnerships with aeronautical and aerospace training centers are expected to be strengthened, as well as the structuring of a niche for applied research and scientific dissemination, which will give the aeronautical complex a significant position in the vanguard of knowledge in the Portuguese landscape.

References

Lappas, I. & Kourousis, K. I. (2016). Anticipating the Need for New Skills for the Future Aerospace and Aviation Professionals. *Journal of Aerospace Technology and Management*, 8 (2), 232–241. 10.5028/jatm.v8i2.616.

Mercer. (2013). *Talent Barometer Survey* [e-book]. Mercer LLC. Retrieved from www.imercer.com/products/2013/talentbarometer.aspx.

Moreira, M. C. (2015). A New Training Center in Portugal: A Unique Project to Boost the Next Generation of Aviation Professionals. *ICAO Training Report*, 5 (1), 28–30.

Paone, M. & Sasanelli, N. (2016). *Aerospace Clusters: World's Best Practices and Future Prospects*. Retrieved from www.defencesa.com/upload/capabilities/space/Intern%20-%20Paone,%20Matteo%20-%20Aerospace%20Clusters.pdf.

Silva, M. F. F. (2012). *The Dynamics of Clusters as Enablers of Corporate and Regional Competitiveness: The Case of the Ribatejo and West Vegetable Clusters – Comparative Analysis with Almería* (Master dissertation, Universidade Técnica de Lisboa, Lisboa, Portugal). Retrieved from http://hdl.handle.net/10400.5/11729.

1.2 Case study – Nurturing the future aviation professional in Africa

Shekoyecenu Gladys Ngbako

Introduction

The African region continues to navigate through different approaches to attract highly skilled professionals into aviation careers by addressing a few predominant myths, providing access to affordable training, addressing skills gaps, and by providing support from states, international and regional organizations, industry and academia. It is anticipated that the demand for trained aviation professionals will continue to rise, and the emphasis to attract more youth is critical. This is particularly important for the African continent as it continues to experience a lack of industry performance and other challenges.

There is no doubt that a large contingent of the current generation of aviation professionals will retire soon, therefore the need for new and additional skilled youth is fundamental to the sustainable growth of the industry. There are more than 720 million African young people, which gives tremendous potential to unlock the power of this human potential. According to IATA the aviation industry forecasts the demand for skilled talents within Africa will double over the next 20 years, with the need to source an additional 20,000 pilots, engineers and technical specialists and other relevant positions (Airlines.iata.org, 2019).

Common myths and challenges

With a region such as Africa, nothing is simple. Government policies, economic and demographic factors, legacy issues and challenges with basic education all place a massive burden on the industry and the possibility of impacting the industry's future.

Progress from initiatives in different parts of Africa has created a roadmap to attract the next generation of professionals, however the rate of change has been slow due to some myths and challenges. The lack of coherent skills in the aviation disciplines and lack of awareness within the next generation of the types of aviation jobs available further compounds the problem. The low participation of the ratio of female involvement in the industry needs further encouragement, as well as the partnership of connecting passionate students into the industry and the availability of access to financial aid.

Initiatives changing the narrative

Several aviation-orientated initiatives have laid out approaches for what is required to turn the status quo around, by challenging both governments and private sector. Among them are Aviators Africa School Club, iConnect Student Association and Experience Aviation in Nigeria; Wonder of Aviation and iFly Academy in South Africa and Dream Alive Foundation in South Africa and Zimbabwe. Other outreach is carried out by the International Women in Aviation Organization which has chapters in several African states including Zambia, Botswana and South Africa. The efforts of the International Civil Aviation Organization's (ICAO's) Next Generation of Aviation Professionals' Initiative helps ensure that enough qualified and competent aviation professionals are available, with centers in Dakar, Nairobi and Cairo.

The two case studies which follow highlight how Aviators Africa Academy and iFly Academy have been able to attract, inspire and retain the next generation of professionals in Africa.

Case study 1: addressing the skills gap, career opportunities and tackling the female barriers in aviation, Aviators Africa Academy (AAA)

The need for skilled professionals in the aviation sector is of the utmost priority. Aviators Africa Academy launched its initiative, Aviators Africa School Club, in April 2018 in partnership with Aviation Development (AviaDev) a platform that is dedicated to growing connectivity to, from and within the African continent.

The aim of the Aviators Africa School Club initiative is to address the anticipated skills gap in Africa with the support of industry experts. The aviation sector is a vast industry with different career options. Yet in Africa due to lack of knowledge transfer, the majority of the next generation of aviators consider flight attendants, pilots and engineers as the only career options in aviation. Through partnership with AviaDev and Women in Aviation (South Africa), the academy has been able to transfer knowledge through outreach, involving aspiring future aviators with innovative and sustainable solutions for challenges in aviation in Africa and connecting the students with industry professionals in Africa and around the world.

The academy aims at inspiring, mentoring and attracting the next generation aviators to ensure that the aviation and aerospace industry in Africa is not lacking in adequate manpower.

Skills gap: the challenge

In order more effectively to address the pressing skills gap the academy has grown rapidly with partnership with Ethiopian Airlines (Africa's biggest airline and contributor of skilled aviation professionals for the region), Airbus Foundation, STEM METS Resources in Nigeria and AviaDev.

African youth are being prepared with the adequate leadership and technical skills to meet and address the myths and challenges in the region. Early learning experiences and primary exposure in science, technology, engineering and mathematics (STEM), aviation and aerospace are critical in preparing the interests of the young population. Through an extensive iteration process and precise mentorship and motivation, interest will be developed towards the diverse career options in aviation.

Although there are no clear solutions to attracting and retaining the new generation of professionals, creating the awareness for them to consider aviation as a career is a first step. To tackle this, AAA sought to create awareness by engaging the youth with outreach events, creating a group platform in some African counties such as South Africa, Rwanda, Ghana and Nigeria and by collaborating with educational institutes to entrench students' interest in the industry. This initiative provides the students with a platform to understand more about the industry and its career opportunities through interactive networking events. AAA is addressing the skills gap challenges, working closely with international and local aviation and training companies.

Case study 2: taking aviation to the local communities in South Africa, iFly Academy

In trying to solve one of the major challenges of accessing suitable funding and getting the opportunity to pursue one's desire to become a pilot in Africa, iFly Aviation Academy was founded in 2017. iFly is an aviation solutions company in Port Elizabeth, South Africa which strives to promote and drive participation between government departments and communities. The core values of iFly are to address the challenges of lack of access to quality aviation experiences for students, particularly those from low-income and under-represented groups in South Africa. Through the combined wealth of experience, industry insights and knowledge, iFly has been privileged to create partnerships with key aviation companies by touring schools in South Africa with personal computer-based flight simulators, giving the students the opportunity to test the sky with a light aircraft.

Financial burden: the challenge

Future aviation professionals in Africa also have a major financial burden placed on the student or their sponsoring company. This financial burden is a major factor for students wishing to enter the aviation industry. For example, the cost of flight attendant training is around US$5,000 for a three-month course and a full pilot training program is around US$68,000. As part of the strategy for partnership iFly has been successful in securing training partnerships where the partners see potential monetary value and driving passion from the students. Collaborating with other agencies has been successful, however key partnerships that can help drive the initiatives have been hard to come by. In some cases particularly the airline industry is not supportive. The engine manufacturing companies such as Airbus, Boeing and Rolls Royce are easier to align with, considering that they already have in-house STEM programs and see the full potential and focus of the growth. As mentioned above, the importance of government involvement is key to the growth and sustainability of attracting, inspiring and motivating the next generation aviators, however the majority of initiatives face difficulties in securing financial backing and support. Due to support from local government, iFly has been able to focus on existing stakeholders' programs and government programs where the initiative can position as facilitators with no cost burden.

The attempt to set up a successful initiative in Africa comes with growing pains, nevertheless iFly has inspired, motivated and given students hope for the future by focusing on establishing as a skills development facilitator that joins the missing dots by connecting young people to funding opportunities, that already exist, and to training institutions. Through the STEM program run in alignment with Airbus and Rolls Royce some of the challenges, such as finances, will enable iFly Academy to involve the local communities to aspire to consider aviation as a career option.

Conclusion

Recognizing that the aviation industry is growing rapidly is critical and requires action to ensure that there are qualified and competent aviation professionals. Therefore, it is imperative to tackle the exciting challenges of building and developing diverse human capital structure for aviation in Africa.

Creating an environment for the next generation aviators in Africa is crucial and the various initiatives are determined to inspire problem solvers, innovative thinkers and builders. Aviators that will solve global strategic challenges and opportunities facing airports and their suppliers by developing new ideas such as smart opportunities in airport retailing, enhancing the passenger experience, airline-airport partnership opportunities and a lot more. All the initiatives are committed to attracting and retaining the brightest professionals for the aviation industry.

Reference

Airlines.iata.org. (2019). *Muhammad Ali Albakri: In pursuit of new talent | Airlines.*[online] Available at: https://airlines.iata.org/blog/2019/06/muhammad-ali-albakri-in-pursuit-of-new-talent [Accessed 20 May 2019].

1.3 Case study – A sustainability perspective on the pilot shortage in Canada

Adem Okal, Angeline Ram, and Suzanne K. Kearns

Sustainable aviation recruitment

Air transport connects us globally. The industry is expected to double within the next two decades, with the number of annual air passengers reaching up to 8.2 billion (International Air Transport Association [IATA], 2018). To support this growth, both additional aircraft and pilots are required. However, the current rate of pilot supply may not support the growth projected.

Sustaining pilot supply is critical considering the economic and social benefits of air transport, for both industry and the general public. Examining the pilot supply and recruitment practices from a sustainability perspective considers the needs of the present as well as the economic and social implications on the future.

This case study presents an example of *unsustainable* recruitment practices within the pilot pipeline in Canada. Following a brief introduction to sustainability, the social and economic dimensions will be discussed in relation to pilot recruitment.

A sustainability perspective

Sustainability is defined as "development that meets the needs of the present without compromising the ability of future generations to meet their needs" (World Commission on Environment and Development, 1987, p. 43). Sustainability proposes a multi-lateral and balanced strategy that considers *economic, environmental* and *social* pillars, with a vision beyond the present, rather than a unilateral assessment primarily driven by economic motivations (Gladwin, Kennelly & Krause, 1995).

The three pillars of sustainability are commonly represented with equal-sized overlapping circles in a Venn diagram as shown in Figure 1.3.1. Balance between the three pillars is rare due to subjective, competing priorities, and the primary focus of each discipline (Hopwood, Mellor & O'Brien, 2005). For example, economists claim that economic growth could prevent poverty and inequality (Hopwood et al., 2005) while environmentalists argue that economic growth exploits natural resources beyond their regenerative capacity resulting in irrevocable environmental degradation (Dresner, 2002).

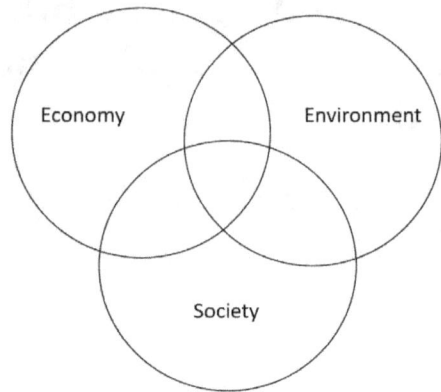

Figure 1.3.1 Venn diagram representation of sustainability.

Despite "social" being included in sustainability models, social sustainability generally receives the least attention in comparison to the economic and environmental aspects (Omann & Spangenberg, 2002). Social sustainability focuses on subjective themes including social equality, justice, cohesion and basic needs. In practice, the economic dimension of sustainability tends to dominate the environmental and social dimensions (Giddings, Hopwood & O'Brien, 2002). Pilot recruitment practices in Canada are primarily associated with the social and economic pillars of sustainability.

Sustainability and pilot recruitment

The pilot career pathway in Canada can be modelled as a progression from student pilot, with an hours-building phase spent instructing or working in the north, to a position within an airline (Figure 1.3.2). (Note that most of the Canadian population lives within a few hundred kilometres of the

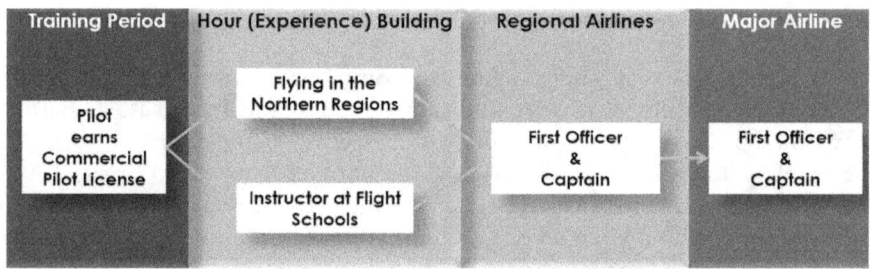

Figure 1.3.2 Model of traditional pilot career progression in Canada.

southern border, where the climate is milder, while the north is made up of smaller rural communities dispersed over large distances.) Acknowledging that several factors (such as regulations) shape pilot career pathways, the increasing demand for airline pilots has a disruptive influence on progression. In this structure, northern air operators and flight schools serve as transitionary employers providing temporary positions before pilots move into more desirable and higher-paid airline pilot positions.

Flight schools in Canada

The demand in air transport has caused two key challenges, flight instructor recruitment and retention. As flight schools are a conduit through which instructor pilots build experience before transitioning to airlines (CAE, 2017) their operations are vulnerable to increasing airline pilot recruitment. Although transitionary, employment at flight schools allows pilots to build flight hours in order to qualify to fly larger aircraft, yet it is very difficult for flight schools to recruit and retain qualified instructors (Canadian Aviation Maintenance Council [CAMC], 2010).

Junior pilots are circumventing the traditional career path, avoiding working in flight schools, to directly accept work within airlines through direct entry cadetships. Cadetships hire pilots with much less experience. The traditional path that required pilots to spend years building flight hours instructing has been reduced to months or eliminated entirely. This limits the availability and experience-level of flight instructors, degrading training quality and capacity, which further exacerbates the pilot supply problem (CAMC, 2010). In the long term, these unsustainable recruitment practices will adversely impact the entire air transport sector's ability to meet the expected industry growth, reducing training capacity and shrinking the pilot supply. Van Dam (2018, p. 1) states "airlines' insatiable demand for pilots threatens to sabotage flight schools' ability to train new ones".

Analysis of pilot recruitment practices shows that airlines would benefit from practices that promote sustainability, such as minimizing the gender gap and motivating minority groups by creating equal access to employment opportunities (Gittens, 2018). Unsustainable recruitment will impact global air transport's capacity and quality of training, adversely impacting air transport's ability to support both the national and international economy. Airlines are compromising Canada's ability to sustain its national air transport by depleting the training capacity of flight schools.

Remote regions in canada

Northern air operators face challenges in comparison to southern airlines. In understanding northern aviation, a brief overview of Canada's geography is critical. Remote regions have small dispersed communities with low populations. Due to geographical disadvantages, satisfying basic needs (such as food and medicine) and reaching public services throughout the year can be difficult. Some remote regions are only accessible through air transport in the winter months (Transport Canada, 2015). For these regions, air transport is essential to their survival (Metrass-Mendes, de Neufville & Costa, 2011).

Traditionally, a junior Canadian pilot's rite of passage starts with northern flying as a stepping stone to future airline jobs in the south. This transience places the northern air operators in a vulnerable position in terms of recruitment and retention. Considering the importance of air transport in remote regions, a high turnover of pilots and unsustainable pilot supply at the north–south axis might threaten air operators and subsequently their ability to serve communities. From a business perspective, transient pilots increase training and operational costs, as training costs would previously result in an operational pilot who would serve many years within an organization. As pilots move on more quickly, businesses have minimal returns on training investments. Jim Heidema, chief operating officer for Northwestern Air (a small regional airline operating 14 aircraft including Cessna 185, 206,and 210, DHC-3 Otter and British Aerospace Jetstream), asserts "it's nice that they [southern airlines] hold our pilots in high regard, but the bad news is they take them from us too soon" (quoted by Thomson, 2017, p. 5). Additionally, unsustainable pilot recruitment and high turnover does not foster a healthy corporate culture focused on safe and efficient operations and continuous improvement through crew resource management, flight safety programmes, enhanced training and scheduling.

Conclusion

The pilot shortage is a crucial issue affecting international aviation. In Canada, both flight schools and air operators in remote northern regions are pathways that develop the professional pilot pool which feeds regional and major airlines. Recruitment and retention within these units are particularly susceptible to changes in the pilot supply.

Unsustainable recruitment practices have started to reduce the training capacity of flight schools which is diminishing the pilot supply for airlines. This practice has broad implications for the economic and social sustainability of air transport. In the context of northern Canada, these practices might lead to air service disruptions compromising vital lifelines providing basic needs and public services. Considering the critical roles of flight schools and air transport in northern Canada, there is a need to reflect on sustainable recruitment methods to mitigate the risk of disruption in air operations and diminishing training capacity.

References

CAE. (2017). *Airline pilot demand outlook: 10-year view.* p. 62.

Canadian Aviation Maintenance Council. (2010). *Human resource study of the commercial pilot in Canada.* p. 123.

Dresner, S. (2002). *The principles of sustainability*. London: Earthscan.
Giddings, B., Hopwood, B. & O'Brien, G. (2002). Environment, economy, and society: Fitting them together into sustainable development. *Sustainable Development, 10*(4), 187–196. doi: 10.1002/sd.199.
Gittens, A. (2018, August 27). *Redoubling our efforts to gain diversity and inclusion: Reflecting on ICAO's Global Aviation Gender Summit*. Retrieved July 1, 2019, from www.unitin gaviation.com/strategic-objective/capacity-efficiency/gender-equality-efforts-to-gain-diversity-and-inclusion/
Gladwin, T. N., Kennelly, J. J., & Krause, T. S. (1995). Shifting paradigms for sustainable development: Implications for management theory and research. *Academy of management Review*, 20(4), 874–907.
Hopwood, B., Mellor, M. & O'Brien, G. (2005). Sustainable development: Mapping different approaches. *Sustainable Development, 13*(1), 38–52. doi: 10.1002/sd.244.
International Air Transport Association. (2018. October 24). *IATA forecast predicts 8.2 billion air travelers in 2037*. Retrieved July 1, 2019, from www.iata.org/press room/pr/Pages/2018-10-24-02.aspx
Metrass-Mendes, A., de Neufville, R. & Costa, A. (2011). Air accessibility in Northern Canada: Prospects and lessons for remoter communities, *7th Forum on Air Transport in Remote Regions*, 1–13.
Omann, I. & Spangenberg, J. H. (2002). *Assessing social sustainability: The social dimension of sustainability in a socio-Economic scenario*, Sustainable Europe Research Institute SERI. Proceedings of the 7th Biennial Conference of the International Society for Ecological Economics, Sousse, 6–9 March 2002. 1–20.
Thomson, J. (2017, June 30). *Northern airlines feeling the strain as Canada faces shortage of 6,000 pilots*. Retrieved from www.cbc.ca.
Transport Canada. (2015). *Comparison of approaches for supporting, protecting and encouraging remote air services: Canada, 2015*. Retrieved from https://assembly.nu.ca/library/GNe docs/2015/001996-e.pdf.
Van Dam, A. (2018, May 21). *Pilot-hungry airlines are raiding flight schools – creating a shortage of instructors to train the next generation*. Retrieved from www.washington post.com
World Commission on Environment and Development. (1987). *Our Common Future*. Oxford: Oxford University Press.

1.4 Case Study – Introducing ALICANTO, the International Association of Aviation and Aerospace Education

Angela C. Albritton, Pascal Revel, and Robert Reid

Aviation is a global, complex industry involving numerous and diverse stakeholders. The industry relies on a highly skilled workforce and competes with other highly technical industries to attract and retain a qualified workforce. At the same time, growth in the aviation industry is surging. Boeing (2018) projects 790,000 new civil aviation pilots and 754,000 new aviation maintenance technicians will be needed over the next 20 years. If the aerospace industry is unable to recruit the skilled workforce it requires, it could have a ripple effect that is felt globally. Many of the competing industries are investing heavily in creating workforce development pipelines, and to fuel its future growth, the aviation industry understands it needs to do the same.

Educational outreach and innovative career pathway programs are emerging as essential to inspiring and recruiting the next generation. Recognizing the need to support future growth and continued stability in aviation, the International Civil Aviation Organization (ICAO) established the Next Generation of Aviation Professionals (NGAP) initiative, to attract and nurture qualified younger aviation professionals that are required to operate, manage and maintain the future international air transport system. Part of the NGAP focus has been to determine ways that industry, academia and government can work together to find more innovative ways to establish career pathway programs and address the growing need for qualified aviation professionals.

The International Civil Aviation Organization's NGAP Summit in 2017 advocated the creation of a consortium of universities to bring in a coordinated voice of academia on subjects relevant to ICAO and other stakeholders, such as the aerospace industry and governments. The network of educational institutions would aim to collaboratively develop initiatives to attract and prepare the next generation, as well as play a leading role to create, publish, distribute, and promote educational programs that serve the needs of the aviation industry and support the education and training of the next generation of aviation professionals. As an organization that represents a collaboration among the aviation and aerospace universities, one aim is to interact with and support the needs of the global set of aviation industry stakeholders with academically supported and informed programs and projects.

Such an initiative was started in 2018 through the collaboration of six respected international aerospace universities: Beihang University in China, Ecole Nationale de l'Aviation Civile in France, Embry-Riddle Aeronautical University in the United States, McGill University in Canada, Moscow State Technical University of Civil Aviation in Russia, and the University of the Witwatersrand in South Africa.

With the encouragement of ICAO, representatives of each of these universities met regularly to create a framework for a new international association of aviation and aerospace universities. The group was keenly aware that ICAO member states have different education systems and workforce development avenues that are often dictated by established accreditation practices, state and regional policies, and various regulations. Rather than focus on the challenges that we knew needed to be addressed as the association matured, the six founding member universities were committed to, and continue to focus on, a common goal of international collaboration and partnership.

The initial group of six looked at existing university consortia for guidance. One of these was the PEGASUS consortium in Europe, which consists of 28 European aerospace universities from 11 different European countries. They collectively graduate more than 2,000 aerospace engineers annually. The PEGASUS model was a good starting point since numerous universities from different countries were involved in its founding. However, it was understood that the European model could not simply be replicated, but would instead need to be modified to allow the development of a framework, structures, and policies that suit an organization of a global nature, with universities from all regions of the world. Additional discussions took place with other aviation and aerospace university consortia in China and the United States. Through many months of fruitful discussions and collaboration, ALICANTO—the International Association of Aviation and Aerospace Education began to come together.

The group strongly committed to ensure that ALICANTO bylaws were flexible and inclusive to find ways to bring in not only the more well-known aerospace universities, but to ensure that barriers were not unconsciously being put in place that would keep out universities with smaller programs. ALICANTO was aware of the important work training organizations were doing to help prepare the future workforce. However, it was believed that the mission of these organizations differs significantly from that of academia. Likewise, conscious consideration was given to the work being done by original equipment manufacturers (OEMs) and other stakeholders in the industry around education and training. Accordingly, it was decided to create two types of membership: a voting membership for universities and a general membership for other stakeholders who support ALICANTO's goals.

Once the group had established the basic framework for our cooperation, ALICANTO was registered as a non-governmental, non-sectarian, non-partisan and non-profit organization in Montréal, Québec. McGill University's Institute of Air and Space Law was chosen as the association's domicile. The creation of ALICANTO was officially announced at the 2nd ICAO Next Generation of Aviation Professionals (NGAP) Summit in Shenzhen, China on December 13, 2018.

The establishment of ALICANTO fills an important gap in the global aviation cooperation framework. Mature associations, such as the International Federation of Airline Pilots' Association (IFALPA), the International Federation of Air Traffic Controllers' Associations (IFATCA), and the Airports Council International (ACI) have been the collective voice of their members. Aviation and aerospace universities have not had one global voice to advocate on their behalf. Increasingly, the highly technical requirements of the aerospace industry require the kind of educated workforce and programs that universities are uniquely qualified to help develop.

Global mission and objectives

ALICANTO's mission is to be a global advocate for aviation education and to represent, promote, and support the interest of its members. The goal is to ensure that graduates are meeting the needs of the industry.

The objectives of ALICANTO are to:

- Represent our members and establish cooperation with various stakeholders, as well as with governments and international organizations;
- Maximize cooperation and mutual assistance among higher educational institutions;
- Assist our members in the development of strategies and actions for attracting and educating the next generation of aviation professionals in a sustainable global society;
- Enhance educational efforts through public awareness of the economic and social importance of civil aviation;
- Create a forum where academics, students, regulators, and worldwide industry can meet, exchange ideas, and conduct research surrounding issues and advances in the field of aviation education, and
- Promote gender equality in aviation and support sustainable development in the field of aviation.

Membership is currently open to universities that meet the ALICANTO eligibility requirements, that is, those universities that regularly deliver at least one higher education degree in aviation and/or aerospace. Members must also be committed to actively participating in the association's activities including at least one annual general assembly meeting.

Next steps

The aviation industry is beginning to adopt innovative education and training solutions to enable optimum learning and knowledge retention. Immersive technologies, adaptive learning, schedule flexibility, and new teaching methods will be needed to effectively meet the educational needs of a wide range of learners. The growing diversity and mobility of aviation personnel will also require instructors not only to be technically competent, but to have cross-cultural, cross-generational, and multilingual skills to engage with tomorrow's workforce.

Some universities already deliver engineering degrees in distance learning formats. Incorporating virtual labs and offering internships enhances these non-traditional education programs. Building more innovative education programs is only one of many strategies to meet the dramatic growth in the need for aviation professionals. Regulators, too, need to stay abreast of changing educational technologies and help expedite approvals through policy changes, if necessary. We have to consider how the strategies and approaches to aviation education and training to which we have become accustomed will not necessarily serve the rapidly changing educational needs of an expanding industry. In brief, many aspects of the way that new aviation professionals have been educated in the past aren't going to work in our future, and aerospace universities can take a leading role in supporting the industry in this changing landscape.

Navigating through this new environment can be both uncomfortable and invigorating at the same time, but is necessary to support continued growth. An ongoing dialogue among industry, academia, and government partners is an essential element in developing the future aviation and aerospace workforce. ALICANTO's primary objective is to support, encourage, and promote that dialogue:

- How many young women and men does the industry need to recruit into aerospace and what can be done to attract them?
- What should the education and training of the future look like?
- How can we maximize training efficiency without compromising safety?
- How will this education be funded and do universities have the necessary resources to prepare the next generation? Are there enough training organizations that can fill the gaps?

It is also important for the aerospace community to understand the barriers that exist for the next generation to enter and/or remain in the field. ALICANTO is committed to understanding those barriers, and collaborating to help the industry and governments address and overcome them. It is often said that the aviation industry does not compete on safety. Similarly, a global, collaborative approach to the problem of developing the next generation of aviation professionals will ensure the industry's stability and strength in the upcoming critical decades of growth.

References

Boeing. (2018). *Pilot & Technician Outlook 2018–2037*. Retrieved June 3, 2019 from: www.boeing.com/commercial/market/pilot-technician-outlook/.
PEGASUS. *PEGASUS Home*. Retrieved June 4, 2019 from www.pegasus-europe.org/

1.5 Chapter – Aviation outreach

Reaching the next generation of aviation professionals

Rebecca K. Lutte and Chenyu Huang

Background

The aviation industry is facing a global professional shortage in many critical areas stemming from a mix of fleet growth, retirements, and increasing worldwide air transportation demand. Boeing projects that 790,000 new civil aviation pilots, 754,000 new maintenance technicians, and over 890,000 new cabin crew will be needed to fly and maintain the world fleet over the next two decades (Boeing, 2018). The regions with the greatest demand are Asia-Pacific, followed by North America (Boeing, 2018). Boeing's forecast is inclusive of commercial aviation, business aviation, and civil helicopter industries. The potential demand from general aviation could further upraise the shortage of aviation professionals. Early in 2011, the International Civil Aviation Organization (ICAO) published a 20-year forecast of global demand of pilots, technicians, and air traffic controllers (International Civil Aviation Organization [ICAO], 2011). Asia, North America, and Europe are the regions with most demand (ICAO, 2011). In addition, the International Air Transport Association (IATA) predicts the total number of air travelers will nearly double to 7.8 billion by 2036 compared to 2016 (International Air Transport Association [IATA], 2017). China, the U.S.A., and India are expected to be the top three leading countries with the fastest growing markets (IATA, 2017). As a result, the growing air transportation market will need more aviation professionals to support safe and efficient air transportation operations. To mitigate the impact from the aviation professional shortage, the aviation industry, government agencies, and nonprofit organizations have conducted a series of initiatives to recruit qualified aviation personnel as well as develop the next generation of skilled aviation professionals.

Outreach defined

Outreach has been widely used as an effective tool to recruit groups that may be difficult to engage in many occupations. Outreach can be defined in a variety of ways (Lutte, 2018) but generally includes the components of targeting and contacting groups, providing resources, information, or services, and ultimately changing behavior in the targeted group (Andersson, 2013; Dewson et al., 2006; Ford et al., 2007). Also common in outreach literature is the emphasis on recruiting underrepresented groups that are "invisible, hidden, or otherwise difficult to engage in a program" (Ford et al., 2007, p. 174). For the purpose of focusing on aviation outreach initiatives, the term aviation outreach is defined below.

Aviation outreach:

> contacting and engaging targeted groups to bring awareness of the career opportunities in the field to recruit the next generation of aviation professionals.
>
> (Lutte, 2018, p. 17)

Aviation outreach model

To address the critical components of an aviation outreach program, the Aviation Outreach Model was developed (Figure 1.5.1). The model focuses on identified essential elements for successful outreach programs based on a review of outreach research (Lutte, 2018). The essential elements include preparation, contact, engagement, sustaining the momentum, and evaluation of results.

Essential elements of outreach:

- *Preparation*: agree on the problem(s) to be addressed, identify goals that focus on the problem(s) identified, establish timeline and budget, identify stakeholders including gatekeepers (defined as those who assist or impede outreach)
- *Contact*: identify specific target groups, identify means to initiate contact, consider strategies to reach underrepresented groups

PREPARATION	CONTACT	ENGAGE	SUSTAIN	EVALUATE
Identify problems	Identify target groups	Implement activities	Incorporate actions to further support	Measure outcomes
Set goals	Make contact	Consider environment		

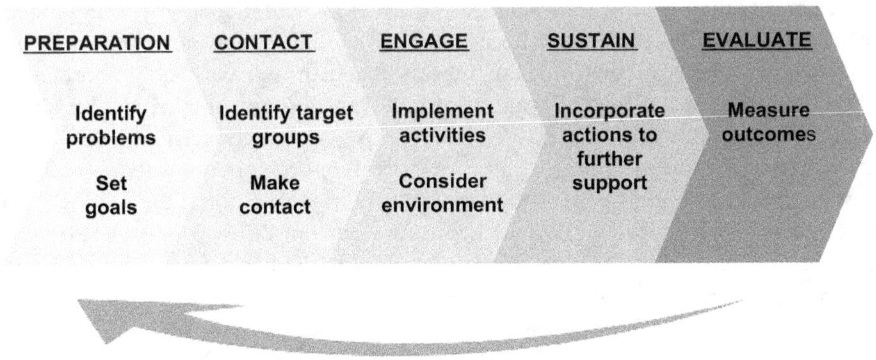

Figure 1.5.1 Aviation outreach model.

- *Engage*: implement the activity for interaction with the targeted group, consider the environment and location relative to the event and location of targeted group, identify threats to safety and develop mitigation strategies to address those threats
- *Sustain*: sustain the momentum by providing next steps to participants, provide a clear path for progress
- *Evaluate*: develop means to measure the results, consider output measures (measures what is produced such as number of participants), consider outcome measures (measures of impact such as changes in behavior), compare results to original goals identified in order to enhance future activities

In order to implement the essential elements of the Aviation Outreach Model, a checklist based on the model and the related Aviation Program Gap Analysis (Lutte, 2018) is provided (Figure 1.5.2). This checklist may act as a resource when establishing an aviation outreach program or as a review of current aviation outreach programs. Based on the model, three aviation outreach programs have been identified as best practices; Experimental Aircraft Association (EAA) Young Eagles, Women in Aviation International Girls in Aviation Day, and Aircraft Owners and Pilots Association (AOPA) High School Initiative (Lutte, 2018). These programs and more are presented in the aviation outreach programs section of this chapter.

Aviation outreach programs: examples from around the world

A diverse group of organizations including nonprofit, industry, university, and government organizations provide a wide variety of aviation outreach programs. A common approach in aviation outreach is to identify the program as STEM-focused outreach; STEM education is defined as the knowledge and skills gained through the study of science, technology, engineering, and math (STEM) subjects (U.S. Department of Education, 2019). The cultivation of graduates who are technically skilled is critical for all countries. The U.S. Bureau of Labor forecasts that the demand for computer occupations will increase by 12.5 percent from 2014 to 2024 and result in nearly half a million new jobs (Fayer et al., 2017). The European Commission reports that Europe will face a shortage of 756,000 information and communication technology employees by 2020 (European Commission, 2017). The skill gap is a global concern as noted in the 2018 World Economic Forum Future of Jobs Report, "the growth potential of new technological expansion is buffered by multi-dimensional gaps across local and global labour markets" (World Economic Forum, 2018, p. 15). A review of aviation outreach strategies that often include a STEM focus provides examples and best practices for further review.

Early in 1935, the U.S. Department of Commerce Bureau of Air Commerce started work with the U.S. National Education Association (NEA) to define and promote aviation education (Federal Aviation Administration [FAA], 2019). The following establishment of FAA and National Aeronautics and Space

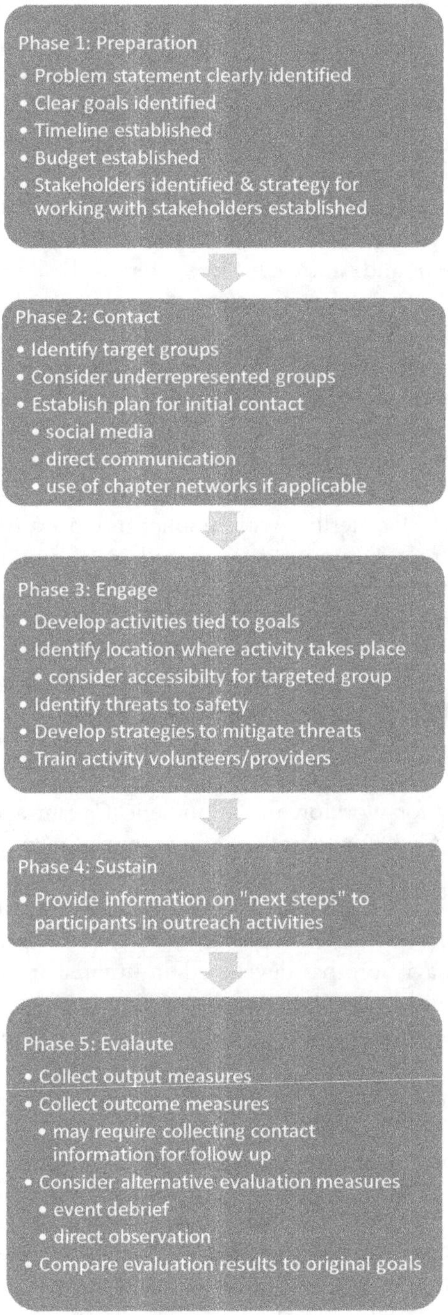

Phase 1: Preparation
- Problem statement clearly identified
- Clear goals identified
- Timeline established
- Budget established
- Stakeholders identified & strategy for working with stakeholders established

Phase 2: Contact
- Identify target groups
- Consider underrepresented groups
- Establish plan for initial contact
  - social media
  - direct communication
  - use of chapter networks if applicable

Phase 3: Engage
- Develop activities tied to goals
- Identify location where activity takes place
  - consider accessibilty for targeted group
- Identify threats to safety
- Develop strategies to mitigate threats
- Train activity volunteers/providers

Phase 4: Sustain
- Provide information on "next steps" to participants in outreach activities

Phase 5: Evalaute
- Collect output measures
- Collect outcome measures
  - may require collecting contact information for follow up
- Consider alternative evaluation measures
  - event debrief
  - direct observation
- Compare evaluation results to original goals

Figure 1.5.2 Aviation outreach model checklist.

Administration (NASA) in 1958 resulted in allocating more resources to aviation education. The FAA STEM Aviation and Space Education (AVSED), created in 1961, is a program supported by government with the mission of helping children and young adults explore the worlds of aviation and aerospace (FAA, 2019). The AVSED Outreach Program was created to prepare and inspire the next generation of skilled professionals for the aviation and aerospace communities, using STEM-based programs (FAA, 2019). Dr. Mervin K. Strickler, Jr, nicknamed the "father of aviation education", joined the FAA in the early 1960s and was a strong supporter of the AVSED program (EAA, 2017). An early leader of aviation education and outreach, Dr. Mervin K. Strickler, Jr. is widely recognized as a distinguished proponent of aerospace education (FAA, 2019; Smithsonian National Air and Space Museum, 2019). With the support of Dr. Mervin and other aviation professionals, the FAA Aviation Education program was mandated under Public Law 94–353 in 1976 (Airport and Airway Development Act, Amendments of, 1976). The FAA's Aviation Education Outreach Program was further supported with Order 1250.2 in 2001 to further promote aviation education and distribute aviation information to all segments of society (FAA, 2001). Partnering with public and private sectors, the STEM AVSED programs target different grades of students around the world with three levels of program, including elementary programs, middle school programs, and high school programs (FAA, 2019). The STEM AVSED helps students learn more about civil and commercial aviation and the critical role of STEM in a young aviator's future by organizing regional and local activities, such as job shadowing, career days, science fairs, field trip opportunities, and workshops for educators.

Outreach programs targeting students in grades K-12 have been implemented as an important strategy for workforce development. Organizations such as Aviation Exploring Posts and Civil Air Patrol Cadet programs function as excellent venues to involve youth in aviation-related activities and stimulate self-esteem and enthusiasm for further involvement in aviation. The Aircraft Owners and Pilots Association (AOPA), as one of the largest and oldest nonprofit organizations dedicated to general aviation, has developed an umbrella program, You Can Fly, to facilitate the sustainable development of aviation professionals (AOPA, 2019a). Confronted with the shortages of current and future aviation personnel, AOPA has created a variety of initiatives to fill the shortage gap. The AOPA High School Initiative is one of those programs developed to expose a diverse group of students to aviation (AOPA, 2019b). Working in partnership with high schools, AOPA delivers real-world preparation for careers in flight and unmanned aircraft systems by providing free STEM based curriculum to participating schools. In addition, AOPA offers flight training scholarships and an annual, teacher focused high school aviation STEM symposium (AOPA, 2019b). The AOPA High School Initiative was identified as a best practice in aviation outreach (Lutte, 2018). For example, the program makes excellent use of school counselors and teachers as gatekeepers to enhance delivery of the outreach program. At the annual AOPA STEM symposium, teachers who participate are also provided with information on aviation career pathways for their students so that they can assist students on next steps towards their journey to an aviation career.

In 1992, the Young Eagles program was created by the EAA to provide children between ages 8 through 17 an opportunity to experience flight in a general aviation (GA) aircraft (EAA, 2019). As of April, 2019, the Young Eagles program has provided over two million young people a free introductory flight (Figure 1.5.3) (EAA, 2019). The program also provides Young Eagles participants with a pathway to continue their pursuits by providing access to free ground school, a student membership in EAA, a free first lesson, and the opportunity to apply for flight training scholarships. As a result, the EAA program was identified as a best practice in aviation outreach and as a prime example of providing next steps to sustain momentum (Lutte, 2018).

Figure 1.5.3 Jodie Gawthrop, age 16, of Westchester, Illinois (left) represents 2 million young people flown in EAA's Young Eagles program with a flight with actor Harrison Ford on July 28 2016 at EAA Airventure Oshkosh in Oshkosh, Wisconsin (EAA photo/Michael Steineke).

University aviation programs often partner with organizations to provide outreach. The Ohio State University Career Eagles Aviation Initiative is a joint initiative to engage and encourage middle and high school students to pursue careers in aviation through academic programs and scholarships (The Ohio State University, 2019). The initiative, a collaboration with the Knowlton Foundation, EAA, and The Ohio State University Center for Aviation Studies was developed as a resource and support system for youth interested in aviation, providing aviation activities throughout the area (The Ohio State University, 2019). The University of Nebraska at Omaha Aviation Institute (UNOAI) hosts an Aviation Exploring post. Exploring is affiliated with the Boy Scouts of America and welcomes young men and women ages 14 to 20. The UNOAI post works with local organizations to provide a range of activities with the overall goal of introducing youth to careers in aviation. Activities include tours, guest lecturers, hands on experience in flight simulators, and a flight experience in an aircraft (University of Nebraska at Omaha, 2019; S. Vlasek, personal communication, May 21, 2019). The Aviation Exploring program has been successful in recruiting students from high school into the university aviation program. Over the past five years, over 180 students participated in the program and 12% of participants went on to enroll in the university aviation program (S. Vlasek, personal communication, May 21, 2019). As noted by Aviation Exploring program director Scott Vlasek:

> I find the Exploring program to be rewarding and beneficial to the students involved. Watching so many of these kids grow from being a sophomore (students aged 15-16) in high school to graduating from our program is such a cool and worthwhile experience. For the Aviation Institute it provides an avenue to recruit students to our program, share information and knowledge about the industry with not only the students but their parents, and to begin to develop future leaders of the industry. Over the past 20 years I have seen kids from Explorers become airline, corporate, and military pilots, work in the airport environment, and become air traffic controllers, dispatchers, and more.
>
> (personal communication, May 21, 2019)

Corporations in the aviation industry engage in a diverse range of ongoing aviation outreach programs to inspire and prepare the next generation of aviators. One example is Boeing's community engagement and education programs (Boeing, 2019). On a publicly available web site, Boeing provides K-12 educational resources including the curiosity machine design challenges developed by Boeing engineers (Boeing, 2019). Airbus provides online and onsite aerospace oriented, STEM based programs targeted to young people throughout the world. Through the Airbus Foundation Discovery Space, information and activities are provided for students, parents, and educators (Airbus, 2019).

One of the largest international aviation outreach programs, The Next Generation of Aviation Professionals (NGAP) initiative, was launched by ICAO in 2009 with the mission of developing strategies, best practices, tools, standards, and guidelines to assist the global aviation community in attracting, educating, and retaining the next generation of aviation professionals (ICAO, 2019a). The ICAO NGAP Progamme was designated as a Global Priority by ICAO in 2016 (Kearns, 2017). Functioning as a global aviation community, NGAP engages with diverse aviation stakeholders including airlines, air navigation service providers, airports, manufacturers, training providers, and universities to focus on aviation outreach, education, and recruitment. To support outreach among youth, ICAO developed many activities and programs targeted to young people. For example, the Future Aircraft Designs and Competitions provides an opportunity to compete with different types of aircraft concept designs to stimulate young people's interest in aviation. In addition, ICAO collaborates with IATA and the Airports Council International (ACI) as joint forces to support the development of tomorrow's leaders of the air transport industry through the Young Aviation Professionals Program (ICAO, 2019a). As part of the NGAP education and development tools, ICAO partnered with the University of Waterloo in Ontario, Canada to develop an online course to introduce students and young professionals to aviation and career opportunities. The Fundamentals of Air Transport course provides a global reach to attract and inform potential aviation professionals (ICAO, 2019b; Kearns, 2017). The course is free, easily accessible in an online format, and available to anyone around the world to explore aviation interests and careers. Subjects include air law, aircraft, operations, navigation, airports, security, environment, accidents, and safety (ICAO, 2019b).

Many aviation outreach programs are dedicated to attracting underrepresented groups to enrich the diversity in aviation professionals. Women in Aviation International (WAI) began in 1990 with the purpose of encouraging and advancing women in all aviation career fields and interests (WAI, 2019a). WAI provides resources and educational outreach programs to educators, aviation industry members, and young people internationally. The WAI Girls in Aviation Day program is targeted to girls ages 8 through 17 (WAI, 2018a). The organization selects a specific day each year for GIAD. Chapters and corporate members of WAI host a variety of events at multiple locations around the world with the singular goal of introducing girls to the world of aviation (Figure 1.5.4). In 2018, GIAD held 99 events in 15 different countries for over 15,000 participants (WAI, 2018a). WAI is also known for the impressive amount of scholarships provided to support their mission. At the 2019 International Women in Aviation Conference, over $875,000 (USD) in scholarships were awarded bringing the total amount of WAI scholarships awarded to over $12,000,000 (WAI, 2019b). An identified best practice in aviation outreach, GIAD is an excellent example of using chapter networks as gatekeepers to reach a wider audience and is a stand out example of targeting underrepresented groups in aviation outreach (Lutte, 2018).

Figure 1.5.4 - WAI India chapter 2018 girls in aviation day

The Organization of Black Aerospace Professionals (OBAP) conducts programs targeted to exposing youth from diverse backgrounds to the aviation industry. The programs, known as Project Aerospace, provide a pathway program for youth with a "cradle to career" focus (OBAP, 2019). The programs include curriculum designed for kids ages 6 through 10, a professional development program where members volunteer as mentors for high school students, and Aerospace Career Education (ACE) Academy summer camps. An active organization in youth outreach, OBAP has awarded $4.8 million (USD) in scholarships and reaches 100,000 youth and young adults annually through their combined programs (OBAP, 2019).

There are also a number of programs targeting underrepresented groups that operate internationally and include a focus on emerging markets. One such example is the Girls Fly Programme in Africa (GFPA) Foundation which provides STEM education and programs to increase awareness of aviation and aviation career opportunities to young women in an effort to continue to strengthen the aerospace industry in Africa (Figure 1.5.5). Currently GFPA is operating in Botswana, Cameroon, and South Africa and is adding operations in Kenya and Uganda (GFPA, 2019). The organization was the first to host an aviation and space camp in Africa, now an annual event. They also participate in the WAI Girls in Aviation Day, hosting events in multiple locations in Africa. The founder of GFPA, Refilwe Ledwaba, the first black woman to pilot a helicopter in the South African Police Service, is an active fixed wing

Figure 1.5.5 Girls Fly programme in Africa Fly for STEM event.

and rotorcraft pilot and mentor to young women interested in aviation careers (Forbes, 2018). The GFPA has conducted outreach to 100,000 youth throughout Africa (GFPA, 2019).

A second example of a program that places emphasis on underrepresented groups and includes emerging markets is Dreams Soar. A global outreach initiative, Dreams Soar has conducted outreach events in 57 countries including Indonesia, Egypt, Thailand, India, and Afghanistan (Dreams Soar, 2019). The mission of the organization is "to inspire the next generation to pursue STEM education and aviation careers" (Dreams Soar, 2019). The key event used to reach that goal was the around the world flight of Shaesta Waiz, the first civilian female pilot from Afghanistan and the youngest woman to complete a solo around the world flight in a single-engine airplane. The highly publicized accomplishment included stops in 22 countries on five continents with 32 outreach events (Dreams Soar, 2019). The global flight was supported by ICAO as part of its NGAP programme (ICAO, 2019c). Dreams Soar continues to focus on global outreach with emphasis on promoting STEM and aviation education to young women.

Conclusion

Aviation outreach programs targeted at raising awareness about the field of aviation and career opportunities will continue to be an essential element to addressing workforce development for the global industry. A large variety of programs exist, provided by an array of stakeholders. It is critical that programs use resources in an effective manner to meet the needed goals. The Aviation Outreach Model and checklist provide a means to explore current and future outreach efforts. One of the most challenging components continues to be evaluation and measuring outcomes (Lutte, 2018). Outcomes, identified as change in behavior, are difficult to determine when programs have large lead times from event to results such as in youth-focused programs. Efforts should be made to capture contact information with participants, to improve the opportunities to track progress towards outreach end goals. Alternative evaluation techniques, such as debriefs with event volunteers and providers and direct observations, may also supplement evaluation measures. Although challenging, efforts to evaluate programs should not be overlooked and lessons learned from the results should be applied to further enhance the outreach efforts. It is a sign of the times that so many diverse groups have invested resources to reach out to the next generation of aviation professionals. Time will reveal just how successful outreach efforts are at meeting the increasing demand for the aviation workforce.

References

Airbus. (2019). Airbus foundation discovery space. Retrieved from www.airbus.com/company/discovery-space.html#Games

Aircraft Owners and Pilots Association. (2019a). History of AOPA. Retrieved from www.aopa.org/about/history-of-aopa

Aircraft Owners and Pilots Association. (2019b). AOPA high school initiative. Retrieved from https://youcanfly.aopa.org/high-school

Airport and Airway Development Act, Amendments of. (1976). Pub. L. No., 94–353.

Andersson, B. (2013). Finding ways to the hard to reach: Considerations on the content and concept of outreach work. *European Journal of Social Work, 16*(2), 171–186. doi: 10.1080/13691457.2011.618118

Boeing. (2018). Pilot & technician outlook 2018–2037. Retrieved from www.boeing.com/commercial/market/pilot-technician-outlook/

Boeing. (2019). Education resources. Retrieved from www.boeing.com/principles/education/explore-by-format.page

Dewson, S., Davis, S., & Casebourne, J. (2006). *Maximizing the role of outreach in client engagement* (Research Report 326). Retrieved from www.employabilityinscotland.com/media/300532/maximising_the_role_of_outreach_in_client_engagement__dwp_research_report__j_dewson_et_al__2006_.pdf

European Commission. (2017). E-skills and jobs in the digital age. Retrieved from https://ec.europa.eu/epale/en/content/e-skills-and-jobs-digital-age

Experimental Aircraft Association. (2017). Introduction to FAA STEM aviation and space education. Retrieved from www.eaa.org/en/eaa/eaa-chapters/chaptergram-articles/2017-10-18-introduction-to-faa-stem-aviation-and-space-education

Experimental Aircraft Association. (2019). Young Eagles. Retrieved from www.eaa.org/eaa/youth/free-ye-flights

Fayer, S., Lacey, A., & Watson, A. (2017). *BLS spotlight on statistics: STEM occupations – past, present, and future*. Washington D.C., U.S: Department of Labor, Bureau of Labor Statistics.

Federal Aviation Administration. (2001). Aviation education outreach program (Order 1250.2). Retrieved from www.faa.gov/documentLibrary/media/Order/1250.2.pdf

Federal Aviation Administration. (2019). About STEM AVSED. Retrieved from www.faa.gov/education/about/

Forbes. (2018, December 24). South Africa's first black female helicopter pilot for SAPS uplifts young women, *Forbes Africa*. Retrieved from www.forbesafrica.com/woman/2018/12/24/in-pictures-south-africas-first-black-female-helicopter-pilot-for-saps-uplifts-young-women/

Ford, C. L., Miller, W. C., Smurzynski, M., & Leone, P. A. (2007). Key components of a theory-guided HIV prevention outreach model: Pre-outreach preparation, community assessment, and a network of key informants. *AIDS Education and Prevention, 19*(2), 173–186.

Girls Fly Programme in Africa Foundation. (2019). About us. Retrieved from www.gfpafoundation.org/about-gfpa/stem-education-programmes

International Air Transport Association. (2017). *2036 forecast reveals air passengers will nearly double to 7.8 billion* [Press release]. Retrieved from www.iata.org/pressroom/pr/Pages/2017-10-24-01.aspx

International Civil Aviation Organization. (2011). *Global and regional 20-year forecasts* (ICAO Doc 9956). Montreal, Canada: ICAO.

International Civil Aviation Organization. (2019a). *Next generation of aviation professionals*. [Press release]. Retrieved from www.icao.int/safety/ngap/Pages/NGAP-Programme.aspx

International Civil Aviation Organization. (2019b). Fundamentals of the air transport system (FATS) elearning course. Retrieved from www.icao.int/safety/ngap/Pages/Fundamentals-of-the-Air-Transport-System-(FATS)-eLearning-Course.aspx

International Civil Aviation Organization. (2019c). Historic "Dreams Soar" round-the-world STEM mission takes flight. Retrieved from www.icao.int/Newsroom/Pages/Historic-Dreams-Soar-round-the-world-STEM-mission-takes-flight.aspx

Kearns, S. (2017). Attracting and informing the next generation of aviation professionals. *ICAO Training Report, 7*(3), 10–13.

Lutte, R. (2018). Aviation outreach model and gap analysis: Examining solutions to address workforce shortages. *Collegiate Aviation Review International, 36*(1), 13–33. doi: 10.22488/okstate.18.100484

The Ohio State University. (2019). Career eagles aviation initiative. Retrieved from https://aviation.osu.edu/careereagles

Organization of Black Aerospace Professionals. (2019). Project aerospace. Retrieved from www.obap.org/project-aerospace

Smithsonian National Air and Space Museum. (2019). Wall of Honor: Dr. Mervin K. Strickler Jr. [Press release]. Retrieved from https://airandspace.si.edu/support/wall-of-honor/dr-mervin-k-strickler-jr

Dreams Soar. (2019). Global outreach. Retrieved from http://dreamssoar.org/global-outreach/

U.S. Department of Education. (2019). Science, technology, engineering and math: Education for global leadership. Retrieved from www.ed.gov/stem

University of Nebraska at Omaha. (2019). Student organizations: Explorers. Retrieved from www.unomaha.edu/college-of-public-affairs-and-community-service/aviation/student-involvement/index.php

Women in Aviation International. (2018a). The results are in: Girls in Aviation Day 2018 a huge success. Retrieved from www.wai.org/news/2018/10/26/results-are-girls-aviation-day-2018-huge-success

Women in Aviation International. (2019a). History. Retrieved from www.wai.org/about-wai

Women in Aviation International. (2019b). WAI conferences. Retrieved from www.wai.org/conference

World Economic Forum. (2018). *The future of jobs report 2018*. Geneva, Switzerland: Author.

1.6 Chapter – STEM and sustainability

Creating aviation professional change agents

Patti J. Clark, Laura Zizka, and Doreen M. McGunagle

Introduction

When we think about Science, Technology, Engineering and Maths (STEM) students we envision them focused intently on data, working in labs and conducting experiments. In the case of aviation students, we can extend that to visual flying or repairing an aircraft. Then the real questions are what are they working on and what is the point? In the simplest terms they are investigating and acquiring knowledge about the environment, materials behavior or computed outcomes. In STEM fields these aspects may be investigated separately (raw) or combined (aircraft). But the true crux of the issue is how these students learn. They learn by doing – touching, viewing and even manipulating items that are tangible and not theoretical. Of course, theory must be comprehended to carry out the experiments or lab work but the application of theory to practice is where a STEM student thrives.

In a world of tangible aspects for STEM students, the concepts of sustainability may seem too abstract to be properly assimilated by them. Arguably, sustainability is best described as a system of systems (Monat & Gannon, 2018) and requires a higher level of understanding beyond concepts and principles. Since the UN declared the "Decade for Sustainable Development" (2004–2015), many higher education (HE) institutions have introduced sustainability into programs and curriculum to develop the student's awareness of sustainability challenges and their economic, social and environmental responsibilities. Nonetheless, the absence of understanding how sustainability goals and challenges are interrelated in context to all three pillars (environmental, economic and social) and all relevant stakeholders is missing from many STEM higher education programs.

To attract and engage aviation students we must make sustainability a part of their studies and reinforce the information with real world examples. Today, knowledge of sustainability varies for students, yet the engagement towards sustainability is crucial to their future. With the evolution of the workforce and the growing needs of the aviation industry, a clear need for concrete sustainability initiatives and actions have emerged. Sustainability in this sense becomes a matter of survival for the future. For this reason, in this chapter, we will attempt to close some gaps in current sustainability studies. Our purpose is to develop a "simple" strategy for integrating all three pillars of sustainability into STEM higher education programs that create authentic engagement and real buy-in from the students that are then replicated in the workplace. Based on the literature and our own research projects, we offer concrete recommendations on how sustainability could be integrated and address the workforce opportunities and challenges that this entails.

Background

The idea that sustainability and subsequently STEM application should focus on the environmental solutions to the world's greatest issues is undoubtedly the largest problem. For the aviation industry, the emphasis is most often placed on environmental issues such as emissions and noise pollution, but the solutions to these issues are embedded in wider political, economic and social frameworks. According to McManners (2016), the aviation industry is one of the most difficult sectors in which to apply sustainability as stakeholder views are highly polarized. For an industry that is embedded in so many areas of the economy it is not difficult to understand the divergent ideas. Manufacturers produce aircraft and the buyers range from general aviation owners to the largest airlines in the world. Maintenance, Repair and Overhaul providers and parts suppliers wield clout through synergistic alliances across the world. Aviation is a global network and today very few have not been touched in some way by the globalization of aviation. Of course, the reach is both good and bad with differing views on sustainability and responsibilities. For current and potential aviation students the discussion can be put into focus from a consumer point of view. How is aviation sustainability relevant to them? We do not have to look far to understand current perspectives. According to McManners, when asked almost all stakeholders find the idea of sustainable flying to be desirable; they just do not see a need or incentive to act now. The results are a lack of awareness and a clear lack of ownership or decision-making power from the potential change-makers.

Another reason why seemingly simple yet possible solutions are squelched is found in the gap between intention/value and behavior/action. Like the stakeholders in the aviation example, students also believe that sustainability is important. They are aware that our current lifestyle is based on unsustainable practices that negatively impact the world, but are reluctant to make lifestyle changes for it (Lambrechts et al., 2018) or give up something they enjoy to make it better (McManners, 2016). However, the good news is emerging generations like GenZ are more aware and sometimes termed Planetary Evangelists due to their holistic views on sustainable initiatives (Mohr & Mohr, 2017). If an academic institution and local community show little interest in sustainability, the students may be disenfranchised towards replicating sustainability principles into their own actions both on campus and later in the workplace. For this reason, addressing sustainability in STEM based aviation programs is crucial to attracting and preparing conscientious leaders of tomorrow.

Sustainability and STEM

STEM can be defined as

> authentic science as participants working in the natural world, working towards a problem, exploring information, using technology, utilizing mathematics, analyzing evidence, developing conclusions, refining questions and methods for future use, communicating results, and recording the results and disseminating information for others to use.
>
> (Burrows et al., 2018, p. 2)

In engineering, for example, students utilize a systems thinking approach to the problem by following these steps. Nonetheless, studies have shown that students do not have an holistic or systems perspective regarding sustainability. Conversely, STEM students compartmentalize sustainability and consider environmental issues more often than social or economic (or political or cultural) (Segalas et al., 2010; Thurer et al., 2018; Zsoka et al., 2013). However, STEM studies, particularly in aviation-related fields must address problems that are complex systems-based and often where no one answer is correct nor satisfactory for all stakeholders involved. With a more applied sense of sustainability from a systems thinking view, aviation STEM students are ideally suited to becoming change leaders of tomorrow.

Creating change leaders

Inherently, change agents have an existing penchant and passion for sustainability issues; they do not have to be convinced about the importance of sustainability and can be the catalysts for the earliest steps toward creating more sustainable solutions. Segalas et al. (2010) posits that engaged engineers are crucial for our future as they can and should be empowered moral and social agents to make society more sustainable (El-Zein & Hedemann, 2016; Zsoka et al., 2013). Indeed, our future depends on engineering students who design activities to sustain rather than degrade the natural environment and enhance human well-being; engineers who can deal with the societal aspects of the technologies they are creating (Segalas et al., 2010). So how do we thread that needle of connecting hard science students like aeronautical engineers, materials scientists, physicists and those in technical fields not only to the broader view of sustainability but to application in the real world?

Teaching sustainability principles

The first opportunity to create or foster connections to sustainability resides in STEM-based programs and students should be prepared for work in a global economy through linking what the students experience (Rus & Yasin, 2015) and learn by doing (Millar, 2014). The tenets or philosophy of sustainability can be accomplished through stand-alone courses, embedded into existing courses at a program or university level (Seto-Pamies & Papaoikonomou, 2016; Sidiropoulos, 2014; Verhulst & Lambrechts, 2015; Zizka & McGunagle, 2017). Additionally, new courses that are interdisciplinary and multidisciplinary and include action-based, real world and work-based contextual environments should be created that offer a collaborative platform for delivery of content and assignments (Clark & Button, 2011; Kennedy & Odell, 2014; Kurland et al., 2010; Mochizuki & Fadeeva, 2010; Muller-Christ et al., 2014; Zizka et al., 2018). From a conceptual level, Figure 1.6.1 illustrates possible approaches to creating sustainability relationships in STEM programs both during studies and beyond, both inside and outside the classroom or campus.

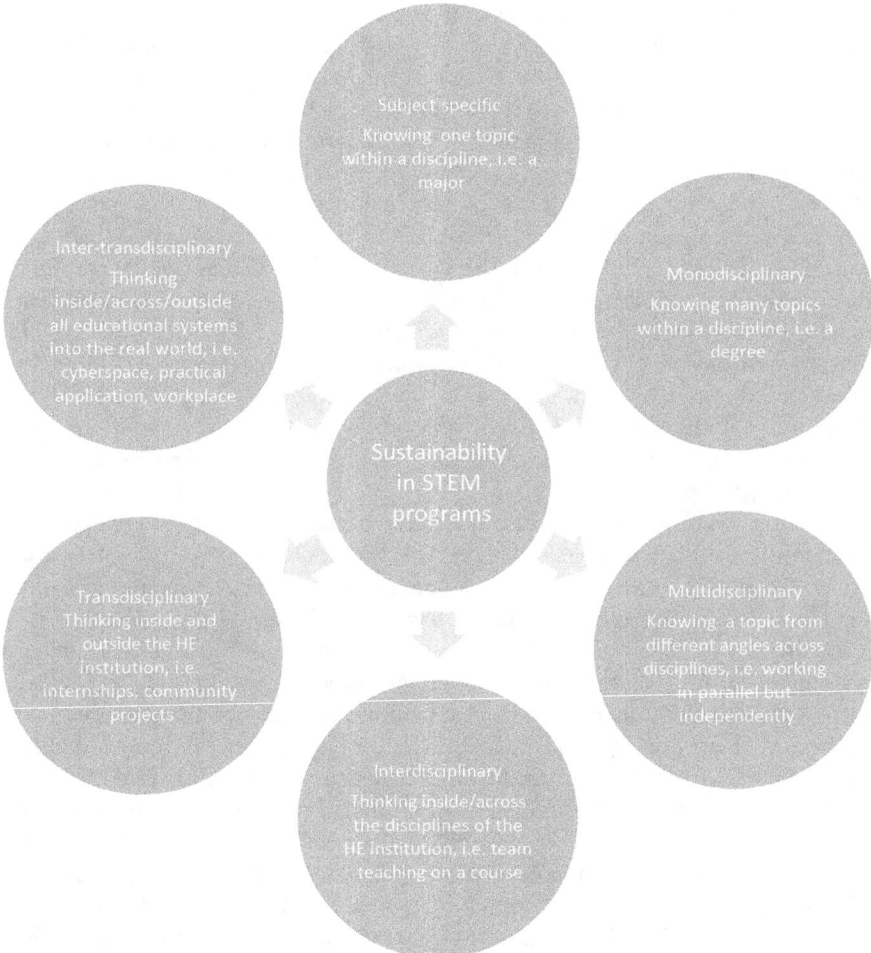

Figure 1.6.1 Methods of including sustainability in STEM education.

As seen in Figure 1.6.1, the options for incorporating sustainability range from subject specific, i.e. one sustainability topic in one specific course and based on one discipline, to inter-transdisciplinary which extends beyond the boundaries of a higher education program and occurs after graduation. Aktas (2015) offered the distinctions between *multidisciplinary, interdisciplinary* and *transdisciplinary* approaches. A multidisciplinary approach offers a weak link and minimal integration between different fields of study where students may work in parallel but are independent of each other, i.e. sustainability is a concept not science and therefore does not overlap into engineering. Interdisciplinary integrates fields of study which have traditionally been considered as separate entities to solve complex problems that cannot be solved using a monodisciplinary framework. Interdisciplinary sustainability is utilized by many colleges to link sustainability to a major field through a specialization or even a linked graduate level degree. While the previous methods are certainly acceptable the needed correlation of systems-based thinking to sustainability is often missed. A more realistic or practical way is transdisciplinary which removes disciplinary barriers to form new groups from different fields to solve many problems over an extended period of time. In this type of learning, a group of science, engineering, math and technical students are presented with problems and must find equitable or sustainable solutions that incorporate the requirements of their disciplines. In short, in a transdisciplinary scenario, the students represent stakeholders in the working world. While the last method is more complex, Zoller (2015) added one further option termed *inter-transdisciplinary* that is defined as an inside and outside perspective that invokes deeper questions and in turn develops higher-order cognitive skills. Therefore, inter, transdisciplinary and even inter-transdisciplinary methods offer better solutions to bringing the needed holistic, out-of-the-box thinking to an increasingly specialized, expert workforce that is necessary to foster sustainable development (Toomey et al., 2015).

Certainly we can see that previous research advocates that STEM programs draw from real-life examples in application of concepts outside the classroom which allows the students to make a connection between disciplines, be more responsive, adaptable, creative and proactive (Egarievwe, 2015; Madden et al., 2013; Prinsley & Baranyai, 2015). Real-world applications of sustainable practices not only raise the awareness of how STEM-related efforts affect the community but also provide the student with engagement between theory and practice.

Moving from concept to application, Zizka et al. (2019) found a link in the top 20 STEM HE institutions and that the sustainability initiatives they implemented enriched the overall community. Therefore, leaders in aviation STEM education should ensure that graduates develop innovative and creative solutions to aviation complex problems by requiring that sustainability is included within their curriculum, both on and off campus. The top-tier STEM HE institutions did not necessarily offer a stand-alone course or two but required specific actions and enterprises be developed as well as executed that benefited the communities in which they resided.

The connecting of context to real world issues is not new and in 2007 Tanggaard discussed the importance of transmitting information across educational context to actual problems by creating a collaborative platform that allows the student to learn through a multi-level approach. Aspects such as weekly readings, media and videos are great resources to assist with filling in some of the gaps on the material. Creation of complex or holistic assignments allows the student to conduct research on current sustainability issues and correlate personal experience with course concepts. The engagement through the course activities and projects provides a robust, engaging learning environment for students.

In the real world, solutions to problems are often economically driven and this is particularly true for sustainability-based issues. Traditional aviation-based engineering and science education has focused on the response to the needs/demands of employers, industry and the marketplace. Recently a more concentrated focus on responsibility for decisions that may have a negative impact on society, environment and resources has transpired (McManners, 2016; Staniskis, & Katiluite, 2016). As noted earlier, our next generation in the workplace deem accountability for actions as very important. This shift provides an opportunity to implement a radical new approach for addressing this issue in how the topics are taught in class and to how they are adapted in the world. McManners stated, "Instead of seeking to make the most economic case sustainable, make the most sustainable solution economically viable" (2016, p. 87). Simply, what McManners is suggesting is a different starting place when incorporating sustainable principles into problems. If the bottom line was actually sustainability and not the typical driver of money; if all decisions and strategies focused on finding sustainable solutions then finding better solutions to the most complex problems would not only be more acceptable, but clearer and better understood by all.

Opportunities

The implementation and consequently attraction to sustainability falls to STEM institutions to incorporate into the mission, strategy and programs. These facets have long been discussed in the literature and many scenarios or approaches are available. Generally, as mentioned before, sustainability principles can be taught through individual courses, individual speakers/ workshops, or individual initiatives, like committees created by students to instigate sustainability changes on campus. Sustainability or sustainable development may be embedded into several or all courses, lead to a certificate, a program and even a degree. In mission and vision statements as part of the overall strategy or as an argument to attain an accreditation like Accreditation Board for Engineering and Technology criteria that includes sustainability principles can be included within the evaluation process. Certifications such as the Assessment Instrument for Sustainability in Higher Education (AISHE) or the Sustainability Tracking, Assessment & Rating

System (STARS) provide an overview of sustainability activities undertaken on campus though not necessarily in the actual content of courses. Perhaps the most important aspect for consideration is that sustainability is not confined to the campus or courses in many schools, but is encouraged outside of the institutions through community partnerships, volunteer work and/or outreach programs. Many STEM programs engage with the community by hosting the outreach programs to encourage younger students, especially girls, to enter the STEM disciplines. While projects that include the community are a common strategy to increase student engagement, another possibility includes collaboration across multiple disciplines and schools.

Current STEM professionals and organizations are uniquely suited to provide mentoring to the upcoming STEM aviation workforce. Sustainability role models or champions provide a physical connection for students to visualize how sustainable development is carried out in design, manufacturing, operations, airlines, airports and the myriad of other sectors in the world of aviation. Even companies or individuals without direct involvement in aviation can provide expertise that may engage STEM aviation students. Systems and design thinking are universal and the concept development can be applied regardless of the product, process or service provided. For true sustainability-minded professionals, the connections to the holistic problem-solving process should be a simple task to articulate and integrate into actionable tasks.

Challenges

Some serious challenges exist to implementing new sustainability initiatives or courses or expanding on sustainability topics currently taught in existing programs or institutions. The first obstacle is buy-in or incorporating sustainable initiatives into the fabric of an organization. While more than 80 percent of U.S. universities have courses related to sustainability, the activities vary from adding sustainability into the existing curriculum to embedding sustainability across full programs. For example, the approach may be through a series of theoretical lectures, or making the institution more sustainable (Segalas et al., 2010). In fact, universities still lag behind corporations and governments in regards to sustainability (Staniskis & Katiluite, 2016) due to lack of money, resources and other structural conditions (Zsoka et al., 2013). Admittedly one of the most serious faults by learning institutions in embedding sustainability is by simply "greening" the curriculum which is not a judicious option and does not lead to greater student engagement or competencies (Segalas et al., 2010). Furthermore, a green curriculum only addresses one aspect of sustainability and with this lopsided approach does not promote pro-sustainability behavior outside of school or later in the workplace (Zsoka et al., 2013). Obviously, there are many opportunities as well as challenges to applying sustainability into the curriculum to increase student engagement. For aviation based programs, the challenges may appear to outweigh the opportunities. However, when approached with foresight and acumen, the actual complexity of the aviation industry offers fertile ground for STEM students to apply sustainable principles through case studies, industry resources and projects.

Inspiring change through application

Case studies based on actual occurrences or problems have long been recognized as a way to connect theory to practice in many professions. Aviation case studies abound and most unconsciously apply sustainable principles through the application of systems-based thinking. As an example, the Lockheed L-188 Electra aircraft accidents are well known and have been examined from many angles. Monat and Gannon (2018, p. 8) pointed out the systems thinking flaws in the engineering and design stages due to a "Failure to adequately address planned and unplanned interactions among system components themselves and between system components and the environment." We can extend the systems thinking application in the example to include the absence of sustainable tenets in product development by applying the same examination of issues. See Figure 1.6.2 for an illustration of how the principles of sustainability applied to the aircraft, yet missed the mark on creating a sustainable product. Note that the money or economic aspect touched on both environmental and social aspects, but the three factors never intersected.

The Lockheed L-188 is only one example although many potential case studies exist based on aviation history and making predictions for the future of the industry. The point is that existing case studies or examples from all areas of aviation can easily be linked to sustainability by using a systems thinking perspective.

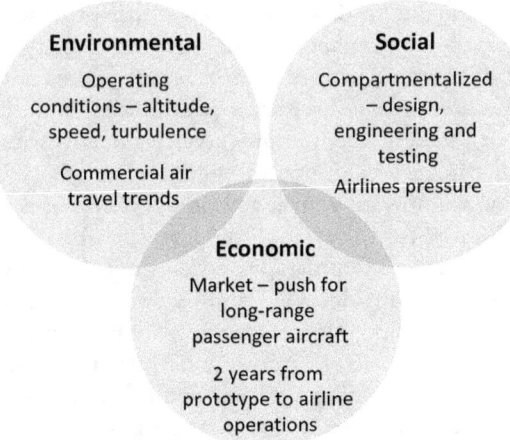

Figure 1.6.2 Lockheed L-188 Electra sustainability.

Resources like Air Transportation Action Group (ATAG), Sustainable Aviation Guidance Alliance (SAGA) and Sustainable Aviation Fuel Users Group (SAFUG) offer a myriad of free sustainability-specific case studies from many sectors of the aviation industry that can be implemented in many types of courses. Industry members from manufacturers to airlines to Maintenance, Repair and Overhaul and many others provide Corporate Social Responsibility reports or separate resources on their websites that can be downloaded for use as sustainability teaching tools. Other more focused organizations like the Aircraft Fleet Recycling Association (AFRA) offer best management practices regarding end of life decisions for aircraft and offer an opportunity for students to examine current processes and future goals. All of the above resources offer opportunities to attract and engage aviation students.

In previous research (Zizka et al., 2019) analyzed 102 community engagement initiatives at the top 20 STEM HE institutions in the U.S. and found all projects fell into the three sustainability aspects of Environmental, Economic and Social. Interestingly, the higher percentage of the programs fell into social initiatives followed by economic and environmental. The community engagement initiatives were conducted both on and off campus. The community engagement involved efforts by the community, students, partners, staff and faculty on both a local and global scale. Zizka et al.'s study found that community engagement was one of the most popular projects for the 20 universities in the form of outreach that inspired students from K-12 to become the next generation of STEM students. Another community engagement initiative discovered was volunteer service that was implemented in the local community and abroad. Several of the universities operated an Office of Community Engagement that promoted community partnerships. A unique requirement for all students at Worcester Polytechnic Institute was the requirement to complete an Interactive Qualifying Project (IQP). The IQP expectation was for students to develop a project that provides a solution based on the intersection of science and technology and society. From a general perspective these initiatives or projects can be implemented for aviation STEM students. The challenges, or in a sense the opportunities, lie in creating aviation-specific initiatives or projects. Community service initiatives may take the form of restoring an aircraft for a local museum, volunteering at airshows, airports and schools and even more innovative projects like upcycling or repurposing aircraft parts into art, tools or for reuse as aviation training artifacts.

Many studies examined different types of learning that could be applied to STEM institutions for introduction and indoctrination of sustainability concepts. Aktas (2015) studied engineering and applied sciences programs that experimented with pragmatic learning and interdisciplinary studies that considered the three sustainability pillars at the same time as the course content(s). Munakata and Vaidya (2015) investigated project and theme-based learning through a creative science project on sustainability that involved multiple disciplines. In their study, STEM students were paired with art students to complete a collaborative video on sustainability practices.

Another relevant innovative project was initiated at a STEM institution in Lausanne, Switzerland. To encourage assimilation of all three pillars of sustainability and offer a truly applied project, the scientists from the STEM institution collaborated with a business and art school in Lausanne. Students were required to work on a multidisciplinary project in teams with a business and art student. Each student brought the best practices and knowledge of their discipline to the project. The STEM student contributed the rigorous scientific process; the business student ensured the economic feasibility; and the art student added the creative touch to satisfy the social affinity aspect. Working in a team, they shared ideas that they would not have otherwise considered. For example, a purely STEM team would have been able to check for scientific flaws or limitations, but not necessarily consider the creative or economic side of the technology or tool they developed. For Aktas (2015), working in a team of different backgrounds, disciplines and perspectives leads to better results and more effective solutions that align with the three sustainability pillars and bring added value to the student learning experience. Similar projects can easily be implemented in aviation STEM programs and may have a positive benefit of attracting business and art students to aviation career fields. We need to remember that our next generation of aviation professionals are already change agents in many ways. The upcoming GenZ group has already solidified their commitment to professions, companies and initiatives that make a positive difference in the world and embrace ethical behavior. As aviation professionals, we must take sustainability as a concept and sustainable development as a process seriously to ensure we attract a sufficient number of STEM students to aviation fields. We cannot accomplish the tasks simply by providing information about what sustainability is, but must integrate authentic resources, case studies and projects into curriculum.

Practical suggestions/recommendations for action

To summarize the suggested actions, for educators/trainers of aviation professionals we offered insight into specific recommendations and activities for teaching or training aviation STEM students and interns. We presented information to assist with debunking common myths and pitfalls often associated with teaching sustainability. Furthermore, the information for STEM educators is one of a need to incorporate all three pillars of sustainability into different types of courses and academic levels Most importantly, application of sustainable tenets must be conveyed through tangible initiatives for STEM students and not approached purely from a theoretical platform.

With community stakeholders the opportunities are many and the authors provided information on current best practices and the potential participation opportunities in applied projects with aviation-focused STEM students such as case studies, field trips, collaborations with airports, aviation companies, internships – perhaps even a consideration for virtual internships. STEM students do not come from equal circumstances and the challenge to communities is to find innovative ways to foster the development of the STEM aviation professionals of tomorrow.

Last but certainly not least, STEM professionals are needed to imprint as well as inspire students by serving as local or regional aviation sustainability champions or role models. It is particularly important to make sure these role models have "change" experience in areas such as advanced manufacturing methods, alternative fuels, solar, environmental and social initiatives. Ideally, these champions should originate from diverse or challenging backgrounds to ensure the message is relevant to emerging and diverse populations. The next generation of social champions is appearing and the focus of the message from the aviation industry must be that we not only care but are taking action to further social equity. This is an imperative in order to attract the needed workforce of tomorrow.

In conclusion, attracting the next generation of aviation professionals requires a 21st-century view of the landscape to prepare students for the opportunities and challenges outside the classroom. Based on previous research and personal experience the authors have generated in the preceding pages an offering of the best of all teaching practices and approaches in order to better prepare the next generation of aviation STEM professionals to become the vital *sustainability thought leaders* needed for the years to come. Our collective future depends on them.

References

Aktas, C. B. (2015). Reflections on interdisciplinary sustainability research with undergraduate students. *International Journal of Sustainability in Higher Education, 16*(3), 354–366. doi: 10.1108/ijshe-11-2013-0153

Burrows, A., Lockwood, M., Borowczak, M., Janak, E., & Barber, B. (2018). Integrated STEM: Focus on informal education and community collaboration through engineering. *Education Sciences, 8*(4), 1–15. doi: 10.3390/educsci8010004

Clark, B., & Button, C. (2011). Sustainability transdisciplinary education model: Interface of arts, science, and community (STEM). *International Journal of Sustainability in Higher Education, 12*(1), 41–54. doi: 10/1108/14676371111098294

Egarievwe, S. U. (2015). Vertical education enhancement: A model for enhancing STEM education and research. *Procedia Social and Behavioral Sciences, 177*, 336–344. doi: 10.1016/j.sbspro.2015.02.354

El-Zein, A., & Hedemann, C. (2016). Beyond problem solving: Engineering and the public good in the 21st century. *Journal of Cleaner Production, 137*, 692–700. doi: 10.1016/j.jclepro.2016.07.129.

Lambrechts, W., Ghijsen, P. W. Th., Jacques, A., Walravens, H., van Liedekerke, L., & van Petegem, P. (2018). Sustainability segmentation of business students: Toward self-regulated development of critical and interpretational competences in a post-truth era. *Journal of Cleaner Production, 202,* 561–570. 10.1016/j.jclepro.2018.07.303

Madden, M. E., Baxter, M., Beauchamp, H., Bouchard, K., Habermas, D., Huff, M., Ladd, B., Person, J., & Plague, G. (2013). Rethinking STEM education: An interdisciplinary STEAM curriculum. *Procedia Computer Science, 20,* 541–546. doi: 10.1016/j.procs.2013.09.316

McManners, P. J. (2016). Developing policy integrating sustainability: A case study into aviation. *Environmental Science & Policy, 57*(C), 85–92. doi: 10.1016/j.envsci.2015.11.016

Millar, E. (2014). The expectation gap: Students' and universities' roles in preparing for life after grad. *Canadian University Report.* Retrieved from https://www.theglobeandmail.com/news/national/education/the-expectation-gap-students-and-universities-roles-in-preparing-for-life-after-grad/article21187004/

Mochizuki, Y., & Fadeeva, Z. (2010). Competences for sustainable development and sustainability: Significance and challenges for ESD. *International Journal of Sustainability in Higher Education, 11*(4), 391–403. doi: 10.1108/14676371011077603

Mohr, K.A.J., & Mohr, E. S. (2017). Understanding Generation Z Students to Promote a Contemporary Learning Environment. *Journal on Empowering Teaching Excellence,* 1(1), Article 9. doi: 10.15142/T3M05T

Monat, J. P., & Gannon, T. F. (2018). Applying systems thinking to engineering and design. *Systems,* 6, 3. doi: 10.3390/systems6030034

Muller-Christ, G., Sterling, S., van Dam-Mieras, R., Adomßent, M, Fischer, D., & Rieckmann, M. (2014). The role of campus, curriculum, and community in higher education for sustainable development: A conference report. *Journal of Cleaner Production, 62,* 134–137. doi: 10.1016/j.jclepro.2013.02.029

Munakata, M., & Vaidya, A. (2015). Using project and theme-based learning to encourage creativity in science. *Journal of College Science Teaching, 45*(2), 48–53. Retrieved from www.montclair.edu/media/montclairedu/csam/cmsproject/project-theme-learning-creativity-science.pdf

Prinsley, R., & Baranyai, K. (2015). STEM skills in the workforce: What do employers want? *Office of the Chief Scientist,* (9), 1–4.

Rus, R. C., & Yasin, R. M. (2015). Cultivating learning: A grounded theory of skills acquisition for vocation in modern apprenticeships. *Procedia - Social and Behavioral Sciences, 174,* 275–282. doi: 10.1016/j.spspro.2015.01.658

Segalas, J., Ferrer-Balas, D., & Mulder, K. F. (2010). What do engineering students learn in sustainability courses? The effect of the pedagogical approach. *Journal of Cleaner Production, 18,* 275–284. doi: 10.1016/j.jclepro.2009.09.012

Seto-Pamies, D., & Papaoikonomou, E. (2016). A multi-level perspective for the integration of ethics, corporate social responsibility and sustainability (ECSRS) in management education. *Journal of Business Ethics, 136,* 523–538. doi: 10.1007/s10551-014-2535-7

Sidiropoulos, E. (2014). Education for sustainability in business education programs: A question of value. *Journal of Cleaner Production, 85,* 472–487. doi: 10.1016/j.jclepro.2013.10.040

Staniskis, J. K., & Katiluite, E. (2016). Complex evaluation of sustainability in engineering education: Case and analysis. *Journal of Cleaner Production, 120,* 13–20. doi: 10.1016/j.jclepro.2015.09.086

Tanggaard, L. (2007). Learning at trade vocational school and learning at work: Boundary crossing in apprentices' everyday life. *Journal of Education and Work, 20*(5), 453–466. doi: 10.1080/13639080701814414

Thurer, M., Tomasevic, I., Stevenson, M., Au, T., & Huisingh, D. (2018). A systematic review of the literature on integrating sustainability into engineering curricula. *Journal of Cleaner Production, 181*, 608–617. doi: 10.1016/j.jclepro.2017.12.130

Toomey, A. H., Markusson, N., Adams, E., & Brockett, B. (2015). Inter- and trans-disciplinary research: A critical perspective. In *GSDR 2015 Brief*. Retrieved from https://sustainabledevelopment.un.org/content/documents/612558-Inter-%20and%20Trans-disciplinary%20Research%20-20A%20Critical%20Perspective.pdf

Verhulst, E., & Lambrechts, W. (2015). Fostering the incorporation of sustainable development in higher education: Lessons learned from a change management perspective. *Journal of Cleaner Production, 106*, 189–204. doi: 10.1016/j.jclepro.2014.09.049

Zizka, L., & McGunagle, D. M. (2017). Sustainability: Exploring gaps in higher education. *Proceedings of the BAM 2017: 31st Annual Conference of the British Academy of Management*, Warwick Business School, Coventry, U.K.

Zizka, L., McGunagle, D. M., & Clark, P. (2018). Sustainability in STEM higher education: It takes an institution to make social change. *32nd Annual Conference of the British Academy of Management*.

Zizka, L., McGunagle, D. M., & Clark, P. (2019). Teaching Sustainability in STEM Classrooms. *Conference Proceedings: Fifteenth International Conference on Environmental, Cultural, Economic & Social Sustainability*, Vancouver, BC, January 17–19, 2019.

Zoller, U. (2015). Research-based transformative science/STEM/STES/STESEP education for "sustainability thinking": From teaching to "know" to learning to "think." *Sustainability, 7*, 4474–4491. doi: 10.3390/su7044474

Zsoka, A., Szerenyi, Z. M., Szechy, A., & Kocsis, T. (2013). Greening due to environmental education? Environmental knowledge, attitudes, consumer behavior, and everyday pro-environmental activities of Hungarian high school and university students. *Journal of Cleaner Production, 48*, 126–138. doi: 10.1016/j.jclepro.2012.11.030

1.7 Professional reflection

The case of Cambodia: challenges in training the next generation of aviation professionals

Jennifer A. Meszaros

ខ្លាពឹងព្រៃ ព្រៃពឹងខ្លា

Translation: The tiger depends on the forest; the forest depends on the tiger

As one of Asia's most promising emerging markets, and despite its highly seasonal visitor numbers, Cambodia has traditionally posted some of the fastest growth rates in the global aviation industry, recording strong double-digit passenger growth in recent years. From 2010 to 2015, Cambodia's aviation market grew by at least 13 percent annually (Center for Aviation, 2017). In 2016, total passenger numbers at Cambodia's three international airports – Phnom Penh, Siem Reap and Sihanouk – handled 7 million passengers, followed by 8 million in 2017 (Cambodia Airports, 2017). A year later, Phnom Penh was crowned the world's fastest-growing major airport as all three airports combined crossed the 10 million passenger mark (Cambodia Airports, 2018; Casey, 2019).

In recent times, visa exemptions and improved air connectivity have greatly increased access to Cambodia and its Southeast Asian neighbors (World Tourism Organization, 2018). Together, the ten member states (Brunei, Cambodia, Indonesia, Laos, Malaysia, Myanmar, Philippines, Singapore, Thailand, and Vietnam) make up the Association of Southeast Asian Nations (ASEAN) – a regional trade bloc that aims to create a common market by 2025. To that end, the ASEAN Economic Community (AEC) was established as a way to promote economic, political, social and cultural inclusion across a region of more than 640 million people with a combined gross domestic product (GDP) of US$2.8 trillion (Sing, 2018).

Air travel and the ASEAN Single Aviation Market (ASAM) open sky policy is part of a larger discussion of the AEC. The relaxations of market access rights within and between sub-regions, which began in the 1990s, has been instrumental in creating an environment where airlines can expand their services and increase their competitiveness to appeal to price-sensitive passengers (Tan, 2013). While ASEAN has significantly deepened its regional integration through multilateral and bilateral agreements, as well as with its own version of an open skies treaty (Tan, 2013), a clearly articulated vision of what a regional identity looks like is difficult to define (Jones, 2004). Rather, ASEAN economies display a remarkable degree of political, social and economic diversity (Acharya, 2017); it is a region united by a trading bloc but divided by political ideologies, cultural norms and economic inequality.

The disparity between nations is quite evident when examining Cambodia's place in the larger ASEAN context. While the Kingdom has been a positive force for the process of regional integration and community building since the 1990s (Peou, 2016), it is difficult to deny the existence of significant economic and social disparities between Cambodia and its more affluent neighbors. Whereas Singapore is consistently rated the richest country in Southeast Asia with a GDP per capita reaching US$64,030 in 2018 (CEIC Data, n.d.a), Cambodia ranks as one of the poorest countries in the region with a GDP per capita of US$1,538.000. (CEIC Data, n.d.b). According to the Asian Development Bank (ADB, 2018a), nearly 70 percent of Cambodians live on less than US$3.20 a day. Approximately 4.5 million people remain near-poor, vulnerable to falling back into poverty when exposed to economic and climate shocks. (World Bank, 2019a). Stubborn pockets of poverty also continue to prevail in remote areas, where households have restricted access to productive resources and education (Levy, 2017). These issues are magnified further when examining Cambodia's youthful demographics; almost two-thirds of the population is under the age of 30. Only 23 percent of the nation's 16 million live in urban areas (World Bank, 2018a).

Since the end of the civil war, the Royal Government of Cambodia has made impressive gains to alleviate poverty through a series of national reforms and initiatives as well as the adoption of the United Nation's Sustainable Development Goals (Sivhuoch & Sreang, 2015). Coordination between non-government organizations (NGOs) and major stakeholders has also been a long-standing feature of the government's Rectangular Strategy – a policy program designed to boost human resources, economic diversification, private sector investment, job creation, and inclusive and sustainable development (Royal Government of Cambodia, 2018). Official estimates show that the percentage of Cambodians living under the national poverty line fell from 47.8 percent in 2007 to 13.5 percent in 2014 (World Bank, 2019a). In 2016, the World Bank revised the status of Cambodia's economy, moving it up a rung from the low-income bracket into lower-middle-income territory after its 2015 gross national income per capita (GNIPC) surpassed the US$1,026 threshold to reach US$1,070. Major social indicators, in both education and health sectors, have also greatly improved including a reduction in mortality rates among women and children (World Bank, 2019a).

Rising inflows of foreign direct investment (FDI), deeper integration in global value chains and a stable macroeconomy have all contributed greatly to poverty reduction (ADB, 2014). Fueled by garment exports and tourism activities, Cambodia's economy has sustained an average growth rate of 7.7 percent between 1995 and 2018, making it among the fastest-growing economies in the world (Ly et al., 2019). With economic growth averaging 7 percent annually, the government expects Cambodia to reach upper-middle-income status by 2030 and become a high-income nation in 2050 (Royal Government of Cambodia, 2018). The World Bank Group classifies upper-middle-income economies as having a GNIPC of at least US$3,996, and high-income economies with a GNIPC of at least US$12,375.

Robust economic growth over the medium term is expected to result in continued poverty reductions; the longer-term outlook, however, depends on Cambodia's ability to productively absorb rising FDI inflows and promote domestic investment against a backdrop of external and internal pressures (World Bank, 2019b). The prolonged expansion of domestic credit growth has overextended the financial sector. The escalating trade war between the United States and China has potential downside risks to Cambodia's growth prospects. Meanwhile, the Kingdom is facing a temporary suspension of its preferential access under the Everything But Arms (EBA) scheme, which could jeopardize economic growth (World Bank, 2019b).

To mitigate potential risks, Cambodia is in various stages of implementing large-scale initiatives and reforms contained in various economic, educational and social frameworks including the government's Rectangular Strategy Phase IV and the newly developed 2019–2023 Cambodia Trade Integration Strategy. Among the key priorities for the government is ensuring that there is enough human capital and institutional capacity-building in higher value-added sectors to diversify and sustain growth (Royal Government of Cambodia, 2018).

ចេះមកពីរៀន មានមកពីរក

Translation: Learn from studying, wealth from working

Research demonstrates that industrialization is more challenging for developing countries as world markets become increasingly competitive (de Almeida et al., 2014). In the case of Cambodia, the country not only has to mitigate external pressures, but the Kingdom must also address a number of institutional, human capital, and infrastructure constraints to boost competitiveness and create a vibrant private sector. This is a daunting task for Cambodia given its not-so-distant history of war and genocide. While it has risen from a fractured state to a leader in poverty reduction (World Bank, 2017) – in a relatively short time period – one third of children under five will experience malnutrition and stunting (World Bank, 2019b), impacting later life outcomes including adult earnings potential (McGovern et al., 2017).

Cambodia also lags behind its neighbors in terms of education and skill, making it difficult for its citizens to work and compete in more advanced markets (World Bank, 2018b). The World Economic Forum's Global Human Capital Report (2017) assigned Cambodia the poorest score in ASEAN for educating and training its citizens to develop a competitive workforce and put their skills to productive use. Findings reveal that only 43 percent of students completed lower secondary level (Grade 7 to 9) in the 2016–2017 academic year; 20 percent graduated from upper secondary (Grade 10 to 12) in the same period (MOEYS, 2017). Not being adequately prepared for school, attending school irregularly, and experiencing poor quality of learning modalities and teaching styles, including corporal punishment, are impacting enrollment rates. Additionally, many parents, especially in rural areas, have difficulty understanding the value of education (Royal Government of Cambodia, 2014).

To a large extent, Cambodia's economic success has been driven on the back of cheap low-skilled labor to manufacturer products for export (World Bank, 2018b). The industrial sector is dominated by garments and footwear manufacturing as well as construction, which contribute substantially toward Cambodia's GDP. Looking forward, the demand for occupations such as garment, agricultural and fishery workers, which accounted for the majority of jobs in the past are not likely the occupations that will drive competitiveness and future job growth (World Bank, 2018b). New mega-trends have emerged including regional integration and a shift toward smart production and value chains will inevitably reshape the country's employment landscape (World Bank, 2018b).

Against this backdrop, the government has ramped up efforts to develop its technical and vocational training institutes (TVET) in order to build the right skillsets for the next generation. Central to this is having enough funds to upgrade its existing TVET system. Since 2015, the country has benefited from an ADB policy-based and project loan of $30 million to renovate its existing TVET systems, strengthen governance and management of its vocational programs, and address gaps in access, quality, institutional capacity and gender equality (ADB, 2019).

While Cambodia has made significant headway towards improving its TVET system, enrollment remains quite low with only 28,702 (20.7 percent females) trainees enrolled in 2017 (ADB, 2018b). Among the key issues impacting enrollment are a lack of consistency, diversity and flexibility in training programs, a lack of awareness about the value of TVET, the tendency for parents to encourage their children to further their studies in general education, limited cooperation and sponsorship from the private sector and a lack of financial resources to fund workshops and technical equipment (World Bank, 2018b). Findings also reveal that the low quality of general education means students lack fundamental numeracy and literacy skills to succeed in TVET programs (ADB, 2016). While TVET graduates are more prepared for the workforce, slow adaptation to the new industrial working requirements and a lack of motivation and interpersonal skills are among some of the key challenges faced by employers (ADB, 2018b).

Beyond this, the research also suggests that there is a lack of interest and willingness among young people to enroll and complete a TVET program (ADB, 2016). Even when TVET is free and accessible, there are still costs involved, such as food and transport, which poses a barrier to disadvantaged youth. Giving up paid employment to study full-time is also an obstacle to enrollment. Finally, there is a negative perception of TVET programs in the public sphere (ADB, 2016).

Looking forward, the government requires a wide range of solutions and industry cooperation to promote TVET as a credible alternative to university (Figure 1.7.1). One method is to promote vocational training as a lifestyle choice (ADB, 2016). Research also demonstrates that there is an urgent need to bridge the gap between education and industry to ensure training providers are more responsive to labor market needs (ADB, 2016).

ចូរកុំវាយតម្លៃមនុស្សតែសំបកក្រៅ

Translation: You cannot judge a book by its cover

In the context of aviation, little is understood about the human capital requirements given the absence of industry-wide data. Rather, studies on the shortage of skilled workers have largely excluded the current and future needs of Cambodia's air transport sector. This is surprising given that the industry – which includes the airlines, the airport operator, air traffic control, general

Figure 1.7.1 Pochentong International Airport inaugural, 1964 (currently known as Phnom Penh International Airport).
© Thongsin Noreak Seung.

aviation, ground handlers, airport security, immigration and customs, aircraft maintenance, and other airport-related activities – directly and indirectly supports roughly 1.7 million jobs (20 percent of Cambodia's working population), and 17 percent of the country's GDP (Sinn Chanserey Vutha, personal communications, May 20, 2019). In looking at the greater region as a whole, activities in Asia-Pacific's air transport sector – and the indirect and induced impacts that flow from that – support over 30 million jobs and contribute to over $700 billion of the region's GDP (IATA, 2019).

While the absence of research makes it challenging to properly plan and execute adequate training programs to support the development and growth of the Kingdom's aviation sector, some information can be gleaned in looking at the available research on the overall shortage of skilled workers. In a 2017 National Employment Agency study, around 47.5 percent of workplaces with vacancies claimed to have experienced recruitment difficulties. When asked why vacancies were hard to fill, the most usual cause (41 percent) was the low number of applicants with the required qualifications. This first reason suggests that Cambodia's education system has not yet produced enough skilled workers to respond to employer requirements (NEA, 2018).

Since 2013, the author has conducted numerous interviews with Khmer aviation leaders and personnel working in Cambodia's air transport sector, revealing insights into current issues (excerpts from these interviews are included at the end of this chapter). All respondents reported that there was a shortage of qualified aviation personnel across all fields varying from pilots and air traffic controllers to ground handling staff and customer care agents. These findings are aligned with the results found by the International Air Transport Association (IATA) when looking at aviation in a global context. According to IATA (2018), attracting and retaining talent across the world remains a challenge; the two biggest barriers are the availability of applicants with the right skill levels and qualifications and the salary demands of new applicants.

តក់១ពេញបំពង់

Translation: Drop by drop fills the container

In 2016, the author founded Aviation in Asia (AIA) – a competency-based outreach program designed to cultivate youth interest in aviation and aerospace. The idea arose from a community need evidenced by a lack of awareness and industry-specific education to support young people to enter the field.

Rather than reinvent the wheel, AIA is based on the principles of ICAO's NGAP initiative and the United Nations' Agenda 2030 Sustainable Development Goals. The program offers free aviation education and mentorship to young people living in Cambodia and the greater ASEAN region. Students have access to a wide variety of resources including Khmer language aviation cartoons and educational material; free community workshops and events are held throughout the year to increase awareness and understanding of aviation careers.

The success of AIA is attributed to the overwhelming support received from people working in Cambodia's civil aviation sector and the Royal Cambodian Air Force. The support of the community has also been instrumental in helping the program reach a large and varied audience across Asia-Pacific, Central Asia, Africa, and the Middle East. Today, Aviation in Asia reaches up to seven million people per month on social media.

In mid-2016, the newly established Civil Aviation Training Center (CATC) in Phnom Penh officially opened its doors, effectively becoming Cambodia's first modern aviation facility. Funded by South Korea's International Cooperation Agency (KOICA) on behalf of the Cambodian and Korean governments, the US$10.1 million center serves as a training arm of the State Secretariat of Civil Aviation (SSCA), boasting a state-of-the-art air traffic control and radar simulator as well as an X-ray room, computer-based training (CBT) classrooms, a library and disability-friendly facilities. To date, the school has trained over 1,000 personnel across the sector in a wide spectrum of courses (i.e., air traffic control, safety management systems, dangerous goods awareness, aviation security, international air law, and aviation English). Recognizing the need to implement internationally recognized standards, the center is now moving towards achieving ICAO TRAINAIR PLUS full membership. Under the program, members make up a global collaborative network that develops, exchanges and benefits from high-quality standardized aviation training materials in such areas including flight safety and training competency development (ICAO, n.d.a).

In late 2018, the CATC launched a public event to highlight the value of Cambodia's aviation sector. Central to this was the promotion of an aviation English course developed by the author to introduce Cambodian nationals to the technical language commonly used across eight subjects (i.e., standard phraseology, human factors, airport operations, the science of aerodynamics, aircraft and engine systems, navigation and technology, aviation hazards and meteorology). In developing the syllabus for Aviation Fundamentals Level 1, the author relied on several sources including the government's Rectangular Strategy Phase IV, the National TVET Policy 2017–2025, findings from the Ministry of Women's Affairs, ICAO's guidelines for aviation English training programs, ICAO's NGAP initiative, ADB TVET findings and market labor research. The author currently teaches this course to both the general public and SSCA students. Additional English language aviation courses are planned for 2020.

In July 2019, the CATC reached another significant milestone with the launch of its third public Aviation Fundamentals course: the number of females enrolled greatly outnumbered the male students. While research demonstrates that women are highly underrepresented in aviation across the globe (Turney, 2018), the achievement was made even more remarkable by the fact that Cambodia continues to be underpinned by harmful gender stereotypes that prevent women from having equal access to rights and opportunities within society (Ministry of Women's Affairs, 2014). Despite the tremendous efforts made by Cambodia's Ministry of Women's Affairs

(MoWA) over the past two decades, societal norms continue to limit a woman's ability to enter higher education and skilled occupations. Women also have less access than men to the resources necessary to expand their businesses due to traditional stereotypes that assign women less power than men in decision-making processes (MoWA, 2014). Harmful social norms are also attributed to wide-spread gender-based violence (Ellsberg et al., 2017); almost one in four women in Cambodia is a victim of physical, emotional or sexual violence (Fulu et al., 2013).

Aligned with the above, Cambodian society, particularly in rural areas, is still guided by the Chbab Srey – a code of conduct for Khmer women (Anderson & Kelly, 2018). Considered an important piece of Cambodian literature, the Chbab Srey is a poem that was orally passed down from the 14th to 19th centuries and later codified in written form. It details a mother's advice to her newly married daughter, dictating how she should behave in society with a focus on showing subservience to her husband and deference towards men (Anderson & Kelly, 2018). In 2007, the MoWA successfully lobbied to have sections of the Chbab Srey removed from the educational curriculum. Today, a truncated version can be found in textbooks aimed at grade eight and grade nine schoolgirls (Anderson & Kelly, 2018).

Further research is required to fully understand why CATC's Aviation Fundamentals course is appealing to young women. The class is relatively small, which makes generalizability difficult. Nevertheless, the upward trajectory of female enrollees can be seen across all three public aviation courses with a near equal split of male and female students. In looking at possible causalities, one factor could be because the instructor is a woman who has actively promoted the value of Cambodia's aviation sector since 2016; CATC also employs a large number of women, including female deputy directors. Another contributing factor could be due to the repeated efforts made by the MoWA and the Cambodian National Council for Women to combat harmful gender-based stereotypes. A fourth factor could be correlated to how young girls and women view other Khmer women in leadership and aviation positions. Albeit few, these women are often described as "idols," regardless if they work in the government, military or private sector (Figure 1.7.2). Similarly, writer Thon Thavry (author of "The Proper Women," which challenges Cambodia's social and cultural norms) and vlogger Catherine V. Harry (vlogger of "A Dose of Cath," which focuses on sexual and reproductive health) have both played crucial roles in questioning the normative expectations of women. Intergovernmental bodies, NGOs and women's resource centers have also been instrumental in reducing poverty, raising health and education standards, and promoting gender equality (McGrew et al., 2004).

Moving forward, both the author and the CATC will continue to identify potential barriers to workforce upskilling and the realization of the benefits of vocational training. The SSCA, Cambodia Air Traffic Services (CATS), and the CATC are also making a concentrated effort to increase industry dialogue and stakeholder engagement to address the current and anticipated shortage

Figure 1.7.2 Image of So Sokna.

Note: So Sokna began her aviation journey in 1992 after receiving an ICAO scholarship to complete an Air Traffic Control degree in Thailand. Her efforts, along with those of her colleagues, have been instrumental in the development and modernization of Cambodia's air traffic services, postwar. So Sokna's husband, Lieutenant Colonel Hul Sangvath, serves as a Chief Flight Operations Officer for the Royal Cambodian Air Force. As a young soldier of the National Army, he fought against the Khmer Rouge forces in the border town of Sisophon. In 1987, Hul Sangvath was sent to study flight operations in Vietnam; after returning to Cambodia, he assumed various roles in both the SSCA and the now-defunct Royal Air Cambodge. Today, their 24-year old daughter Darapich Hul carries on the legacy of her mother, working at Phnom Penh's control tower as an air traffic controller.

of skilled and multi-skilled workers. Meeting internationally recognized standards, expanding public outreach activities and increasing coordination across the industry also remains a priority.

ចង្កឹះមួយដាយកាច់ ចង្កឹះមួយបាច់កាច់មិនបាក់

Translation: A bunch of sticks cannot be broken

In 2009, ICAO launched its NGAP initiative, a platform designed to raise awareness and engage stakeholders on the forecast shortage of aviation personnel. In line with this view, the program promotes cooperation and coordination within the global aviation and education community to attract, educate and retain the next generation of aviation professionals. To date, the NGAP program has conducted several workshops at the global and national level and supports a wide range of aviation youth activities in various countries. The initiative also offers a Fundamentals of the Air Transport System course, and releases newsletters and forecasts that explores the shortage of aviation personnel (ICAO, n.d.b).

Recognizing the importance of engaging the next generation to ensure a sustainable aviation system, the Civil Aviation Authority of Singapore (CAAS) adopted the NGAP program in 2015 by kicking off a highly visible public outreach program designed to raise aviation awareness. The first campaign, entitled the "Heart of Aviation Explorer," was a mobile exhibition bus boasting interactive displays. The bus traveled to roughly 30 schools over one year and appeared in various public spaces. Complementing the campaign were pop-up outdoor displays as well as an aviation resource kit that was distributed to students (CAAS, 2015).

In 2016, Singapore launched the SkillsFuture initiative to provide citizens with opportunities to upgrade their skills in various sectors including aviation, regardless of their starting point in life. Under the program, nationals aged 25 and older are eligible for an open credit of $500 (SGD) from the government to pay for a wide range of approved skills-related courses. The SkillsFuture Credit aims to encourage citizens to take ownership of their skills development and lifelong learning (Government of Singapore, 2019a). Other initiatives include an Aviation Manpower Program, which provides two scholarships: an Aviation Horizons Scholarship, which enables companies to recruit and sponsor Institutes of Higher Learning (IHL) graduates; and the Aviation Youth Outreach Seed Fund, which supports youth aviation interest activities (Government of Singapore, 2019b).

The regulatory regime of CAAS has also been instrumental in boosting human capital. In 2018, authorities shortened the licensing period of aircraft maintenance engineers (AME) to reduce barriers to entry for young people, build its AME pool and reduce training costs (Government of Singapore, 2019b). Meanwhile, CAAS's training arm, the Singapore Aviation Academy (SAA), is reconfiguring its program in line with the NGAP mandate to offer a greater number of globally-recognized programs and certifications. The school is also one of the first training organizations to achieve ICAO TRAINAIR PLUS full membership (Government of Singapore, 2019b).

Overall, Singapore has spent considerable time, money and effort in understanding the needs of its aviation workforce through various studies and surveys. In doing so, the CAAS has been better able to align itself with the recommendations set out by ICAO's NGAP program. These efforts have significantly paid off. In 2018, ICAO and Singapore inked an agreement for a new five-year, six-million-dollar program, which will see 40 new scholarships and 600 new fellowships being made available to the next generation of aviation professionals. The initiative supports the ICAO's No-Country-Left-Behind (NCLB) and NGAP initiatives (Government of Singapore, 2018).

In 2019, a total of 120 fellowships and 15 scholarships were made available and extended to government officials (aged 35 and below) of developing ICAO Member States. At the time of writing this chapter, nine Khmer aviation professionals attended training in Singapore under ICAO's NGAP initiative.

While Cambodia does not enjoy the same level of socio-economic status as its ASEAN neighbor, the country does understand that the success of its aviation industry is driven by a skilled workforce. In 2018, the Ministry of Education, Youth and Sport held Cambodia's first-ever Air and Tech Show – a three-day event designed to cultivate youth interest in aviation and technology. The event was held at the Royal Cambodian Air Force base and attracted a number of corporate sponsors including Airbus and Cambodian helicopter company Helistar. Over 9,000 students attended the event with many bussed in from the provinces (Muonvichny Tan, personal communications, July 31, 2019).

At Cambodia Airports, executives are laying plans to develop an airport management diploma program in conjunction with a Singapore university to raise workforce skills and qualifications. Critical to this plan is developing a partnership with a local university (Philippe Araujo, personal communications, May 10, 2019). Today, Cambodia Airports employs roughly 1,800 Khmer staff including 18 airport trainers that cover 106 airport skills (Norinda Khek, personal communications, May 16, 2019). To attract new talent, the airport periodically hosts career fairs and public events throughout the year.

In evaluating the scenario for current and future workforce demand, it is well documented that the Asia-Pacific region is achieving unprecedented long-term growth in civil aviation, generating high regional economic impacts. Cambodia sits in the heart of this growth but has yet to fully prepare itself to meet the demands of a rapidly changing industry. In light of this, greater synergy between all industry players – from the authority and the airports to the airlines and the training school – should be ramped up to support the country develop the necessary human resource skills to cater to the specialized requirements of aviation. With concentrated effort and coordination among key stakeholders, the Kingdom can develop its own systematic approach to ensuring that there are enough qualified and competent professionals to manage the current and future demands of its air transport system.

The following four recommendations aim to support the medium to long-term development of Cambodia's aviation workforce, including: research and data collection; public aviation outreach activities; aviation course development; and media involvement.

Research and data collection

- Strengthen collaboration between the public and private sector to share and disseminate information
- Develop a national aviation workplace skills study; conduct a national aviation training needs assessment annually; compare research to global findings
- Disseminate research work and findings to the aviation sector and relevant ministries
- Develop an electronic system for understanding real-time labor market trends
- Assess the role of private and public training providers in skills development and their incentives to train the workforce

Public aviation outreach activities

- Strengthen collaboration between the public and private sector; establish a working group to develop and implement a consistent and meaningful public outreach campaign
- Allocate public and private funds to support the successful implementation of public outreach activities
- Strengthen collaboration between industry and education providers to ensure aviation activities are disseminated to primary, secondary and university students.
- Align outreach activities with ICAO's NGAP initiative; use Singapore's NGAP program as a model

Aviation Course Development

- Define aviation training priorities based on comprehensive research work and findings
- Continue to develop CATC as a national flagship aviation center, a role model for all aviation institutes and a learning and experience sharing forum
- Offer affordable and flexible learning pathways (i.e., weekend and night courses)
- Encourage gender equality, and equity and access for people with disabilities when promoting aviation courses
- Develop aviation scholarships and fellowships for existing aviation personnel and the general public
- Encourage private sector involvement in the development of internationally recognized aviation programs
- Include aviation training in the national TVET policy
- Ensure courses are supported by the right capital investment to ensure students have the necessary resources (i.e. machinery) to be successful
- Reconfigure existing programs to align with internationally recognized standards
- Strengthen cooperation between industry and education providers including curriculum development, and internship and apprenticeship programs to reinforce classroom learning, and practical applications of theory
- Monitor programs to reduce duplication and increase efficiency
- Plan investments for improving and expanding aviation programs and infrastructure

Media Involvement

- Develop a social marketing and communication strategy to attract students to aviation by linking learning, earnings, and career possibilities; market courses, attractive jobs, careers, and lifestyles

- Encourage gender equality, and equity and access for people with disabilities when promoting aviation courses

This is a time of unprecedented opportunity for Cambodia to unlock its economic and social potential and deepen its engagement with the regional market. At the same time, recruiting, hiring and training staff are costly endeavors for the aviation industry. The rapid pace of change in aviation will likely shift the needs of companies and government entities; these transformations, if managed wisely, could lead to new jobs and economic prosperity in Cambodia, but if managed poorly, pose the risk of widening skills gaps and hampering productivity and safety within the sector.

Taking the lessons learned from the global community, Cambodia can be viewed as fertile ground to develop strategic and tactical solutions to address training and upskill constraints in the aviation industry while creating an environment that will allow the next generation to lead.

CODA: A (very) brief and oversimplification of external intervention, war and genocide in Cambodia

Since the dawning of the earliest polity in the Mekong Delta, Cambodia has had an intimate relationship with war. Scattered and second-hand text from Chinese sources reveal ancient warlords conquered as they expanded their territories across the loose network of pre-Angkor states Funan (Pelliot, 1903) and Chenla (Vickery, 1998); The battles of men, gods and demons still whisper from the bas reliefs of the once-mighty Angkor Empire.

More modern times hold fewer secrets. The rise of competing hegemonies between Thailand and Vietnam saw Cambodia's power considerably weaken throughout the 17th and 18th centuries. Facing suzerainty from Siamese rulers, the Kingdom succumbed to French protection in 1863, later sparking anti-French sentiments and rebellions in the years to come (Chandler, 2018).

In 1945, Japan's coup de force in Phnom Penh gave impetus to a new young King – his Highness Norodom Sihanouk – and his movement towards securing Cambodia's independence from France in 1953 (Osborne, 1969). Towards the end of the 1960s, however, the country was thrust back into the arena of political disorder and conflict. The US secret bombing campaign of Cambodia during the Vietnam War coupled with the overthrow of Prince Sihanouk and Lon Nol's rise to power had effectively installed a new form of terror (Kiernan, 1989). Propagandizing the American bombings to great effect (United States Central Intelligence Agency, 1973), the Khmer Rouge army rose to power and with astonishing brutality obliterated the educated and the elite in pursuit of a radical agrarian utopia. Money, free markets, schools, private property, and traditional Khmer culture were abolished, and buildings such as schools, pagodas, and government institutes were transformed into death camps and granaries (United to End Genocide, 2016). The Cambodian Genocide Program at Yale

University estimates the number of deaths under the Khmer Rouge totaled roughly 1.7 million (21percent of the population of the country).

In 1980, the United States Central Intelligence Agency (CIA), released a report in what could be the first methodical attempt to analyze the statistical impact of Pol Pot's regime (1975–1979). While time has revealed a series of flaws in its reporting, the document reveals a common theme that has been the basis of much literature since.

> Even were food and health conditions to improve markedly, a rebuilding of Kampuchean society would be a long process. The executions under Pol Pot effectively wiped out the leadership echelon, and the extreme conditions suffered during the last five years have decimated the adult labor population. There are few Khmers to replace the dynamic segments of society. The ranks of those over 20 years old are thin, and the numbers within those ranks possessing skills are few…[the] revitalization of the country would be a lengthy and difficult undertaking…Their health is fragile, and their training has been curtailed. Survival is their goal… Whether [children] will be healthy and vigorous enough – or whether there will be enough of them – to eventually fill the jobs and occupations needed for a functioning society is highly questionable.
>
> (CIA, 1980)

Figure 1.7.3 Pochentong International Airport, 1979.

Note: Pochentong International Airport shortly after the fall of the Khmer Rouge, 1979. Right beneath the tower rests the Democratic Kampuchea flag, waiting to be removed.
© Thongsin Noreak Seung

Figure 1.7.4 An Antonov An-24RV – Kampuchea Airlines, 1989.
© Thongsin Noreak Seung

Since the reconstruction of society, beginning in the 1980s, Cambodia has been engaged in a process of rebuilding its political, legal, economic, social, and educational institutions. To this end, any evaluation of Cambodia's civil aviation sector needs to be undertaken in the light of the prevailing historical context.

Aviation voices

> In Cambodia, cabin crew positions are often viewed as a glamorous career choice. We need to change public perception. People need to be aware of the special skills sets required to become cabin crew. They need to understand that aviation is about safety and security. This begins with educating the community.
> Phanakry Chheav, SSCA Cabin Crew Inspector

> In Cambodia, students lack awareness of aviation as a career path. Early exposure to aviation education is therefore critical. We need to have programs at both the primary and secondary school level if we are to inspire the next generation.
> Samnang Putheany, Corporate Sales Manager, Cambodia Airways

> There are 3Rs that Cambodia requires: Right trainers, right training centers and right media. First, Cambodia needs to bring existing aviation

professionals together who can provide general knowledge, theory and guidance. These people could be working in Cambodia now or in nearby countries. Second, Cambodia needs the right institutes equipped with the right resources to facilitate trainers and trainees. Third, the media plays a very important role in educating and motivating students – this area should not be overlooked.

CATC Aviation student Botto Sean, age 32

I only joined Aviation Fundamentals because of my brother; I didn't realize that aviation is not just about airplanes, it's about something bigger. Aviation for me can still be hard at times, but it is understandable. I think this class is pretty complex for someone my age but it is just easy enough to comprehend.

CATC Aviation student, Watha, age 11

The aviation industry is a brand new world for Cambodians, however, it's not that different from any other working environment that employs more men than women. I am currently completing a Diploma in Civil Aviation Management at the Singapore Aviation Academy and I am the only woman in a class of 34 candidates from all over the world. Women are very underrepresented in the aviation industry – in Cambodia and across the globe. Overall, there needs to be more aviation education and workforce opportunities for women to train and upskill. When you have opportunities in aviation, learning more about the industry becomes an addiction.

Voeunrath Soporlita – Flight Dispatcher, SSCA

We are a nation still struggling to play catch-up with the rest of its neighbors. However, we must also recognize that today's youth are not like their parents. They did not emerge from a war with a sense of duty to rebuild the nation's social and economic systems. Owning property, building a business and saving money was critical post-war. Today, there is a shift in values; globalization has inspired our young generation to strive for other things that include traveling and seeing the world. They are disconnected from past horrors.

In knowing this, I have had to change my perspective about the new generation. We all need to change in how we view today's youth if we're to respond to the shifting dynamics of our aviation sector.

To this end, our focus should be developing educational programs at the primary and secondary level to introduce children to the benefits of an aviation career. We need to look at implementing an ICAO NGAP program.

Deputy Director-General and SSCA
Spokesman Sinn Chanserey Vutha

To get people into aviation, Cambodia needs the involvement of related stakeholders from both the public and private sector. This is necessary to raise awareness and understanding of aviation among Cambodian youth at the primary, secondary and university level.

Aviation Student Ouch Lyeak, age 23

Don't let the words "but you're a woman" stop you from following your dreams. Look up at the sky, spread your wings and fly. We're all born with a pair of wings, but it's your decision as to whether you have the courage to fly or remain invisible.

Rathanakunthea Chem, Personal Licensing Officer,
SSCA, on her advice to other women

Acknowledgement

At Phnom Penh International Airport, Human Resource Project and Development Manager Thongsin Noreak Seung mentors and trains the next generation of aviation professionals. In addition to training airport staff, Thongsin is a highly regarded public figure known for his commitment to raising aviation and aerospace awareness.

Thongsin began his aviation journey in the 1980s – a challenging and precarious period in Cambodian history. As part of post-conflict reconstruction efforts, Thongsin was one of approximately 250 people who was sent to the former Soviet Union between 1981 and 1985 for aviation training. He became an aeronautical engineer and has since assumed various roles in Cambodia's aviation sector.

An avid photographer, Thongsin has a collection of approximately 500 photos of the Khmer Air Force over three time periods: 1954 to 1970, 1970 to 1975 and 1975 to 1979. Many photos in his collection, which includes never-seen-before images, were taken by Thongsin's late uncle.

Thongsin hopes to work with a publisher to develop a dual language photography book to pass down to the next generation. The author extends her deep, heartfelt gratitude to Thongsin for his ongoing support and his contribution towards this chapter.

References

Acharya, A. (2017). The Evolution and Limitations of ASEAN Identity. *ASEAN@ 50 Volume 4, Building ASEAN Community: Political-Security and Socio-cultural Reflections*, 25–38.

Anderson, E., & Kelly, G. (2018). From Schoolgirls to "Virtuous" Khmer Women: Interrogating Chbab Srey and Gender in Cambodian Education Policy. *Studies in Social Justice*, 12(2), 215.

Asian Development Bank. (2014). *Cambodia Diversifying Beyond Garments and Tourism Country Diagnostic Study* [Report] Retrieved from www.adb.org/sites/default/files/publication/149852/cambodia-diversifying-country-diagnostic-study.pdf

Asian Development Bank. (2016) Policy Priorities for a More Responsive Technical and Vocational Education and Training System in Cambodia. Retrieved from www.adb.org/sites/default/files/publication/217341/cambodia-tvet.pdf

Asian Development Bank. (2018a). Asian Development Bank and Cambodia Fact Sheet. Retrieved from www.adb.org/sites/default/files/publication/27757/cam-2018.pdf

Asian Development Bank. (2018b) Cambodia: Technical and Vocational Education and Training Sector Development Program (Second Tranche). Retrieved from www.adb.org/sites/default/files/project-documents/46064/46064-002-pr-en.pdf

Asian Development Bank. (2019). Cambodia: Technical and Vocational Education and Training Sector Development Project. Retrieved from www.adb.org/sites/default/files/project-documents/46064/46064-002-esmr-en_1.pdf

Cambodia Airports. (2017). Crossing the 8-million Passenger Mark, the 3 International Airports Break a Record. Retrieved from https://corp.cambodia-airports.aero/en/press-release/crossing-8-million-passenger-mark-3-international-airports-break-record

Cambodia Airports. (2018). Cambodia's 3 International Airports Hit Record High 10 million Passengers. Retrieved from https://corp.cambodia-airports.aero/en/press-release/cambodias-3-international-airports-hit-record-high-10-million-passengers#targetText=About%20Cambodia%20Airports%3A&targetText=In%202017%2C%20the%20number%20of,International%20Airport%20handled%20338%2C000%20passengers

Casey, D. (2019). Asia Dominates List of Fastest-Growing Airports. Retrieved from www.routesonline.com/news/29/breaking-news/283239/asia-dominates-list-of-fastest-growing-airports/

CEIC Data. (n.d.a). Singapore GDP per Capita. Retrieved from www.ceicdata.com/en/indicator/singapore/gdp-per-capita

CEIC Data. (n.d.b). Cambodia GDP per Capita. Retrieved from www.ceicdata.com/en/indicator/cambodia/gdp-per-capita

Center for Aviation. (2017). Cambodia's International Market Grows by Another 10% as Chinese Visitor Numbers Surge. Retrieved from https://centreforaviation.com/analysis/reports/cambodias-international-market-grows-by-another-10-as-chinese-visitor-numbers-surge–329459

Chandler, D. (2018). *A History of Cambodia*. Routledge.

Civil Aviation Authority Singapore. (2015). CAAS Kicks Off Year-Long Campaign to Promote Aviation Careers with Mobile Aviation Exhibition. Retrieved from www.caas.gov.sg/about-caas/newsroom/Detail/caas-kicks-off-year-long-campaign-to-promote-aviation-careers-with-mobile-aviation-exhibition/

de Almeida, M. D. G. F., Mbate, P. M., Rangette, A., & Scheffczyk, A. (2014). Enhancing UNIDO's Industrial Capacity Building Tools. Retrieved from www.equip-project.org/wp-content/uploads/2018/01/UNIDO-Report-Final-new.pdf

Ellsberg, M., Vyas, A., Madrid, B., Quintanilla, M., Zelaya, J., & Stöckl, H. (2017). Violence against Adolescent Girls: Falling through the Cracks. Manuscript in preparation.

Fulu, E., Warner, X., Miedema, S., Jewkes, R., Roselli, T., & Lang, J. (2013). *Why Do Some Men Use Violence against Women and How Can We Prevent It?* —Quantitative Findings from the United Nations Multi-Country Study on Men and Violence in Asia and the Pacific. Bangkok: UN Partners for Prevention.

Government of Singapore. (2018). Singapore and ICAO Establish New Programme to Develop the Next Generation of Aviation Professionals. Retrieved from www.caas.gov.sg/about-caas/newsroom/Detail/singapore-and-icao-establish-new-programme-to-develop-the-next-generate-of-aviation-professionals/

Government of Singapore. (2019a). Skills Future Credit. Retrieved from www.skillsfuture.sg/Credit

Government of Singapore. (2019b). Preparing Tomorrow's Aviation Workforce. Retrieved from www.caas.gov.sg/who-we-are/our-organisation/our-publications/publication-details/publication/preparing-tomorrow-s-aviation-workforce

International Air Transport Association. (2018). IATA Aviation Human Resources Report 2018. Retrieved from https://www.iata.org/publications/Pages/aviation-human-resources-report.aspx

International Air Transport Association. (2019). Asia-Pacific. Retrieved from www.iata.org/about/worldwide/asia_pacific/Pages/index.aspx

International Civil Aviation Organization. (n.d.a). ICAO Global Aviation Training. Retrieved from: www.icao.int/training/Pages/TPP-Training-Packages.aspx

International Civil Aviation Organization. (n.d.b). About NGAP. Retrieved from www.icao.int/safety/ngap/Pages/NGAPInitiatives2.aspx

Jones, M. (2004). Forging an ASEAN Identity: The Challenge to Construct a Shared Destiny. *Contemporary Southeast Asia*, 26(1), 140–154.

Kiernan, B. (1989). The American Bombardment of Kampuchea, 1969–1973. *Vietnam Generation*, 1(1), 3.

Levy, S (2017). Graduation-Based Social Protection for Cambodia's Extreme Poor: A General Equilibrium Analysis of Economic and Poverty Impacts. Retrieved from www.undp.org/content/dam/cambodia/docs/ResearchAndPublication/Re.%2018%20Jan%202018_Social%20Protection%20Report%202017%20English.pdf

Ly, S., Sanchez, M., Miguel, E., Phim, R., Ky, L., Tong, K., Provo, A. M., Nagpal, S., Vashakmadze, E. T. (2019). *Cambodia Economic Update: Recent Economic Developments and Outlook* (English). Cambodia Economic Update. Washington, DC: World Bank Group.

McGovern, M. E., Krishna, A., Aguayo, V. M., & Subramanian, S. V. (2017). A Review of the Evidence Linking Child Stunting to Economic Outcomes. *International Journal of Epidemiology*, 46(4), 1171–1191. doi:10.1093/ije/dyx017.

McGrew, L., Frieson, K., Chan, S., & Anderlini, S. N. (2004). Good Governance from the Ground Up: Women's Roles in Post-conflict Cambodia. Hunt Alternatives Fund.

Ministry of Education, Youth and Sport. (2017). Public Education Statistics and Indicators 2016–2017. Retrieved from www.moeys.gov.kh/en/emis/2461.html#.XOt5SIgzbIV

Ministry of Women's Affairs. (2014). Gender Relations and Attitudes: Cambodia Gender Assessment. Retrieved from www.kh.undp.org/content/dam/cambodia/docs/DemoGov/NearyRattanak4/Neary%20Rattanak%204%20-%20PB%20Gender%20Relations%20and%20Attitudes%20Eng.pdf

National Employment Agency. (2018). Skills Shortages and Skills Gaps in the Cambodian Labour Market: Evidence from Employer Survey 2017. Retrieved from www.nea.gov.kh/images/survay/ESNS%202017-Final-05282018.pdf

Osborne, M. E. (1969). *The French Presence in Cochinchina and Cambodia: Rule and Response (1859–1905)*. Cornell University Press.

Pelliot, P. (1903) Le Fou-nan.

Peou, S. (2016). Cambodia: From Isolation to Involvement in Regional Community Building. In L. T. Lee, & Z. Othman (Eds.), *Regional Community Building in East Asia* (pp. 57–80). Routledge.

Royal Government of Cambodia. (2014). National Strategic Development Plan (NSDP) 2014–2018. Retrieved from www.cdc-crdb.gov.kh/cdc/documents/NSDP_2014-2018.pdf

Royal Government of Cambodia. (2018) Rectangular Strategy for Growth, Employment, Equity and Efficiency: Building the Foundation Toward Realizing the

Cambodia Vision 2050. Phase IV of the Royal Government of Cambodia of the Sixth Legislature of the National Assembly. Retrieved from http://cnv.org.kh/wp-content/uploads/2012/10/Rectangular-Strategy-Phase-IV-of-the-Royal-Government-of-Cambodia-of-the-Sixth-Legislature-of-the-National-Assembly-2018-2023.pdf

Sing, C. C. (2018). A Resilient and Future-Ready ASEAN. Retrieved from https://asean.org/storage/2018/11/AEIB_4th-Issue_r1.pdf

Sivhuoch, O., & Sreang, C. (2015). An Analysis of Cambodia's Preparedness for the Implementation of Sustainable Development Goals: Challenges, Opportunities and Financing.

Tan, A. K. J. (2013). Toward a Single Aviation Market in ASEAN: Regulatory Reform and Industry Challenges (No. DP–2013–22).

Turney, M. A. (2018). Attracting Women to Aviation Careers: What Recent Studies Reveal. *The Collegiate Aviation Review International*, 18(1).

United States, Central Intelligence Agency. (1973). Efforts of Khmer Insurgents to Exploit for Propaganda Purposes Damage Done by Airstrikes in Kandal Province, Intelligence Information Cable, May 2, 1973, Directorate of Operations, declassified February 19, 1987.

United States, Central Intelligence Agency. (1980). Kampuchea: A Demographic Catastrophe. Retrieved from www.mekong.net/cambodia/demcat.htm

United to End Genocide. (2016). The Cambodian Genocide. Retrieved from http//endgenocide.org/learn/past-genocides/the-cambodian-genocide/

Vickery, M. (1998). Society, Economics, and Politics in Pre-Angkor Cambodia: The 7th–8th Centuries. Centre for East Asian Cultural Studies.

World Bank. (2017). *Cambodia – Sustaining Strong Growth for the Benefit of All. Overview*. Washington, DC: World Bank Group. Retrieved from http://documents.worldbank.org/curated/en/620151496155751423/Cambodia-Sustaining-strong-growth-for-the-benefit-of-all-a-systematic-country-diagnostic

World Bank (2018a). Urban Population. Retrieved from https://data.worldbank.org/indicator/SP.URB.TOTL.IN.ZS?locations=KH

World Bank (2018b). *Cambodia Economic Update: Recent Economic Developments and Outlook (English)*. Cambodia economic update. Washington, DC: World Bank Group. Retrieved from http://documents.worldbank.org/curated/en/888141543247252447/Cambodia-Economic-Update-Recent-Economic-Developments-and-Outlook

World Bank. (2019a). *The World Bank in Cambodia*. Retrieved from www.worldbank.org/en/country/cambodia/overview

World Bank (2019b). *Cambodia Economic Update: Recent Economic Developments and Outlook. Selected issue investing in Cambodia's Future: Early Childhood Health and Nutrition* [Report] Retrieved from http://documents.worldbank.org/curated/en/843251556908260855/pdf/Cambodia-Economic-Update-Recent-Economic-Developments-and-Outlook.pdf

World Economic Forum (2017). Global Human Capital Report 2017. Retrieved from Ministry of Education, Youth and Sport. 2017. "Public Education Statistics and Indicators 2016–2017." Retrieved from www.moeys.gov.kh/en/emis/2461.html#.XOt5SIgzbIV; www3.weforum.org/docs/WEF_Global_Human_Capital_Report_2017.pdf

World Tourism Organization (2018). UNWTO Tourism Highlights. Retrieved from www.e-unwto.org/doi/pdf/10.18111/9789284419876

Yale University (n.d.) Introduction to Cambodian Genocide Program. Retrieved from https://gsp.yale.edu/introduction-cambodian-genocide-program

1.8 Professional reflection – A Great Britain perspective on aviation skills

Simon Witts

Preamble

Great Britain's role in the global aviation industry can be charted via many milestones and initiatives, yet whatever is chosen as the 'start', one factor has dominated, and will continue to dominate the whole industry, and that is the *people*.

People come in all shapes and sizes, ethnicity and diversity but the common factor that relates to this unique industry is the thought, word and deed of that person, individually or as part of a team, that has been translated into a magnificent flying machine.

Over the decades, this application has led to vehicles of all types that operate on water, above it, in the extremities of the atmosphere and in outer space. Without people at all levels, the ingenuity, experimentation, development and refinement would have led to this fledgling industry failing to launch at all. In the early days of flying, the human spirit shown in adventure was endless as was the funding for all and many differing types of taking to the air. It is at the end of this age that I became aware of this exciting area called aviation.

My journey in aviation started at the age of 4 at the Farnborough Air Show in 1962. I vividly remember climbing into a Westland Widgeon helicopter and being captivated and knowing that something in aviation would be in my future. Born into an aviation family it was likely that I would be infected by that bug that only true aviators will recognise – an all-consuming passion for anything that flies. This was followed by meeting many amazing people that made this industry tick, from test pilots/airline pilots/military pilots to air traffic controllers, to engineers and cabin crew, to airport/heliport teams and operations teams. So, the die was cast that, to my mind, *people* made this industry and somehow I needed to become one of them.

So, how does this relate to a skills shortage?

Well, as I approach the later stages of a fantastic career that has given me many privileges and enabled me to meet and work with many, many great people, I am now consumed by what has actually led to this critical shortage of people and to find my own small part in the solution. That the aviation industry needs the right people now to enable its continued growth is a worrying situation, particularly in the United Kingdom (UK), a country that has a strong history of collaborating across boundaries and achieving prior sustained growth in aviation. Alongside the people issues, the matter also has a very significant economic and social issue.

When presented with an opportunity to do something different in 2010, I set about creating a vehicle to play my part in a change to address the shortages. I was convinced that what was needed was a brand new approach and, after a couple of years of broadening my base of knowledge around the UK and international skills system, in 2013 I set about a 'positive disruption' approach that would change the dynamics of the skills industry to achieve a positive outcome. I realise now that what has gone into building the Aviation Skills Partnership (ASP) approach is largely my own experiences throughout my career, coloured also by those around me (including that of my wife and children). I could not have created the organisation at the start of my career as I had simply not experienced the challenges, pitfalls and hurdles that existed if you were setting out to reach the top of your chosen area (I didn't even have a high ambition but ended up realising that dream by taking every opportunity that I was given – driven by a hunger for experience, knowledge, information and challenge).

Looking back, the main elements that I can now reflect on that led to my eventual ASP-led campaign include:

- A childhood filled with all aspects of aviation achievement, experiences and knowledge – meeting many iconic people and realising that they were actually ordinary people doing amazing things;
- An education that equipped me with significant theoretical aviation knowledge but little or no practical experience – Queen Mary University of London (that delivered the first Aeronautical Engineering Course in the UK in the early part of the 20th century) did all that they could to give me a great academic education. That this included the experience of a week's stability and control flying at Cranfield University was one of those 'embedders' that I realise transformed my understanding of complex flight and stability equations;
- A first employer that 'blooded' me in practical aspects of engineering and flight test across the world – I realise now how fortunate that I am that the then world's largest helicopter operator (still led then by iconic personalities) gave me this opportunity straight from university;
- Employment that followed filled with great people that stretched my knowledge, experience and tested my limits;
- The experience of flight-testing aeroplanes and helicopters around the world;
- Restructuring and running large maintenance, engineering and training departments of large airlines;
- Running all of the operational aspects of an airline across (what I eventually coined as) the six areas of aviation – engineers, pilots, airport, operations, cabin crew/crew and Air Traffic Control;

- Having the opportunity to create a nationally significant first Aviation Academy;
- Experience of establishing a new industry-facing subsidiary for the CEO of one of the world's oldest awarding organisations that created qualifications that reflected academic, practical and people skills.

All of these became the ingredients in my plan to create a vehicle to make a difference.

Initially, working with the Royal Aeronautical Society (of which I have been a member since student days, latterly a Fellow), I produced a paper 'Towards a UK Aviation Skills Plan' that was published by the society in October 2013. This complemented work that I had instigated in 2011 (more later) with great people from the UK Civil Aviation Authority (CAA) and a highly experienced higher education practitioner and visionary. Working with industry, UK government, educators and associations on the concept of a new skills pathway into one of the six areas of aviation – pilot training, the working group launched a unique practice-based pilot degree framework that, in turn, led to a full pathway back to the age of 7, followed by a similar approach in the other five areas. This approach achieved significant success across a number of measures including the direct feed into a major airline in a manner never before achieved.

So, what of this approach and its successes and failures? In this reflection I have set out to explain the approach taken through working with the four elements that are, I consider, the focal points for the actions that are needed to connect into a national aviation skills plan including:

- industry;
- people and parents;
- educators and trainers;
- government and regulators.

I have also illustrated the development of the first Aviation Skills Manifesto that was launched in 2016 and that is approaching the end of its third year of delivery and which, in its new form, is planned to lead to the launch of a Charter for Aviation Skills in 2019. It is intended that this be put forward to the International Civil Aviation Organization (ICAO) as a major initiative for the Next Generation of Aviation Professionals (NGAP).

Within my reflection, where possible, industry and personal cases are drawn from all four areas above and, where practicable, include academic input from schools, colleges, universities and national training providers.

From the start I have set out to define aviation as the part of the industry that operates the vehicle, be it fixed-wing or rotary-wing, civil or military, large or small, piloted remotely or on-board. The six areas encompass the main operating roles (engineering, pilot, air traffic, airport, operations and cabin crew). Within these areas are, of course a myriad of support areas exist, from finance to marketing, leasing to logistics and so on.

My approach

At the time of writing, the aviation (operating) industry in the UK is at an all-time high in terms of volume of flights, operational deployments on missions, orders for aircraft and therefore the need for people.

This aviation industry status sits alongside the UK's position as the number one aerospace manufacturing country in Europe and number two in the world as well as a buoyant and growing space sector. In terms of aviation skills, though, and the supply of people, in general, the industry largely still trains its own people to its own (and regulatory) standards. There are a number of reasons for this approach, including:

- the gap between the delivery point of people from the education and training system to the 'ready for work' point;
- the regulatory need for accountability for training to sit within, for example, the operator, airport or maintenance organisation.

In 'Towards a UK Aviation Skills Plan' referenced earlier, it was suggested that the 'dis-integration' of a national training system (exemplified by, for example, Royal Aircraft Establishments at Farnborough/Boscombe Down/Bedford, the National Gas Turbine Establishment, Royal Signals and Radar Establishment at Malvern and such like) had led to a breakdown in the supply chains of people. Registering a strong family link (since my father, uncle and cousins attended RAE Farnborough on fully-funded apprenticeships) these national centres produced the people that were needed predominantly for the strong and 'hungry for skilled people' military. The benefit, though, was that, with the flow of people from military to civil being relatively strong and regular, these people ended up in the aviation operational roles.

Such a national training system, whilst apparently centralised and government-controlled has demonstrated a system that worked and that resulted in a sustainable supply of skilled people for the industry. Right now, it is far from clear that the establishment of a centralised government training system is the answer, however, a national framework that standardises the approach may well be an answer, linking together the educators and trainers that deliver the specialised training. More of that later.

From an industry perspective, the aviation industry – the operating industry – is fragmented and physically spread but with a common core of need across the UK – from the deepest south-west to the Highlands and Islands. So how does the industry coordinate its approach and signal a renewed push for the training industry to provide it with the right skilled people at the right time? Enter at stage right the Aviation Skills Manifesto in 2016, written and launched by Aviation Skills Partnership on behalf of the aviation industry to illustrate, frame and encapsulate the seven areas that need to happen at the same time to create a sustainable supply of appropriately skilled people. It was connected to government by the launch location – the UK House of Commons – and the visionary launch Member of Parliament, but was independent of the need for government resources, including funding.

Why then was there no single, all-encompassing policy already in place that the industry could get behind? The answer, I believe, lies in the way that the aviation industry is categorised in the UK and the sector coding for the industry.

In the early 2000s, twenty-five UK Sector Skills Councils were established to represent all aspects of industry as a means of channelling government support and to garner industry leadership across the main industry sectors. Aviation was categorised as passenger transport and therefore categorised with, for example, rail, buses, taxis and passenger ferries. Whilst, as far as the civil sector is concerned, the descriptor accurately reflects the purpose of the industry, when it comes to the skills needs and requirements, they are patently very different and the training programmes and regimes entirely non-transferable due to the regulatory system, amongst other areas. There was a benefit to the approach in terms of funding, since the UK government provides very significant programme and skills support but when spread across twenty-five Sector Skills Councils and then looking at the needs within each sector, the funding and direct support dwindled. Also, the skills needs of the aviation industry were ill-defined and relatively invisible in terms of demographics and data. Coupled with this, where the operationally focused industry was challenged to operate its training regimes in alien and unknown national skills and qualifications territory to create a version of transferability, it created somewhat of a mismatch in the systems that were meant to be joined together and common (if common funding was to be achieved). Although some early successes could be highlighted, progress in aviation was significantly curtailed when, in the late 2000s, the Sector Skills Councils were asked to become self-funding which led (in a number of cases, including aviation) to an inability to continue to fund many necessary skills activities. This left a vacuum and for a few years, the aviation skills agenda in the UK was left rather unsupported by the systems that had been set up to support it.

In 2011, with much personal support and encouragement and with the initial support of a number of organisations and key individuals, I decided to set up a new independent industry initiative to create, as one of the key areas of aviation, a single national pilot training pathway. Supported at senior level by many visionary people including within the UK CAA and the UK National Apprenticeship Service, it was designed to be new, different and outcome focused. At the first meeting, twenty-five operators and airlines were represented, and the group set itself challenging targets.

If a catalyst for this work was needed, the event that sticks in my mind was the student story which I had directly experienced and which, in many ways, became the spark that led me to establish ASP.

Let me summarise the story, as it exemplifies the situation that has existed all over the UK – and possibly many other areas of the world. This student, a young lady, was one of a group who had been studying at university and who had attended a presentation and panel that I had been part of one evening in the north of England when I was at a large regional airline (establishing a new type of training academy having completed my part of the post-sale integration of another large regional airline). A panel debate, which included skills, had completed and I was approached by a group of students who replayed their story. They were just completing their university degree that was badged as something along the lines of an aviation degree that included pilot studies. The lead student had wanted to be a pilot since she was eleven years old and had saved up all of her money to fund the degree. However, she realised, after starting, that the pilot training was an additional cost as were the aviation regulator examination fees that they were asked to sit. What no one had told her, and I bore the brunt of her frustration, was that the pilot training was not at the level required for the industry and nor were the regulator examinations real or accredited. They were merely mock examinations (i.e., past practice papers). Further, if this was not enough, towards the end of her final year, she had written to every airline in the UK and those that had replied had effectively said that she may as well have applied directly through their training partners and not gone to university at all. Such was her (justified) frustration that she and her ten colleagues said 'we have not met you before but you are from the industry, this is your problem, what are *you* going to do about it!' This had a really powerful effect as I felt, as a senior representative of the industry, that I had let her down in some way. Coupled with this, how was it that a bright set of individuals were being disconnected from their chosen goal – and they were all female too (the UK is, I believe, currently sitting at around 6 per cent females as a percentage of the overall pilot population – my youngest daughter is on the verge of becoming one of them).

So, returning to the group that was set up, you can see that it had a powerful stimulus. To reinforce the message, I asked the student to present her situation to the assembled group and most were speechless and agreed that we needed to do something about it. Henceforth a new working group was born – many present were touched by this very human story that illustrated a potential breakdown in the skills pipeline.

So, what did the group set out to achieve and why is it relevant to this story? Well, it became a driven group of people determined to encapsulate every element of the issue when applied to just one area – pilot training – but also had immediate and powerful connections across to the other areas of aviation and beyond. Yes, in itself, the working group had a unique set of ingredients – people. These people, variously, had been through their own journey to get to their position and when put together and compounding our experience, we were able to illustrate what turned out to be akin to a supply chain approach to providing the right people with the right skills at the right time. Chaired by a great and visionary leader from the UK CAA mentioned earlier, and excellently coordinated by an expert in Higher Education, the working group reached its planned conclusion in a relatively short time. At the time, it had strong representation with virtually every type of body around the table. The group took each element of the skills requirements of the job – airline pilot – and constructed a 'perfect world' approach to achieving an 'output' of a person with the right skills in the right job. It also showed the multi-lateral nature of the work required to achieve a sustainable result across a nation, or internationally.

My personal experience of helping to set up and run the group led me to the formation of, first, the Aviation Skills Network and then the ASP. The fledgling organisation worked alongside partners to utilise the output of the group and set about completing the validation of the framework with a selected university. It rapidly became a practice-based degree that fully integrated the regulated pilot training to become a line co-pilot with an airline and that, at the point of graduation, was set at the completion of the regulated base and line training. Furthermore, it was also a UK Higher Apprenticeship and was therefore able to attract funding. The programme went live in 2014 with three pilot training organisations and still operates today.

In terms of a conclusion to the issue, though, this one programme and one area of aviation was only really scratching the surface. What was needed was a systematic approach across all areas of aviation and capable of being delivered all across the UK (and internationally) and ensuring that it was accessible to all.

So, with my then Advisory Board, I decided in late 2015 that we needed a national platform from which to embed the initial three years of experience of operating ASP as an independent, non-aligned organisation that could work with any company or body to drive towards a sustainable supply of appropriately skilled people. To this end, in January 2016, on the third birthday of ASP in the UK House of Commons, we launched the Aviation Skills Manifesto, a seven-point plan that would not need to rely on government funding and that would, at least, cover its own costs.

This plan revolutionised our way of focusing on the issues with our partners and also helped to organise and launch the plan to take the issues and resolutions forward. The approach taken was to systematically create a movement that would meet the global/growing need for a sustainable supply of skilled people in aviation. It would do this by working collaboratively with the right partners to develop and deploy the right pathways. These would connect back from the required jobs and would be designed and developed from existing or developing programmes using the facilities and equipment that the pathways and programmes need. Following this with the appropriate knowledge and information, inspiration through heritage and recognition for achievement, completed the cycle.

Building on the success of the pilot pathway approach referenced earlier of creating practical and achievable routes for real people into their dream roles, I realised that whilst pilot training academies were largely available and accessible and that simulation and emulation already played a large part in the training, the same could not be said of the majority of the other areas of aviation (particularly when looking at aviation engineering, cabin crew and airport roles, for example). Therefore, the plan was hatched to design, from the ground up, a new generation of training academies that could connect directly and seamlessly with aviation jobs and support the aviation education and live-aircraft based practical training that was needed, back to the age of seven. Alongside this, existing facilities would be re-purposed or recognised. Three locations in the UK for new academies were targeted to host the first of these and very quickly, through a combination of events and circumstances, a plan was agreed between local government, stakeholders and industry to set up a project in the east of England. In an incredible demonstration of how quickly stakeholders can move, the organisations came together, leading to, just three years from first concept to opening, a world-first. In so doing, the team unwittingly unearthed a powerful and unique long-forgotten aviation history for the city and the region, but that is a matter for another time.

Such it was that this building was opened in 2017 by a senior ambassador of the aviation youth movement followed, in 2018, by official recognition of its significance – to inspire the next generation of aviators. Personally, I probably didn't fully appreciate the significance that this first academy would have for our model. First, we were all heads-down working with partners to ensure that the facility could accommodate the first practice-based engineering degree students undertaking the programme that fully integrated regulatory training with a full Honours degree. Nonetheless, the significance dawned mostly though the feedback of the people visiting from across the country and internationally. What occurred to me was that the academy itself encapsulated all seven aspects of our Aviation Skills Manifesto in action, namely:

1. Skills Policy – the academy set the focus for the east of England skills strategy for aviation, placing aviation back on the agenda as a viable sector for a region that had hitherto focused on agriculture, agri-tech, energy and tourism, amongst others. The power of this alone cannot be underestimated when coupled with the historic aspects of area 6 below.
2. Partnerships – dubbed 'a coalition of the willing' we had brought together partners that would not usually sit in the same room, truly uniting under one banner, public sector, educators, trainers, industry.
3. Pathways – the first full pathway to go live (aviation engineering) resulted in instant recognition by key employers as one of the places to go to recruit (please excuse the cliché) 'job-ready' people.
4. Academies & Hubs – the creation of the first academy has already created the need for similar academies elsewhere.
5. Knowledge & Information – of course, all of the activity mentioned here and undertaken elsewhere would not be worth it if the opportunities were not communicated.
6. Heritage – little did we (or many others at the time) know that in selecting Norwich, we had landed on one of the birthplaces of aerospace in the UK. A city recognised as being the second city in the UK in the 18th century, its aviation roots were only really known for housing a famous RAF station and being the birthplace of Air Anglia, to become AirUK, a leading regional airline and the first regional jet operator in the UK with the Fokker F28.

What we had not realised was the even more significant past. By chance (a factor that has occurred many times in my own personal and ASP's journey), at a lunch I sat opposite what turned out to be a senior member of the Museum Service. Faced with one week to go until the media launch of the academy, we knew that the 'why Norwich?' question, as to the choice of the location for the first academy, had one of our weakest answers. So, asked 'do you know of any killer facts why Norwich would be the right location?', he and his team turned up trumps. It turned out that Norwich was the home of the first metal-built aircraft in the UK, the Boulton and Paul P.10. Built as a prototype for the Air Ministry and fledgling Royal Air Force at a time when the world spruce supplies were drying up (post World War I), Mr North and his design team obviously saw this as an exciting but natural extension of their work building everything out of metal – from lighthouses to fridge cabinets. In 1919 when the prototype appeared at the Salon du Bourget in Paris, it caused a storm as it also featured the first application of composite material (Bakelite-Dilecto). We had happened on a people skills story of its own and that, without the academy activity, may well have remained buried in the annals of history.

Building on this story, we have been able to bring famous stories and people to life through events and inspire the next generation based on the exploits of the past.

7. Accreditation and Awards – last, but not least, we wanted to make sure that any activities run through the academy were recognised formally and academically or through some form of accreditation.

At the time of writing, with the first academy approaching its second official birthday as it realizes the dreams and aspirations of aviators, amongst other locations, ASP is embarking on a new and exciting chapter in its development. In its first six years, ASP as a fast growing organisation with a very willing and capable team, sometimes faced an identity challenge as it did not appear to conform to the structures and approach associated with skills organisations. It also faced challenges in the way that it operated and relied heavily on the willingness of a large number of people, too many to mention here, to make the model work. I was fortunate to be able to work with an Advisory Board full of iconic people who also believed that if we did not do anything, the whole industry faced the sort of challenges that none of us thought we would see – a shortage of the right people coming into the industry that we know and love.

After three years of operating the Aviation Skills Manifesto, in 2018, as we were looking to relaunch the Aviation Skills Manifesto and bearing in mind my 2013 paper 'Towards a UK Aviation Skills Plan', I thought, together with my peerless Strategy Board led by an excellent Chairman, that we should work towards something that could replace the manifesto with a new and updated approach.

At this point, and in hindsight, at the perfect time to take the next step on the journey, after a chance conversation with a member of ASP's Strategy Board late in 2018, ASP was fully acquired on 6 February 2019 by Pennant

International Group plc (see earlier). So, ASP is being powered onto the next stage in its journey by this great news and the success is sure to be underpinned. I am really looking forward to playing my small part in guiding the newly re-energised ASP into an updated plan, in full collaboration with its partners.

The industry that I know and love is built with partnership and collaboration at its core and, with this new dawn, I sincerely hope that all partners will embrace the opportunity to create something truly special and to support a cause which has the real ability to change lives, realise dreams and ensure that sustainable supply of the right skilled people that the industry needs so much.

In this reflection, I have tried to highlight a few of the key aspects that I believe have helped to transform the approach to aviation skills. As but one person in a huge industry, there are numerous more worthy examples I am sure that can be referenced but, for me, the key lessons and take-aways include:

1. Our business, aviation, has been, is and will be for many years heavily people focused. Operating at all skills and experience levels, without people we would be nowhere and there would be no aviation industry.
2. Some of our best leaders have worked their way through the system, experiencing many aspects and sometimes learning the hard way.
3. Aviation people are a rich blend of pioneers, innovators, disruptors, planners, deliverers, reflectors and improvers. I could write an entire book on the influence that the people that I have met and worked with have had on me. People that work against all odds, never take no for an answer. People that believed in me, invested time in me, set me seemingly next to impossible challenges and that helped me to learn from the many incredible experiences that I am really fortunate to have had.
4. We can achieve so much if we set our minds to it and if we work together.
5. There are many valuable lessons that we have learnt that can be reflected forward to re-energise future activities.
6. Quite often the simplest solutions are the best – I will often categorise achievements as common sense as I believe that, fundamentally, that is what they are based on.
7. Role models are vital. People need to draw from people that they value and respect. Role models are not celebrities but people who single-mindedly set themselves goals that they tirelessly pursue.

So, my simple advice to anyone involved in any area of aviation skills is to:

a. Set down why you are doing what you are doing – why do you need to do it and what will the outcomes be.
b. Identify who you will do it with. Most successes that I have been involve in involve partners and collaborative working. In some cases too, unlikely combinations of people often create spectacular results.

c. Create a common core, a pathway, that bonds and unites the activity and design it in reverse, starting with the outcome first. Be inspire by what we have achieved in the past. Make sure that any pathway achieves proper milestones and accreditation, reflecting achievement of goals and outcomes. Assure competence and not just knowledge.
d. Create the infrastructure that is needed – do not settle too quickly for a compromise or second-best solution.
e. Ensure that people know what you are doing – communication and information is key and can build and unite teams and outcomes.

Last but not least, people are the key to the future of aviation skills. People of all types and from all backgrounds. People who are drawn to playing a part in our amazing industry and working together to deliver incredible results over a relatively short amount of time in our whole civilization.

My small story is but one of billions and we need to harness every element of all those experiences out there to bring ourselves back into a position where we can enjoy and rely on a sustainable future for aviation.

2 Educating the next generation of aviation professionals

Section introduction

Suzanne K. Kearns

As you read through this volume, you will note that the three NGAP themes (attract, educate, and retain) are not completely distinct – as significant overlap exists between the three. This is particularly true for the role of education. For example, attract overlaps with education, as young adults must be educated about opportunities within the sector. Likewise, a key element in the retention of professionals is providing developmental opportunities so young working adults can advance in their careers to feel fulfilled and eventually move into leadership positions. Similarly, attraction does not only refer to youth, as professional organizations must consider how to recruit transitioning professionals to enhance their ranks, and thus attract and retain overlap as well (see Figure S2.1). Ultimately, the three themes are intended to provide some structure when considering NGAP issues rather than discrete boundaries between initiatives.

It can be argued that educational research in aviation, despite its critical importance to every aspect of operations, has been undervalued in comparison to other disciplines. For example, for decades there has been a focus on aviation psychology, which is critically important. However, as psychology provides insights into the nature of human limitations, it requires the expertise of the educational field to transfer that information into effective teaching and transfer of learning. The editors of this book (with

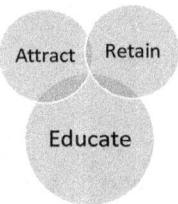

Figure S2.1 The overlapping NGAP themes: attract, educate, and retain.

backgrounds in secondary, tertiary, and professional education) advocate for education as an academic area that must be further advanced within the aviation community. Areas such as curriculum, instructional methodologies, standards, assessment, and program evaluation are uniquely housed within those with educational backgrounds.

Consequently, the education theme has emerged as the central theme of the NGAP sub-discipline. Considerations explored within Section II of the book include modern training approaches, technologies, accomplishments, and partnerships:

2.1 **Case Study** – Higher Education in aviation for Portuguese-speaking countries: Portugal's perspective *by Rui Castro e Quadros*

   This case explores how Portuguese universities are supporting the development of future young African professionals. The case also reports on the LusoAvia project, a conference that brings together aviation professionals from all Portuguese speaking countries.

2.2 **Case Study** Industry – pilot training partnerships: A case study *by Rebecca K. Lutte and Russell W. Mills*

   How airlines are partnering with educational institutions to create a pipeline of talent, that flows directly into professional positions, is discussed in this case. This includes an in-depth look at the US-based 'United Aviate Program' and the European 'Lufthansa Group Flight Academy'.

2.3 **Case Study** – How work influences cabin crew learning: A situated learning perspective *by Maria F. Larrea, Steven Hodge, Yoriko Kikkawa, and Timothy J. Mavin*

   Cabin crew training involves activities and social interactions that aren't explicitly included in training programs. This case discusses a qualitative study that sought to understand the influence of operational experience on learning in comparison to formal training in cabin crew professional development.

2.4 **Chapter** – Multi-piloted Operations *by Alan Martinez, R. Joseph Childs, and Dan Sutliff*

   Ab initio pilot training, meaning teaching people with no previous flight training, is explored in depth within this chapter. Discussions include the implementation of the multi-crew pilot license (MPL) incorporating competency-based education (CBE). The political constraints of MPL adoption in the United States are also discussed.

2.5 **Chapter** – Ensuring success by using the 4 A's of learning *by Mary Niemczyk*

   This chapter takes a generational perspective on aviation education by focusing on Gen Z. Gen Z, defined as people born after 1997, will play critical roles within the future of global air transport and thus their education is of importance. The '4 A's of Learning Model' is presented – Active, Associate, Anticipate, and Awareness.

2.7 **Chapter** – Engaging practices for training the new generation of aircraft maintenance technicians *by Karen Jo Johnson and Denis Manson*

Learning technologies are likely to play an increasing role within future training of maintenance technicians – yet questions remain about how to ensure courseware is effective considering the technical and hands-on nature of this field. This chapter presents some guidance on educational technologies, including e-learning, virtual reality, and learning management systems.

2.7 **Chapter** – Language education for ab ignitio flight training: A plan going forward *by Jennifer Roberts and Alan Orr*

As English language proficiency is required for many aviation professionals, this presents a critical challenge for world regions where English is not a first or national language. This chapter discusses strategies for the implementation of English for Specific Purposes (ESP) language training for ab initio pilots using Content-Based Language Teaching (CBLT) and Task-Based Language Teaching (TBLT).

2.8 **Professional Reflection** – Mixed reality to augment the next generation of aviation professionals *by Lori J. Brown*

This professional reflection highlights work associated with virtual, augmented, and mixed reality to support aviation education. In addition, to guide educators, practical suggestions on the implementation of these technologies are included.

2.9 **Professional Reflection** – The solution of customized aviation English: Training the aviation maintenance technician *by Anne E. Lomperis*

This work describes four pillars of customized infrastructure that must be established to support English language development of maintenance technicians: 1) teacher training, 2) curriculum development, 3) program design for implementation and delivery, and 4) testing for aviation maintenance.

2.10 **Professional Reflection** – Evidence-based training: The story *by Michael Varney and John Scully*

The authors describe the development of evidence-based training (EBT) within this professional reflection. The EBT story, from origin through to modern-day implementation, is outlined along with lessons learned through the process.

2.1 Case study – Higher education in aviation for Portuguese-speaking countries
Portugal's perspective

Rui Castro e Quadros

Introduction

Creating a single airspace in the African continent will undoubtedly lead some of its major countries to top positions. Cape Verde and Angola, Portuguese speaking countries, will certainly lead in fulfilling their needs with regard to the training of young executives, especially in higher education. Portugal, by its common language ties and its long tradition in commercial aviation, will be able to help thousands of young African Portuguese speakers.

Students from the countries belonging to the Community of Portuguese Speaking Countries (CPLP), such as Angola, Brazil, Cape Verde, Guinea Bissau, Mozambique, São Tomé and Príncipe and East Timor – Portugal excluded) are the most representative group amongst the foreign students who attend higher education in Portugal.

Regarding Portugal's role in training young people in aviation courses, this case highlights the importance and influence that higher education has on the future of young people in Portuguese-speaking communities.

The African Union Commission Agenda for 2063 (African Union Commission, n.d.), created a major project, the Single African Air Transport Market (SAATM) (International Transport Association, 2019). The African Union clearly wants to make a major impact on the economy by creating a single African Air Transport Market and a single passport for all Africans. The initial commitment was signed by eleven countries: Benin, Cape Verde (Portuguese speaking country), Côte d'Ivoire, Egypt, Ethiopia, Kenya, Nigeria, Rwanda, Republic of Congo, South Africa and Zimbabwe.

The concept of liberalization of air transport in Africa arose in 1988 with the adoption of the Yamoussoukro Declaration, followed a few years later by the Yamoussoukro Decision in 1999. This decision provided full liberalization of intra-African air transport, the possibility to adopt the five traffic rights freedoms for scheduled flights, allow capacity and frequency adjustments, and the free allocation of tariffs. Full implementation will lead to a single aviation area, where trade, services and the free movement of goods will lead to a remarkable development in the single area.

InterVistas Consulting study prepared for IATA in 2014 'Transforming Intra-African Air Connectivity: The Economic Benefits of Implementing the Yamoussoukro Decision' explored the potential benefits of intra-African liberalization (InterVistas, 2014). The analysis examined the impact of liberalizing air markets between 12 countries within four sub-regions of Africa: North (Algeria, Egypt, Tunisia); East (Ethiopia, Kenya, Uganda); South (Angola, Namibia, South Africa) and West (Ghana, Nigeria, Senegal). Angola, a Portuguese-speaking country, according to the same study, is expected to increase the volume of passengers by 153 percent (after liberalization). The increase in the aviation activity will bring more investment, more tourism, more productivity and a considerable increase of employment in the airline industry.

InterVistas's report states that liberalisation between the 12 countries is estimated to generate 155,100 jobs in aviation (15,300 jobs in Angola), tourism and the wider economy and to contribute US$1.3 billion to annual GDP (about 0.07 percent of the GDP of the 12 countries).

Portugal's role

After the colonial period and much because of historical ties, Portuguese universities have become the obvious path for all young Africans who speak and write in Portuguese.

The cooperation policy began in the 1970s, through agreements with the postcolonial states, and almost immediately after their independence. It has developed in a more organized way since the end of the 1980s, when education became one of the main frames of the Portuguese government. Between 1995 and 2012, the number of foreign students, nationals of the CPLP attending higher education institutions in Portugal, experienced a significant growth. From 4,000 students in the academic year of 1995/96, it had grown to close to 15,000 in 2011/12, representing a cumulative annual growth of 7.9 percent (DGEEC, 2015).

Portugal's higher education enrolment for the year of 2017/18 (Registration of Registered Students and Graduates of Higher Education [RAIDES, 2017]) had reached 372,753 students. The foreign student community represents 7.5 percent of the total (28,129).

From the Survey on the Registration of Enrolled Students and Graduates of Higher Education, DGEEC (2017/2018), the total number of native students from the CPLP countries is 19,544, 56 percent of which are from Brazil. Angola (16 percent) and Cape Verde (13 percent) are the most represented countries after Brazil. Also included are Mozambique, São Tomé and Principe, Guinea Bissau and East Timor. During the year 2017/2018, and according to the same source, of the total number of students in transport, only 24 percent come from private sector higher education. This is challenging since the costs to attend aren't subsidized by the origin countries.

Programs

Aeronautical Engineering is taught in public universities, but Aviation Management and Aeronautical Sciences courses are offered only by private institutions. The leading institutions for management degrees are ISEC Lisboa and Lusófona University of Lisbon. In 2019, according to Lusófona University Annual Report and Accounts for 2017–2018, 16 percent of its students come from Lusophone countries. In the aeronautics courses, which include the undergraduate and master's degrees from ISEC Lisboa, students coming from Portuguese-speaking countries represented 30 percent of the total enrolment in the academic year 2017 and 2018 (according to ISEC's Academic Services, Lisbon, 2019).

The public institutions National Civil Aviation Authority (ANAC) and the National Navigation Services (NAV Portugal, 2017) are also engaged with the African Portuguese-speaking countries as far as training programs are concerned. According to the NAV's Annual Activities Report, Cape Verde was the country which mostly received training by NAV Portugal.

In 2018, ANAC (National Civil Aviation Authority [2018]) had training cooperation programs with the Civil Aviation Authority of Mozambique, Guinea Bissau, São Tomé e Principe and various activities within the community of Lusophone Civil Aviation Authorities (CAACL).

In 2018 the Absant Group (2019), a private Portuguese training company operating in the civil aviation sector reported that, of the total of its graduates, 10.9 percent come from Portuguese speaking countries.

As can be seen from the presented data, professional training provided by both public (ANAC and NAV) and private entities (Absant Group, Lisbon) is oriented towards already established professionals, to those who need updates and initial training.

As previously mentioned, the higher education institutions which have more students coming from the communities of the CPLP are also privately held.

Regarding non-academic training, public and private entities are the main providers of training services in Portugal. Public entities work to pre-established agreements, and in an institutional way. Given their profit-driven nature, the Portuguese private entities end up equally working for public entities. For both airline industry and higher education, the training is performed by privately held institutions.

Steps for the near future

African airlines, airports and governments should continue to support the single African Air Transport Market by strengthening the International Civil Aviation Organisation's compliance standards, supported by a sustainable air transport system. Connectivity, alliances and agreements, and hub development are imperative.

Governments should include in their programs the training of executives and technicians. An efficient and robust air transport system can only be ensured by having qualified human resources.

For Portugal and for the cooperation between Portuguese-speaking countries there is a great opportunity in training young Africans. This investment is high, and the authorities must strive to give opportunities to young people to have the resources to do so.

It is unfavourable for the new generations in Portuguese-speaking countries, because the training is costly and only exists in private companies. Difficulties are a reality, since the training is expensive, some are sponsored by public entities, others coming from the private sector. There should be specific agreements between Portuguese-speaking African countries and Portugal in the crucial areas of civil aviation.

The emergence of the Ponte Sor aviation cluster, managed by the City Hall of Ponte de Sor, and the LusoAvia (Portuguese Commonwealth Leaders Summit), can become the specialized political, economic and teaching platform young African students need.

References

Absant Group Portugal. (2019). Internal communication, May 2019.
The African Union Commission. Flagship Projects of Agenda 2063. Retrieved from: https://au.int/en/agenda2063/flagship-projects.
Direção Geral de Estatísticas da Educação e Ciência. (2015). Retrieved from: www.gepe.min-edu.pt/np4/68/%7B$clientServletPath%7D/?newsId=69&fileName=relat_rio_artigo___DGEEC21052015.pdf.
International Transport Association. (2019). The Single African Air Transport Market (SAATM). Retrieved from: www.iata.org/policy/promoting-aviation/Pages/saatm.aspx.
InterVistas. (2014). Transforming Intra - African Air Connectivity: The Economic Benefits of Implementing the Yamoussoukro Decision. Retrieved from: www.iata.org/publications/economics/Reports/InterVISTAS_AfricaLiberalisation_FinalReport_July2014.pdf.
Isec Lisboa, Serviços Académicos. (2019). Internal communication, April 2019.
National Civil Aviation Authority. (2018). Annual Activity Report (2017). Retrieved from: www.anac.pt/SiteCollectionDocuments/Informacao_Gestao/Relatorios_Gestao/ragc2017.pdf.
NAV Portugal. (2018). Relatório e Contas (2017). Retrieved from: www.nav.pt/docs/NAV/informação-sobre-a-empresa/relatório-e-contas/relatório-e-contas-2017.pdf?sfvrsn=4

RAIDES. (2017). Principais resultados - Inscritos 2017/2018. Retrieved from: www.dgeec.mec.pt/np4/958.html

Universidade Lusófona de Humanidades e Tecnologias. (2019). Relatório Anual 2017-18 (De acordo com o Art.º 159º do RJIES). Retrieved from: www.ulusofona.pt/pt/media-ref/relatorio-anual-2017-18/download/relatorio-anual-2017-18.pdf.

2.2 Case study – Industry–pilot training partnerships

Rebecca K. Lutte and Russell W. Mills

Introduction

Facing an unprecedented period of pilot demand globally, airlines have taken bold steps to attract and retain pilots. The number of air transport passengers is forecast to nearly double in the next twenty years (IATA, 2018). Freight demand is growing at twice the rate of capacity (IATA, 2018). Pilot demand forecasts predict a need for 635,000 new pilots globally by 2037 to meet forecast demand (Boeing, 2018). New airline pilots generally come from one of the following pathways: military, university training environments, general aviation training environments, or airline-focused academies. In the environment of fierce competition for pilots (Lutte, 2018), airlines have developed strategies to target and recruit perspective pilots to join their specific airline. These strategies range from university-focused partnerships to identify and hire talent early in their training careers to ab initio airline training for pilots who are trained from day one in an airline- and crew-focused environment. This case will explore two pilot training–industry partnerships, the United Airlines Aviate program and Lufthansa Aviation Training. These two programs are a sign of the times and represent unique approaches by industry to address the global pilot supply challenge.

Industry programs to attract pilots

Across the globe, many airlines have developed partnerships with universities and colleges that develop clear career pathways for students while also allowing carriers to identify and secure talent earlier in the training process. These partnerships, commonly referred to as cadet programs, are agreements between institutions of higher education and airlines that provide a combination of financial incentives, employee benefits, mentorship, and preferential hiring consideration including a guaranteed first officer position to students who commit to a specific regional or mainline carrier. Additionally, many of these cadet programs involve agreements between more than one carrier, with several containing "flow programs" that allow cadets to move from a position at a regional carrier to a mainline carrier after a certain period of time or experience. Cadet programs provide airlines with access to talent at an earlier stage of the training process and allow them to recruit students while still in an institution of higher education. A recent analysis by the authors found that as of early 2019, regional carriers had entered into over 175 agreements with over 70 institutions of higher education in the United States, with mainline carriers such as Delta Air Lines, United Airlines, and JetBlue having over 25 such agreements with 15 institutions of higher education (Lutte and Mills, 2019). The analysis found that while these cadet programs vary greatly in terms of the incentives used to recruit pilots, the common denominator is a conditional offer of employment to a flight student while still in college.

Another approach to address the pilot supply challenge, and one that is more prominent outside the US, is airline-focused flight training academies. These ab initio style programs are focused on a line flying experience and multi-crew environment from day one with emphasis on standard operating procedures that may even be airline specific. Airline flight training academies are playing an increasing role in pilot supply. In 2016, approximately 6,500 airline pilots hired were trained in airline-focused academies compared to approximately 3,000 from military, university backgrounds, or those who transitioned from business aviation to airlines (CAE, 2016). We will further explore pilot hiring programs and airline training academies by developing a case study of one pilot hiring program, the United Aviate program, and an airline training academy program, Lufthansa Aviation Training.

Pilot hiring program: United Aviate

The United Airlines Aviate program is designed to provide a clear pathway for perspective pilots to land a position at United Airlines. Aviate focuses on partnerships between United Airlines, select regional carriers operating as United Express, and select university aviation programs. Recruits can enter the program as a university student from the partner schools. University students who meet the requirements and successfully complete the selection process are offered conditional employment while still in training at their university. In addition to a conditional employment offer, the student will receive a variety of financial and other incentives including sign-on bonuses from the regional airlines and mentoring from current pilots at United Airlines. The pathway for university student participants includes flying for one of the United regional airline Express partners. United monitors the training and performance of participants throughout the program. Once the participant is flying for the regional airline partner, he/she will have a direct path to United and will be eligible to enter the United hiring pool when the participant meets the minimum service requirements for flight time and length of employment at the regional partner, and maintains an acceptable performance and training record with the regional partner carrier (United, 2019).

Airline training academy: Lufthansa Aviation Training

Lufthansa Aviation Training (LAT), a subsidiary of Lufthansa Group, offers a different type of path for recruitment of airline pilots, providing ab initio pilot training for recruits, new to the industry, who want to pursue a career as an airline pilot. Using multiple training sites in Germany, Switzerland, and the United States under the European Flight Academy brand, LAT takes zero time pilots and prepares them for employment at a Lufthansa Group airline or other European airline. Training includes ground instruction and flight training at multiple locations. A focus on multi-crew operations and use of advanced simulators are essential elements of the program. Total time for completion is 20 to 28 months from the start to eligibility for employment at an airline (European Flight Academy, 2019). An advantage to the plan is the deferred payment financing option. While cost is prohibitive for many prospective airline pilots, the Lufthansa pathway offers an alternative financing plan. Using this option, students can defer the payment for the duration of training. In this model, training fees will be deducted from the pilot's salary when the pilot begins employment upon completion of training (European Flight Academy, 2019). Lufthansa Aviation Training produces about 500 pilots a year, enough to meet annual attrition rates of the Lufthansa Group pilots (Catchpole, 2018).

Conclusion

Given the demand for pilots globally, competition for pilots has motivated airlines to develop programs to attract and retain pilots early in their training. Such programs provide evidence of just how competitive the market is globally. While there is significant variation between cadet and airline training programs, they often focus on developing predictable career progression pathways for students to move to a career as a pilot by reducing barriers to entry to the profession through the use of financial incentives (such as bonuses or deferred payments for training costs) and preferential selection for openings within an air carrier. Given the forecast demand, the industry can expect an expansion of these programs with even more benefits offered to the participants to entice them to join the ranks of professional airline pilots. The success of these programs to enhance the pipeline for the next generation of aviation professionals could ultimately benefit both the airlines and the training providers that support them.

References

Boeing. (2018). *Commercial market outlook 2018–2037*. Seattle, WA: Author.
CAE. (2016). *Airline pilot demand outlook 10 year review*. Montreal: Author.

Catchpole, D. (July 18, 2018). Lufthansa aviation training turns to virtual reality. *AINOnline*. Retrieved from www.ainonline.com/aviation-news/aerospace/2018-07-18/lufthansa-aviation-training-turns-virtual-reality

European Flight Academy. (2019). Becoming a pilot. Retrieved from www.european-flight-academy.com/en

IATA. (2018). *IATA annual review 2018*. Montreal: Author.

Lutte, R. (2018). Pilot supply at the regional airlines: Airline response to the changing environment and the impact on pilot hiring. *Journal of Aviation/Aerospace Education and Research, 27*(1). https://doi.org/10.15394/jaaer.2018.1749.

Lutte, R. & Mills, R. (2019). Collaborating to train the next generation of pilots: Exploring partnerships between higher education and the airline industry. *Industry and Higher Education*. https://doi.org/10.1177/0950422219876472

United (2019). Aviate. Retrieved from: https://www.unitedaviate.com/aviate-program-career-paths/attending-a-university

2.3 Case study – How work influences cabin crew learning

A situated learning perspective

Maria F. Larrea, Steven Hodge, Yoriko Kikkawa, and Timothy J. Mavin

Introduction

The role of cabin crew has become more substantial both for safety and commercial reasons in recent years. Their work involves social interactions with different people (e.g., passengers and pilots) in different situations ranging from routine flights to inflight medical emergencies. For cabin crew training, airlines have adopted different strategies and methods. However, the impact cabin crew work has on their learning process is not considered, nor is the work considered as part of the curriculum.

For this study, it is important to differentiate two concepts related to researching the relationship between formal training as an influence on learning and cabin crew work as an influence on learning. The theory of situated learning (Lave & Wenger, 1991) was applied in this study to understand the learning that arises from context, like cabin crew work. According to this theory, cabin crew work can be regarded as a type of 'social practice' or structured, contextualised social engagement that generates learning and is characterised by special skills and knowledge, power hierarchies, a sense of the value or mission of the work, and a set of work identities. With respect to current aviation industry training theory, cabin crew work has been defined as any task performed by them under the requirement of the airline during a flight duty (International Civil Aviation Organization, 2014). On the other hand, social practice refers to the interaction of newcomers and old-timers to gain mastery in a social practice (Lave & Wenger, 1991). The point is made because within the industry, the term 'practice' often refers to simulated exercises during training. To avoid confusion, within this chapter simulated exercises will be referred to simply as 'training'.

This chapter presents the results of a small qualitative study conducted with cabin crew members of an airline operating in the Tasman Sea region. The study aimed to understand how initial training and earlier experiences at work influence learning of cabin crew from the perspectives of situated learning. The chapter first provides an outline of theory and research related to cabin crew training and situated learning, which inform a conceptual framework used for this study. Second, it describes the case context involved in the study, followed by methods used for collecting and analysing data. Moreover, the results of the qualitative study are discussed, and diverse contributions of the study are considered.

The literature

Although studies on the work of cabin crew have increased in recent years (Damos et al., 2013), the role of the cabin crew is underrepresented in the aviation literature, especially regarding their learning processes. Research on cabin crew training emphasises the need for effective training due to the complexity of their work context. Primarily, research has focused on training effect on performance. For example, a study that tested the retention of skills and knowledge in cabin crew 12 months after their training found the majority failed to demonstrate the expected first aid performance (Mahony et al., 2007). The study also found that time limitations in training and a lack of real-life scenarios affected performance. Another study assessing instruction on controlling unruly passengers concluded that training did not reflect the realities of work and therefore was not effective (Rhoden et al., 2008). These studies stressed these situations are becoming increasingly frequent and therefore require training strategies that replicate the work context to develop the skills expected of the cabin crew.

On the other hand, studies on pilot training have also investigated training effects in performance. For example, the concept of transfer of training has been applied to determine quantitatively how learning in a training context (i.e., simulators) contributes to the performance in a real work context, also called positive transfer (Kearns, 2007). Likewise, the incorrect application of procedures learned in training into work, or negative transfer, has been the cause of investigations for being related to aviation accidents (Borgvall et al., 2007). For a positive transfer of training, the use of realistic simulators or role-play in class is needed, in addition to exercises in work teams that favour the acquisition of skills for work (Kearns, 2007). Thus, learning in real work contexts has also been highlighted as fundamental for pilot training.

The contemporary framework of safety training for cabin crew by the International Civil Aviation Organisation (ICAO, 2014) has begun to be incorporated by airlines worldwide. This framework is a competency-based education (CBE) approach intended to facilitate the standardisation of learning outcomes. Competency-based education is programme design, training and assessment that refers to written statements about expected training outcomes (Kearns et al., 2016). Implementation of CBE by the ICAO is based mainly on behavioural objectives theory (Hodge, 2007) because the approach is believed to promote homogenous, controlled and observable performance (Tennant, 2002). Learning objectives are achieved by external stimuli of a teacher, in controlled environments such as a classroom (Cunningham et al., 2007), and ignore individual and social responses (Cohen et al., 2007). However, in work contexts where human performance and social interaction are complex, a more holistic approach is beneficial for learning (Anderson et al., 1996; Gonczi, 1999). In particular, Kearns et al. (2016) discussed the need for a CBE model for aviation training that considers the complexity of the lived social context in which knowledge and skills are applied—a context termed a 'social practice'—for curricular development.

Lave and Wenger (1991) first proposed the theory of situated learning to understand the learning trajectory of apprentices whose training took place through participation in the social practice of a skilled occupation. According to the authors, only under these circumstances does meaningful learning occur. Lave and Wenger distinguished a 'learning curriculum' from a 'teaching curriculum'. The latter refers to what is explicitly taught by old-timers and others with teaching responsibilities. The learning curriculum, in contrast, is the impact of work itself on learning. In modern training systems such as competency-based cabin crew training, the teaching curriculum is initially delivered by instructors using the units of competency to inform instructional activities. What is of particular interest to this study is how the 'learning curriculum' created by authentic cabin crew work, contributes to learning.

It should be noted that the situated learning perspective has been criticised for ignoring the contribution of individuals' cognition to learning (Anderson et al., 1996). This issue is especially relevant to educational programmes such as cabin crew training in which individual responsibility is stressed. Situated learning theory is also criticised for failing to engage with the complex realities of modern society in which people cross numerous 'social practices' as they learn, thus increasing the difficulties of contemporary learners as they negotiate multiple demands (Fuller, 2007). Despite these arguments, situated learning helps us to appreciate the influence of social context in the growth of cabin crew knowledge and skills and offers a complementary perspective to that of formal initial training.

The case

This case study focused on cabin crew training within an airline serving on short-haul flights on small turbo-prop regional aircraft with only two cabin crew. The formal or 'teaching curriculum', developed using the framework for *cabin crew safety training* proposed by ICAO (2014), consists of a three-week classroom-based training programme followed by one week of on-line training (i.e., in the aircraft flying with passengers). During the first three weeks, the trainees attended classroom lectures and eventually, aircraft familiarisation. They were assessed for their competence weekly through computer-based tests. The lectures, led by an instructor, focused mainly on safety aspects (e.g., characteristics of the aircraft's emergency equipment, evacuation procedures). Later, during on-line training, the trainees had their first contact with the actual work context, although they were not acting as part of the crew. The trainees observed routine procedures of cabin crew on actual flights (e.g., service delivery, cabin safety checks), and gradually assumed duties under the instructor's

96 Maria F. Larrea et al.

supervision. Finally, their performance in-flight was assessed, as a regulatory requirement of the country's Civil Aviation Authority.

Study methods

This study explored the cabin crew's perceptions of the contributions of initial training and earlier experiences at work to prepare them for work. A qualitative study using an ethnographic approach was proposed, since it provides an insider perspective of a group's culture, in its social context (Creswell, 2013). Aviation, traditionally, has been studied quantitatively; qualitative studies have been limited but show the advantage in understanding social interactions within the industry (Ferroff et al., 2012). This study involved seven individual interviews with cabin crew who joined a regional airline in the past two years (referred to as P1 through P7). Later, the data collected was analysed thematically to articulate themes within the participants' expressions (Creswell, 2013). Finally, the data collected was triangulated with literature and theoretical concepts to deepen and extend the analysis and to frame the conclusions and recommendations of the study.

Findings

Figure 2.3.1 summarises the findings concerning the initial training curriculum and the contribution cabin crew work has on learning. The results are discussed below under five categories when: (a) work confirms training, (b) work modifies training, (c) work contradicts training, (d) work does not confirm training, and (e) when work is not taught during training. The expressions of some participants are used to exemplify these categories.

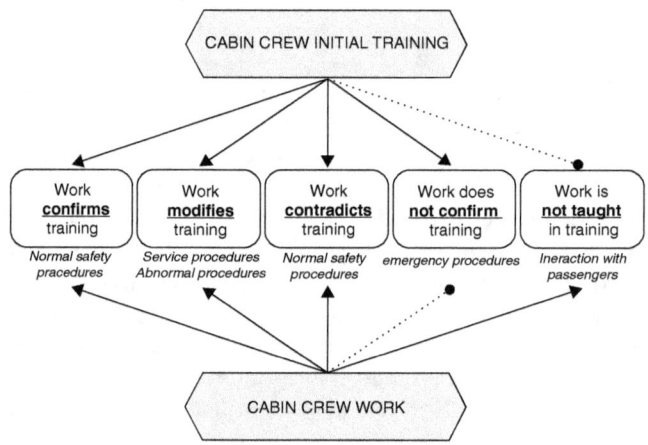

Figure 2.3.1 Research findings on the relationship between formal training and cabin crew work (Larrea et al., 2019).

1. **Work confirms training** Participants expressed that routine duties, such as emergency equipment checks and service delivery, complied with the procedures taught during training. 'We do our checks at the start of each flight, we'll check the safety equipment, 95% of the procedures are what I learned in those four days of on the-job-training' (P7). Interacting with their trainers and colleagues during the on-line training and in regular flights allowed the participants to consolidate knowledge.
2. **Work modifies training** The participants mentioned that their experienced colleagues modify certain procedures, such as the delivery of services, in order to perform them more efficiently. The perception of the participants is that experiences at work modified to adapt to unexpected situations, such as interaction with passengers, and to perform more efficiently under time pressure. For example, P6 declared: 'I'd be following their lead, because they would be quicker. Then, I'd see the way they do it. So, next time I do it myself, I'll do it that way'. Observing the different practices of their colleagues prompted the participants to develop their own work style, that subsequently gave them greater confidence in their own performance.
3. **Work contradicts training** 'At this stage, I definitely do the procedures, but I do take on what other people do. I don't learn from bad habits. I have noted the difference between what they do and what the manual says' (P2). It was also perceived that some modifications made while at work could produce learning that was contrary to formal training. The participants did not report these behaviours as intentional violations but rather as efforts to expedite processes during time-critical moments in flight, as expressed by P7: 'We do have a rule book essentially. You're only going to change something if it's beneficial, not if it's going to be detrimental'. Interestingly, their perceptions towards this practice were diverse: Some of them rejected the practice emphatically, while others minimised their consequences.
4. **Work does not confirm training** 'I know you can't practice an emergency, but in the back of my mind, if something happens, there's still that question of *would I perform?*' (P5). Participants *perceived* insufficient preparation lead to reduced levels of self-confidence to perform in emergencies. The perceived insufficient preparation stems from the fact that these duties are not part of routine work, and training was unrealistic.
5. **Work is not taught in training** 'I'm still learning now about different ways you can handle situations. Actually, jump on the plane, and you get an older cabin crew you asked the question you've never heard before. And that is your training for future reference' (P3). The participants mentioned that there are situations in the work context that are not part of the training, such as the daily interaction with passengers. However, the influence of more experienced colleagues was identified as a valuable source of new learning.

Discussion and recommendations

This chapter described a case study of cabin crew learning across formal training and experiences in the real-life setting of work. Five categories of interactions between formal learning and learning situated at work were identified, which were alternative categories to those established in transfer of training studies for pilot training. Although the findings show the importance of formal training, a greater contribution of learning situated in the work context was found, mainly due to the social interaction of the new cabin crew members with their experienced colleagues. More specifically, evidence under *the work confirms training theme* indicated the effectiveness of the initial training in normal safety and service procedures. However, the other four themes—*work modifies training, work contradicts training, work does not confirm training* and *work is not taught in training*—revealed divergence between initial training and experiences at work. The findings of these themes emphasised that the participating cabin crew gained substantial learning in their work context.

Moreover, regarding non-routine work (e.g., emergency training), more realistic training facilities are needed to improve their readiness and, therefore, ensure they can perform appropriately if a situation occurs. Since resource limitations were acknowledged in this study, such as the limited access to simulators in regional airlines, it is challenging for the industry to find a way to address this need for cabin crew training. Finally, learning can be compromised due to confusion and contradiction between the observed practice and training. In some cases, it could lead to complacency with behaviours that could potentially affect the passenger's satisfaction or flight safety. Therefore, the airline managers should closely monitor the practices that could inhibit learning.

The contributions of this study are diverse. First, the findings help expand knowledge about cabin crew learning, which to date has been limited. Second, this study expands the understanding of the concepts previously studied in aviation training, such as the transfer of training, as it provides a qualitative perspective to contemporary concerns of the industry (e.g., human performance and social interrelations). Finally, the complexity of the cabin crew role facilitates critical analysis of the dominant model of competency-based education and the potential of situated learning theory to contribute to aviation industry training programmes.

References

Anderson, J. R., Reder, L. M., & Simon, H. A. (1996). Situated learning and education. *Educational Researcher, 25*(4), 5–11.

Borgvall, J., Castor, M., Nählinder, S., Oskarsson, P. A., & Svensson, E. (2007). *Transfer of training in military aviation.* Sweden: Command and Control Systems, Swedish Defence Research Agency (FOI).

Cohen, L., Manion, L., & Morrison, K. (2007). *Research methods in education*. Abingdon, UK: Routledge.

Creswell, J. W. (2013). *Educational research: Planning, conducting, and evaluating quantitative and qualitative research* (4th ed.). Boston, MA: Pearson.

Cunningham, T., Gannon, J., Kavanagh, M. B., Greene, J., Reddy, L., & Whitson, L. (2007). *Theories of learning and curriculum design: Key positionalities and their relationships*. Ireland: Dublin Institute of Technology.

Damos, D. L., Boyett, K. S., & Gibbs, P. (2013). Safety versus passenger service: The flight attendants' dilemma. *The International Journal of Aviation Psychology, 23*(2), 91–112.

Ferroff, C. V., Mavin, T. J., Bates, P. R., & Murray, P. S. (2012). A case for social constructionism in aviation safety and human performance research. *Aeronautica, 3*, 1–12.

Fuller, A. (2007). Critiquing theories of learning and communities of practice. In J. Hughes, N. Jewson, & L. Unwin (eds.), *Communities of practice: Critical perspectives* (pp. 17–29). New York, NY: Routledge.

Gonczi, A. (1999). Competency-based learning: A dubious past—an assured future? In D. Boud, & J. Garrick (eds.), *Understanding learning at work* (pp. 180–196). London, UK: Routledge.

Hodge, S. (2007). The origins of competency-based training. *Australian Journal of Adult Learning, 47*(2), 179–209.

International Civil Aviation Organization (2014). *Cabin crew safety training manual* (Doc 10002). Montreal and Canada: International Civil Aviation Organization.

Kearns, S. K. (2007). *The effectiveness of guided mental practice in a computer-based single pilot resource management (SRM) training program*. (Doctoral dissertation) Minneapolis, MN: Capella University.

Kearns, S. K., Mavin, T. J., & Hodge, S. (2016). *Competency-based education in aviation. Exploring alternate training pathways*. Surrey, UK: Ashgate.

Larrea, M. F., Mavin, T.J., Hodge, S., & Kikkawa, Y. (2019, September 4). Cabin crew training with a situated learning perspective. Paper presented at the PACDEFF CRM and Aviation Human Factors Conference, Gold Coast, Australia.

Lave, J., & Wenger, E. (1991). *Situated learning. Legitimate peripheral participation*. Cambridge: Cambridge University Press.

Mahony, P. H., Griffiths, R. F., Larsen, P., & Powell, D. (2007). Retention of knowledge and skills in first aid and resuscitation by airline cabin crew. *Resuscitation, 76*(3), 413–418.

Rhoden, S., Ralston, R., & Ineson, E. M. (2008). Cabin crew training to control disruptive airline passenger behavior: A cause for tourism concern? *Tourism Management, 29*(3), 538–547.

Tennant, M. (2002). *Psychology & adult learning* (2nd ed.). London, UK: Routledge Falmer.

2.4 Chapter: Multi-piloted operations

Alan Martinez, R. Joseph Childs, and Dan Sutliff

Introduction

Ab initio training for multi-piloted cockpits and the Multi-Crew Pilot License (MPL) continues to be adopted worldwide by the aviation industry but, as of 2019, not in the United States. Universities in the U.S. are well suited to introduce and enhance multi-crew training for student pilots as part of their graduation requirements for the Restricted-Airline Transport Pilot (R-ATP) certification. In this chapter, we discuss the historical development of multi-crew training for air transport category aircraft and the factors leading to the adoption of MPL by the International Civil Aviation Organization (ICAO). We will review the status of multi-crew training in the U.S. and also discuss the emergence of competency-based education (CBE) as an instructional design and assessment methodology to improve the quality of aviation training. Finally, we consider the role of university aviation programs in providing enhanced training beyond the current minimum Federal Aviation Administration (FAA) requirements to successfully meet the challenge of training future aviation professionals.

Cockpit teamwork

Transport category aircraft require pilots to operate as teams and successful teamwork is essential in today's complex sociotechnical aviation system. Successful individual performance does not ensure effective team performance. Cockpit team performance requires team level knowledge, skills, and attitudes (KSAs) and team members must thoroughly understand the unique roles performed by each member of the team and the interdependencies of those roles (Delise et al., 2010). Until the advent of cockpit team training and evaluation in the late 1970s and early 1980s, traditional pilot training focused on error-free individual pilot skills with little emphasis on teamwork and successful interaction with other members of the flight crew (Tullo, 2010). Cockpit team training, known also as Crew Resource Management (CRM), introduced psycho-social skills and management to the cockpit team environment, and the cockpit workload shifted from traditional "stick and rudder" skills to managing the flight crew team in a highly automated aircraft (Harris, 2011). With a team-based focus, individual pilot skills were now part of larger team-based skills designed to improve team performance and increase safety (Flin et al., 2008).

Over the next two decades, cockpit team training would see five generational shifts as new initiatives in human factors research emerged (Transport Canada Civil Aviation, 2019). By the late 1990s, researchers began to acknowledge the ubiquity and inevitability of human error and the natural limitations of human performance and explored cockpit team interactions as error countermeasures. Tullo (2010) suggests that cockpit teamwork is the focus on the "proper response to threats to safety and the proper management of crew error" (p. 55). The essence of threat and error management (TEM) is not the prevention of human error but the stopping of adverse consequences through detection and correction. Cockpit teamwork is better understood in terms of frameworks instead of generations. Threat and error management is found in the risk management sixth framework that includes risk and resource management and resilience training (Farrow, 2019). It remains prevalent in cockpit team training programs today, though some argue that risk management initiatives are ineffective in helping flight crews innovate, increase situation awareness, develop shared mental models, and enhance cockpit teamwork required in today's complex highly-automated aviation environment (Fraher, 2011).

Multi-crew pilot training

In legacy civilian pilot training, cockpit teamwork training normally occurs at the point in the pilot's flight hour experience progression where an aircraft type rating in a multi-crew cockpit is required. Until then, fight training and experience take place in light propeller-driven single-engine (SE) and multi-engine (ME) aircraft specifically designed and certified for single-piloted operations. Though the aspiration of many pilots is to fly in transport category multi-piloted cockpits, training standards and learning pathways in legacy training programs from the beginning, i.e. ab initio, strictly focus on single-pilot learning outcomes in course curricula designed to meet Private and Commercial licensing requirements. The reasons can be attributed to the legacy regulatory environment and training cost constraints that favor single-pilot operations. After achieving Private and Commercial certificates, flight experience normally occurs within general aviation as a Certified Flight Instructor (CFI). Functioning as a CFI can undoubtedly increase pilot in command (PIC) abilities, and "captainship" (Embry-Riddle Aeronautical University Associate Professor, personal communication, March 29, 2019), but the nature of the CFI's light piston-powered single pilot aircraft environment does little in, and may in fact be counterproductive to, developing cockpit teamwork skills essential for operating air transport category aircraft that are designed and certified for multi-crew operations

(Wikander & Dahlstrom, 2014). Furthermore, the aspiring airline pilots who depend on gaining the total hours toward the ATP via the CFI route often lack cross-country experience (Bjerke & Malott, 2011). The lack of multi-crew experience is further exacerbated by the common "ready-entry career structure" system which promotes the accumulation of flight hours to meet the ATP 1500 flight hour requirement in cockpits vastly different than those used for airline transportation (Kearns et al., 2016).

Alternative pathway for multi-crew training

In 2002, ICAO established the Flight Crew Licensing and Training Panel (FCLTP), to consider new pilot licensing and training standards that were safe, effective, and efficient ways to train and develop multi-crew flight operations proficiencies earlier in a pilot's training process. The general view among the 64 members from 18 ICAO states and 5 international organizations was that modern training methodologies and flight training technology could improve pilot certification and training standards (International Air Transport Association [IATA], 2015; Wikander & Dahlstrom, 2014). The panel sought new and optional alternatives to the traditional hours-based licensing approach for multi-piloted cockpit environments. Leveraging imprecise and broad guidance found within the ICAO regulations for alternative licensing pathways, the panel determined a multi-crew licensing approach providing an airline pilot training pathway with a multi-crew focus. See Kearns et al. (2016) for a review of the panel's overall structure of the competency approach. Based on the panel's recommendations, multi-crew licensing was reviewed by the ICAO Air Navigation Commission (ANC) and approved by the ICAO Council in November 2006 and distributed as an amendment to Annex 1 – Personal Licensing and Procedures for Air Navigation Services, Training (PANS-TRG) Doc 9868. The MPL was the first major update to licensing provisions since 1948 (Schroeder & Harms, 2007). Several updates have been made to Doc 9868 since the original inclusion of MPL with the approval of the second edition in 2015 (ICAO, 2016).

Multi-crew pilot license (MPL)

The foundational element of the MPL is competency-based ab initio training in multi-piloted cockpits that is complementary to currently existing licensing requirements, emphasizing flight simulation training devices (FSTDs) (Wikander & Dahlstrom, 2014). The MPL is also designed to be consistent with the FAA's Advanced Qualification Program (AQP) which promotes a systematic task analysis methodology and training design for flight crew evaluation (FAA, 2017a). And similar to the AQP, the MPL integrates cockpit team training with individual flying skills, systems knowledge, and flight simulation in a multi-crew environment with embedded CRM and TEM elements. Using the instructional systems design (ISD) performance task analysis principle of "beginning with the end in mind," the multi-crew pilot license (MPL) is "determinedly designed for multi-crew airline operations" (IATA, 2015, p.8).

MPL training design

The MPL training scheme is divided into four sequential training stages: 1) core flying skills; 2) basic; 3) intermediate; and 4) advanced (see Table 2.4.1).

The training design of the MPL focuses on the performance outcome of a transport category aircraft first officer (FO)/second-in-command (SIC) crewmember. According to ICAO (2016), the first two stages are foundational and "are of the utmost importance as the student starts to develop core technical, interpersonal, procedural, and aircraft-handling skills that underpin the competencies of an MPL" (p. II-1-1-A-1). The use of flight training devices and CRM/TEM principles are introduced in core flying skills and continue throughout all training parts. What is unique about the MPL training design is that immediately after core flying skills, student pilots are introduced to the multi-crew environment and associated PF and PM teamwork interactions, which then carry forward into the rest of the training. The intermediate stage introduces high-performance transport category aircraft and line-oriented flight training (LOFT) that provides the opportunity for the student pilots to practice procedures, maneuvers, and line operations, CRM, and TEM in a full simulated multi-crew environment (FAA, 2015). The strength of LOFT is the integration of technical skills and CRM in a "real-world, real time" simulation that evaluates both individual and team member performance. The final stage is advanced, which is a culmination of previous stages and similar to a transport category aircraft type-rating. Both the intermediate and follow-on advanced stage utilize the highest level of full-motion flight simulation to fully replicate a multi-crew environment in an advanced technology cockpit including flight guidance and flight management systems.

MPL First Officer (FO)/Second in Command (SIC) crewmember competencies

The strength of the ISD process is the systematic functional/task analysis, which identifies the subcomponents of the first officer/second-in-command flight crewmember "job," which in this case, is the instructional goal of the MPL program. The job is further divided into functions, tasks, sub-tasks, and possibly sub-task elements. The purpose of functional/task analysis is to help determine what the learner needs to know or to perform as a competent first officer FO/SIC. A competent FO/SIC crew member is someone with the requisite skills, knowledge, and attitudes that can *fully* participate in a complex sociotechnical aviation industry (Kearns et al., 2016). A *fully participating* FO/SIC crewmember possesses a specific set of knowledge, skills, and attitudes that contribute and enhance the overall team performance

Table 2.4.1 MPL training stages

Stages of Training	Areas of Training	Training Equipment – Crew Position Focus	
Advanced Type rating training in air carrier operations environment	• CRM • TEM • LOFT • All weather scenarios • Landing • Abnormal procedures • Normal procedures • Upset prevention and recovery	Aircraft: Turbine Multi-engine Multi-crew FSTD: High fidelity transport category aircraft	Pilot Flying & Pilot Monitoring
Intermediate Application of multi-crew operations	• CRM • TEM • LOFT • Multi-crew • Instrument • Abnormal procedures • Normal procedures	FSTD: High performance, multi-engine turbine aircraft	Pilot Flying & Pilot Monitoring
Basic Introduction of multi-crew operations	• CRM • TEM • PF/PM interaction • IFR cross-country • Night • Instrument • Upset prevention and recovery	Aircraft: single or multi-engine FSTD: Higher fidelity level	Pilot Flying & Pilot Monitoring
Core flying skills Single pilot training	• CRM • TEM • VFR cross-country • Solo flight • Basic instrument • Flight Principles • Cockpit procedures • Upset prevention and recovery	Aircraft: single or multi-engine FSTD: Lower fidelity level	Pilot Flying

Source: ICAO (2016) and ICAO (2018).

(Oser et al., 2000). The functional/task analysis identified nine functions (competency units) which were then divided into 56 tasks (competency elements), with applicable performance criteria (ICAO, 2016). For the original MPL training process, the competency units follow the normal flight sequencing of ground operations/pre-flight operations, takeoff, climb, cruise, descent, approach, landing, and after landing operations, and include TEM application. The Approved Training Organization (ATO) systematically designs and develops training based on competency units, elements, and associated performance criteria. The ATOs are given the flexibility to design their instructional program based on training objectives and derived competency elements and it includes some type of learner assessment and evaluation and structured initial operating experience (IOE) which is acceptable to the licensing authority (ICAO, 2016).

Aviation industry reaction to MPL

The initial reaction to the MPL was positive but was mixed with some concerns and misconceptions. A common misconception was that the MPL approach was a regulatory response to a global pilot shortage. According to Schroeder and Harms (2007), the panel's recommendations and subsequent changes were entirely due to the antiquated licensing provision standards and practices found in the current ICAO Annex 1. It was the panel's belief that worldwide pilot training had not kept in step with industry practices nor reflected the latest advances in flight simulation. However, even before the 2006 Annex 1 update, the European Cockpit Association (ECA) and International Federation of Air Line Pilots' Association (IFALPA) expressed concerns with the MPL licensing process and lack of required flight hours (Wikander & Dahlstrom, 2014). In 2008, the Air Line Pilots Association, International (ALPA) white paper questioned the training and licensing provisions of the MPL process and because the concept was "new and unproven" suggested additional safety oversight was needed as compared to the traditional pilot licensing approach (p. 5). The same year, IFALPA (2008) once again voiced concern by arguing that the "MPL philosophy is a new and yet unproven concept and is therefore a significant departure from existing pilot instruction methodologies" and argued for a "scientific" analysis of the MPL to prove that MPL philosophical soundness met safety levels provided by "traditional training methods" (p. 1).

By 2010, 30 ICAO countries had adopted the MPL approach and only 12 courses existed (Wikander & Dahlstrom, 2014). In October of 2011, IATA published the first edition of Guidance Material and Best Practices for MPL Implementation. In December of 2013, ICAO held an MPL Symposium to keep its promise to review the MPL concept and evaluate the program's successes, challenges, and proper way forward (ICAO, n.d., p. 21). The goal was to improve upon MPL existing standards and guidance material and bring together those associated with MPL throughout the world. A major conclusion was the need for more industry data on current MPL programs which led to data collection efforts shortly thereafter (Wikander & Dahlstrom, 2016).

A symposium workshop, plus MPL advisory board findings and ATO site visits, revealed concerns about basic flying skills, airmanship, CRM, and Air Traffic Control (ATC) situational awareness of pilots trained using the MPL process (IFALPA, 2014). The ECA published their position shortly after the symposium stating MPL had not proven to reach the equivalent safety of "traditional pilot licensing and training programs" (2013, p. 4). Interestingly, IFALPA recently co-authored the second edition of guidance material for MPL implementation with IATA representing a collaborative effort toward harmonized MPL best practices around the globe suggesting a more positive view by industry of the MPL concept (IATA, 2015). The guidance document sources ATOs conducting MPL courses, MPL advisory boards, MPL surveys and interviews, pilot training conferences, workshops, panels, and results from the ICAO 2013 MPL Symposium. Despite industry concern, MPL training around the world continued to increase. By 2014, 52 ICAO countries (states) had adopted the MPL approach with 22 active courses thus indicating a growing global acceptance of the MPL training concept (Wikander & Dahlstrom, 2014).

Current state of MPL

According to the Global MPL Course Tracker, as of December 2018, there were 39 ATO MPL programs in the world (IATA, 2018). Since 2013, the number of MPL graduates increased from 785 to 3433 and MPL students increased from 2330 to 5667. This suggests ATOs around the world are finding the MPL a viable training option for the next generation of aviation professionals. Despite initial concerns and misconceptions and any current skepticism, recent MPL survey data shows a strong belief and support for the MPL training concept (Wikander & Dahlstrom, 2016).

Competency confusion

Recognizing the complex sociotechnical aviation system and the unseen potential for dangerous flight situations, an international working group established evidence-based training (EBT). The EBT methodology defines pilot "core" competencies for air carrier operations according to threats collected in accidents, incidents, flight operations, and training (Evidence-Based Training by Varney in this volume; ICAO, 2013). Leading to better training outcomes, EBT technical and non-technical core competencies are similar to skills historically identified as FAA CRM critical skills and European nontechnical (NOTECHS) skills (FAA, 2004; Flin, 2019, IATA, 2013). The strength of the EBT core competencies is the link to specific actions, which represent a prescribed set of behaviors leading to an overall performance aspect (Flin & Martin, 2001). The goal of behavior markers (indicators) is to minimize observer judgments, reduce ambiguities, and help identify underlying deficiencies in cockpit teamwork (Flin, 2019; Flin et al., 2008).

Early developers of the MPL recognize that the original nine competency units identified vis a vis different phases of flight did not fully meet the definition of a competency, thus creating confusion about the MPL systematic approach, instructional outcomes, and connection with later published EBT pilot core competencies, competency descriptions, and associated behavioral indicators (Rosenkrans, 2014; Wikander & Dahlstrom, 2016). The original flight phase task headers as competencies created a misalignment in the global aviation training industry with EBT where competency assessments are considered disconnected from specific tasks (M. Varney, personal communication, May 18, 2019). The most recent MPL guidance attempts to clarify competency-based training by using an input-output model (IATA, 2015). Effective application of the pilot core competencies (input) results in successful aircraft handling in all phases of flight (output). The input-output model was only a stop-gap measure to address the confusion between EBT pilot core competencies and MPL competencies units/elements (D. Harms, personal communication, May 27, 2019). A proposal by the recently established Competency-Based Training and Assessment Task Force now aligns ICAO's EBT and MPL competency-based training and assessment methodologies but the amendments to Annex 1 – Personal Licensing and PANS-TRG Doc 9868 as of the date of this chapter are still in draft form awaiting final approval (ICAO, 2018).

Summary

While there has been debate and skepticism about the MPL since ICAO adoption in 2006, the value of multi-crew training for pilots preparing to become competent first officer/second-in-command flight crewmembers is difficult to dispute. The process and implementation are influenced by cultural, political, and economic factors unique to each country. And while many aviation regulatory organizations embrace ab initio multi-crew training and the move from experience-based flight hour requirements to pilot competencies, some still perceived the MPL as unsuitable.

Multi-crew pilot training in the United States

As of this writing, multi-crew pilot training and certification as used by ICAO member countries are not part of the U.S. regulatory requirements. In fact, the measure of pilot training and qualification remains a specific amount of flight hours. Training is conducted under Title 14 Code of Federal Regulations (CFR) Federal Aviation Regulations (FARs) § 61 or § 141 which outline required training times and/or flight experience minimums for pilot certificates and ratings. Under § 61, pilots are required to have 250 hours of flight time to be eligible for a commercial pilot certificate, and until 2013, this, along with an instrument rating, *qualified* a pilot to act as a first officer/second-in-command flight crewmember. The only mention of a multi-crew environment occurs during instrument training under § 61.65(b)(10) which requires ground training on CRM, including crew communication and coordination.

In 1974, the FAA published FAR § 141 with the goal of providing "equivalent levels of aeronautical experience in less time than required by § 61" (FAA, 1993, p. 1). Pilot training schools accomplish this by utilizing FAA approved structured training programs and experienced chief instructors. They also must undergo periodic surveillance by the FAA. Under § 141, a pilot is eligible for a commercial certificate after receiving 120 hours of training beyond that required for the private pilot certificate and the instrument rating, each of which require 35 hours, for a total of 190 flight hours (FAA, 2017b).

FAA/Industry Training Standards (FITS)

A serious effort toward *more efficient pilot training* came in the early 2000s in the form of FAA/Industry Training Standards (FITS). A FITS curriculum can further reduce training times through the use of "real-world, real time" scenarios, similar to LOFT mentioned earlier. Since FITS curricula need only be "accepted" by the FAA rather than "approved," FITS offer the flexibility to incorporate multi-crew concepts if so desired, keeping in mind that the practical test must be accomplished as a single pilot. Rather than the 120 flight hours of commercial pilot training required under § 141, a FITS student is eligible for the practical test upon demonstrating proficiency in core concepts such as risk management, aeronautical decision making, situational awareness, and single pilot resource management along with the requisite knowledge and skills (FAA, 2006). With FITS there is the potential to reduce commercial flight training hours by more than half, therefore, producing commercially certificated pilots with approximately 130 flight hours. Beyond FAR § 141, and a FITS curriculum, there are currently no prescribed methods to achieve additional efficiencies in initial pilot training in the United States. However, there are changes occurring to make pilot training more relevant to the operational environment.

Airman Certification Standards (ACS)

In 2016, the FAA began replacing the Practical Test Standards (PTS) with the Airman Certification Standards (ACS). Rather than a purely task-oriented approach to the practical test, the ACS adds the aeronautical knowledge and risk management elements that support each task. The ACS provides a clear, single source set of standards to be satisfied to qualify for a pilot certificate or rating (FAA, n.d., p. 20). While able to introduce multi-crew concepts during training, there is currently no regulatory determination at the commercial pilot level of whether a pilot is headed for commercial operations as a single pilot or as a member of a multi-crew cockpit.

Restricted airline transport pilot certificate (R-ATP)

On February 9, 2009, a high-profile regional airline accident focused attention on multiple aspects of air carrier pilot qualifications. The National Transportation Safety Board (NTSB) final report of the Colgan Air Flight 3407 accident raised questions about FO/SIC training and flight hours requirements. Specifically, should a SIC be held to the same training and flight hours requirements as a PIC? And, what is the relative importance of a pilot's academic coursework and flight training quality to the total number of flight hours? Ironically, pilot professionalism and the adequacy of a pilot's exposure to a multi-crew environment were also called into question. In July 2010, the FAA chartered the Flight Officer Qualification Aviation Rulemaking Committee (FOQ ARC) to develop recommendations. In August 2010, Public Law 111–126 was signed into law directing the FAA to modify ATP certification requirements in the interest of air carrier safety (Airline Safety and Federal Aviation Administration Extension Act, 2010). Based on these recommendations, the FAA published the Final Rule on Pilot Certification and Qualification Requirements for Air Carrier Operations in July 2013. The rule required an FO/SIC in air carrier operations to hold an ATP certificate. However, pilots could qualify for a restricted privileges airline transport pilot certificate (R-ATP) that modified the 1500-hour flight time requirement and age minimum of 23 years. At the age of 21, military-trained pilots qualify for the R-ATP certificate with 750 hours of flight time. Those with a bachelor's degree with an aviation major from an approved college or university qualify with 1000 hours total flight time, and those with an associate degree from a similar institution, with 1250 flight hours. The R-ATP allows a pilot to serve as SIC in air carrier operations.

Airline transport pilot certification training program

The final rule also required ATP certificate candidates to complete an ATP Certification Training Program (ATP-CTP). The ATP-CTP requires 30 hours of classroom instruction that includes multi-crew operations such as communications, checklist philosophy, and CRM. Ten hours of training in an FSTD that represents a multi-engine turbine airplane are also required (Federal Register, 2013a). However, the entire ATP-CTP can be completed in one week, bringing into question its long-term efficacy in producing and evaluating multi-crew competencies.

Enhanced qualification program

In 2016, the Air Carrier Training Aviation Rulemaking Committee (ACT-ARC) submitted recommendations it received from the ATP Workgroup (ATP-WG) for an Enhanced Qualification Program (EQP). The ATP-WG had been tasked with exploring alternative pathways to an R-ATP. Their proposal involves prerequisites, candidate assessment, and integrated academic and flight training. The goal is for a pilot candidate to acquire the requisite knowledge and skills for transport category aircraft in a shorter time period. The recommendation establishes *competencies* needed for safe operations in a multi-crew environment. The EQP is designed to integrate academic training with "immersion training for multi-crew operations in transport category airplanes in a realistic air carrier operating environment" (FAA, 2016, p. 11). Successful completion of an EQP results in flight time credit toward the R-ATP by one of two proposed alternative methods. The first is a 250-hour credit in addition to that achieved through military training or completion of a college degree-based aviation program. The second allows qualification for the R-ATP with 500 hours of total flight time regardless of the pathway (military or collegiate) prior to entering the EQP. A § 121 air carrier is responsible to submit an EQP to the FAA for approval (FAA, 2016).

Current U.S. regulatory environment

The current political realities in the U.S. may hinder adoption of MPL or the EQP. Along with pilot unions, families of the victims from Colgan Air Flight 3407 remain a strong voice against lowering any total hour requirement. As one FAA Administrator gave his personal opinion, "I would guess that MPL is a non-starter with the FAA, and for some good reasons. I would imagine that the Colgan 3407 families and ALPA would be against it as well" (D. Lundgren, personal communication, April 27, 2019). This was demonstrated by the presence of Colgan Air Flight 3407 families at the Senate confirmation hearings for FAA Administrator Stephen Dickson in May 2019. In his prepared statement to the Committee, Dickson (2019) emphasized the importance of balancing changes brought on by technological innovations in crew automation with existing safety systems. He also acknowledged that the influx of a new generation of pilots requires improvements in safety and performance outcomes. When questioned about the 1,500 flight hour ATP, Dickson supported current rules and would not seek changes that would lower safety standards (Oster, 2019).

Summary

Multi-crew pilot training in the United States has largely been left up to initial hire training at the airlines and is most recently associated with the ATP-CTP. While U.S. airlines are starting to recognize the benefits of ab initio training, there currently is no civilian path to the right seat of a transport category aircraft other than the legacy single pilot training and qualification mandated by the FAA. Some American air carriers have begun pseudo ab initio programs that take carefully selected applicants through the system of single pilot training and time building in a variety of creative ways, but none are specifically designed to provide dedicated multi-crew pilot training and advancement to transport category jet aircraft cockpits based on core competencies. JetBlue's Pilot Gateway Program has been around since 2016 and utilizes a contract flight training provider to qualify applicants for positions with other operators with which JetBlue has agreements. There, applicants can build the flight time that will eventually allow them to become first officers in JetBlue aircraft (N. S. Hocking, personal communication, May 8, 2019). In contrast, Lufthansa's ab initio pilot training program has been in operation for decades and relies on a rigorous selection process. Selected applicants in their program are funneled directly from initial pilot training into preparation for multi-crew qualification in transport category jet aircraft through a training curriculum based on competencies alone (T. Lippincott, personal communication, May 1, 2019). We applaud the continued refinement of the ICAO MPL concept in countries where the political milieu and regulatory environment are favorable. Given the current political realities in the U.S., it is unlikely the FAA will, in the near future, lower total time requirements below the current R-ATP rules or as proposed in the EQP or adopt the MPL. But there are opportunities to move toward more widespread adoption of multi-crew training as enhancements in the U.S.

University flight training

Besides the previously discussed § 61 or § 141 vocational non-accredited flight school or independent certified flight instructor, a second way to acquire pilot certificates and ratings is through regionally accredited institutes of higher education that offer aviation-related college or university degrees. Most of the later are authorized to issue the R-ATP certificate. Though non-IHEs (institutions of higher education) or vocational schools offer lower total prices and the flexibility to complete training in a timelier fashion, that training is accomplished through a substantial quantity of hours flown in low-cost single-engine aircraft. Hence, there is little economic incentive to pass on the costs of added value in complex aircraft or quality enhancement beyond the minimum FAA hour requirements to earn a pilot certificate (S. Markhoff, personal communication, April 10, 2019). On the other hand, academic institutions conduct flight training in the context of a broad general education, instill more rigor, and provide the opportunity for students to access state and federal financial aid. While only regionally accredited higher education schools are eligible to certify students to apply for the R-ATP, it normally takes four years to earn the degree and often an additional year as a CFI to build up the 1,000 total hours for R-ATP certification. In terms of time to qualify for first officer positions at regional airlines, the vocational route is faster. However, the universities provide enhanced training through requirements outlined in § 61.160.

The guiding principles of the R-ATP, as outlined in Advisory Circular (AC) 61–139, is that students earn academic credit for course work beyond the minimum required for the Instrument Rating and Commercial Certificate. This added value should "improve and enhance the knowledge and skills of a person seeking a career as a professional pilot" (FAA, 2013, p. 6). R-ATP certifications must also offer some type of multi-crew team training. This is normally accomplished in a course labeled CRM/human factors and/or in a capstone regional airline transition course. Students learn the history and evolution of cockpit teamwork, aspects of interpersonal relationship skills, and behavior dynamics in multi-piloted cockpits. Some universities use FTSDs or Advanced Aviation Training Devices (AATD) representing transport category aircraft allowing students to practice PF and PM procedures including checklists, flows, and call outs. The training is usually associated with some type of advanced training option or jet transition course which combines aircraft systems training with multi-crew training similar to Line Operational Simulations (LOS) experience. Students shopping for flight school options should understand the primary benefit of the 1,000 hour R-ATP isn't the saving of flight time. It is the *quality* of training, enhanced aeronautical knowledge, and CRM skills development required to operate safely at the airlines that are the differentiators.

Emerging best practices

The University Aviation Association (UAA) and Aviation Accreditation Board International (AABI) provide guidance on best practices that exceed the minimum required standards and support academic research to enhance instruction. In the absence of regulatory requirements or standards set by specialized accreditation boards, training methods and learning outcomes related to multi-crew training seem to be idiosyncratic to the university. This in part is based on the self-regulated nature of accreditation in the U.S. For instance, AABI does not prescribe the curriculum for flight education programs other than it must lead to *national certification*. But it does require outcome assessment and institutional quality enhancement programs consistent with the school's mission and program goals (AABI, 2018). As long as universities graduate students that meet the FAA national standards it is left to universities to decide how and when to introduce enhanced training beyond the minimum.

Based on the authors' anecdotal survey of university catalogs and interviews with professors, the advanced training where multi-crew operations are often introduced occurs toward the end of the curriculum and are usually not integrated into § 141 ab initio training. However, recent efforts at Oklahoma State University (OSU) to integrate multi-crew training into § 141 are having positive results. In a CRM course, students were introduced to multi-crew training in a Redbird MCX, motion simulator AATD configured as a light twin. Students were randomly selected to work as a crew and alternated roles as PF and PM. They encountered aircraft maladies and live ATC events in which crew coordination and the first-officer assertiveness were critical to positive outcomes. This form of multi-crew training is now required of all OSU students (Vance, 2017). Notable is that this training is now included in the § 141 Commercial certification, which means it is integrated into the pilot training, rather than being a stand-alone CRM multi-crew course. Best practices will emerge as more universities publish similar multi-crew training studies, including virtual reality (VR) and mixed reality (MR) training devices. Hopefully, these will be endorsed by industry and academic stakeholders and become recognized standards even if the FAA never adopts an MPL or the recommendations of the multi-crew features of the proposed EQP.

Competency-based education (CBE)

Universities should adopt CBE as a means to develop curriculum and grant academic credit. Competency-based education differs from the traditional seat-hour means of granting academic credit by requiring students to demonstrate competency on all entire learning outcomes. Students are not passed just because they sit in a classroom for a 45 hours semester and earn 70 percent on a comprehensive final exam. Nor, does the accumulation of 1,500 flight hours alone and passing an ATP-CTP course prepare a student to successfully operate in transport category air carrier operations. In a CBE model, students must demonstrate competency in 100 percent of the learning outcomes as assessed by a rubric with specific behavioral markers. Hence, the quality of aviation training curriculum must be designed to develop measurable knowledge and behavioral skills (Kearns et al., 2016). ICAO's pilot core competencies are an excellent foundation for targeted multi-crew performance outcomes. The UAA position statement supports universities adopting innovative competency-based training techniques and endorses efforts such as the Air Carrier Enhanced Pilot Training (ACE) program, which led to the CBE-based EQP recommendations from ACT ARC. The position paper emphasized the unique role universities have in providing more comprehensive and structured training that goes beyond simple time-building as a way of qualifying professional pilots (UAA, n.d.).

Universities in the U.S. may utilize Title IV funding to pay student tuition for CBE-based programs provided the CBE measures progress using clock hours. However, there are provisions by which Title IV under 34 CFR 668.10 can be used experimentally purely in a direct assessment program in lieu of clock hours as a measure of learning (Competency-Based Education Reference Guide, 2016). At this point, there are no known U.S. institutes of higher education offering a CBE aviation-related degree based on the latter. On a global scale, the industry is moving more toward competency-based instructional methodologies and measurable outcomes as a primary means to measuring proficiency as opposed to classroom seat hours or logbook flight hours (Kearns et al., 2016). The Flight Safety Foundation punctuates the urgency to adopt CBE and EBT training methods, "It cannot be assumed that critical skills and knowledge will be obtained only through hours in the air" (2018, p. 1). This is self-evident in the MPL design being adopted in multiple countries (states) outside of the U.S. It's time for U.S. universities to lead with CBE multi-pilot training as part of their degree requirements, and as the Flight Safety Foundation suggests, partner with ICAO and industry to define expected quality and performance.

University aviation curricula

Universities should consider where to place multi-crew and cockpit team training as an enhancement to in their FAA minimum required curriculum. In the MPL model, it is introduced early after core flying skills are mastered (ICAO, 2016). A logical place to start would be during the latter part of the instrument rating training or during time building during the commercial training phase. This could be done concurrently with an academic course in cockpit teams with embedded simulation so that the crew skills are practiced. The goal here is a competency-based approach that engenders teamwork and the pilot core competencies. Sessions could be recorded and assessed for behavioral markers and students could observe themselves from recordings as a means to learn. This method of self-regulation is useful for improving performance (Zimmerman & Schunk, 2011). The solution lies in a competency-based strategy that de-emphasizes individual performance and accentuates team performance. Innovations should be based on established learning theory and initiated as a means to improved training outcomes more efficiently. As data are gathered and studies published, a body of evidence will emerge to benefit all stakeholders. The first universities that lead with multi-crew CBE innovations will likely provide a catalyst for system-wide change.

Conclusion

As described in this chapter, civilian flight training is evolving in response to improve the quality and efficiency of preparing pilots to fill the global labor shortage expected through 2035. The introduction of MPL based on a competency-based education (CBE) model is gaining traction worldwide. The benefit of MPL over the traditional single pilot legacy certification system in the United States is that it enables ab initio training to prepare airline pilots to master skills and qualify based on the quality of training rather than solely on the number of flight hours. While there has been innovation and improvements in aviation training in the U.S. in the past decades, there is yet the political will to reduce total flight hours for first officers below the 1,000 hour R-ATP option through an accredited university. We encourage U.S. universities to modify their § 141 curriculum and graduation requirements to increase the quality of their multi-crew training and the use of ICAO pilot core competency methodology. There is inspiration in ICAO's MPL training model and the ACT ARC's EQP recommendations for the university aviation curriculum. As innovation in aviation training produces evidence of quality results from multi-crew training, this may influence policymakers to consider adoption of the MPL, or at least EQP in the U.S. However, the time may be short as we move towards fully autonomous aircraft. For air transport category aircraft with increased cockpit automation, where there were once three pilot seats, there are now only two, and the trend is likely to continue.

References

Air Line Pilots Association, International (2008, April). *Safety Committee Statement of Position: The Multi-crew Pilot License (MPL)*. Washington, DC: Author. Retrieved from http://crewroom.alpa.org/SAFETY/DesktopModules/ALPA_Documents/ALPA_DocumentsView.aspx?itemid=13553&ModuleId=13545&Tabid=3205

Airline Safety and Federal Aviation Administration Extension Act of 2010, Pub. L. - 111–216, 124 Stat. 2349. Retrieved from www.congress.gov/111/plaws/publ216/PLAW-111publ216.pdf

Aviation Accreditation Board International (February 2018). Accreditation Criteria Manual FORM 201. Retrieved from www.aabi.aero/about-aabi/forms-and-publications/

Bjerke, E. & Malott, D. (2011). Impacts of Public Law 111-216: Will the flight instructor career path remain a viable option for aspiring airline pilots? *Collegiate Aviation Review International*. 29. 1–9. doi:10.22488/okstate.18.100414

Competency-Based Reference Guide (July, 2016). U.S. Department of Education. Retrieved from https://experimentalsites.ed.gov/exp/pdf/CBEGuideComplete.pdf

Delise, L. A., Gorman, C. A., Brooks, A. M., Rentsch, J. R., & Steele-Johnson, D. (2010). The effects of team training on team outcomes: A meta-analysis. *Performance Improvement Quarterly*, *22*(4), 53–80. doi:10.1002/piq.20068

Dickson, S. (2019, May 15). Prepared statement of Stephen M. Dickson, nominated as Administrator of the Federal Aviation Administration. Retrieved from www.commerce.senate.gov/public/_cache/files/78b3e4d8-8758-4f55-bece-76dd7a2c4ae6/BD2130BBD2D5CD1222521E1A45549F29.dickson-witness-testimony.pdf

European Cockpit Association (2013, December). Position paper on Multi-Crew Pilot License. Retrieved from www.eurocockpit.be/sites/default/files/eca_position_paper_mpl_13_1219_f.pdf

Farrow, D. R. (2019). A regulatory perspective II. In B. G. Kanki, J. Anca, & T. R. Chidester (Eds.), *Crew Resource Management* (3nd ed., pp. 465–487). London, UK: Academic Press.

Federal Aviation Administration. (1993). *Pilot school certification* (Advisory Circular 141-1A). Washington, DC: Author. Retrieved from www.faa.gov/documentLibrary/media/Advisory_Circular/AC%20141-1A.pdf

Federal Aviation Administration. (2004). *Crew resource management training* (Advisory Circular No 120-51E). Washington, DC: Author. Retrieved from www.faa.gov/documentLibrary/media/Advisory_Circular/AC_120-51E.pdf

Federal Aviation Administration. (2006). *FAA/industry training standards (FITS) questions and answers.* Washington, DC. Retrieved from www.faa.gov/training_testing/training/fits/media/fits_qa.pdf

Federal Aviation Administration. (2013). *Institution of higher education's application for authority to certify its graduates for an airline transport pilot certificate with reduced aeronautical experience* (Advisory Circular No 61–139). Washington, DC: Author. Retrieved from www.faa.gov/documentLibrary/media/Advisory_Circular/AC_61-139.pdf

Federal Aviation Administration. (2015). *Flightcrew member line operational simulations: Line-oriented flight training, special purpose operational training, line operational evaluation* (Advisory Circular 120-35D). Washington, DC: Author. Retrieved from www.faa.gov/documentLibrary/media/Advisory_Circular/AC_120-35D.pdf

Federal Aviation Administration. (2016). *Air Carrier Training Aviation Rulemaking Committee (ACT ARC) Recommendation 16–8: Enhanced Qualification Program.* Washington, DC: Author. Retrieved from www.faa.gov/about/office_org/headquarters_offices/avs/offices/afx/afs/afs200/afs280/act_arc/act_arc_reco/media/2016/ACT_ARC_Reco_16-8.pdf

Federal Aviation Administration. (2017a). Advanced qualification program (Advisory Circular 120-54A, Change 1). Washington, DC: Author. Retrieved from www.faa.gov/documentLibrary/media/Advisory_Circular/AC_120-54A_CHG_1.pdf

Federal Aviation Administration. (2017b). *Part 141 pilot schools, application, certification, and compliance* (Advisory Circular 141-1B). Washington, DC: Author. Retrieved from www.faa.gov/documentLibrary/media/Advisory_Circular/AC_141-1B.pdf

Federal Aviation Administration. (n.d.). *Airman certification standards information brochure* Washington, DC: Author. Retrieved from www.faa.gov/training_testing/testing/acs/media/acs_brochure.pdf

Federal Register. (2013a). *Pilot certification and qualification requirements for air carrier operations.* Retrieved from www.govinfo.gov/content/pkg/FR-2016-01-04/pdf/2015-32998.pdf

Flight Safety Foundation (2018, March). *Position paper: Pilot training and competency.* Alexandria, VA: Author. Retrieved from: https://flightsafety.org/wp-content/uploads/2018/03/FSF-position-paper-pilot-training-and-competency-FINAL-03-01-18.pdf

Flin, R. (2019). CRM (non-technical) skills: A European perspective. In B. G. Kanki, J. Anca, & T. R. Chidester (Eds.), *Crew Resource Management* (3nd ed., pp. 185–206). San Diego, CA: Academic Press.

Flin, R., & Martin, L. (2001). Behavioral markers for crew resource management: A review of current practice. *The International Journal of Aviation Psychology*, 11(1), 95–118.

Flin, R., O'Conner, P., & Crichton, M. (2008). *Safety at the sharp end: A guide to non-technical skills.* Surrey, England: Ashgate.

Fraher, A. L. (2011). Thinking through crisis: Improving teamwork and leadership in high-risk fields. New York, NY: Cambridge University Press.

Harris, D. (2011). *Human performance on the flight deck.* Surrey, England: Ashgate.

International Air Transport Association (2013). *Evidence-based training implementation guide.* Montreal: Author. Retrieved from www.iata.org/whatwedo/ops-infra/training…/ebt-implementation-guide.pdf

International Air Transport Association (2015, July). *Guidance Material and Best Practices for MPL Implementation* (2nd ed.). Montreal, Quebec: Author. Retrieved from www.iata.org/whatwedo/ops-infra/training-licensing/Documents/guidance-material-and-best-practices-for-mpl-implementation.pdf

International Air Transport Association (2018, December). *MPL Courses Global Tracker*. Retrieved from www.iata.org/whatwedo/.../MPL%20documents/mpl-courses-global-tracker.xlsx

International Civil Aviation Organization (n.d.). *Multi-crew Pilot Licence Symposium*. Retrieved from: https://www.icao.int/meetings/mpl/Pages/default.aspx

International Civil Aviation Organization (2013). *Manual of evidence-based training* (Doc 9995). Montreal: Author. Retrieved from www.icao.int/SAM/Documents/2014-AQP/EBT%20ICAO%20Manual%20Doc%209995.en.pdf

International Civil Aviation Organization (2016). *Procedures for Air Navigation Services: Training* (Doc 9868) (2nd ed.). Montreal: Author.

International Civil Aviation Organization (2018, August). *Proposals for the Amendment of Annex 1 and the PANS-TRG consequential to Amendment 5 to the PANS-TRG*. Montreal: Author.

International Civil Aviation Organization (n.d.). *Multi-Crew Pilot Licence Symposium*. Retrieved from www.icao.int/meetings/mpl/Pages/default.aspx

International Federation of Air Line Pilots' Associations (2008, February). *IFALPA Multi-Crew Pilot License (MPL) Checklist for Member Associations* (08HUPBL02). Retrieved from www.ifalpa.org/media/2062/08hupbl02-mpl-checklist.pdf

International Federation of Air Line Pilots' Associations (2014, June). *Multi-Crew Pilot License (MPL)* (15POS03). Retrieved from www.ifalpa.org/publications/library/multi-crew-pilot-license-mpl-1650

Kearns, S. K., Mavin, T. J., & Hodge, S. (2016). *Competency-based education in aviation, exploring alternate training pathways*. Surrey, England: Ashgate.

Oser, R. L., Salas, E., Merket, D. C., Walwanis, M. M., & Bergondy, M. L. (2000). Can applied research help Naval Aviation?: Lessons learned implementing crew resource management training in the Navy. *Transportation Human Factors, 2*(4), 331–345. Retrieved from www.tandfonline.com/toc/hzzj20/current#.VQdUb-F2V9s

Oster, C. (2019, May). Senate holds FAA Administrator's confirmation hearing. *Eno Transportation Weekly*. Week of May 13, 2019. Retrieved from www.enotrans.org/article/senate-holds-faa-administrators-confirmation-hearing

Rosenkrans, W. (2014, June). *Timely Refinements*. Retrieved from https://flightsafety.org/asw-article/timely-refinements/

Schroeder, C., & Harms, D. (2007, November). MPL represents a state-of-the-art ab initio airline pilot training programme. *ICAO Journal, 62*(3), 15–16, 31–32. Retrieved from www.icao.int/publications/journalsreports/2007/6203_en.pdf

Transport Canada Civil Aviation (2019). *Crew resources management (CRM)*. (Advisory Circular 700-042). Ottawa, ON: Author. Retrieved from www.tc.gc.ca/en/services/aviation/reference-centre/advisory-circulars/ac-700-042.html

Tullo, F. J. (2010). Team and organizational factors. In B. G. Kanki, J. Anca, & T. R. Chidester (Eds.), *Crew Resource Management* (3nd ed., pp. 53–72). London, UK: Academic Press.

University Aviation Association (n.d.). *Air carrier enhanced pilot training program (ACE) program*. Retrived from www.uaa.aero/position_papers.php.

Vance, S. M. (2017). The value of collegiate FAR 141 jeopardy-crew resource management (CRM)-simulation event. *Journal of Aviation/Aerospace Education and Research, 26*(2). doi:10.15394/jaaer.2017.1730.

Wikander, R., & Dahlstrom, N. (2014). *The multi crew pilot licence: revolution, evolution or not even a solution? -A review and analysis of the emergence, current situation and future of the multi-crew pilot licence (MPL)*. Retrieved from www.researchgate.net/profile/N_Dahlstrom/publication/297368588_The_Multi_Crew_Pilot_Licence_-_Revolution_Evolution_or_not_even_a_Solution_-_A_Review_and_Analysis_of_the_Emergence_Current_Situation_and_Future_of_the_Multi-Crew_Pilot_Licence_MPL/links/56de9b3e08aed4e2a9

Wikander, R., & Dahlstrom, N. (2016, May). *The multi crew pilot licence part II: The MPL data – capturing the experience. A review and analysis of the results from a global online survey on the worldwide experiences with the multi-crew pilot licence*. Retrieved from www.researchgate.net/profile/N_Dahlstrom/publication/304062538_The_MPL_Part_II_The_MPL_Data_-_Capturing_the_Experience/links/576535af08ae1658e2f48171/The-MPL-Part-II-The-MPL-Data-Capturing-the-Experience.pdf

Zimmerman, B. J., & Schunk, D. H. (2011). *Handbook of self-regulation of learning and performance*. New York, NY: Routledge.

2.5 Chapter – Ensuring success by using the 4 As of learning

Mary Niemczyk

Generational differences

Categorizing individuals into generational cohorts can be a useful tool to analyze changing societal perspectives over time. These cohorts are typically comprised of individuals who have been impacted by similar occurrences in their environment during adolescence, which is a very transitional stage of life (Dimock, 2019). During this stage, people are enduring a broad range of developmental changes physically, emotionally, socially, and cognitively (Eagleman, 2015; Science of Adolescent Learning, 2018). In addition, they are typically becoming more independent from their parents, and starting to experience various individual and life challenges, which often result in strong perspectives about the world. Likewise, major occurrences, such as wars, technological advances, economic cycles, and societal changes can also cause deep, long-lasting impressions.

Because of these shared experiences, generations tend to form a persona or set of characteristics and behaviors by which they are defined. This persona may include attitudes towards work, technology, gender roles, religion, race, family, and value systems. These attitudes not only provide commonality within each generational group, but also the distinction between generational groups making each one somewhat unique. These attitudes seem to permeate the generation becoming influential elements in the mind-set of its members. Interestingly, these generational traits tend to remain fixed as the members age and seem to become lifelong attributes which can provide generations strength in society (Schuman & Scott, 1989; Strauss & Howe, 1997; Zemke et al., 1999). It is important to note, however, there may be individuals within the generational cohort who do not display all of the behaviors and characteristics of the particular generation, therefore it is important not to stereotype, but to treat people as individuals.

The distinction between where one generation ends and another begins is not an exact science, yet their boundaries are not arbitrary either. In addition to the shared formative experiences, the span of birth years is also considered in an attempt to make a generational cohort equivalent to preceding generations so that meaningful comparisons can be made. The names and birth years used to categorize generations may vary slightly, but the most common are: G.I. (born before 1936), Silents (1937–1945), Baby Boomers (1946–1964), Gen X (1965–1980), Millennials (1981–1996), and Gen Z (1997–2012). Each generational span is somewhat similar in the number of years, except for the Baby Boomers who are defined by the documented increase in post-WWII births in 1946 and substantial decline after 1964 (Dimock, 2019; Strauss & Howe, 1997; Zickuhr, 2011).

Generational Characteristics of Gen Z

As younger generations emerge and begin replacing older generations in societal roles, there tends to be a "generational shift" whereby attitudes and values of the upcoming generation tend to take hold (Johnson & Wilson, 2008; Mitchell, 1995). This applies not only to how they view their environment and world, but also to what is essential in their personal, academic, and professional lives. Like all generations, Gen Z has experienced events uniquely different to those experienced by previous generations. The most evident are the economic downturn in the late 2000s and the rapid advances of technology, both of which have distinctively influenced the perspectives and aspirations of this generation.

During the late 2000s and early 2010s, most of the world's developed economies, especially those in North America and Europe, were tremendously affected by the Great Recession that lasted approximately two years. The impact was far reaching and the lives of many Gen Z members were personally affected. Some of their parents lost their jobs and some were even displaced due to subsequent loss of homes. Living through this period has caused a majority of Gen Z members to have deep-seated concerns about financial security and consequently, they tend to be sharply focused on obtaining a meaningful education that will prepare them for a secure career (The New Generation of Students, 2019).

The rapid advances in and ubiquitous use of technology have also had a profound effect on this generation. Growing up in an online world, Gen Z is accustomed to getting information anytime and anywhere. With the availability of broadband internet, this generation has had access to more information than any other generation at their age. Born at nearly the same time as the internet was becoming prevalent, they are true digital natives (Seemiller & Grace, 2017).

Career preparation and an active, technologically based instructional environment appears to be a priority for members of Gen Z (Crouch, 2015). To effectively engage with them and enable them to be productive aviation employees, it is vital to consider their needs and desires. This alignment can also improve recruitment and retention by demonstrating to Gen Z their importance to the aviation industry (Niemczyk & Ulrich, 2009).

Learning preferences

Each generation has experienced instructional strategies throughout their education that were used somewhat consistently, whether it be a classroom with one teacher who might have required students to read aloud and work problems at the chalkboard, to the utilization of film strips, educational TV, micro-computers, and most recently Smartboards. These educational experiences influenced the manner in which students study thereby establishing their learning preferences and strategies (Johnson & Wilson, 2008; Shrock, 1995). For Gen Z, the proliferation of the internet and other technologies has not only caused them to expect faster and more interactive learning environments (*Gen Z in the Classroom*, n.d.), but neuroscience research has shown that the availability and rapid delivery of digital information has caused the brains of Gen Z members to develop differently than the brains of individuals in previous generations. These differences need to be considered when designing and developing instruction and to ensure members of this generation understand how to become successful learners (Eagleman, 2015; Noonoo, 2018).

Learning strategies

There is a great deal of literature offering suggestions regarding the instructional strategies most beneficial for teaching Gen Z, much of it emphasizing the use of digital textbooks, video, interactive learning systems, and other similar educational technologies. Conversely, there appears to be a limited focus on the learning component of the educational process.

Oftentimes it is assumed that students have some understanding of how to learn effectively and strategically. Unfortunately, they do not necessarily develop effective learning strategies automatically and research has found that many students utilize the same learning strategy for all educational activities (Rachal et al., 2007). Some may even continue to struggle with learning successfully throughout their collegiate programs, then into the workplace.

Most students have not considered how learning occurs and simply study material provided by their instructors using the best learning strategies they know. A recent survey found that globally, Gen Z high school students use memorization as their primary learning strategy 76 percent of the time (*Gen Z in the Classroom*, n.d.). Unfortunately, this strategy may not be effective for many learning outcomes and may cause the student frustration due to their inability to remember the information when needed as well as perhaps not knowing the information well enough to achieve the desired learning goal.

It is critical that Gen Z understands how to study and learn not only for their academic success now, but also for their success in the aviation industry. With the vast amount of information available and requiring to be mastered while working in this dynamic, complex industry, it is essential that success in learning be a certainty. If these individuals do not know how to use a variety of learning strategies, it may be difficult for them to learn no matter how well the instruction is designed or delivered. As the industry continues to evolve in the use of online, self-directed instruction it is essential that this generation of self-described independent, self-reliant learners have a toolbox of strategies they can use for any learning situation.

Before discussing learning strategies and the attributes of a successful learner it is important to have an understanding of the human memory system.

The human memory system

The information processing view is the most common perspective used to explain how memory works (Anderson, 1995). This view compares memory to a computer system – information enters the system, is stored, and then retrieved when necessary.

As humans, our five senses are constantly being bombarded by stimuli from our environment. The information received by our sensory receptors is actually stored in our sensory memory for a few brief moments, about one to three seconds. Therefore, for a few seconds, a wealth of data from our experiences remains intact. During this brief period, we have a chance to select information for further processing. Even though we are constantly being bombarded with stimuli, it is difficult for us to perceive every sound, temperature change, movement, and smell. By paying attention to certain stimuli and ignoring others, we are able to select what information we are going to process and move along in the memory system (Eagleman, 2015; Medina, 2008).

Our ability to attend to something is also very limited. There is much discussion about attention spans diminishing, though this notion is apparently only supported by anecdotal evidence. It is important to note, however, that Gen Z are accustomed to searching and finding information as they need it. They may not, therefore, be willing to spend time on material that does not appear necessary or interesting. This generation has grown up in a world where information is available instantaneously, and they seem to be impatient with traditional, sequential training and instruction.

It is notable that members of all generations now appear to have challenges paying attention or focusing for extended periods of time. Because of the non-stop communication environment in which we live, many of us are often distracted by vibrations, buzzes, rings or other types of notifications that draw us away from what we are doing. This apparent inability to focus or not miss out on anything or even a fear of missing out, FOMO, is often referred to as continuous partial attention. Continuous partial attention is literally defined as paying partial attention continuously (Continuous partial attention, n.d.). There are countless things in our environment competing for our attention, but in order for us to learn, we need to be fully attentive to be able to select the appropriate information to be processed further in our memory system.

Short-term memory

Information that we focus on enters our short-term memory next. The duration and capacity of this storage area is extremely limited, with a considerable amount of research finding that new information can be stored there for only about 15–30 seconds. The capacity for storage is also very limited and is most often supported by Miller's Law of 7, which states that as humans we can store about seven plus or minus two (or five to nine) separate items or chunks of information (Miller, 1956). More recently, however, there is some evidence suggesting the duration and capacity of our short-term memories has diminished since that aspect of our memory is not being used as much due to our overreliance and convenience of storing information on our various electronic devices, especially cell phones.

Short-term memory should be considered a passageway into long-term memory as opposed to a secure storage area. Students who utilize memorization strategies are actually storing information in their short-term memories. Due to its limitations, information stored there needs to be constantly activated or rehearsed by continuously repeating the information, a practice referred to as maintenance rehearsal. Once this rehearsal stops, the information disappears quickly.

Long-term memory

For information to be usable, it needs to be stored in long-term memory. In contrast to short-term memory, long-term memory seems to have an unlimited storage capacity and duration. Information stored there are joined together through a rich network of interconnections, in a very organized fashion. In order to effectively store information in long-term memory, students need to integrate the new information they are learning with prior knowledge, information they already know, or to form connections and associations among the various aspects of the skills and concepts they are currently trying to learn.

The importance of learning strategies

In general, most educational activities are instructor-led, and students attempt to carry out the instructional activity using the learning strategies they know (Zimmerman, 1989). As individuals move into the workforce, many may participate in classroom style trainings, but online and self-paced training methodologies are being employed more often. Learning in these types of environments can be challenging as there is usually limited interaction with instructors or other students.

For most students, the set of learning strategies they know about may be limited, and they may actually use the same strategy for all educational tasks (Rachal et al., 2007). Most students have not had any formal instruction in how, when, and why to use various learning strategies. The strategies used may have been developed through personal trial and error in completing homework assignments and studying for tests. The effectiveness of the strategy is typically determined by how well they performed on the educational task. If they did as well as expected, the strategy is often considered effective. If not, they often become frustrated and may even give up since they may not be aware of other learning strategies.

Knowing which learning strategy to use for each learning situation is also critical; the learning strategy used should be appropriate for the desired learning outcome or goal. The use of learning strategies appropriate to the learning situation is empowering in that it provides individuals with control over their learning process. With the explosion of knowledge and information and the demands for lifelong learning in every aspect of aviation, this is a skill critical to the success of Gen Z.

Memorization

As stated previously, many Gen Z members use memorization or rehearsal strategies for learning most frequently. This generation is not alone, as in general this is perhaps the learning strategy used most often. For many individuals, this is the only strategy they are familiar with as it is typically used for first learnings – such as learning the alphabet and multiplication tables – and is carried forward into their early academic careers where foundational knowledge is being developed. During this period of education, memorization may prove to be effective, but as students move through their academic programs and even into their careers where conditional knowledge is required, these strategies will prove to be inadequate.

Rehearsal strategies promote rote-learning – information is learned in a strictly verbatim manner, without attaching any meaning to it. The use of these strategies supports the acquisition of declarative knowledge, verbal knowledge, or knowledge of facts (Anderson, 1995). Students with declarative knowledge may be able to state a definition or identify a location on a map, but they may not be able to explain the details of the concept, only simply repeat the information they have memorized. The use of these types of strategies may be appropriate for lower level cognitive learning objectives such as naming, listing, or identifying. For example, if a student needs to learn facts, terms, names, and rules of which they may not have any prior knowledge, the best strategy to use initially may be rehearsal. For example, a new aviation student attempting to learn airport identifiers may use a memorization strategy.

These strategies essentially enable students to temporarily store information in their short-term memory, which is limited in regards to capacity and duration. To keep information active, students need to use continuous repetition to hold something in memory, conducting maintenance rehearsal. Some common examples of rehearsal strategies include the use of flashcards, repeating key terms aloud, re-reading, and repetitive writing. Although rehearsal strategies may assist students in getting information into their short-term memories, they fall short of being able to effectively move information into long-term memory where it can be used at a later time.

Most students using these strategies feel as though they are studying intensely because of the time and effort spent trying to memorize course material. Their perception is quite accurate, because using a rehearsal strategy is a relatively slow and ineffective way to learn new information. Although rehearsing information is better than doing nothing at all with it, overall, memorization is a relatively ineffective way to learn. Information can be remembered more easily and utilized more effectively when using association and anticipation strategies.

The specific learning strategies used when trying to learn new information affects one's ability to remember and use that information at a later time, it is therefore critical that members of Gen Z become informed about other learning strategies so they can be successful learning in any educational situation.

The 4 As of Learning

There is a significant amount of educational psychology research that has examined the characteristics of successful learners, asserting that successful learners have the skills and ability to learn in a variety of instructional situations (Medina, 2008; Zimmerman, 1989). They can adapt their learning techniques as necessary because they understand how their brain works and how to use the appropriate learning strategy for the desired learning goal. They approach instructional tasks with a high degree of confidence that they can accomplish the task correctly and also understand that learning is an active process. Essentially, successful learners are **actively** engaged with the material and make **associations** between new information and prior knowledge. They **anticipate** uses and applications of this information and have an **awareness** of when they are learning the material, and possibly more importantly, when they are not (Mayer, 2014; Mayer & Wittrock, 1996; Zimmerman, 1989).

In summary, to be successful students need to do the following:

- **Actively** work with the information
- **Associate** new information with prior knowledge
- **Anticipate** uses and applications for the information
- have **Awareness** of when they are learning and when they are not (Niemczyk, 2009; Figure 2.5.1).

Active

To learn effectively, students need to be actively engaged in the learning process. The development of knowledge requires the learner to "do" something with the information being presented, instead of simply attempting to absorb information in a passive way (Anderson, 1995; Medina, 2008). Members of Gen Z have a strong desire to be fully involved in their education and state that the ideal learning situation for them is one in which they can participate in the instructional process. Many of these individuals are observers

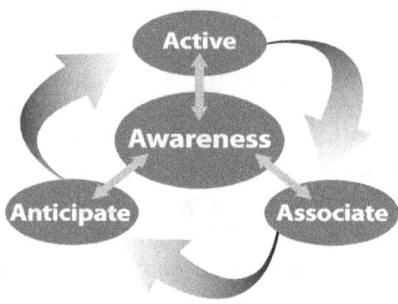

Figure 2.5.1 The 4 A's Model of Learning.

first – they prefer to initially watch someone complete an instructional activity then they'll attempt to replicate it. For many members of this generation, the resource they rely on the most is YouTube (Seemiller & Grace, 2017).

Because of the depth and complexity of aviation concepts and skills, Gen Z members need to use learning and comprehension monitoring strategies that will enable them to become cognitively engaged. They need to invest effort to make connections, elaborate, translate, organize, and reorganize in order to think and process deeply, so that they can perform successfully in this unique environment.

Using distributive practice techniques

Being an active learner also means taking control of the various aspects of the studying and learning process. One way to greatly enhance the effectiveness and efficiency of learning is to encourage Gen Z members to develop a study plan which facilitates their studying in a distributed manner.

Many individuals may not begin to study until several days before or even the night before an exam. This ineffective technique, referred to as massed practice or cramming, does not allow for the learning of complex information in a short time span. When relying on massed practice, Gen Z will most likely be utilizing memorization or rehearsal strategies, providing for only the ability to state, recite, or identify information, a very low level of cognition. A more productive method is to study a little bit every day. This method not only improves learning but is also more conducive to members of Gen Z, who prefer to obtain information quickly and in short durations of time. Studying for as little as 20 to 30 minutes at a time each day is more beneficial than attempting to study for several hours in one sitting.

Not only will distributed practice techniques increase the acquisition of knowledge, but they can also assist in alleviating test anxiety by providing Gen Z members self-assurance knowing they studied for several days as opposed to several hours.

Associate

As stated previously, cognitive scientists have discovered that information stored in long-term memory is organized and interconnected (Anderson, 1995; Medina, 2008). Consequently, new information can be learned more easily when it can be connected to prior knowledge or to an overall organizational structure. In addition, research has also demonstrated that illustrations and diagrams supported by text assists students to learn more deeply and facilitates storage of information in long-term memory more readily than when information is presented from a single source, such as text only. The use of both graphics and text causes the learner to use two different cognitive processing systems which enhances retention of the information.

Association strategies group separate pieces of information into meaningful chunks or patterns that can assist students in understanding relationships between what they are learning and what they already know. Meaningful patterns and connections are easier to remember than discrete items. Unfortunately, many students tend to organize concepts as a list of separate facts, rather than being interrelated. When younger members of Gen Z are being introduced to new content or skill, it is important that the instructor assist them in making the connection to previously learned information, as they may not yet have a significant knowledge-base of the material and may be unable to recognize the connection between concepts.

Examples of association strategies include diagramming, categorizing, flowcharting, classifying, hierarchies, maps, models, and matrices. All of these types of structures enable students to depict relationships between the various components of the material.

Presenting instructional material in an organized way can be very effective as students can then use the instructor's association diagram to assist them in learning. Research has found, however, that recall can be improved even more when students create their own association scheme. To make learning more effective, encourage Gen Z individuals to develop their own diagram and to actively think about the relationships that exist among the various aspects of a concept, or the relationships that exist between multiple concepts while creating the diagram. To reinforce and deepen their knowledge, Gen Z students should envision themselves in their current or future aviation role and explain the concepts they are depicting to a peer or colleague. It is important to reinforce to students that the information on the diagram should not simply just be re-read or memorized as that would be a rehearsal strategy and may not be appropriate for the learning goal.

Developing these types of diagrams enhances learning in many ways, especially for members of Gen Z. This generation prefers not to read large amounts of text and is accustomed to having information at their fingertips. In using these techniques, several pages of notes can be consolidated into one diagram, greatly reducing the amount of text needed to be read. In addition, when humans recall information from memory, our brain "sees" the information as a picture (Medina, 2008). There are a couple of clichés that aptly describe this, such as, "A picture is worth a thousand words" and "I can see that." Even though they are clichés they are scientifically confirmed as diagrams and graphics are a more efficient and effective way to represent information. Since Gen Z prefers learning that is visually based, association strategies may be a welcome addition to their study strategy toolbox.

Anticipate

Gen Z members, in general, have indicated they are career driven with college being a pathway to a good job. They want to be able to immediately apply the knowledge and skills they are learning to their profession (Seemiller & Grace, 2017). Anticipation strategies enable them to do just that, as these strategies focus on making the information personal, by providing meaning, relevance, and context. Essentially, these strategies increase one's knowledge of a concept by elaborating and expanding on the various aspects of the concept.

Anticipation can be thought of as a process of broadening and deepening the understanding of the material presented. To use anticipation as a learning strategy, Gen Z members should envision themselves in their future career role, whether it be a pilot, manager, dispatcher, controller or any other function. When learning new skills and concepts, they should envision themselves in that environment and consider the context of when, how, and why they might use that skill or concept. By elaborating and expanding upon the material in this way, they will enhance meaning by making the new information personal, relevant, and contextual.

Information that is personal, meaningful, relevant, and contextual can be remembered for a lifetime. By visualizing themselves and using information and skills learned in a situated context, Gen Z individuals can emulate the emotions and feelings of experiences in a specific time and place. This technique can utilize episodic memory, which associates what, when, and where, something occurred. A similar technique, chair flying, is often used by flight students. When chair flying, flight students visualize themselves sitting in the cockpit of an airplane. They perform the physical, verbal, and cognitive aspects of a flight scenario by using their hands and feet to move the imaginary flight controls, verbalizing air traffic control requests, and even resolving possible abnormalities encountered during the flight. Learning strategies, such as these, can enhance positive transfer which is essential for success in an ill-defined environment like aviation.

Developing higher levels of cognition

Anticipation strategies are active learning strategies. When using these strategies, students are actively engaged with the material, critically thinking about the concept and its relationships to other concepts (Zimmerman, 1989).

Research has shown that part of the benefit gained from using anticipation learning strategies comes from the mental processing conducted while critically thinking about the concept.

The use of anticipation strategies will provide Gen Z with conditional knowledge or knowing how and why to do something. This type of knowledge is essential in a multitude of aviation situations as it enables individuals to analyze, evaluate, problem solve, and conduct other high-level cognitive processing skills. In order for Gen Z to utilize information completely and in an integrative manner, it is important for them to have a strong foundation of conditional knowledge allowing them to apply information in unique and complex situations.

Learning objectives

Students may not always understand the goal of an instructional activity which could prevent them from either not learning the content well enough or even cause them to focus on less important aspects. To ensure they are aware of the desired outcome of instruction, it is important they be informed of the learning objectives for the particular assignment, unit of instruction and course. The verb in the learning objective will inform them of how well they should know the information and what learning strategy they should use (Anderson & Krathwohl, 2001). For example, if the learning objective is for students to be able to *explain* the Five Freedoms of the Air as opposed to simply *listing* them, they should use an association learning strategy and not just memorize the Five Freedoms which would enable them to simply list them.

Bloom's Revised Taxonomy (Anderson & Krathwohl, 2001) is the most utilized resource for developing learning objectives for instructional tasks (see Table 2.5.1). The following table includes verbs commonly used to specify desirable student behaviors at various levels of cognition. As you review the table from left to right, you can see that the level of cognition increases from that of declarative knowledge to conditional knowledge. Included at the bottom of the table are the learning strategies to be used for each of the desired outcomes.

Awareness

Central to the success for Gen Z individuals is for them to become aware of every aspect of their learning. This self-awareness, or metacognition, involves assessing all aspects of their learning process (Zimmerman, 1989). It starts with focusing on the learning objectives, assessing whether they have any prior knowledge of the knowledge and skills, evaluating the learning strategies they should use, and determining whether their study process is effective. To become self-aware, or metacognitive of their learning, they should consider the following:

Table 2.5.1 Bloom's Revised Taxonomy with Appropriate Learning Strategies

	Remember	Understand	Apply	Analyze	Evaluate	Create
Verbs	list	explain	apply	analyze	evaluate	Create
	locate	describe	solve	categorize	select	design
	write	discuss	examine	compare	choose	develop
	find	classify	complete	contrast	decide	devise
	state	identify	demonstrate	explain	justify	formulate
	identify	interpret	illustrate	demonstrate	recommend	combine
	name	recognize	operate	differentiate	criticize	plan
	match	report	produce	distinguish	estimate	construct
	repeat	select	calculate	appraise	defend	formulate
	recite	translate	manipulate	deduce	determine	propose
Learning Strategy		**Rehearsal**	**Associate Anticipate**			

Source: Adapted from Anderson, L.W., Krathwohl, D.R., (Eds.) (2001). *A taxonomy for learning teaching and assessing: A revision of Bloom's Taxonomy of Educational Objectives.*

- Assess what they already know about a topic and connect the new information they are learning to this prior knowledge.
- Determine the desired outcome the instructional task as stated in the learning objectives. Ensure that they can do what the verb in the learning objective states.
- Select the learning strategies appropriate for accomplishing the desired learning activity – rehearsal, association, or anticipation.
- Continuously monitor their comprehension. Asking themselves, "Is this making sense?"
- Determine any gaps in their knowledge and use other resources to assist in completing their understanding of the concept.

Gen Z members can assess their acquisition of the requisite knowledge and skills very easily by determining whether they can describe the concept or even teach it to someone, or if it is a skill can they demonstrate it successfully. If not, they should assess whether the learning strategy they are using is appropriate for the learning outcome and possibly use another strategy. Most importantly, they should be able to accomplish the action described by the verb in the learning objective. By constantly being aware of their progress, monitoring their comprehension, and making necessary adjustments Gen Z can be successful in any learning situation (Zimmerman, 1989).

The 4As model of learning can support an individual's success in any educational environment. Based on neuroscience research, the four steps in this model correspond with how the human brain receives, stores and is able to retrieve information (Niemczyk, 2009). Encouraging members of Gen Z to use this model will ensure their success not only in their academic programs but also in the workplace, as well. By making personal growth and development a priority, members of this generation will thrive and be significant contributors to the aviation industry.

Aligning and engaging with Gen Z for success

Gen Z members place a high priority on growth and are keenly driven toward success both in their academic programs and careers. Members of this generation cite career progression as their primary focus followed by fulfilling work and stability (Crouch, 2015). The experiences of living through the Great Depression in the late 2000s seems to have resulted in their intense aspirations for financial security.

Strongly driven toward the achievement of their goals, this generation is seeking academic programs and companies that can offer them the necessary resources and pathways to realize them (The New Generation of Students, 2019). Providing this generation with opportunities for growth and personal development is essential. Whether they are in an academic or corporate classroom, Gen Z members have a strong desire for success in learning and equipping them with the 4 As of learning is essential.

References

Anderson, J. R. (Ed.) (1995). *Cognitive psychology and its implications*. New York: W.H. Freeman.
Anderson, L.W., Krathwohl, D.R. (Eds.) (2001). *A taxonomy for learning teaching and assessing: A revision of Bloom's Taxonomy of Educational Objectives*. New York: Longman.
Continuous partial attention. (n.d.). Retrieved from https://lindastone/net/qa/continuous-partial-attention/
Crouch, B. (2015, May 22). How Generation Z will disrupt the workplace. Retrieved from http://fortune,com/2015/05/22/generation-z-in-the-workplace/
Dimock, M. (2019, January 17). Defining generations: Where Millennials end and post-Millennials begin. Retrieved from https://pewresearch.org/fact-tank/2019/01/17/where-millennials-end-and-generation-z-begins/dimock_mike-4_160X240/
Eagleman, D. (2015). *The brain*. New York: Pantheon Books.
Gen Z in the classroom: Creating the future. (n.d.). Retrieved from http://adobeeducate.com/genz/
Johnson, B., & Wilson, S. (2008).Responding to generational differences in business education: Challenges and opportunities. *Business Education Forum, 62*(3), 40–44.
Mayer, R. E. (2014). *Multimedia learning*. New York: Cambridge University Press.
Mayer, R. E., & Wittrock, M. C. (1996). Problem solving transfer. In D. Berliner & R. Calfee (eds.), *Handbook of educational psychology* (pp. 287–303). New York: Macmillan.
Medina, J. (2008). *Brain rules*. Seattle: Pear Press.
Miller, G. (1956). The magical number seven, plus or minus two: Some limits on our capacity for processing information. *The Psychological Review, 63*, 81–97.
Mitchell, S. (1995). *The official guide to the generations* (1st Ed.). Ithaca, NY: New Strategist Publications.

The new generation of students: How colleges can recruit, teach, and serve Gen Z. (2019). [NextGenStudents_ExecutiveSummary_v5_2019]. Retrieved from connect.chronicle.com

Niemczyk, M. (2009). *Improve your learning and performance in the classroom: Strategies for success.* Kearney, NE: Morris Publishing.

Niemczyk, M., & Ulrich, J. (2009). Workplace preferences of Millennials in the aviation industry. *International Journal of Applied Aviation Studies, 9*(2), 207–219.

Noonoo, S. (2018, June 26). This neuroscientist explains why today's kids have different brains. Retrieved from www.edsurge.com/news/2018-06-26-this-neuroscientist-explains-why-today-s-kids-have-different-brains

Rachal, K., Daigle, S., & Rachal, W. (2007). Learning problems reported by college students: Are they using learning strategies? *Journal of Instructional Psychology, 34*(4), 191–199.

Schuman, H., & Scott, J. (1989). Generations and collective memories. *American Sociological Review, 54*(3), 359–381.

Science of adolescent learning: How body and brain development affect student learning. (2018, August). Retrieved from http://all4ed.org/wp-content/uploads/2018/08/Science-of-Adolescent-Learning-How-to-Body-and-Brain-Affect-Student-Learning.pdf

Seemiller, C., & Grace, M. (2017). Generation Z: Educating and engaging the next generation of students. Retrieved from Wiley Online Library (wileyonlinelibrary.com) by American College Personnel Association and Wiley Periodicals. DOI: 10.1002/abc.21293

Shrock, S. A. (1995). A brief history of instructional development. In G. Anglin (ed.), *Instructional technology: Past, present and future* (2nd Ed.), pp. 11–19. Englewood, CO: Libraries Unlimited.

Strauss, W., & Howe, N. (1997). *The fourth turning.* New York, NY: Broadway Books.

Zemke, R., Raines, C., & Filipczak, B. (1999). *Generations at work: Managing the clash of veterans, boomers, Xers, and nexters in your workplace.* New York: AMACOM. Electronic reproduction. Boulder, CO: NetLibrary, 1999.

Zickuhr, K. (2011, February 3). Generations and their gadgets. Retrieved from www.pewinternet.org/2011/02/03/generations-and-their-gadgets/

Zimmerman, B. J. (1989). A social cognitive view of self-regulated academic learning. *Journal of Educational Psychology, 81*(3), 329–339.

2.6 Chapter – Engaging practices for training the new generation of aircraft maintenance technicians

Karen Jo Johnson and Denis Manson

Introduction

Aircraft maintenance training at the basic level, within government regulated colleges and schools worldwide, is emerging from two decades of relative inertia. Online options for presenting courseware are becoming more commonplace to support distance education in innovative new blended or hybrid delivery modes. The promise of virtual and augmented reality techniques is starting to gather momentum to assist with enabling these flexible delivery options. Yet the myriad of options can be confusing. What should we do and how should we do it? Does my school really need to change? The short answer is: Yes! We need to change to attract, train, and retain a new and demanding generation of people. We cannot rely on the romance of aviation to lure new aircraft maintenance technicians and engineers when other industries are paying more and providing interesting and challenging workplaces and professional development. In an industry characterized by constantly evolving technologies we need to seek instructional technologies to match, creating better ways of conducting our business, or risk falling behind in growth, profitability and market relevance (MRO Network.com).

Current situation

Boeing's 2018 Technician Outlook predicts a need for over 750,000 aircraft technicians through to the year 2037. The 2018 ATEC Pipeline Report found that departing mechanics are on pace to surpass entering mechanics 4:3 through 2037. Both statistics lend proof to what is already known about the inevitable personnel shortage on the horizon. In the 172 Federal Aviation Administration (FAA) Aviation Maintenance Technician (AMT) schools in the USA, only 1 in 2 traditional seats are currently being filled, leaving room for an additional 17,000 students (ATEC, 2018). This doesn't consider the creation of e-learning environments that have the potential to reach even more prospective trainees.

A pressing question is how can AMT schools structure and work efficiently, to better cater for the needs of the industry and, at the same time, accommodate a new generation of learners? One way allowed by the FAA, is to offer distance delivery of lecture-based content, where students study a portion of the prescribed training program remote from a bricks and mortar school. These programs seek to exploit e-learning techniques 'to build job transferable knowledge and skills' (Clark & Mayer, 2016, p. 10) and have the potential to reach more students and fill some of those 17,000 empty training places.

In 2015, the FAA released initial guidance through Advisory Circular 147-3b and Order 8900.1 on procedures for AMT schools to seek approval to offer instruction via distance education. Prior to this guidance, AMT schools were only permitted to deliver content in a synchronous face-to-face setting. The FAA documents lay out details of how an AMT school should propose their distance delivery plans, including blending it into the school's existing program and operations manual. While the guidance does not specify which FAA Part 147 subject areas can be included in the distance delivery, it does give examples of subjects that are better suited for this. It also provides guidelines for practical lab projects that could be delivered with e-learning. As with guidance for the creation of a traditional FAA Part 147 program, the distance delivery guidance does not provide information on the instructional design of the content.

Concurrently, while hybrid training for AMT schools is gaining momentum and legitimacy in the United States, other parts of the world are experiencing further emerging variations of the distance education paradigm. Recently, a niche market has emerged in western AMT institutions to offer a 'twinning' arrangement with training institutions in countries with a burgeoning middle class and expanding aviation industry, such as India and China. An example of this is Aviation Australia (2019), a European Aviation Safety Agency (EASA)/Civil Aviation Safety Authority (CASA) Part 147 college headquartered in Australia, partnering with host colleges in Sri Lanka and Malaysia.

The twinning arrangement allows the two colleges to share responsibilities, explicitly allowed under EASA (2014b) regulations. The EASA foundation modules of instruction, Modules 1–6 and 8–10, are conducted in the host country. Then the more complex modules and practical consolidation is conducted in the better resourced and equipped college. This arrangement allows the host college to advertise, select, and enroll students according to local needs and capability, while the responsibility for provision of course materials, quality assurance of the tuition, and final issue of qualification is that of the partnering college.

Delivery of courseware away from the confines of the governing college could be seen as a problematic aspect of these relationships. Requirements for time tracking, verification of identification, course sequencing, and evidence of completion are obvious sticking points for approval processes. But as AMT schools research and build cases for developing and implementing newer delivery technologies for their in-house and distance education, a number of strategies and resources are emerging which can also be used to exploit and enhance the distance education component of the hybrid or twinning arrangement. These newer training technologies show promise to ease and enhance the facilitation of out-of-classroom tuition and distance education (Martin-Gutierrez et al., 2017), be it hybrid delivery, twinning arrangements, or other e-learning constructs.

Adapting for the new generation of learning

Newer generations of students have been entertained in their learning from an early age and adult learners too expect a certain level of entertainment with their education (Vai & Sosulski, 2016). As such, there exists an expectation of a more adaptive and interactive learning environment than what is typically provided in traditional classrooms. While AMT programs will always require the physical demonstration of technical skills, the use of interactive digital tools and online learning environments that allow students to manipulate and explore relative concepts on their own time and away from brick and mortar schools will be welcomed. Aviation Maintenance Technician schools should intimately understand these technologies and their usefulness and be prepared to include them in their classes so that both instructors and students can benefit from their affordances.

Hybrid delivery and twinning arrangements are examples of how AMT schools may first consider the move into e-learning and investing in newer training technologies. But this should not be the only impetus for modernizing some of the more traditional methods and media. At the very least, the programs that move into the hybrid/twinning space will invest time and effort into transforming some of their older courseware and delivery techniques in accordance with current research and best-practice. This investment should provide information and guidance for other organizations who follow track.

The architectures and interactivity of e-learning environments can be classified into three categories: information acquisition, response strengthening, and knowledge construction (Clark & Mayer, 2016). Most classes benefit from design that combines elements from all three structures. Instruction begins with presentation of the content that promotes recall, followed by examples, practices, and feedback that involve a significant amount of interaction between the learner, the delivery platform (such as a Learning Management System, or LMS), and instructor. Instruction closes with opportunities for learners to build knowledge while finding solutions to problems requiring the highest level of interaction between content, technology, and resources. This interaction requires e-learning students to learn more, though, than just the content. They must become familiar with the technological tools required by the online learning environment and technologies utilized within (Anderson, 2002).

Learning Management System platforms have tools to enable the delivery of content and facilitate interaction among students and instructors. The use of these tools depends on them being suitable for a program's intended student population with a focus not on the distance, but on the intentional interactions afforded by the technology, created by the instructors and students (Vrasidas & Glass, 2002). In other words, when designing course material for distance delivery, emphasis should be placed on the benefits to interaction provided by the technology regardless of the space and time between instructors and students, however small or large they may be.

Interaction between the LMS, students, and instructors is a key point when developing effective e-learning programs (Vai & Sosulski, 2016) and also when adhering to regulatory requirements for distance delivery and twinning programs. The geographical separation of students and instructors can create a challenge to the most important aspect of instruction; communication (Clark & Mayer, 2016). Likewise, the benefit of asynchronous instruction afforded by distance delivery, can be a barrier to adequate communication. To this point, the guidance provided by the FAA calls for a clear and concise plan for providing e-learning students with practical communication strategies. Depending on the LMS used, the delivery platform could include discussion forums and internal emails that allow for asynchronous communication in which messages are exchanged between users at different times and chat rooms and online meeting spaces for synchronous communication where messages between users are exchanged at the same time. Using all of these options will allow for optimal interaction at critical points during the delivery of instruction. Discussion forums and group emails create archived records that can be accessed any time while chat rooms and online meetings can be recorded to provide the same. As with traditional face-to-face programs, office hours can also be maintained, during which students can call in or meet online individually with instructors.

Whether offering asynchronous and synchronous meeting spaces or building interactive learning scenarios or providing links to additional resources, the learner must have an unambiguous understanding of when and how to use these opportunities for interaction when they are available. E-learning technologies allow content and activities to be interactive both within themselves and with the learner, depending on the level of instruction required. This learner control is a key component to whether a student will succeed or fail, especially in online learning environments (Vrasidas & Glass, 2002), so care must be taken when designing the interface and control options. Yet caution is advised, as Scheiter (2014) explains, as offering control to newer learners during instruction can sometimes cause cognitive overload. That is, learners with more content knowledge will benefit more from the autonomy because their level of knowledge also means they have a better innate understanding of when and how to use those interactions.

One thing is certain though, AMT instructors repurposing the same presentation slides and written worksheets used in a traditional classroom into an e-learning format will not develop an effective and engaging e-learning course. Instructors who have facilitated classes in both modes know first-hand how different they are. When considering the development of a hybrid program, the current instructor group and their collective abilities in online delivery and development are crucial factors. While some may be reluctant to adopt this new realm of online content development and delivery, others may already have useful knowledge and skills. There are vast amounts of creative digital tools available to instructors for use in the development of computer-based content, some of which are already being used in traditional face-to-face classrooms (Filgo, 2017). However as institutions carry out their online content development, they will still need the subject matter expertise of AMT instructors to ensure the quality and accuracy of the content.

Considerations in instructional design for the new generation of learners

Technologies

Once the platform and the three-way interaction (between the students, the LMS, and the instructor) is determined, careful thought must be applied to the learning content of the AMT subjects. Since the adoption of PowerPoint presentations in the 1990s and the subsequent evolution of PowerPoint-to-Flash conversion and then 'rapid authoring' software, very few significant changes have been made to the way basic AMT classroom materials have been presented.

Over the last 20 years, aircraft OEMs, the military, and some larger and well-funded training organizations have made significant progress using new generation digital training resources. Indeed, for right or wrong, the aerospace industry is often quoted by other industries as being well-resourced leaders in the use of augmented reality (AR) and virtual reality (VR) for technical training. But the use of more complex e-learning technologies has not been widely adopted at the AMT instructional level mainly due to cost restraints and a general conservatism. Things are slowly changing and, prompted by the need to keep abreast of market demands, some AMT schools are investing in the development of AR and VR assets. Other digital techniques are also being used, such as 360-degree photography and video (360) using image capture and editing tools of the type developed by Virtual eTraining (virtualetraining.com).

Whatever the technology or delivery mechanism, any development of training resources should follow consistent design guidelines. Hays and Singer (1989) argue, while the goal of training is to improve job performance, decisions in training development are often blurred by hardware-centric considerations, making the training event fit in with the capability of the selected hardware. It is important to strive for the reverse and assess the available technology in light of what is best for the training.

New technology tools such as AR, VR, and 360 will be especially valuable in flexible delivery situations such as hybrid delivery and twinning. These tools represent engaging ways of delivering content while exploiting asynchronous and synchronous delivery methods. They enhance relevant and interesting subject content. They strive to develop knowledge, workplace familiarization, and skill development. All these things intimately reflect the student self-direction, interaction, and autonomy that we strive to achieve with a robust online delivery philosophy. Implementing some of these resources aims to provide a series of student-focused, engaging, and immersive learning opportunities within the current courseware while also providing for concurrent improvement in learning and retention, as noted by Madathil et al. (2017). Resources that the authors know are planned, already built, or in the process of being built using these methods are:

- Theoretical concepts, such as aerodynamics, hydraulics, and electrical/electronic theory;
- Duplication or simplification of individual components, hardware, tooling, aircraft systems, gas turbine engines, entire aircraft;
- Duplication or simplification of the environments in which aircraft are situated, such as hangars, ramp areas, taxiways/runways, airspace and incident/accident scenes;
- Job tasks, for example marshalling, towing, pre-flight inspection, component removal and installation, flight control rigging, servicing and ground handling tasks.

Research on the migration of traditional courseware elements into new generation methods such as AR, VR, and 360 shows that these technologies will have the ability to enhance most current delivery of basic AMT curricula, including their use in hybrid/distance offerings (Pantelidis, 2010; Madathil et al., 2017). If well-constructed, the new techniques benefit the new generation of learners, keen for interactivity and self-direction, exploiting the blurred lines between entertainment and education. However, colleges need to keep focus on what is best for achieving the necessary learning outcomes. Care must always be taken with the instructional design, and schools must implement meaningful, effective, and authentic learning opportunities not just use VR/AR for the sake of using the next hyped piece of technology.

Another prime consideration when designing training materials for alternate realities is the question of cognitive overload (Dunleavy et al., 2009). This is a paradox for less experienced designers who may believe that a goal of VR or AR is to replicate the real world as faithfully as possible, the so-called 'digital twin', with training information added. But, just as the real world can be overwhelming and confusing for new trainees, so too a virtual environment with too much detail can be counterproductive for training, especially when combined with a great deal of sensory stimulation.

Assessment

A significant problem for any form of distance education lies in the fact that institutions are not just delivering content in an attempt to impart knowledge. They strive to influence skills, opinions, and attitudes in order to make students truly job-ready. With this goal in mind, schools must seek the best way to capture the technical, non-technical skills (NTS), such as communication, teamwork, and problem solving, and behaviour sets that characterize a successful student and hopefully a capable future AMT.

Assessing students in alternate reality environments has challenges. Next generation learning spaces encapsulate the affordances of both physical and virtual spaces and yet many assessment tasks are still designed as if students occupied only one. Instructional designers need to provide more authentic, meaningful tasks that will engage students in using the full range of their capabilities and available resources, both physical and virtual (Crisp, 2014).

Schools are charged then with not only delivering interesting and immersive training material, but gathering student assessment markers that may not be immediately apparent when trainer/assessor and student are remote from each other. Developing methods for assessing technical competencies and appropriate attitudes and behavioural markers in online and virtual environments are particularly important (Crisp, 2014). Assessing attitude as an extension of knowledge and skill-based assessments acknowledges the importance of students comprehending the serious nature of their work, the ramifications of error, and the awareness of techniques to mitigate human error before it has undesirable consequences. Whatever the delivery mode, this requirement will never disappear.

Yet another, more in-depth form of assessment that is becoming prevalent with the increasing use of more interactive technologies is what Van Eck et al. (2018) explain as 'stealth assessment' (p. 281) in which the interactions that the learner has with the technology are digitally recorded. This data that shows what and how many times students clicked on/used/viewed can then be inspected for evidence of the acquisition of knowledge by the learner. This stealth assessment can be particularly effective with gamified training events, where learners progress through a game-play environment that can incorporate workplace competency markers. The learner may be motivated by those game-play elements – collecting points, avoiding peril, or levelling up. But, in effect, their progress through the game demonstrates the building of skill and knowledge.

Challenges to the new generation

Aside from tackling issues inside the online and traditional classrooms, programs can also be challenged by the opinions and attitudes of aviation regulators who, while being conscious of trends within the industry, often display inertia in changing regulations to move with the times. Examples of this, immediately pertinent to aircraft maintenance training, include prescriptive time requirements for course durations and the regulatory definition of 'face-to-face'. While technologies can provide verification of students' identity such as proctoring services (examination supervision) and webcams, these options often come at a cost to either the institution, student, or both. Simpler solutions to implement can include the use of time tracking elements within an LMS and pop-up windows requiring students' action to confirm their attendance and continued presence. AR/VR tools also have the capability to confirm identity and time inside of the technology. Following up distance delivery of any format with robust assessments can also indicate a student's level of interaction with course materials and provide program inspectors with proof of student engagement.

Notwithstanding the expected improvements in delivering hybrid training or facilitating twinning arrangements, there are understandably major challenges for any AMT school considering a departure from basic e-learning or a more traditional face-to-face training and these should be addressed with planning, research, and consultation when necessary. Some of these challenges include:

- Lack of understanding of available technology options;
- Time and cost of developing or otherwise acquiring resources;
- Internal/external infrastructure capability;
- Hardware choice, cost, and acquisition;
- Difficulty developing and capturing student assessment markers;
- Instructor resistance to newer technologies.

Of the almost unlimited opportunities to develop new digital resources or migrate existing courseware into a VR, AR or mixed reality setting, where and how should an AMT college start? The answer to that question has as many answers and permutations as there are schools and colleges. It is a highly specific situation, depending on budget, manpower, organizational direction, appetite for risk, in-house capability, tolerance for disruption and the suitability of individual subjects and topics. Broadly, the questions that institutions and organizations should initially ask themselves are: What could we do? and How could we do it?

What could we do?

An underlying premise when selecting a strategy is one of economics and practicality. The typical AMT school will not build a complete suite of new generation VR/AR/360 training resources to satisfy an entire curriculum or to improve its courseware to better facilitate distance/hybrid delivery. This would be inordinately expensive and time-consuming. Therefore, unless we are considering a greenfield college, one being set up from scratch, with a large budget for resource development, decisions will always have to be made by AMT schools about what part of the existing courseware may be converted to these new media.

Chapter – Aircraft technician training   141

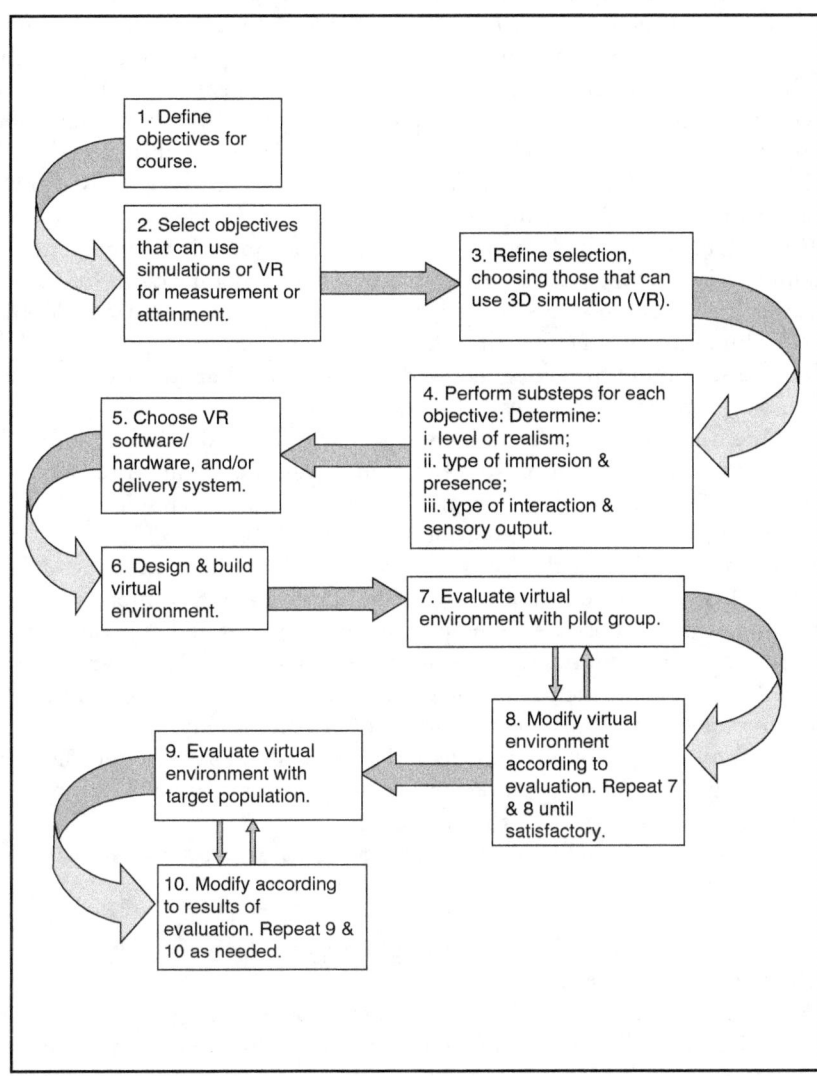

Figure 2.6.1 Pantelidis Model. Copyright 1997, 2009 by Veronica S. Pantelidis, Ph.D., East Carolina University, USA.

When trying to decide what new generation training resource to build or acquire first, the almost overwhelming range of choices can be counterproductive. Often people see something new and interesting and grasp at it, whether it comes from a presentation made by a slick and expensive company, a website, an online article, or a YouTube video that someone considers 'innovative'. Sometimes personal biases can influence decisions. A better way to choose 'What could we do?' would be to engage with a process to objectively analyse the possible options for when and where to use VR and other developments. A number of options exist. Pantelidis (2010) proposes a simple, 10-step model for development of virtual resources which is self-explanatory, if somewhat impractical when developing a resource in a commercial setting (Figure 2.6.1). Pantelidis describes the model as being useful for making decisions about when to use VR (and, by extrapolation, AR and 360) in any one course.

While succinct and deceptively simple, the model is impractical in a commercial setting because evaluation and modification of a VR environment is not an open-ended process when contracting a development firm to build to a specification. A scoping and quoting process will be undertaken to define the work required and the cost. Variations to that scope will incur further cost. Thus, Pantelidis' model works well when the development is carried out by university students in a multi-faculty effort, but for a commercial setting, a pre-development analysis is required to define the work required, rather than depending on evaluation results to inform modification(s) to the virtual environment (Steps 7–10).

A similar objective methodology drawing on Pantelidis' model, but with more emphasis on pre-development analysis can be achieved more simply via a spreadsheet listing possible development opportunities and applying a rating scale derived from a series of questions, see Figure 2.6.2. The rating scale provides a score which becomes objective evidence to inform the development. If a particular opportunity doesn't rate highly, then this is a flag which may prevent it progressing to a deeper analysis. At the very least, the spreadsheet provides a framework for the first questions to be asked, which is the most important step. An extract is shown.

Questions asked should consider organizational characteristics as well as individual subject areas. For example:

- Are there existing resources that can be repurposed?
- Is anyone else doing it?
- Can an asset be purchased instead of developed?
- What is the degree of difficulty (expense) to develop or otherwise acquire?
- What is the degree of educational benefit by moving into VR/AR? Some subjects lend themselves to a new treatment, some subjects are best taught using a whiteboard;
- If you plan on on-selling to recoup costs, what is the size of the potential market?
- Are there other groups who can leverage off this development. For example, if you build an aircraft with a hydraulic system can the interior be enhanced and be used for cabin crew training?
- How strong is the perceived 'need' for this development opportunity?

	Subject Matter				Development			
	Interesting Subject Score 1–10	Technically Complex Score 1–10	Information Available Score 1–10	Likely Time / Cost / Difficulty Score 1–10	Availability of Resources Score 1–10	Chance for 'Wow' Factor Score 1–10	Level of Immersion Required Score 1–10
Propeller Theory	5	7	8	7	5	5	2
Aircraft Certification/Continuing Airworthiness	6	7	7	7	5	5	3
CPCP/Ageing Aircraft	6	7	7	6	5	4	4
Reliability Programs	6	7	7	6	5	4	3
CDCCL / Fuel tank safety	6	7	7	7	7	8	8
Ethical decision- making	7	6	6	6	6	8	8
Servicing Task (ground handling)							
Weight and balance for load control	7	7	8	7	8	8	8
Service/replenish galleys	5	9	8	8	7	7	7
Pushback and towing	7	8	8	7	8	8	9

Figure 2.6.2 Developmental Rating Spreadsheet (unpublished) Copyright 2018 by Senseability Studios Pty Ltd.

- Are there subjects or topics that are not taught well, via qualitative (e.g., feedback) or quantitative (e.g., exam results) markers?
- Will a new resource replace targeted curriculum elements adequately, i.e., satisfy the same learning outcomes? If not, what are the shortfalls and the blended learning options?
- Is it possible to use an alternative method with lesser fidelity to reduce the expense? For example, a series of 360-degree photographs can be just as effective as a detailed virtual environment, at a fraction of the cost.
- Are there any tech requirements for the users, e.g., headsets, tablet devices, wifi, high speed internet, computer specifications?

A third and more comprehensive analysis process can be achieved by using a commercial consultancy service. For example, a VR/AR development company, ACHIEVR. (2019) has developed a set of enterprise tools for 'Rapid Design Modelling', 'Cost Modelling', and 'Strategic Alignment' which they claim significantly reduces planning, scoping, and development time for VR experiences. This process is designed to provide expertise and advice on selecting likely opportunities for new VR/AR courseware, culminating in a design document specifying costs, time, and hardware required.

If a VR/AR/360 asset is being purchased for implementation, the European Aviation Safety Agency (2014a) gives guidance by providing a table of 'The Quality of a Digital Learning Resource'. This table provides objectivity for AMT schools to assess the suitability of any digital learning resource that is, or is planned on being, implemented. A score is given to 20 individual assessment items, for an overall score out of 100. Obviously, the higher score, the more superior the resource. Categories for assessment are:

- Academic quality;
- Pedagogical quality;
- Didactic quality; and
- Technical quality.

Experience and lessons learned from more advanced organizations are now being more seriously investigated by AMT schools. Some schools are building assets themselves for their own use, others are building for on-selling. Outside commercial entities too are working on the development of online AMT modules that can be subscribed to by educational institutions, such as that of the University of Clemson's Workforce Development platform (General Curriculum Pilot, n.d.). In some cases, digital development companies retain ownership of the intellectual property when creating resources to customer specifications. This keeps the development price low for the initial customer, and the development company can then repurpose or re-sell the resources to other training organizations at a price much lower than it would cost for any other school to develop themselves. An example of this is Staples VR (staplesvr

.com) who developed B787 and A320 aircraft models initially for a project for Jetstar Airlines. While Jetstar could negotiate on final ownership of the models, the creative effort invested by the developers means, by default, they retain intellectual property rights to the end product. Staples VR can then repurpose the digital assets for another client. For example they could use the hangar environment to create a platform for aviation health and safety training or re-sell the complete aircraft models for another purpose (at a lower price than the original development).

Collaborative efforts between schools, while not yet common, appear to be a potential and logical step to keep costs down, though regardless of who develops the online content, the major concern is that the design of the online content maximizes the affordances available with online learning tools.

How could we do it?

In general terms, if AMT schools wish to explore the possibility of designing and creating new digital course content, they have three broad options:

- **Build the material themselves** – this requires specialist expertise for the instructional design, 3D modelling, coding, and gameplay elements. If using university resources in a multi-faculty cooperative effort, this will require a large amount of coordination and supervision. 360-degree photography and video has become a little easier over the last few years. Software packages allow end-users to edit the images and embed resources to create meaningful training events;
- **Contract an external developer to build** – this requires a commitment from the AMT instructors to act as subject matter experts to devise the specifications and storyboard and commit to regular liaison with the developers;
- **Purchase a copy of an existing product outright or on a subscription basis** – this is by far the less expensive option, but depends on whether the product is actually for sale, who owns the intellectual property, and whether the product suits the intended use.

If practitioners decide to develop a VR/AR asset from scratch, or decide to convert an existing resource to a VR/AR/360 opportunity, care must be taken to ensure the training intent and objectives are preserved as the development takes place. The question of fidelity of virtual learning spaces and models is an important consideration when designing learning tasks for both experienced and non-experienced participants (Hays & Singer, 1989). Similar to the range of flight training devices, a number of possibilities exist, from inexpensive, simple developments with limited functionality, through to highly complex, hugely expensive replicas of real-world objects and environments. Comprehensive storyboarding is the mechanism for this and should be careful to include the assets that are normally incorporated in the institution's delivery methods.

Training professionals understand the importance of storyboarding. When storyboarding for VR/AR, the fundamentals are the same, in that words and pictures may be used to build a description of the intended training experience. But in a virtual environment there are extra considerations, especially in the areas of describing the user experience and user interaction, i.e., what will the student have to *do* in the VR/AR/360 experience to satisfy the targeted learning outcomes and how they will do it? Coupled with this, training in a virtual environment may encourage in-depth interaction and have more options for user interface with the materials. It may employ self-directed exploration and therefore not have a linear flow like other training formats, so linking and relationships between individual scenes may be more complex (Wilson et al., 2002).

Moving towards the future

As these assets and techniques evolve, it is expected that the scenarios in which they are used will become more complex and detailed. More and more supplementary information and assessment tasks will be built in to the material, encompassing game-play elements where appropriate. In keeping with the interactive nature of the technology, there is likely to be more emphasis on meaningful simulated tasks which familiarize and test practical skills. There will also be further and more complex opportunities to provide interactive, scenario-based training to develop and challenge NTS, such as communication, teamwork, leadership, decision-making, creativity, and problem-solving (Passos et al., 2016).

The immersive, self-directed, exploratory nature of these experiences allow them to complement distance/hybrid/twinning arrangements, as they lend themselves to autonomous and asynchronous participation and, importantly, provide motivation for students (Beluce & de Oliveira, 2015). Again, the instructional design of the experience has an influence on its usefulness as an autonomous learning tool, with both the technical and the pedagogic elements contributing to the learning space (Gardner & Elliott, 2014).

Developing aviation maintenance training in an online learning environment can be an adventurous and daunting undertaking for AMT schools. Economic and pedagogic decisions need to be made. Successful programs will need to balance carefully the use of e-learning technologies with the limitations of governing regulations. As hybrid and twinning arrangements gain popularity and extend into other initiatives, it is expected that distance education demands will generate further research and opportunities in this space. Lessons are being learned and shared. Collaborative efforts and consultative services are becoming more prevalent.

Coupled with robust mechanisms for student communication, interaction, and self-direction, new immersive courseware elements can only benefit our new young and redirected learners. Choices range from simple interactive PowerPoint lessons to advanced virtual reality trainers but it is the appropriateness of the technology and its effective incorporation into the traditional classroom activities that will attract and retain this next generation of aviation maintenance professionals, and the future generations of students to come.

References

ACHIEVR. (2019). Retrieved from www.achievr.io/
Anderson, Terry (2002). Revealing the hidden curriculum of e-learning. In Vrasidas, C. & Glass, G.V. (Eds.) *Distance Education and Distributed Learning* (pgs. 115–133). Greenwich, Connecticut: Information Age Publishing.
Aviation Australia. (2019). Retrieved from www.aviationaustralia.aero/
Aviation Technicians Education Council. (2018). *The 2018 Pipeline Report*. Jenks, OK: ATEC. https://www.atec-amt.org/pipeline-report.html.
Beluce, A. C., & Oliveira, K. L. D. (2015). Students' motivation for learning in virtual learning environments. *Paidéia (Ribeirão Preto), 25*(60), 105–113.
Clark, R. C., & Mayer, R. E. (2016). E-learning and the science of instruction: Proven guidelines for consumers and designers of multimedia learning. John Wiley.
Boeing Company. (2018). *Technician Outlook: 2018-2037*. Retrieved from www.boeing.com/commercial/market/pilot-technician-outlook/2018-technician-outlook/
Crisp, G.T. (2014), Assessment in next generation learning spaces In K. Fraser (Ed.), *The Future of Learning and Teaching in Next Generation Learning Spaces (International Perspectives on Higher Education Research Volume 12)*, (pp. 85–100). United Kingdom: Emerald Group Publishing.
Dunleavy, M., Dede, C., & Mitchell, R. (2009). Affordances and limitations of immersive participatory augmented reality simulations for teaching and learning. *Journal of Science Education and Technology, 18*(1), 7–22.
European Aviation Safety Agency. (2014a). *New Training Methods and New Teaching Technologies* (Notice of Proposed Amendment 2014-22). Retrieved from www.easa.europa.eu/sites/default/files/dfu/NPA%202014-22.pdf
European Aviation Safety Agency. (2014b). *Commission Regulation (EU) No 1321/2014 ANNEX IV (Part 147) 147.A.145(d) - Privileges of The Maintenance Training Organisation*. Retrieved from https://eur-lex.europa.eu/legal-content/EN/TXT/PDF/?uri=CELEX:02014R1321-20190305&from=EN
Filgo, Kelly. M. (2017). DIY simulations: The case for using them and where to find them. *Aviation Technician Education Council Journal, 39*(2). Retrieved from www.atec-amt.org/journal-archive.html
Gardner, M., & Elliott, J. (2014). The Immersive Education Laboratory: Understanding affordances, structuring experiences, and creating constructivist, collaborative processes, in mixed-reality smart environments. *EAI Endorsed Transactions on Future Intelligent Educational Environments, 14*(1).
General Curriculum Pilot for Aviation Maintenance Technicians. (n.d.). Retrieved from https://cecas.clemson.edu/cucwd/clemson-engineers-lend-a-hand-to-students-programming-robotic-arms-copy-copy/
Hays, R. T. & Singer, M. J. (1989). *Simulation Fidelity in Training System Design*. New York: Springer-Verlag.
Madathil, K. C., Frady, K., Hartley, R., Bertrand, J., Alfred, M., & Gramopadhye, A. (2017). An empirical study investigating the effectiveness of integrating virtual

reality-based case studies into an online asynchronous learning environment. *Computers in Education Journal, 8*(3), 1–10.

Martín-Gutiérrez, J., Mora, C. E., Añorbe-Díaz, B., & González-Marrero, A. (2017). Virtual technologies trends in education. *EURASIA Journal of Mathematics Science and Technology Education, 13*(2), 469–486.

MRO Network.com. Retrieved from www.mro-network.com/emerging-technology/opinion-ad-out-alignment-industry-40, 7 May 2019.

Pantelidis, V. S. (2010). Reasons to use virtual reality in education and training courses and a model to determine when to use virtual reality. *Themes in Science and Technology Education, 2*, 59–70.

Passos, C., Nazir, S., Mol, A. C., & Carvalho, P. V. (2016). Collaborative virtual environment for training teams in emergency situations. *Chemical Engineering Transactions, 53*, 217–222.

Scheiter, K. (2014). The learner control principle in multimedia learning. In R. E. Mayer (Ed.), *The Cambridge Handbook of Multimedia Learning* (pgs. 487–512). New York: Cambridge University Press.

StaplesVR. (n.d.). Retrieved from www.staplesvr.com/

Vai, M., & Sosulski, K. (2016). *Essentials of Online Course Design: A Standards-Based Guide*. New York, NY: Routledge.

Van Eck, R. N., Shute, V. J., & Rieber, L. P. (2018). Leveling up: Game design research and practice for instructional designers. In R. A. Reiser & J. V. Dempsey (Eds.) *Trends and Issues in Instructional Design And Technology* (pgs. 277–285). New York: Pearson.

Virtual eTraining Software. (n.d.). Retrieved from www.virtualetraining.com/products-and-services/

Vrasidas, C. & Glass, G.V. (2002). *Distance Education and Distributed Learning*. Greenwich, CT: Information Age Publishing.

Wilson, J.R., Eastgate, R.M., & D'Cruz, M. (2002). Structured development of virtual environments. In K. Stanney (Ed.), *Virtual Environment Handbook*, (pp 353–378). Mahwah, NJ: Lawrence Erlbaum Associates.

2.7 Chapter – Language education for ab initio flight training
A plan going forward

Jennifer Roberts and Alan Orr

Aviation is the most global of all industries, and its presence in parts of the world where English is a foreign or second language is growing exponentially. Resulting from this growth is an almost desperate need for aviation personnel, forecasted to most dramatically impact regions of the world where English is neither a first nor a national language (see Airbus, 2019; Boeing, 2019). In fact, 35 percent of the new pilots needed are predicted to be in the Asia-Pacific region. Since English is the lingua franca of aviation operations, as mandated by the (ICAO, 2010), training programs for these new pilots should include an English language component to enable safe and efficient communication among aviation operational personnel. With the anticipated growth of air travel will come more congested airways which will, in turn, create less talk time available on the radio; therefore, it will be essential for communication to be timely, concise, and accurate (Kay, 2019, May 8). The future of air travel will be more crowded, with new routes, more airports, and busier operations. The demographics of those piloting the aircraft in this emerging airspace will likely shift to include more non-native English speakers (NNES) with less operational experience. The next generation of aviation professionals (NGAP), despite their first language backgrounds, will inevitably need the English language to interact with the pilots, air traffic controllers, cabin crew, maintenance technicians, and flight instructors of the world.

Language in aviation is a high-profile, critical area. In nearly every aspect of aviation operations, the English language pervades. Its multidimensional effects on safety are seen in its use in operational and safety manuals; maintenance records and checklists; audio warnings on the flight deck; training seminars in the classroom; and in radiotelephony communications between pilots and air traffic controllers. English is also commonly used as the language of instruction in training. Increasingly, NNES ab initio students travel to English speaking countries to obtain pilot licenses and then proceed through the pipeline to work as flight instructors who will eventually become airline pilots all over the world. Beginning this journey with a safe and effective level of English language proficiency allows for a smooth, cost-efficient, and timely flight training experience. English training for this particular population of the NGAP, then, must be carefully planned and executed to prepare for the communicative situations likely to be faced during training.

This chapter sets forth an ideal English language training process for NNES ab initio NGAP that is meaningful, cost- and time-efficient, and safety-oriented. To make the case for such training, the chapter identifies and explains aviation English for ab initio flight students as an occupational-specific subset of English language that differs from general English proficiency. The chapter then outlines a process for providing pre-flight school language instruction by using an assessment instrument for placement followed by training for those students who lack adequate aviation English language proficiency. Such aviation English curricula are recommended to be grounded in the language teaching approaches of Content-Based Language Teaching, Task-Based Language Teaching, and English for Specific Purposes (ESP). The macro objective of this chapter is to promote the considerations and processes that are necessary to implement for ensuring that the large population of NGAP whose first language is not English are adequately prepared for flight training. While effective language proficiency training has numerous benefits—including facilitating operational content learning during flight school and clear communication in a multilingual and multicultural industry—the more important benefit is that effective language proficiency training will help maintain aviation safety.

Aviation English

A concise and comprehensive definition of the construct of aviation English is difficult to provide given the numerous contexts in which it is used (ICAO, 2010). English permeates beyond just pilot-controller communications on the radio; it is also used to facilitate Crew Resource Management (CRM) among multilingual flight crews, to exchange messages using controller-pilot data link communications (CPDLC), and to provide recurrent training from organizations like Flight Safety International. The need to participate in English-medium ab initio flight training is likely just the start of how the NGAP will utilize English throughout their training and careers.

International Civil Aviation Organization Language Proficiency Requirements

In 2003, the International Civil Aviation Organization (ICAO) adopted the Language Proficiency Requirements (LPRs), mandating that any pilot or air traffic controller operating internationally must minimally be rated as Operational Level 4 (ICAO, 2010). However, the LPRs are only applicable to professional pilots and controllers, and the evaluation criteria refers to their use of standard phraseology and plain language in the communicative domain of radiotelephony. Standard phraseology aims to facilitate clear communication between pilots through a catalogue of phrases designed to avoid ambiguity and influence from languages other than English (ICAO, 2016). The words and phrases prescribed in ICAO Document 9432, *Manual of Radiotelephony* (ICAO, 2007) cover a wide array of possible situations that may arise by flying, but their limitations create the need for mixtures of standard phraseology and general English to be used when necessary (Kukovec, 2008). General English within and beyond the specific domain of aviation operations is called "plain language." The ICAO (2007, 2010) implores that plain language follow the same principles of standard phraseology in that it should be as unambiguous as possible. On the surface, this notion is sensible; yet, plain language is susceptible to a wide variety of linguistic influences that are likely to invite ambiguity and obscure clarity in communication. Examples of these influences include the use of region-specific idioms, the use of strategies and phrases for repairs, sociolinguistic factors, and more. Avianca Flight 052, an example that is visited later in this chapter, demonstrates the potential consequences of ambiguous speech in the phrase, "We just running out of fuel." Whether the first officer's use of the word "just" was intended to specify that something had happened immediately before (e.g., "We've just had lunch"), or to minimize a fact (e.g., "I'm just kidding") was not conveyed clearly to the controller and resulted in a fatal crash ("Avianca 052", 1990).

Aviation English as a teachable form of English

It is important to acknowledge the complexities of aviation English, as it includes the specialized use of language for radiotelephony; at the same time, it is also used in multiple contexts for operations within the aviation industry. In the field of applied linguistics, language used in a specific domain is called English for Specific Purposes (ESP). English for Specific Purposes requires knowledge of technical vocabulary and patterns of language use specific to an industry and its related registers, also known as situations of language use (Alderson, 2009). For example, when considering a skill such as speaking, a pilot must have the specific ability to comprehend and produce technical aircraft-related utterances during communications with air traffic control, but also have the broader ability to participate in recurrent training, interact with the crew onboard, report information to maintenance personnel, and so on (ICAO, 2009).

Aviation English is also likely to be used in high stakes, time-sensitive situations (see Alderson, 2009). Being proficient is having the ability not only to choose spoken words and phrases that deliver clear, unambiguous messages, but also the ability to produce these words and phrases with the phonological accuracy necessary to be understood. Aviation English involves the ability to receptively comprehend messages as well, often without the help of visual cues and potentially through merely suprasegmental indications such as intonation and stress patterns. The occupational demands for English language use in the aviation industry are high, and they differ drastically from other linguistic contexts. Lack of adequate language proficiency is likely to impact both safety and efficiency of operations (Hutchins, Nomura, & Holder, 2006). For these reasons, aviation English, in all contexts, deserves quality training programs, quality instructors, and a realistic and fair time investment.

The ab initio flight training context

Ab initio flight training organizations in the United States are experiencing a push to get students through quicker and more cost-effectively than before, due to the pressure facing the airline industry to hire new pilots and keep the National Airspace System operating efficiently and safely (Circelli, 2018). In regions experiencing the demand to produce large numbers of pilots but lacking the capacity to do so, it is common to send trainees to countries such as the United States, Canada, or Australia for flight training. Many students come to flight schools in English speaking countries through contracts with airlines (Dusenbury & Bjerke, 2013) that place limits on the amount of training time permitted. However, the pressure to produce pilots quickly should not give way to compromising the achievement of adequate English proficiency; it is of utmost importance that all licensed pilots minimally have ICAO Operational Level 4 English proficiency.

During flight instruction in English speaking countries, training is almost certainly provided in English, typically by speakers of English as a first language; yet, as Emery (2015) points out, there is even an increasing trend for non-English speaking countries to also use English as the Medium of Instruction (EMI). Ground and flight instructors, while well versed in operational information, are unlikely to be versed in strategies for accommodating English language learners. They are liable to use a fast speech rate and regional accent in addition to idioms—all of which may impede comprehension for international students. It is not surprising that non-native English speaking students report a variety of challenges in the EMI flight training environment, including communicating with their instructors and air traffic control; keeping up with the pace of training; taking aural tests and completing ground school listening tasks; and learning technical terminology (Nishikawa & Nawata, 2019). Linguistically, this context presents operational, procedural, and conceptual content through a variety of mediums. Lectures, videos, and on-site training (e.g., on the flight deck, during pre-flight) require listening skills and strategies. Texts used in both ground school and the flight training environment require reading skills and strategies. Interactions with flight instructors and air traffic controllers require real-time listening and pragmatic speaking skills. Even for native speakers of English, the linguistic proficiency necessary to acquire and demonstrate mastery of flight training content can be challenging.

The listening, speaking, and reading skills required to be successful in the EMI training environment are similar to English for Academic Purposes (EAP) skills. Students need to use the English language as a tool in their training to learn ground school topics, such as aircraft systems, airport operations, aerodynamics, and aviation weather, and to prove their mastery of this knowledge through oral and written examinations. Most commonly, students learn in a classroom modality, seated at desks listening to instructor lectures, perhaps using multimedia tools like videos or digital presentations. This input must be aurally received, comprehended, and reproduced through notetaking, and later, in examinations.

Furthermore, students are asked to read long, information-dense texts, such as the Federal Aviation Administration's *Pilot's Handbook of Aeronautical Knowledge* or Jeppesen's *Guided Flight Discovery: Private Pilot*, and utilize procedural documents during operations, such as Quick Reference Handbooks (QRH) and written checklists. Finally, interacting in an intelligible, fluent, and clear manner with their peers and flight instructor is necessary to exchange information, ask questions, and participate in hands-on training in the flight deck.

Academic skills are likely to be helpful in this context, but according to a 2019 survey of ab initio flight students at an institution in Japan, only 20 percent of students reported that intensive academic English preparation classes were useful overall in terms of the skills needed in flight training (Nishikawa & Nawata, 2019, May 8). To illustrate the limited effectiveness of academic skills, consider that many academic English programs place a heavy emphasis on writing instruction because written compositions are often used as assessments in higher education. Instructional time is often dedicated to the topics of rhetoric and the compositional structures used in research paper writing. These writing skills may be limited in their helpfulness within a flight training context. Furthermore, EAP training does not account for the nuances of the industry-specific complexities of aviation English such as its technical vocabulary and commonly employed phrases. A solution to this disparity between approaches is a comprehensive program which prepares students specifically for the language demands of ab initio flight training conducted in English, drawing from principles of both traditional EAP and English for Specific Purposes, with substantial attention given to the fact that these NGAP students are likely learning English as a tool to learn how to fly.

A plan going forward

Because ICAO does not regulate ab initio flight training as strictly as commercial operations, member states have implemented a wide variety of testing and training policies. Regardless of this reality, the following recommendations for admissions and training are applicable for all ab initio training contexts as a way to begin systematizing the process and establishing quality standards moving forward.

The admission process

Currently, there is no official criteria for admission into a flight school. Unlike universities which require certain scores on standardized exams, flight schools may use a variety of evaluative instruments to select new trainees. In some cases, they may not screen students at all. With no formal specifications for the design or administration of such evaluations, results across training organizations are inconsistent and unreliable. Evidence has shown, however, that pre-screening does have predictive power. Dusenbury and Bjerke (2013) found that higher English proficiency scores on English exams correlate with student success in flight school, specifically as an indicator of performance on oral exams and a lower total number of hours required to complete training. When students without adequate English language proficiency are admitted into flight school, the consequences can be substantial, especially when students are traveling abroad for their instruction. Aside from the demotivating frustration of being unable to communicate about content and procedures, students who face difficulties in the classroom due to English proficiency may be required to take unexpected time off from flight instruction for language remediation. Situations like these become costly detours and create unwelcome clogs in the organization's system. Furthermore, searching for a nearby aviation language program may prove futile, as most English programs focus only on general and academic skills, rather than skills specific to a flight school context.

Flight training programs must have an efficient and valid screening process for ab initio pilots (Dusenbury & Bjerke, 2013). Despite being commonly used as an entrance exam for flight schools (Campbell-Laird, 2006), the Test of English as a Foreign Language (TOEFL) measures English language ability to perform academic tasks at the university level (Educational Testing Service, 2019) and is not a good indicator of overall success in the specific domain of ab initio flight training. Most commonly, a test taker's score is reported holistically; that is, the final reported score is combined from a test-taker's reading, writing, listening, and speaking sub-scores. The use of this evaluation as a determination for entrance into flight training is problematic because students may excel in reading and writing, but lack the listening and speaking skills needed in flight training (Albritton, 2007). Students who are more adept at passive language skills such as reading may be able to progress through the classroom courses of ground school only to be "grounded" once they are required to communicate over the radio.

Other flight schools rely on the ICAO LPRs to screen students, but as Emery (2015) notes, doing so is a misuse of the LPR descriptors because they are written to test the English proficiency of pilots and controllers who have completed their professional flight training already. Moreover, they are designed to test English proficiency within the context of radiotelephony only; they are not written to test for flight training readiness. Furthermore, ICAO (2009) states that placement tests should refer only to subject matter that is familiar to the student population, suggesting that ab initio and professional pilots require different tests (Friginal et al., in press). As ICAO does not produce assessment instruments and only develops and maintains standards, the type of assessment instrument to use in this domain remains an open question.

A standardized method of testing for non-native English speakers ab initio flight students is undoubtedly needed, rather than the ad hoc use of tests that may not be appropriate for the context (Albritton, 2007). An ideal measurement tool would be adapted from the ICAO LPRs and take into account the specific language-related functions required for flight school. Currently, the LPRs assess language skills related to primarily listening and speaking in radiotelephony communications (comprehension, pronunciation, structure, vocabulary, fluency, and interaction). An assessment of English proficiency for flight school readiness would partially maintain this focus but also shift to the skills required for instructional interaction. Speaking descriptors would focus on pronunciation, structure, and fluency related to the functions of explaining, describing, asking questions for clarification, and recognizing and repairing breakdowns. Listening descriptors would focus on comprehension in dialogues, lectures, and videos. Reading descriptors would also be needed to assess the ability to comprehend complex, technical texts. To comply with ICAO's (2009) recommendation, successful performance on the test should not require any previous aviation knowledge or radiotelephony skills, as students will not yet have been exposed to this information (Emery, 2015).

The use of these specialized proficiency descriptors would enable flight schools to establish a threshold for English proficiency. Currently, this threshold for entrance into ab initio flight training has not been established in the same way that ICAO Operational Level 4 for commercial pilots and controllers has been. This type of assessment instrument, however, can serve as a basis for enrollment decisions, with the option of admitting only students who meet the threshold, or admitting students but providing them with a path forward for achieving the necessary language proficiency. Considering the industry pressure to produce new pilots, the latter option is preferred, providing, if required, supplementary language training before operational training begins (Mell, 2004).

Language training solutions

The preferred approach for aviation English language training is Content-Based Language Teaching (CBLT) (see ICAO, 2009, 2010). This approach, also known as Content-Based Instruction, maintains a dual commitment to teaching specific subject matter, or "content," while also teaching language. The amount of instruction that is dedicated to either content or language instruction can be adjusted in line with the goals of the course (Stoller, 2004). Content-Based Language Teaching is effective in the pre-flight language training context because it is often intrinsically motivating for students as the flight topics are of shared interest among the students and instructor. International Civil Aviation Organization Document 9835 (2010) Section 7.5 states that using relevant content in the aviation English classroom "doubles the value of required language learning time by pairing language with important safety content" and allows the "time spent on language learning [to have] a positive impact on progress." For the instructor, having a consistent context for language teaching keeps a course focused and forces the instructor to employ the teaching techniques that best enable students to acquire the language skills necessary to achieve specific goals. All language teaching and learning, then, is purpose-driven and avoids the artificial separation of language and content (Mathews, 2014).

A training program for ab initio flight students should utilize a curriculum that contains tasks and language skills like those typically found in ab initio training environments (Friginal et al., in press). The types of tasks in the classroom should mimic those that will occur in the "real world" setting of flight training, including tasks such as listening to a lecture, answering questions from an instructor, participating in a debriefing, reporting an incident, or taking an oral exam. This practice of replicating, as closely as possible, real world activities ("target tasks") with classroom activities ("pedagogical tasks") is known as Task-Based Language Teaching (TBLT) and focuses on accomplishing meaningful learning objectives through the completion of relevant tasks (Bygate, Skehan, & Swain, 2001). Task-Based Language Teaching is similar to scenario-based training in that it allows students to practice completing tasks in an environment that affords learners the opportunity to pause, ask questions, clarify, negotiate, discuss, and even start over before performing the task in the operational environment (Friginal et al., in press).

To prepare students for ab initio flight training in the medium of English, an approach using CBLT and TBLT can provide meaningful aviation content acquisition with the development of language skills specific to the training context. The content utilized throughout the course should be appropriate for ab initio students, with consideration given to both the operational knowledge-level and the English skill-level of the learners (Friginal et al., in press). Authentic flight training material should be utilized in the classroom, through creative means of adaptation done by the curriculum developer. It is important to emphasize to all stakeholders involved that this instruction does not take the place of content instruction in flight school; instead, the content helps to prime the students for flight training when their English proficiency, reinforced by the curriculum, is at an appropriate level for success.

Currently, there are few commercial textbooks available for aviation English, none of which focus exclusively on preparing the ab initio flight student. For this reason, it is recommended to use a tailor-made program designed in-house or by a reputable institution, illustrating in its design a consideration for the specific demographic of learners being trained (Lin et al., 2014; Paramasivam, 2013). Courses designed for this population of students should utilize foundational aviation topics and a learner-centered approach. Again, it is vital that students enter into the flight training environment with adequate language proficiency, considering the level of investment and the realistic possibility of a safety incident due to inadequate English (Emery, 2015).

An aviation English course for ab initio flight training

Language learning is not a quick process. The number of hours required varies depending on both intrinsic factors (e.g., motivation, attitude, and learning style) and extrinsic factors (e.g., type of instruction, quality of the instructor, and learning environment) in combination with a student's starting proficiency level. In a flight training context, if, after being assessed, it is determined that a trainee does not meet minimum entrance-level proficiency requirements, it is recommended that a student take part in an English language course specifically designed for the flight training context. In this such a course, obtaining operational proficiency may require, at times, up to 800 hours of quality language acquisition (Mathews, 2008). What is important is that the time spent in language learning is meaningful, and is done with a quality curriculum, a trained instructor, and within realistic and fair time parameters for measurable improvement.

Activity types. To illustrate the use of content and language integrated into a meaningful lesson, consider the topic of basic aircraft parts (fuselage, wings, empennage, landing gear, and engine). This content can serve as a vehicle for language learning both in its delivery and in how students are asked to demonstrate understanding. In an ideal lesson, objectives should cover both content and language, and use creative techniques to allow students to work on tasks that enable them to develop the communicative competence they need to recognize and repair breakdowns, ask for clarification, explain information, describe situations, and justify observations (Kay, 2019, May 8), all while developing operational content knowledge. Consider the differences between abbreviated versions of two lessons on the basic parts of an aircraft in Box 2.7.1 and Box 2.7.2.

Box 2.7.1 Lesson A: parts of the aircraft

Acquisition of knowledge

Students activate prior knowledge through discussion while viewing visual representations of aircraft. A compelling video is shown which covers the five basic parts of an aircraft and the parts' functions. Students take notes using a pre-made graphic organizer. To review content, students tape strips of paper with components and functions on a large print out of a Cessna 172 projected on the board. Then, students receive either a component or a function and circulate around the room to find their "match" through asking and answering information-seeking questions (e.g., "Do you have the part that generates lift?").

Demonstration of knowledge

Using the transcript from the video, students paraphrase a section of the text which describes a single part. Students meet with others who paraphrased the same part to compare, negotiate, and decide on a final version. Then, groups are formed so that each of the five aircraft parts includes one representative per group. Together, students then dub over the original video, altering their paraphrases as needed to match the pace of the video. As a group, the students will present their dub to the class by playing the video without sound and providing the narration themselves, making sure to include all key information (Roberts, 2017).

Box 2.7.2 Lesson B: parts of the aircraft

Acquisition of knowledge

Students are given a short reading that explains the five basic parts of the airplane which is read alone. The teacher then asks students brief comprehension questions, calling on students one-by-one to answer. To review, multiple choice questions are given such as the following:

1   The wings _____ lift as air flows around them.

    a   generate
    b   generates
    c   generating
    d   has generated

2   The empennage _____ the aircraft while flying.

    a   stabilizer
    b   stabilizes
    c   stabilizing
    d   has been stabilize

Students complete a matching exercise with a part on the left and a description of its function on the right. The teacher reviews the answers with students by calling on students one-by-one.

Demonstration of knowledge

Students take a multiple choice quiz about the content of the reading. The quiz is ten questions long, with questions such as the following:

1   What kind of landing gear allows for easier landings?

    a   tricycle
    b   stationary
    c   conventional
    d   adjustable

2   What type of engine is found in most general aviation aircraft?

    a   turbine
    b   multi-bladed
    c   reciprocating
    d   battery-powered

A quality curriculum will include a substantial amount of exposure to aviation vocabulary, giving students a head start in ground school and possibly a confidence boost due to increased familiarity (Friginal et al., in press). The lessons in Box 2.7.1 and Box 2.7.2 provide exposure to important vocabulary and content, but the differences in the way that the content is delivered and in the inclusion of participatory activities highlight disparities in their likely effectiveness.

In Lesson A, students have ample opportunities to work together, negotiate meaning, ask clarification questions, and collaborate. Perhaps more importantly, they have opportunities to produce language through peer interaction and oral presentations that are directly related to the content. Challenging the students to describe parts of an aircraft at a pace which matches the visuals of the video requires precise timing and fluency, and cannot be done without using both content knowledge and linguistic skills.

On the other hand, Lesson B artificially separates the content and language focus. Students work in isolation without meaningful interaction and notably could answer the multiple choice questions in the review and the final activity either using *only* grammar skills (subject-verb agreement and tenses) or *only* content knowledge. There is no necessary integration of English language skills and aviation content.

Another example of utilizing aviation content as a vehicle for language learning focuses on human factors. Human factors serve as an interesting example in that the topic is relevant throughout the aviation industry and can bring awareness for students to the specific role that language itself can play in communications. While ICAO advocates for unambiguous and direct use of language, sociolinguistic factors can interfere with communication, nonetheless. This issue appears to be present in the communications preceding the Avianca Flight 052 crash during which the First Officer does not adequately convey a fuel emergency and is caught in the pragmatics of communicating with the Captain who lacks English proficiency, and with ATC ("Avianca 052" 1990). The First Officer uses phrases such as "I think," reducing the urgency of the communication when requesting priority handling and illustrating limited control of pragmatic norms of English, likely influenced by culture (Friginal et al., in press).

A lesson on human factors can provide a brief overview of the topic done in lecture-style by the instructor, followed by an explanation of ICAO's SHELL Model (see ICAO, 2018). Emphasis can be placed on liveware-to-liveware communications as seen in CRM when working with multinational crews. Hofstede (1991), as cited in Engle (2000), identifies three dimensions for understanding and leveraging culture in CRM: power-distance (PD), uncertainty avoidance (UA), and individualism vs. collectivism (IND). Students can be asked to reflect upon and research their own national cultures on these dimensions by making use of Hofstede Insights' online tool called "Compare Countries." Using Engle's (2000) recommendations for ideal placement on each dimension for CRM—low PD, high UA, and low IND—students can determine how CRM could best be taught to aviation professionals from their countries and present their ideas to the class. To extend the activity, transcripts of the Avianca 052 accident can be investigated to see how culture and language may have been contributory causes of the crash.

This activity introduces relevant content (e.g., Avianca 052, the SHELL model, and Hofstede and Engle's dimensions) to flight students endeavoring to become commercial pilots. The content here serves as a vehicle for introducing common vocabulary terms for human factors and CRM. The language skills that are exercised are listening, as the foundational information is explained by the instructor, and speaking, as students work together and share their ideas for CRM training with the class. When it comes to the productive portion of the lesson focused on speaking, it can be helpful to provide students with explicit instruction on the language forms that will be needed, which is referred to as "language for the task" (Folse, 2006). In this lesson, the grammatical constructions that make up the language for the task might focus on language used for provisions of examples ("for example/instance," "in a case/situation where/in which," "at times," etc.). Students use these phrases to explain the common cultural practices in their nationalities. Moreover, expressions of necessity (modals by degree of emphasis such as "should vs. could" and it-cleft sentences such as "it would be helpful to," "it is necessary that," and "it is imperative to") could be pre-taught to enable students to describe an ideal CRM culture for their nationalities. These grammatical forms employed for the activity result in increasing students' proficiency as they engage with content related to critical concepts for clear communication.

Conclusion

By articulating the issues related to non-native English speakers ab initio NGAP and by providing a description of an ideal screening tool and language teaching approach for pre-flight school language training, this chapter provides a path forward that moves towards standardizing the flight training process while emphasizing quality and safety. The complexity of English as a lingua franca in the industry and in flight training contexts should not be underestimated. Successful ab initio English language training requires an appropriate proficiency assessment tool to determine readiness for flight training and an informed curriculum that ensures language learning is relevant and purposeful.

As it currently stands, the lack of regulation for English language training (see ICAO, 2009) creates problematic conditions when ab initio flight school students do not have the necessary English skills to succeed in flight school or communicate effectively during radio communications. Establishing effective language assessment and language training practices for the aviation industry is essential. With such growth expected in the aviation industry, especially in regions where English is neither a first nor a national language, it is simply not sufficient to piece together language assessments and curricula for other contexts and apply them to flight training in hopes that they will be effective. Assessments and curriculum need to be purposefully constructed to ensure their validity and efficacy.

Safety remains at the forefront of the aviation industry because of its high stakes nature (Atak & Kingma, 2011), although decisions are often balanced with monetary cost due to the financial realities of the industry (see ICAO, 2009). One purpose of providing targeted English language instruction is to ensure that students are appropriately trained from the beginning so that further costs are not incurred later when problems arise. In effect, employing effective aviation English assessment and training is an investment in the future of the NGAP so that they are prepared to communicate well in this rapidly growing industry.

References

Airbus. (2019). Global market forecast: 2018-2037. Retrieved from www.airbus.com/aircraft/market/global-market-forecast.html

Albritton, A. (2007). *ICAO language proficiency in ab-initio flight training*. Paper from Second ICAO Aviation Language Symposium, Montréal, Canada. Retrieved from www.icao.int/Meetings/AMC/MA/Second%20ICAO%20Aviation%20Language%20Symposium%20(IALS-2)/24.Albritton.pdf

Alderson, J. C. (2009). Air safety, language assessment policy, and policy implementation: The case of aviation English. *Annual Review of Applied Linguistics*, *29*, 168–187.

Atak, A. & Kingma, S. (2011). Safety culture in an aircraft maintenance organization: A view from the inside. *Safety Science*, *49*(2), 268–278.

"Avianca 052: Aircraft Accident Report. January 25, 1990." (1990). NTSB/AAR-91/04. Washington, D.C.: National Transportation Safety Board.

Boeing. (2019). Pilot outlook: 2018 – 2037. Retrieved from www.boeing.com/commercial/market/pilot-technician-outlook/2018-pilot-outlook/

Bygate, M., Skehan, P. & Swain, M.. (Eds.). (2001). *Researching pedagogic tasks: Second language learning, teaching, and testing*. London: Longman.

Campbell-Laird, K. (2006). Pedagogical approaches to aviation phraseology and communication training in collegiate flight programs. *Collegiate Aviation Review*, *24*(1), 25–41.

Circelli, D. (2018). National Training Aircraft Symposium tackles pilot shortage and critical aviation industry issues. *Embry-Riddle Newsroom*. Retrieved from https://news.erau.edu/headlines/national-training-aircraft-symposium-tackles-pilot-shortage-and-critical-aviation-industry-issues/

Dusenbury, M., & Bjerke, E. (2013). Predictive power of english testing: Training international flight students. *Journal of Aviation/Aerospace Education & Research*, *23*(1). Retrieved from http://commons.erau.edu/jaaer/vol23/iss1/5.

Educational Testing Service. (2019). About the *TOEFL iBT®* test. Retrieved from www.ets.org/toefl/ibt/about?WT.ac=toeflhome_aboutibt_180910

Emery, H. (2015). Aviation English for the next generation. in A. Borowska & E. Adrian (Eds.) *Changing Perspectives on Aviation English Training* (pp. 8–34). Warsaw, Poland: University of Warsaw.

Engle, M. (2000). Culture in the cockpit: CRM in a multicultural world. *Journal of Air Transportation World Wide*, *5*(1), 107–114.

Folse, K. S. (2006). *The Art of Teaching Speaking*. Ann Arbor, MI: University of Michigan Press.

Friginal, E., Mathews, E., & Roberts, J. (in press). *English in Global Aviation*. London, UK: Routledge.

Hutchins, E., Nomura, S., & Holder, B. (2006, September 7). The ecology of language practices in worldwide airline flight deck operations: The case of Japanese airlines. In Rouzeau, F., Corker, K., & Boy, G. (Eds.) *Proceedings of International Conference on Human-Computer Interaction in Aeronautics*, Seattle, WA (pp. 290–296).

International Civil Aviation Organization (ICAO). (2007). *Manual of Radiotelephony (Document 9432-AN/925)*. Montreal, Canada: International Civil Aviation Organization.

International Civil Aviation Organization (ICAO). (2009). *Guidelines for Aviation English Training Programmes (Circular 323-AN/185)*. Montreal, Canada: International Civil Aviation Organization.

International Civil Aviation Organization (ICAO). (2010). *Manual of Implementation of The Language Proficiency Requirements (Document 9835-AN/453)* (2nd ed.). Montreal, Canada: International Civil Aviation Organization.

International Civil Aviation Organization (ICAO). (2016). *Air Traffic Management (Document 4444-ATM/501)* (16th ed.). Montreal, Canada: International Civil Aviation Organization.

International Civil Aviation Organization (ICAO). (2018). *Safety Management Manual (Document 9859)* (4th ed.). Montreal, Canada: International Civil Aviation Organization.

Kay, M. (2019, May 8). *Changing traffic, changing communication dynamics: Training for the next generation of pilots and controllers.* Presentation at the International Civil Aviation English Association conference, Tokyo, Japan.

Kukovec, A. (2008). Teaching aviation English and radiotelephony communication in line with the newly established International Civil Aviation Organization Language Proficiency Requirements for pilots. *Inter Alia, 1*, 127–137.

Lin, J., Wang, A., & Zhang, C. (2014). Integrating curriculum design theory into ESP course construction: Aviation English for aircraft engineering. *Open Journal of Modern Linguistics, 4*(2), 219–227.

Mathews, E. (2008). Aviation English training: How long does it take? [article]. Retrieved from: http://www.aeservices.net/English/How-Long-does-it-Take.pdf

Mathews, E. (2014). The value of content-based aviation English training for the aviation industry. Second ICAO Aviation Language Symposium, Montréal. Retrieved from icao.int/Meetings/AMC/MA/Second%20ICAO%20Aviation%20Language%20Symposium%20(IALS-2)/17.Mathews.pdf

Mell, J. (2004). Specific purpose language teaching and aviation language competencies. *First ICAO Aviation Language Symposium*, Montreal.

Nishikawa, M. & Nawata, Y. (2019, May 8). *Identifying the English language skills required by non-native English speaking pilot trainees during flight training.* Presentation at the International Civil Aviation English Association conference, Tokyo, Japan.

Paramasivam, S. (2013). Materials development for speaking skills in aviation English for Malaysian air traffic controllers: Theory and practice. *Journal of Teaching English for Specific and Academic Purposes, 1*(2), 97–122.

Roberts, J. (2017). Responding to the unique needs of aviation English students. *ESP-IS Newsletter*, October 2017. Retrieved from http://newsmanager.commpartners.com/tesolespis/issues/2017-09-26/4.html

Stoller, F. L. (2004). Content-based instruction: Perspectives on curriculum planning. *Annual Review of Applied Linguistics, 24*, 261–283.

2.8 Professional reflection – Mixed reality to augment the next generation of aviation professionals

Lori J. Brown

Introduction

In order to meet the needs of a new generation of learners we must consider the training demands and skills required over the next few decades. As new generation aircraft become more prominent on the global front, advances in airplane technology will drive new training demands. According to Boeing (2018): 'As airlines continually invest to improve the quality and efficiency of their operations, new training curriculums and methodologies will need to be adopted to keep pace with innovation' (pg. 1–3). We are seeing new trends using technology to break long-held, industrial age training paradigms, which hold promise to change the way we look at training for the future. Methodologies such as mobile and distance learning solutions are becoming increasingly popular as a flexible alternative to traditional classroom instruction, and newer technologies such as virtual reality (VR), augmented reality (AR) and mixed reality (MR) are being tested as a way to improve engagement with a new generation of learners to improve training efficiency and knowledge

The Next Generation of Aviation Professionals (NGAP) entering the industry today respond differently to various teaching and learning styles and digital information. In addition, the airlines now have more emphasis on digital content in training and operations. We have also seen an increased use of VR, AR Gaming and MR in military training and assessment programs to decrease training footprints while improving efficiency of training (GAO, 2018). The United States Air Force (USAF) developed the Pilot Training Next (PTN) program to reduce their training footprint from 12 months to 6 months and enhance training curriculums to inspire and develop modern airmen (USAF, 2019). The USAF notes: 'that since the integration of augmented and virtual reality use in PTN, there have been measurable benefits from the addition of the technology' (USAF, 2019).

Technology solutions in aviation training

The operation and maintenance of modern aircraft requires an understanding of several interrelated human and machine components requiring practice and immersion. The aviation educational experience can be enhanced with serious gaming, augmented, mixed and virtual reality. Researchers Bhagat et al. (2018) have found that depending on the type of task, various technologies have advantages and disadvantages with the added ability to embed artificial intelligence (AI), provide necessary feedback and aid in cognitive retention and transfer of skills.. Bhagat et al. (2018) also note that

> such technologies can change the way we train and assess, allowing us to accelerate learning and enable students to master knowledge, skills and ability (KSA) with increased situational awareness. Each technology offers its own pros and cons which need to be considered carefully before investing development time for use as a training solution.

We are also seeing this trend in other industries such as medical training and operations where MR, AR and VR are being touted as the key to training medical students by replacing textbooks (Albrecht et al., 2014). A recent study showed that participants trained with the help of 3D virtual environments were able to maintain better situational awareness and performed effectively within a simulated scenario as compared to those trained with a conventional training method (Nazir et al., 2015). Another recent study also concluded that advanced training methods and environments can be one way to improve performance, reduce errors and enhance safety (Kluge et al., 2014).

The use of MR and AR in the training of pilots is a relatively recent innovation and little research has been published on its efficacy compared to conventional training methods. To evaluate possible benefits for NGAP training, Western Michigan University (WMU), College of Aviation (USA) has integrated an AR application called JetXplore into their curriculum to teach aircraft systems using the Microsoft HoloLens device (AOPA, 2018) These examples will be explored throughout this chapter, however it is important to first differentiate between VR, AR and MR technologies applications in aviation.

Virtual Reality (VR) is widely used in the aviation industry and is becoming more and more affordable for end users. At the same time NGAP want to be well-prepared for their professional career and expect more engaging content and opportunities for application of theoretical knowledge related to their career. Students can benefit greatly when having the opportunity to practice application of the technical skills required to operate aircraft which can be accomplished with VR and other immersive technologies.

Virtual reality simulates a virtual world that users can interact with to 'transport' them elsewhere. VR is able to immerse the user through closed visors or goggles, with the option to add haptics (feel) with the use of haptic gloves or finger mounts. VR can be useful for singular operations such as: reviewing a special qualification airport to allow the pilot to experience the terrain and surroundings before actually flying the approach; learning a procedure or checklist, and practicing maintenance or other operational functions; allowing cabin crew to familiarize themselves with cabin layout and emergency equipment locations or perform a virtual cabin safety check; providing pilots the opportunity to practice flight procedures, flows or experience malfunctions; and giving maintenance technicians the opportunity to observe and practice maintenance procedures in a virtual environment.

We have also seen this trend starting to emerge in other areas such as cabin crew training at Japan Airlines and non-destructive testing (NDT) for maintenance. A recent study noted that 'VR simulators are effective 3D learning objects which can be used for enhancing deliverables of aviation maintenance and other technology driven education' (Rupasinghe et al., 2011).

VR environments also come with a few disadvantages. VR requires expensive gaming computers, heavy devices and not easy to execute in a traditional classroom compared to AR which can be deployed inexpensively using smart devices like smart phones and tablets (Bhagat et al., 2018). Due to the fact that the entire virtual world has to be created in 3D, this can be costly in both time and finances, difficult to change and in some cases causes VR sickness caused by lag (Tiiro, 2018).

Augmented Reality (AR) differs from VR as it takes our real world surroundings and adds something, such as a virtual engine or an aircraft checklist (see Figure 2.8.1). In general, AR glasses/goggles are lighter and more comfortable than VR head mounted devices, and are usually wireless. AR blends 3-dimensional (3D) virtual content with the real world and also provides opportunities to the users to touch, rotate, and manipulate the virtual objects; this feature is absent in VR. As a result, users can interact with virtual content using hand gestures, eye movement and speech – while continuing to interact with instructors and other students. AR can be viewed on a headset, goggles or with any smart phone or tablet as well. AR can provide a total immersive experience which allows the instructor to interact and give immediate feedback to the student. Additionally, this allows the trainee to see technical manuals, checklists and step by step instructions to decrease heads down time and loss of situational awareness (Nazir et al., 2015).

AR is prevalent in many industries including automotive, education, hospitality, aviation, healthcare, retail, construction, oil mining, and maritime. Civilian companies have embraced AR to help with training specific technical tasks such as piloting, maintenance and aircraft inspections. In aviation, operational tasks such as aircraft maintenance can be augmented with procedures, checklists and manual information to create a hands-free environment.

Lockheed Martin has also successfully integrated AR in modern fighter jet maintenance programs for aircraft inspection (Lockheed Martin., 2014). Prominent universities, Japan Airlines, Air New Zealand, Airbus and Boeing have also integrated AR into their aviation training and operations programs (Brown, 2017).

166 *Lori J. Brown*

Figure 2.8.1 Virtual jet engine laboratory example.

While there is a limited body of scientific evidence looking at the efficiency of AR and the ability to engage NGAP in the aviation domain, we can draw from other studies. Bhagat et al. (2018) conducted a study with Taiwan students to evaluate the effectiveness of using AR-based formative assessment for improving students' learning achievement and increase motivation. According to Bhagat et al. (2018), 'The results indicated that using the AR-based formative assessment improved not only students' learning performance but also increased learning motivation effectively compared with a traditional formative assessment approach.'

Several research studies (Bhagat et al., 2018; Cai et al., 2014; Serio et al., 2013; Zhang et al., 2014; Ferrer-Torregrosa et al., 2015) have evaluated the efficacy of AR to enhance traditional education methods to improve education, assessment and engagement. Similarly, Akcayir et al., (2016) investigated the effectiveness of AR technology in enhancing science laboratory skills for first-year university students. Such studies found that 'AR technology not only helped the students to improve their laboratory skills and positively affected their attitudes towards physics' (Akcayir et al., 2016). In another study, researchers found that AR helped create an active learning environment which also resulted in better learning outcomes and motivation (Cai et al., 2017; Wang, 2017; Yilmaz and Goktas, 2017). Conversely, Chang et al. (2016) conducted a quasi-experimental study in which they compared an AR system (ARFlora) with digital video learning. The results did not show any significant differences in learning achievement. However, they reported that the AR system assisted the students in retaining knowledge learned more effectively compared to video learning, and enhanced higher motivation, both of which can lead to improved learning over time.

Mixed Reality (MR) is often used synonymously with AR and has all of the attributes of AR and adds spatial sound, 3D geo-mapping and computer-superimposed holographic enhancements to a user's real-world environment. MR is the evolution in human, computer and environment interaction made possible by advancements in computer vision, graphical processing power, display technology and input systems. While VR limits the participant to the artificial digital world, MR is the result of blending the physical world with the digital world. Modern MR headsets such as the Microsoft HoloLens range from US$1000–US$5000 per unit and offer many features such as: digital computing, hand tracking, eye tracking, 3D sound and artificial intelligence. Although MR is perceived as the technology of the future, the term mixed reality is not new as it was originally introduced in a 1994 paper entitled 'A Taxonomy of Mixed Reality Visual Displays' (Milgram & Kishino, 1994).

MR is making its way into aviation classrooms (Figure 2.8.2), airlines and maintenance facilities. MR has the potential to be a powerful constructivist learning technology that supports machine learning, adaptive syllabus, AI and data collection and brings content to life in an engaging and cost-effective manner. MR has already shown great promise to transform the way we maintain aircraft and train aviation professionals and has the potential to transform the way students see and learn from their surroundings. MR Technologies are currently widely used in the medical and automotive community and have recently been adapted by aerospace industry companies such as Lockheed Martin, Pratt & Whitney, Bell Helicopter, Academia, Air

Figure 2.8.2 Classroom assessment with holographic jet engine viewed through the Microsoft HoloLens.

New Zealand, TAE Aerospace, Air France, Japan Airlines, Boeing and Airbus. MR has also been demonstrated as a valuable assessment tool, allowing students to demonstrate proficiency in learning outcomes and acquire higher-order thinking and performance skills to succeed in today's world (Brown, 2017).

The Microsoft HoloLens MR devices and immersive headsets are at the forefront of immersive technologies and, rather than replace existing practices and workflows, we can enhance them with such technologies. According to recent studies (Kluge et al., 2014), engaging students with interactive 3D learning objects can improve safety, efficiency and lead to higher motor excitability and increased working memory performance-which makes MR attractive for NGAP training.

Benefits of using MR to train the Next Generation of Aviation Professionals

For a generation that has been raised on interactive technologies, bringing MR into the classroom and curriculum can promote active learning, engagement, contribute to NGAP retention, make the information easier to understand and improve student learning outcomes. This is supported by Travis (1995), who notes: 'Actively engaging students motivates deeper thinking about course content, brings additional energy to a classroom, and can help an instructor pin point problem areas'. Felder & Brent (2005) also included active learning in their recommendations for teaching and assessment methods that work, noting among other things that active learning is one of Chickering and Gamson's (1987) 'Seven Principles for Good Practice'.

Through interactive MR the students can experience and be assessed with interactivity on a variety of aviation subjects. While using MR the student interacts with the 3D content with their voice, eye movement or hand gestures. With eye and hand tracking embedded in MR devices the user is able to turn holographic dials, flip on toggle switches, push buttons and increase thrust levers just as they would in the real aircraft. This is imperative to support the training concept of 'Train the way you fly and fly the way you train' so that no negative training takes place. This type of interaction is conducive to pilot, flight attendant and maintenance technician training for NGAP. Examples include: cockpit procedures, flows, aircraft familiarization, practicing opening doors for cabin crew and maintenance practice. Although this type of training promotes muscle memory and immersion, it does not provide any haptic 'feel' unless students wear a haptic glove. There are some new companies on the forefront of developing haptics for AR and MR, however the technology is not ready for broad application.

In addition to training, there is the ability to build the assessment into the interactive 3D models, so that students can analyze and troubleshoot real-world aircraft problems and systems. This type of pedagogy can enhance current methods and creates a learner-centered environment to provide authentic opportunities for students to apply knowledge, skills and ability and to be assessed on what they have learned at a deeper level.

Getting started with MR

Although new technologies can be engaging, increased technology is not always the best method to achieve the specific training outcome desired. Therefore, it is important to first define the problem or gap in your training, then evaluate the best solutions – which may or may not involve VR, AR or MR. It is helpful to first ask yourself: What do you expect the user to be able to know, do and demonstrate after they complete the training? What knowledge, skills and ability do students need to have after completing the course? and How will you measure that students are achieving the intended learning outcomes?

Use your current assessment data to provide you with the information you need to get started. Assessment should be a constant 'feedback loop' with ongoing data gathering to improve student learning outcomes. The goal of assessment, whether for an academic department or airline training program, is to provide clear student learning outcomes. Learning outcomes using many taxonomies are written using measureable verbs (Anderson & Krathwohl, 2001) that can be very useful to training developers and educators to construct optimal learning experiences for the assessment plan.

The assessment feedback loop (Figure 2.8.3) demonstrates how outcomes are assessed, how data is gathered, a comparison between learning outcomes and assessment data to validate current training methods or point to gaps, improvements or enhancements needed.

Feedback loop example:

1. Create learning outcomes based on Blooms' Taxonomy which clearly define knowledge, skills or ability students should possess after completing the training module or course.
2. Align learning outcomes with instructional strategies and assessments.
3. Assess the learning outcomes.
4. Analyze the data gathered from the outcomes assessed and identify training gaps or insufficiencies in knowledge skills or ability.
5. Compare training methodologies to determine the most suitable method to improve learning outcomes or fill training gaps.
6. Implement new or enhanced training methods and start the process again to validate new training methodology.

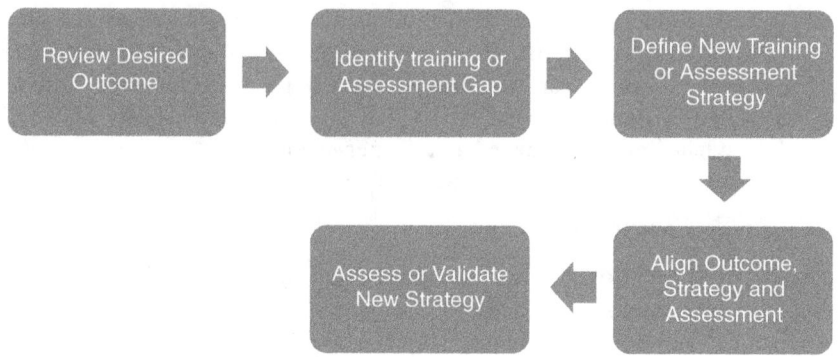

Figure 2.8.3 Feedback loop example.

Bhagat et al. (2018) note that

> although AR and MR are growing in use as a teaching pedagogy, we have yet to established when and with which learners and learning tasks AR is an effective approach Therefore, it is important to align the learning outcomes, instructional and assessment strategies. If assessments, objectives and methods are misaligned it creates a disconnect between the content scope, breadth, depth and rigor of assessments.

See Table 2.8.1. for aviation-specific examples.

Aviation operations and maintenance require several interrelated human and machine components, which require practice, immersion and the ability to apply knowledge and demonstrate skills and ability. 'Applying' in the aviation context refers to situations where learned material is used, applied or demonstrated skills transfer of combined cognitive and psychomotor objectives. Therefore, learning objectives which fall in the area of applying knowledge or skills to carry out or use a procedure, are particularly well suited for 3D interactive experiences (see Table 2.8.1).

Before selecting MR or any other technology as a training or assessment strategy, it is important to set realistic expectations and understand the limitations of the technology. It is prudent to create a small training module such as a micro-simulation to fill a specific gap and validate the results in a beta test first.

Building and designing MR

Building and designing MR content is easier and less expensive than it may appear. One user- friendly platform which is widely used to build virtual content is Unity. The Unity basic developer edition is free to use as long as you are not commercializing content over $100,000. Designing 3D models can be time consuming however, there are many models already built which can be purchased

Table 2.8.1 Examples of aviation-related learning objectives, assessments and methodologies

Learning objective	Examples of aviation-related assessment activities	Examples of appropriate methodologies for instruction and assessment of aviation-related objectives
Interpret Classify Compare	Activities that require students to: classify, categorize, compare and contrast two or more theories, events, or processes.	This can include classroom discussion, papers or interpretation of schematics depending on the subject matter. For technical subjects, printed images or electronic depictions of aircraft schematics such as synoptic displays allow students to interpret system conditions, compare systems states, etc. Classification can be accomplished with labeling, matching or drag and drop activities.
Apply Execute Perform Demonstrate	Activities that require students to: use procedures, solve problems, or complete tasks.	Performance labs or assessments can utilize serious gaming, interactive 3D models experienced in VR, AR, MR or simulation to allow the student to practice, apply and demonstrate knowledge, skills and ability to execute checklists or implement procedures. Example include: Virtual Preflight, Cockpit Flows, Practice Quick Reference Handbook (QRH) malfunctions, cabin safety check, aircraft familiarization and maintenance operations.
Analyze	Activities that require students to: determine how aircraft components, systems and crew function together, and troubleshoot malfunctions	Can include discussion, papers, projects or research. Examples include: accident investigations, case studies, papers or labs using written manuals, documents, serious gaming or video.

rather affordably on commercial sites. Once the model and interactivity are complete you will need to 'optimize' and load the model on the platform of your choice such as PC, tablet, smart phone, virtual headset or AR/MR Goggles.

Adaptive learning

An advantage of today's data-rich environment is the ability to assess knowledge gaps as they occur to create adaptive learning opportunities (Boeing, 2018). Adaptive learning changes the presentation of material in response to student performance based on learning analytics to create a zone of optimal learning. With AI and machine learning we can create an 'adaptive syllabus' based on an individuals' estimated maximum cognitive loads to help students learn at a faster and more efficient rate than traditional methods (USAF Space Command, 2018). We have seen evidence of this in aviation as demonstrated in the US Air Force PTN program (USAF, 2018a).

Mixed reality in aviation training examples

The ability to operate and correlate knowledge can be gained with MR immersive experiences and assessments. With 3D interactive graphics, the student can practice procedures in MR. MR is integrated as interactive 3D knowledge objects. Using Blooms' Taxonomy in the cognitive domain, learning objectives can be refined to create more meaningful student outcomes and mapped to reflect expected student assessment goals. This gives the student the ability to analyze and troubleshoot by seeing, hearing and interacting with a real system fault assessment.

Built on this concept, universities have embraced this technology in aviation academic programs (AOPA, 2018) using interactive MR assessment and training applications depicting modern aircraft. The aim of such programs was to integrate MR into existing aviation curricula assessments to improve learner outcomes, provide deeper learning opportunities, increase engagement and enhance retention – through immersion and practice to improve the quality of performance and assessment of specific course outcomes.

Examples of MR training applications offer a 360-degree holographic replica of the Bombardier CRJ-200 aircraft (Figure 2.8.4) with built-in assessments and scenarios for specific technical training tasks. Each element in the cockpit has a built in 'hook' with narration and textual information to

Figure 2.8.4 CRJ-200 Mixed Reality JetXplore 3D application example.

allow the user to explore the cockpit to familiarize themselves or participate in focused micro-simulations for specific task practice, training and assessment. Students can interact with the mobile 3D laboratory using the Microsoft HoloLens – a hands-free digital computer representing the cockpit as a holographic image in the room, which can be preceded or followed up with a PC, tablet or phone version.

Beyond creating interactive applications for the virtual environment, a significant goal is to reduce the gap between expensive simulators and the classroom. The pedagogical material development can be extended to integrated AR micro-simulations and assessments in the classroom as interactive 3D knowledge objects.

Assessing virtual and mixed reality serious games in aviation education

It is becoming more prevalent to see virtual content migrating into Serious Games (SG) to measure higher learning, requiring critical thinking and decision making skills. SG are developing a reputation with some educationalists as a useful supplementary approach for teaching and learning. According to Bellotti et al. (2013), data analysis and evaluation methods for technology-assisted learning and assessment are still underdeveloped because of different perspectives in evaluation. Thus, development of systems and tools able to support provision of effective feedback is a major requirement for a new generation

Two important issues for SG are how the learning is assessed and how assessment is integrated into an SG application (Hainey et al., 2013). Depending on the task and the level of Blooms' Taxonomy assessed, SG can have formative and summative assessments, embedded and external assessments (Hainey et al., 2013). Existing frameworks (Sliney & Murphy, 2008) for the integration of such assessment into a SG application can be adapted for aviation training.

The record of serious game play should be aligned with specific 3D learning objectives for the respective course or training module. See the example below depicting a record of game play for a CRJ200 Engine Start malfunction. The 3D learning objectives assessed are: recognize start malfunctions and apply proper abort procedures.

The process of how the leaner arrived at the end result is recorded and can be delivered immediately as feedback to the learner, the instructor or both, as shown in Box 2.8.1 (Bellotti et al., 2013).

It is important to note that not all training programs have the skillset and financial means to create and offer SG, however it is important to not overlook the use of personal smart phones and tablets to create cost-effective and mobile AR experiences, such as the new AR enhanced textbooks.

> **Box 2.8.1 Example record of aviation game play**
>
> 1301:00 Student entered 3D interactive cockpit and started the APU successfully
>
> 1302:01 Student engaged engine 1 starter, added fuel at 22% N2
>
> 1302:10 N2 was not spooling up past 25% N2 due to failed ignitor
>
> 1302:15 Student aborted the start with 'incorrect' Quick Reference Handbook procedures
>
> 1303:00 Student was asked to analyze the reason for the malfunction and justification for the incorrect start procedure

AR text books to enhance aviation education

While not everyone has the ability of having technologies like the Microsoft HoloLens in the classroom, most of us do have a smart phone. With image recognition we are able enhance current and future print media and 'overlay' experiences such as checklist, 3D models, video, procedures or interactive training modules. This is similar to an invisible QR code which is mapped to a corresponding image, video, training module or URL. Researchers have recently created the first aviation textbook for NGAP with AR overlays to

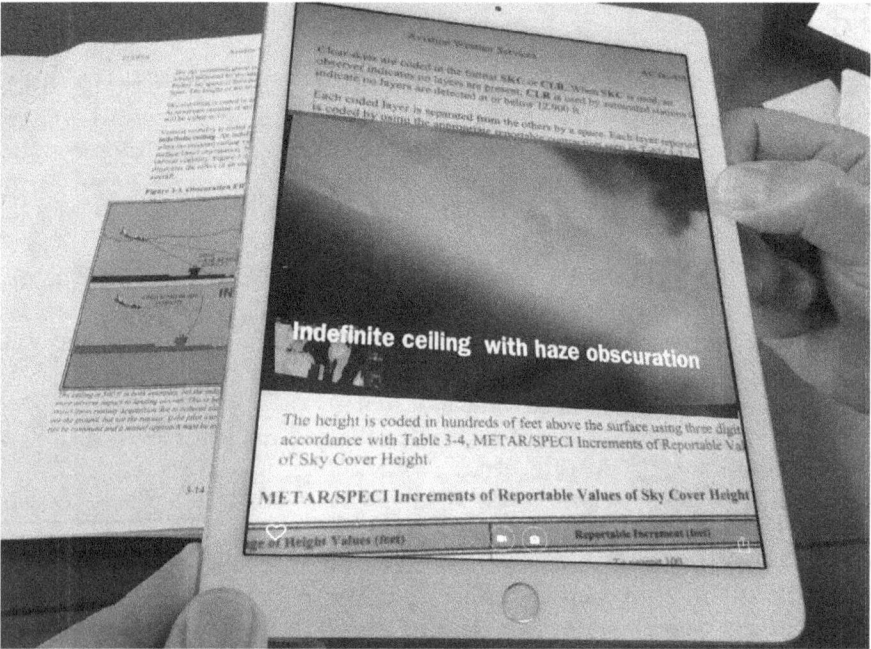

Figure 2.8.5 New aviation textbook with augmented reality.

allow students to interact with the images in an Aviation Weather textbook (see Figure 2.8.5). The students download the free application called 'WeatherXplore' (funded by the Federal Aviation Administration [FAA] Next Gen Weather Technology in the Cockpit Program [WTIC]) from Google Play or Apple iTunes store to use the camera in their phone or tablet to see the hidden content. This technique can also be used by airlines and training providers to overlay content, such as video of procedures, flows over checklists or manual information.

Benefits of AR embedded in aviation weather educational content

The advantages of AR extend past aircraft systems, maintenance, pilot and cabin training to many aspects of aviation education, such as weather. 'Interpreting and understanding weather products is critical to hazardous weather avoidance, and previous studies have indicated that improving understanding of weather and weather products can improve pilot decision making, situational awareness and increase flight safety' (King et.al., 2017; Latorella & Chamberlain, 2002). The ability to understand weather knowledge is further complicated by the difficulty of representing and describing 3D information on paper, which is a consequence of the 2D nature of printed materials. AR, experiential learning modules, real life video and micro-simulations are powerful learning and assessment tools which are making their way into aviation and are transforming the way pilots can see and learn from their surroundings (Whitehurst et al., 2019), which can be integrated into existing and new printed material with AR.

'These AR enhancements can include interactive 3D models, Experiential Learning Modules, assessments, video, scenario based training or links to URL information' (Brown, 2017). With image recognition software the weather-related AR enhancements can be invisibly 'over-laid' onto the image, graphic or text such as an Advisory Circulars (AC) or text book. This type of personalized learning can meet NGAP challenges in an engaging, mobile and cost-effective way.

Through FAA-funded Weather Technology in the Cockpit (WTIC) research team activity, the WTIC team has defined and addressed several research-based gaps affecting pilot decision-making and weather information technology use. Specifically, the ability gap: Lack of ability of pilots to correlate, interpret, and apply weather information related to weather factors (Whitehurst et al., 2019).

In the study (Whitehurst et al., 2019), participants described the traditional weather theory curriculum as 'boring'. 'Book weather' is not very helpful by itself when it comes to applying the weather knowledge, but by pairing it with AR realistic scenarios can solidify the 'book weather' knowledge to allow pilots to see the big picture. The study recognizes that the inclusion of interactive experiential training modules can help pilots develop the ability to visually recognize changes in weather patterns and the dynamic effects of those changes on the safety of their flight. As a result the team focused on developing an augmented reality application to disseminate some of this rich content to the General Aviation (GA) population through an AR application called 'WeatherXplore' (sponsored by the FAA NextGen WITC program).

The free WeatherXplore application serves as an example of how we can augment text books, printed material such as checklists to engage NGAP with affordable AR. The app is available on Google Play and iTunes store and works with the users' phone or tablet. The WeatherXplore application is a demo app which connects digital content with aviation educational material to the FAA Aviation Weather Services Advisory Circular AC 00-45H chg. 1., the FAA Aviation Weather Advisory Circular AC 00-6B (FAA, 2018b) and the book 'Aviation Weather' with Augmented Reality (Brown & Whitehurst, 2019). *To see the demonstration, download the WeatherXplore app from your app store on your phone or tablet, press the button which looks like a camera and hold your phone or tablet over the image in* Figure 2.8.6.

Other examples of overlays contained in the demo include: figures linked to their respective URL; examples for video of a real flight over a sectional chart; video of actual weather conditions such as the development of a thunderstorm in time-lapse photography; tutorial videos describing a new weather product and experiential weather training and assessment modules for scenario-based weather latency and estimating visibility. Although the

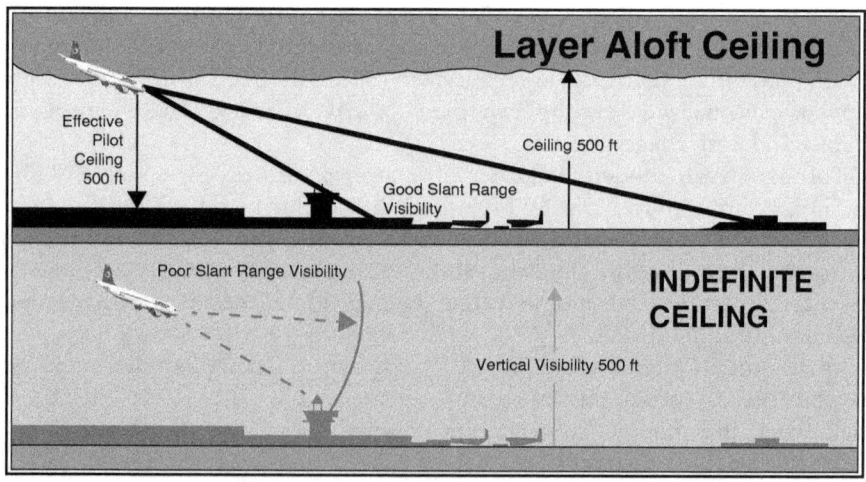

Figure 2.8.6 'Layer Aloft Ceiling vs. Indefinite Ceiling' (from Federal Aviation Administration, 2018b, pp. 16–19).

Figure 2.8.7 Estimating visibility trigger images for Experiential Education training module.

WeatherXplore application was developed for weather-related education, this method can be used in any aspect of aviation.

To improve correlation, understanding and retention of weather topics, the addition of scenario-based experiential training is included in the app demo. This type of scenario-based training includes Experiential Education (ExpEd) exercises in which pilots must interpret and understand weather information and provide appropriate decisions based on their understanding and correlation of the weather information (Whitehurst et al., 2019). *To see the demonstration, download the WeatherXplore app from your app store on your phone or tablet, press the button which looks like a camera and hold your phone or tablet over the image in* Figure 2.8.7.

Discussion

Virtual platforms such as MR are bringing forth a new paradigm of aviation training, where we have the ability to take the analog world and superimpose digital artifacts. AR and MR can safely simulate difficult to replicate scenarios, promote active engagement, evaluate based on performance tasks, virtually create new equipment for training, enhance printed material and allow training anywhere, anytime. Unlike other advanced technologies, MR is intuitive and offers a natural means of interaction with AI integration for adaptive learning. This approach has several practical advantages compared to VR. Not only is it much less likely to trigger discomfort associated with VR sickness, but the ability to overlay holographic elements onto real-world environments makes MR particularly suited for training and education of NGAP. It can be suggested that MR offers the potential for deeper knowledge retention in aviation training, while actively engaging NGAP.

Virtual platforms will not fully replace high fidelity simulation in the near future; however, they are a cost-effective way to bridge the gap between classroom and simulation, while offering experiential learning opportunities to improve outcomes. Additionally, multiple AR/MR glasses can be used to allow others to view the same 3D perspective train as crews or experience instructor interaction.

It is important to consider that many game-based virtual assessments are still only used for formative purposes, providing one summary score as an indicator of a construct (De Klerk & KATO, 2017). With the psychometric models improving (Mislevy et al., 2014), we might see virtual assessment being used for a summative or credentialing purpose in the future. Future research should focus on investigating virtual platforms in higher-stakes assessment. It is critical that efforts to develop game-based assessments be evaluated with high standards of scientific integrity to ensure they are valid and reliable (Kato, 2012).

The Internet of Things (IoT), machine learning and automation will play a key role in improving training for the NGAP workforce for the future. It is possible that MR will become mainstream for the airline industry and offer transformative solutions to existing problems.

References

Akcayir, M., Akcayir, G., Pektas, H., Ocak, A. (2016). Augmented reality in science laboratories: The effects of augmented reality on university students' laboratory skills and attitudes toward science laboratories. *Computers in Human Behavior*, 57, 334–342. doi:10.1016/j.chb.2015.12.054

Albrecht, U., Kuebler, J., Zoeller, C., Lacher. M., Muensterer, O., Ettinger, M., Klintschar, M., Hagemeier, L. (2014). Google Glass for documentation of medical findings: Evaluation in forensic medicine. *J Med Internet Res*. 16(2), e53. doi:10.2196/jmir.3225

Anderson, L., Krathwohl, D. (2001). *A Taxonomy for Learning, Teaching and Assessing: A Revision of Bloom's Taxonomy of Educational Objectives: Complete Edition*. New York, NY: Longman.

AOPA. (2018). Aviation Professor bridges real, artificial worlds, JetXplore holographic learning enhances training. AOPA e-pilot, Flight Training edition. www.aopa.org/news-and-media/all-news/2018/march/12/aviation-professor-bridges-real-artificial-worlds

Bellotti, B., Kapralos, K., Moreno-Ger, P. (2013). User assessment in Serious Games and Technology-Enhanced Learning. *Advances in Human-Computer Interaction*, Article ID 120791, 2 pages, 2013. doi:10.1155/2013/120791

Bhagat, W., Liou, J., Spector, M., Chang, C. (2018). To use augmented reality or not in formative assessment: A comparative study. *Interactive Learning Environments*. 27(5–6), 830–840. doi:10.1080/10494820.2018.1489857

Boeing. (2018). "Pilot & Technician Outlook 2018-2037". www.boeing.com/commercial/market/pilot-technician-outlook/

Brown, L. (2017). Augmenting the next generation of aviation training with holograms. ICAO Training Report Vol. 7 pp 22–25. www.icao.int/publications/journalsreports/2017/icao_training_report_vol7_No3.pdf

Brown, L., Whitehurst, G. (2019). *Aviation Weather with Augmented Reality*. Avotek Publishing. (in press).

Cai, S., Chiang, F., Sun, Y., Lin, C., Lee, J. (2017). Applications of augmented reality-based natural interactive learning in magnetic field instruction. *Interactive Learning Environments*, 25(6), 778–791.

Cai, S., Wang, X., Chiang, F. (2014). A case study of augmented reality simulation system application in a chemistry course. *Computers in Human Behavior*, 37, 31–40. doi:10.1016/j.chb.2014.04.018

Chang, R., Chung, L., Huang, Y. (2016). Developing an interactive augmented reality system as a complement to plant education and comparing its effectiveness with video learning. *Interactive Learning Environments*, 24(6), 1245–1264.

Chickering, A., Gamson, Z. (1987). Seven principles for good practice in undergraduate education. *AAHE Bulletin*, 3–7 Mar 1987.

De Klerk, S., Kato, P. (2017). The future value of serious games for assessment: Where do we go now? *Journal of Applied Testing Technology*, 18 (Sl), 32–37.

Federal Aviation Administration. (2018a). Advisory Circular AC 00-45H - Aviation Weather Services - Change 1. Retrieved from www.faa.gov/documentLibrary/media/Advisory_Circular/AC_00-6B.pdf

Federal Aviation Administration. (2018b) Advisory Circular 00-6B. Retrieved from www.faa.gov/regulations_policies/advisory_circulars/index.cfm/go/document.information/documentID/1030235

Felder, R. M., Brent, R. (2005). Understanding student differences. *Journal of Engineering Education*, 94, 57–72. doi:10.1002/j.2168-9830.2005.tb00829.x

Ferrer-Torregrosa, J., Torralba, J., Jimenez, M., García, S., Barcia, J. (2015). ARBOOK: Development and assessment of a tool based on augmented reality for anatomy. *Journal of Science Education and Technology*, 24(1), 119–124. doi:10.1007/s10956-014-9526-4

GAO-18-113. (2018). DOD needs to reevaluate fighter pilot workforce requirements. Published: Apr 11, 2018. Publicly Released: Apr 11, 2018. www.gao.gov/products/GAO-18-113

Hainey, T., Connolly, T., Chaudy, Y., Boyle, E., Beeby, R., Soflano, M. (2013). Assessment integration in serious games. *Information Science Reference*. doi:10.4018/978-1-4666-4773-2.ch015

Kato, P. M. (2012). Evaluating efficacy and validating health games. *Games for Health: Research, Development, and Clinical Applications*, 1(1), 74–76. doi:10.1089/g4h.2012.1017 PMid:26196436

King, J., Ortiz, Y., Guinn, T., Lanicci, J., Blickensderfer, B.L., Thomas, R., DeFilipis, N. (2017). Assessing General Aviation Pilots' Interpretation of Weather Products: Traditional and New Automated Generation Products. *Proceedings of the Human Factors and Ergonomics Society Annual Meeting*, 61(1), 94–98. https://doi.org/10.1177/1541931213601489

Kluge, A., Nazir, S., Manca, D. (2014). Advanced Applications in Process Control and Training Needs of Field and Control Room Operators. IIE Transactions on Occupational Ergonomics and Human Factors, 2 (3–4): Human Factors in Advanced Applications for Process Control.

Latorella, K., Chamberlain, J. (2002). Graphical Weather Information System Evaluation: Usability, Perceived Utility, and Preferences from General Aviation Pilots (No. 2002-01-1521). *SAE Technical Paper*. doi:10.4271/2002-01-1521.

Lockheed Martin. (2014). Accelerating Augmented and Virtual Reality for Richer Lockheed Martin. Retrieved from: Visualization in Training. www.lockheedmartin.com/us/news/features/2014/141124

Milgram, P., Kishino, F. (1994). A taxonomy of mixed reality visual displays. *IEICE Trans. Information Systems*, E77-D(12), 1321–1329.

Mislevy, R.J., Oranje, A., Bauer, M., von Davier, A.A., Hao, J., Corrigan, S., Hoffman, E., DiCerbo, K., John, M. (2014). *Psychometric Considerations in Game-Based Assessment*. New York, NY: Institute of Play.

Nazir, S., Sorensen, L. J., Overgård, K. I., Manca, D. (2015). Impact of training methods on distributed situation awareness of industrial operators. *Safety Science*, 73, 136–145.

Rupasinghe, T. D., Kurz, M. E., Washburn, C., Gramopadhye, A. K. (2011). Virtual reality training integrated curriculum: An aircraft maintenance technology (AMT) education perspective. *International Journal of Engineering Education*, 27(4), 778.

Serio, A.D., Ibáñez, M.B., Kloos, C.D. (2013). Impact of an augmented reality system on students' motivation for a visual art course. *Computers & Education*, 68, 586–596.

Sliney, A., Murphy, D. (2008). Jdoc: A serious game for medical learning. Proceedings of the 1st International Conference on Advances in Computer-Human Interaction, ACHI 2008. 39. 131–136. doi:10.1109/ACHI.2008.50.

Tiiro, A. (2018). Effect of visual realism on cybersickness in virtual reality. http://urn.fi/URN:NBN:fi:oulu-201802091218.

Travis, J. (1995). Alienation from learning. *Journal for a Just and Caring Education*, 1, 434–449.

US Air Force. (2019). PTN innovations move to undergraduate pilot training. Air Education and Training Command Public Affairs/Published March 14, 2019. www.af.mil/News/Article-Display/Article/1784958/ptn-innovations-move-to-undergraduate-pilot-training/

US Air Force, AETC. (2018a). Pilot instructor training 'embraces change' through virtual reality. Air Education and Training Command Public Affairs/Published October 22, 2018. www.aetc.af.mil/News/Article/1667413/pilot-instructor-training-embraces-change-through-virtual-reality/

US Air Force, Space Command. (2018). Researchers test virtual reality adaptive flight training study. 14th Flying Training Wing Public Affairs/Published January 12, 2018. www.afspc.af.mil/News/Article-Display/Article/1414771/researchers-test-virtual-reality-adaptive-flight-training-study/

Wang, Y.-H. (2017). Exploring the effectiveness of integrating augmented reality-based materials to support writing activities. *Computers & Education*, 113, 162–176.

Whitehurst, G., Brown, L., Nicolai, D., Bradley, J. (2019). The effect of experiential education on pilots' VFR into IMC decision-making. *JAAER*, 28(2), 39–40.

Yilmaz, R., Goktas, Y. (2017). Using augmented reality technology in storytelling activities: Examining elementary students' narrative skill and creativity. *Virtual Reality*, 21 (2), (June 2017), 75–89. doi: 10.1007/s10055-016-0300-1

Zhang, J., Sung, Y. T., Hou, H. T., Chang, K. E. (2014). The development and evaluation of an augmented reality-based armillary sphere for astronomical observation instruction. *Computers & Education*, 73, 178–188.

2.9 Professional reflection – The solution of customized Aviation English

Training the aviation maintenance technician

Anne E. Lomperis

I. The economic context of the next generation of aviation professionals (NGAP)

A. NGAP in the context of the worldwide economy

The aviation sector is so significant in the world economy it is important to engage the next generation of aviation professionals to address the industry's labor shortage. The Air Transport Action Group (www.atag.org, Facts & Figures tab) establishes the value of this sector in the following categories:

- If aviation were a country, it would **rank 20th in the world** in terms of gross domestic product (GDP), generating **$704.4 billion of GDP per year**, considerably **larger than some members of the G20** (and around the same size as Switzerland).
- By 2036, it is forecast that aviation will **directly contribute $1.5 trillion to world GDP**.
- **Over 65 million [65.5] jobs** are supported worldwide in aviation and related tourism.
  Of this, **10.2 million** people **work directly in the aviation industry**.
- Worldwide, the amount contributed to the global economy by aviation jobs is roughly **4.4 times higher** than that contributed by other jobs.
- In 2017, **over 4.1 billion passengers** were carried by the world's airlines.

The aviation sector represents basic infrastructure for any modern economy. The stakeholders involved in this sector form a wide-ranging and interconnected map of global players. (See www.atag.org/our-publications/latest-publications.html. Download pdf for Aviation Industry Stakeholder Map 2018.) To name some of these players, they include:

- Airlines and associated personnel, education and training, [professional associations,] unions, manufacturers, suppliers, flight services [particularly Maintenance-Repair-Overhaul/MRO facilities], and financiers

- Airports and associated companies (e.g., construction), air navigation service providers (ANSPs), regulatory agencies, global associations, cross-industry representative groups, and government entities
- User groups and sellers, including tourism, passengers, [businesses that transport cargo, shippers,] and media/marketers

B. Economic development priorities and policies

The activities of all these players are set in the dynamics of national or regional economic development needs and priorities. By analyzing the economic development priorities and policies that individual countries may be pursuing, the prospects for engaging the next generation aviation professionals become clearer. Some of the most common, current policies are listed below. Which of these does the aviation sector need to consider in a given country in the context of engaging new professionals?

- Nationalization of the labor force (e.g., in countries where government revenues used to support a citizen-subsidized lifestyle and the labor force used to be largely composed of third-country nationals)
- Diversification away from a single-commodity economy into "downstream derivatives" or expansion into a multi-commodity, multi-sector economy
- Increased employment of target populations (e.g., male youth; women, in general; unemployed and under-employed)
- Increased training – and access to training – of target populations
- Increased employment in sectors with labor shortages
- Increased training in sectors with labor shortages
- Setting of policies for foreign study and return commitments
- Review of migration trends (e.g., outgoing, incoming, root causes, economic impact/benefit) and setting of associated policies
- Review of population trends (e.g., birth rates, retirement rates, proportion of the employed supporting retirees) and setting of associated policies
- Outsourcing to reduce labor costs or increasing local nationals to fill outsourced domestic positions
- Supporting new business models (e.g., increased entrepreneurship, formation of regional coalitions)

C. The economic need to address the labor shortage in the aviation sector

Among the economic development needs, priorities, and policies identified above, the aviation sector recognizes it has serious labor shortages. However, economies can't run and flourish without a fully functioning aviation sector. Yet, these aviation shortages are only increasing. Boeing makes the following projections for new employee demand in the following positions in given world regions from 2019-2038 (www.boeing.com/commercial/market/pilot-technician-outlook/, see Table 2.9.1).

Given such worldwide, regional, and national shortages in the aviation sector, all categories of populations for economic development will need to be considered for engagement:

- National citizens new to work, as well as third-country nationals
- Countries new to meeting the demand for an aviation sector at all – and all positions within the sector
- Target populations – male youth and women, the unemployed and underemployed, the young and not-so-young
- Immigrants and refugees. Their employment needs could be a natural match for the aviation labor shortage. Tech-savvy Syrian refugees have formed themselves into a group of "techfugees" (S. Brown, personal email communication, April 3, 2019, 1:30 pm ET)
- Foreign students studying in, but not staying in, their countries of study; and students returning from foreign study to complete commitments to their home countries.

New economic policies may need to be developed to bring some of these populations into aviation. For example, all next generation aviation professionals will need training. And, dependent on the profiles of some NGAPs, new policies may need to be put in place to increase training, to improve access to training, and to make other accommodations to facilitate

| New Employee Demand by World Region and Client Category, 2019–2038 ||||
World Region	Pilot	Technician	Cabin Crew
Asia–Pacific	266,000	266,000	327,000
North America	212,000	193,000	176,000 *
Europe	148,000	137,000	194,000 *
Middle East	68,000	69,000	104,000
Latin America	54,000	52,000	53,000
Africa	29,000	27,000	30,000
Russia & Central Asia	27,000	25,000	30,000
Total	**804,000**	**769,000**	**914,000**
Client Category			
Commercial	645,000	632,000	881,000
Business	98,000	93,000	33,000
Helicopter	61,000	44,000	

* Out of decreasing sequence/order
World regions with non-English official languages will have high demand for Aviation English training.

Table 2.9.1 New Employee Demand by World Region and Client Category, 2019–2038
Source: Compiled and adapted by Anne E. Lomperis, 27 July 2019, from *Boeing's Market Outlook: Pilot & Technician [& Cabin Crew] Outlook, 2019–2038.*

success in training. Perhaps even new business models will need to be introduced to provide this expansion, access, and accommodation in training.

One area of training that is receiving more recognition is English capability. In 2003, the International Civil Aviation Organization (ICAO) of the United Nations set a deadline of March 2008 for English language proficiency at Level 4 and above (up to 6) for all pilots flying international routes and for all air traffic controllers serving international airports and routes. To date, Aviation Maintenance Technicians (AMTs) must meet this same proficiency requirement. (More at III. E. Testing below, however.)

Considering the world regions identified above, it is notable that the demand for new aviation employees is highest where English training will be needed – in Asia/Pacific. And, except for native English-speaking countries in North America, Europe, and Australia/New Zealand, all other countries and regions of the world will need English training, as well.

In fact, because English training is needed to access technical training, and technical training is needed to bring more employees into the labor force, English training is actually critical to reducing the labor shortage in aviation.

Given this demand for English training – and the critical role it plays in reducing the labor shortage, it is incumbent upon the aviation sector to become more knowledgeable about English training. The next section looks at the infrastructure that is needed to provide appropriate English training to the aviation sector. The following section explains basic, relevant concepts in customized English training, with examples from Aviation Maintenance Technology (AMT). The final section discusses implications for advocacy, visibility, and wide audiences in the whole endeavor to develop English capability needed in the aviation sector.

II. Appropriate infrastructure

A. *The distinction between General English and Aviation English*

A guiding principle to providing English training in the aviation sector is that it must be appropriate. What is appropriate can depend on where aviation trainees are geographically located. If they are non-native English speakers who are living, or newly arrived, in an English-speaking country, they may need English for general, consumer purposes to function and integrate into society. They will need such General English to navigate transportation, housing, schooling, health care, shopping, banking, and other consumer services. However, most of the projected future labor force is located outside English-speaking countries – and they can function "just fine" as consumers in their own countries. They don't need this General English for consumer purposes. Rather, they will likely only need English for their aviation training or jobs. So, this English training must be customized to aviation as Aviation English (AE).

This latter specialization of Aviation English is relatively new, though. It is not widely familiar or well understood in aviation circles. Even within the

English teaching profession, such customization of English training to a given industry sector is so new that terms to describe it are often used loosely and incorrectly. In fact, very few English teachers worldwide have ever been trained in how to do this customization of English for the workplace. Instead, it is more likely that people have heard of General English. So, unfortunately, when English training is provided to aviation trainees at all, it is usually General English. This may be helpful, if they do indeed need General English to function in an English-speaking country. But if not, then it is a relative waste of time, when they could benefit much more from targeted Aviation English that will help them learn the highly technical English of this aviation sector.

Another complicating factor is assessing trainee proficiency for placement into an appropriate level of English training. Typically, a General English placement test is given to determine this level. However, in the case of aviation maintenance, no Aviation English test has been developed yet that is relevant to AMT-specific technical training or job performance. The current ICAO Level 4 proficiency testing is correlated to the Aviation English of pilots and air traffic controllers in their unique areas of job performance. So, if maintenance technicians are given any English placement test at all, it will most likely be a General English test. And they will then be placed into a corresponding General English course. As above, this may be inappropriate and must be remedied. (See further discussion under II.B.4. Test Development for AMT and III.E. Testing.)

B. *Infrastructure needed: four pillars*

So, what infrastructure in needed to ensure that customized Aviation English training is actually provided? In the most essential sense, the following "pillars" are needed:

1. English teacher training in how to customize to Aviation English
2. Aviation English curriculum and training material development, allowing for different levels of proficiency
3. Aviation English program design for implementation and delivery of training
4. Eventual development of a dedicated Aviation English test for AMT:
    - once a curriculum is finalized upon which to base the test
    - and the test allows for measuring different levels of proficiency
    - and has versions for initial placement, achievement along the way, and final mastery.

To put these four pillars in place, given initiatives are needed.

1. *Customized Aviation English teacher training*

First, education about and advocacy for such teacher training is needed. Most English training programs will assign a General English teacher to deliver such training, without any thought to the preparation this teacher might need. And these teachers themselves may even be resistant to the whole idea of having to develop their own materials and customize training to an industry sector. They may try to find a commercial textbook that comes as "close as possible" to their own sense of that sector and "make it work."

Instead, these teachers need assurance there is a systematic process of needs assessment and collaboration with industry experts that leads to customization. This may seem daunting to some General English teachers, but it can indeed be taught, especially through onsite modeling of the process. (See III. Basic Concepts in Customized English Language Teaching, including B. The Best Practices.)

Likewise, the aviation side also needs assurance. They may legitimately wonder how English teachers can "teach their own aviation subject matter" without being qualified insiders themselves. Key here is to clarify that English teachers never claim to be subject matter experts (SMEs). Their role is to collaborate with the SME to learn about these job tasks, but then analyze the job tasks for the English needed to carry them out. It is this specific, job-task English that they teach. (See examples in III. D. Sample Analysis for an Authentic AMT English Approach.)

It is true, though, that there is very little workplace English teacher training available around the world to prepare them to do customization. Some university programs that offer a Master of Arts degree in Teaching English to Speakers of Other Languages (MATESOL) mention the specialty of English for Specific Purposes (ESP) in passing in an overview course. They may even discuss the branches of ESP, which are English for Academic Purposes (EAP) and English for Occupational Purposes (EOP)/Workplace English. With very few exceptions, though, EOP will not be addressed any further and no practical, onsite experience to develop a curriculum and deliver a program will be provided.

So, universities could well look toward playing a more intentional role in Workplace English teacher training in the future, given the lack of it and the great demand for it. In the meantime, they could play a helpful role today in arranging certification for teacher trainees who do receive this training in more entrepreneurial ways.

Currently, any operational Workplace English teacher training is typically provided on an individual project basis by a consultant or lead teacher who does have background and experience in this specialty. This also appears to be the case for Aviation English teacher training.

However, some of these Aviation English consultants have begun to offer free-standing, short courses in Aviation English teacher training at given locations around the world (www.nile-elt.com; second week option for AE teacher training). A very few aviation-related schools also offer a teacher training option (www.maycoll.co.uk/aviation-english/index.htm). Others are beginning to plan for this.

Key to offering effective Aviation English teacher training is to build in access to SMEs for collaboration on site at the actual aviation facilities of their trainees. Other aspects and stages of the teacher training may be offered online or through other technology-mediated innovations.

So, this author proposes that where these components can be brought together – access to aviation facilities and SMEs; and knowledgeable Aviation English teacher trainers – regional consortia are developed around such a center. These centers may also transform some teacher training content into technology-mediated modes of delivery.

Additional training may also be provided to these teachers in how to go back to their home locations and set up entrepreneurships, or a small business model, for delivering this Aviation English training to aviation clients in their own vicinities.

The center for the regional consortium can continue to stay in touch with all these teacher trainees and provide ongoing support on a membership or subscription basis.

2. Customized Aviation English curriculum development

Further, the very process of teacher training at these workplace-based centers should depend on a seasoned EOP teacher trainer. This professional should be able to model the needs assessment and SME collaboration process that leads to customization. Then a customized curriculum and training materials should also be developed, as a next step in the process.

In addition, universities and other entities that are engaged in Aviation English research should also be brought into the effort. For example, one group of researchers studied aircraft maintenance manuals for Aviation English training applications (Friginal et al., 2019).

And Embry-Riddle Aeronautical University (ERAU) maintains a large library of aviation resources, including those related to Aviation English. As reported by one of their Aviation English faculty, also a contributing author to this volume:

> ERAU has just published the 2019 supplement to the Language as a Human Factor bibliography. Our library updates this [bibliography] each year with new publications in aviation English. You can find the supplement here: https://commons.erau.edu/db-bibliographies-lhuft/4/. The full bibliography is here: https://commons.erau.edu/db-bibliographies-lhuft/.
> (Roberts, J., personal email communication, April 24, 2019, 10:29 am, ET)

All these sources of research can make valuable contributions to the improved knowledge, design, and professionalism of Aviation English training materials.

3. Customized Aviation English program design

Implementation and delivery of Aviation English training must also be planned to be appropriate. (See also below, III. B. The Best Practices, discussion of program design.)

At the macro level, appropriate modes of delivery need to be determined: classroom/workshop/in-person instruction; technology-mediated instruction through online innovations; or some blend of both.

Finding and scheduling instructors will also need to be arranged. Hopefully, though, the above teacher training programs, with their onsite components, will feed teachers directly into Aviation English program positions.

At the micro level, such issues as trainee identification/selection, schedule/frequency of lesson engagement, total hours, program length, and repeat cycles will need to be worked out.

4. Customized test development for aviation maintenance

Eventually, a collection of individual curricula can be built up that can be drawn upon to develop an Aviation English test for maintenance. However, it is advised that testing experts through relevant professional associations undertake the actual development of this test, with consultation from industry experts. These associations include the International Language Testing Association (ILTA) and the American Association of Applied Linguists (AAAL). These groups have already formed internal constituent groups that focus on Aviation English. There are undoubtedly other relevant professional associations around the world to be identified and brought into the effort, as well.

C. Funding

All this takes funding, of course. Securing such support is another task for building up infrastructure. So, the aviation sector and the language training sector need to come together intentionally to develop a message and strategy to advocate for this funding. And this message must also educate about appropriate, sound models for customized Aviation English training – in the four pillars of teacher training, curriculum development, program design and delivery, and testing for maintenance.

Likely sources of funding must be identified and lobbied with this strategic message. These sources may include Ministries of Transportation and associated Civil Aviation Authorities, other regulatory agencies, all industry participants, any of their foundations, industry and professional associations, development agencies, and other entities to be discovered.

III. Basic concepts in customized English language teaching

A. The four contexts of Workplace English

All stakeholders – the aviation sector, language teaching professionals, and funding sources – would do well to understand some basic concepts about customized English language teaching. This grounding will help them discern appropriate and sound models for this teaching. In this section, the focus will be on English for the aviation maintenance technician, as an aviation position for which much development of such English support is needed. Considerable attention has already been given to English training for pilots and air traffic controllers. Initiatives for training the maintenance technician are in very early stages.

To go now into a little bit more depth, customized Workplace English typically deals with four client contexts: Administration, Operations, Social Responsibility, and Human Resources. For example, under Operations and Social Responsibility, the maintenance trainee will need English to do tasks such as those laid out in Table 2.9.2.

AMT English training will thus need to be customized to such language tasks as these. As has been said, this customization to industry, or Workplace English, for AMT is in very early stages. Textbooks have been published for pilot and air traffic controller English. Very few are available for AMT trainees. And for those that are out there, they will need to be analyzed carefully for authentic customization to job task. Given the very limited nature of Workplace English teacher training and the dearth of those with any extensive experience, the authors of these training materials may not be attuned to pursuing job task customization. The quality of such training materials may be an issue. Their authors may carry over many practices from General English, which is their default comfort zone. (See below in III. D. Sample Analysis for an Authentic AMT English Approach for examples of such General English tendencies.)

B. The Best Practices

So, how does a Workplace English teacher prepare high-quality AMT English training materials? How is authentic customization done? To address these and many related issues, an experienced group of ESP specialists undertook a 9-year initiative to develop international standards, or best practices, in workplace language training (Friedenberg, Kennedy, Lomperis, Martin, and Westerfield, with contributions from van Naerssen, 2003, 2014). They also formed carefully constructed review teams in (about) 45 countries to provide valuable input. Strategically, creation of these teams also engendered buy-in, adoption, and ongoing sustainability of the Best Practices.

Table 2.9.2 Workplace contexts: key business activities or workplace factors and sample language-related tasks

Contexts	Key business activities or workplace factors	Sample language-related tasks	AMT English specific tasks
Operations	Installation, Inspection, Alteration, Maintenance, Repair of Equipment	Read manuals to repair or maintain equipment	Read Civil Aviation Authority (CAA) (e.g., US Federal Aviation Administration/FAA) and manufacturer manuals, service bulletin updates, and advance directives to repair/maintain aircraft
	Record Keeping	Keep records, such as to enter tasks completed into work logs	Follow prescribed format and cite pertinent sources to fill out (write in) entries in maintenance log
	Teamwork	Interact with coworkers and superiors related to a specific issue or process	During shift turnover, report work completed or in progress and give or receive/clarify instructions for work to be completed
Social Responsibility	Safety	Warn others about a safety hazard	Identify a safety issue with a piece of equipment or a particular tool or a "tricky" or sensitive procedure
	Regulatory Agency Requirements or Best Practices	Document compliance with a regulatory requirement	Cite a given manual appendix and numbered section, with work date, to certify an inspection completed for air worthiness

AMT English training will need to be progressively customized to the specifics of AMT job tasks.
© Anne E. Lomperis, 7–28,31–19

These Best Practices cover aspects of entrepreneurship for actually developing a business plan and marketing workplace language training services to clients. They also lay out in detail the process involved in this signature customization. The key to this process is that the language trainer conducts a thorough and systematic needs assessment on site in collaboration with industry experts. Through this process, the language trainer gains knowledge of the job tasks and job culture, which can then be analyzed for the English capabilities needed in the workplace. This process leads to targeted customization that produces desired results in improved English on the job. These results, in turn, yield compelling return on investment (ROI), as high as 531 percent (Martin and Lomperis, 2002).

This process can be expressed as the Customization Formula: Needs Assessment (NA) in collaboration (COLL) with industry experts leads to customization (CUST) that produces results (RESULTS) and high ROI. In shorthand:

NA + COLL → CUST → RESULTS + HI ROI

It is also important to add that, in this process, needs assessment occurs at different times, with different audiences, and for different purposes. Organizational Needs Assessment, or ONA, is actually conducted first with upper management to learn about corporate level goals, priorities, and trends; to understand operations; to explain and obtain buy-in for the customized approach of EOP; and, in practical terms, to end up with a sound program design. Put succinctly, one purpose of the ONA is to inform program design.

A quick example of the importance of conducting ONA first can be drawn from a land-based oil exploration and production worksite. ONA revealed that all staff worked in shifts based on 7-day schedules, as seen in Table 2.9.3.

Table 2.9.3 Staff schedules at oil exploration and production worksite: 7-day increments

Staff categories	7-day schedule increments
Drill hands	7 days on – 7 days off
Supervisors	14 days on – 14 days off
Managers	21 days on – 21 days off
General Manger	28 days on – 28 days off

Work shifts set the design for program and curriculum.
© Anne E. Lomperis, 7-28-19, 8-1-19

Thus, the program design needed to be based on this 7-day schedule. One could not automatically assume and transfer a typical academic semester schedule to this worksite. Further, this program design then informed curriculum design. Again, materials could not be developed on a semester basis, but needed to be organized in 7-day modules.

Similarly, AMT training programs, though basically following an academic schedule, may have variations in the day and week that accommodate both classroom and workshop modes of instruction. An EOP curriculum design would then need to follow these accommodations for program design.

The second major type of needs assessment is Instructional Needs Assessment, or INA. In this part of the process, the language trainer, again in collaboration with industry experts, determines the direct needs for language training. Industry experts now include the anticipated trainees and appropriate others at the worksite at different levels within the organizational structure; e.g., coworkers, supervisors, department heads. Here, INA informs curriculum design, as originally shaped by program design.

The Best Practices discuss INA at great length. Two overarching questions apply for the trainee: (1) what tasks do you do in your job; and (2) what language do you need to do these tasks? The language trainer is also trying to identify the gap to bridge between the trainee's current proficiency (Present Situation Analysis, PSA) and target proficiency (Target Situation Analysis, TSA) as needed for effective job performance.

C. The hot air balloon of customization

One final point to emphasize about the customized curriculum derived from this process of needs assessment and collaboration is that lessons are driven by job tasks. These job tasks are derived from key business activities and workplace factors within the EOP contexts of Administration, Operations, Social Responsibility, or Human Resources. As stated above, the language trainer then analyzes the English needed for these job tasks, applying various linguistic frameworks. These may include notions and functions, genre analysis, discourse analysis, strategic competence, work-worker-workplace situations, sociolinguistics, and pragmatics. This is where language trainers "work their magic" to identify key language patterns for Aviation English training. These patterns could relate to high-frequency or critical job tasks. (See below D. Sample Analysis for an Authentic AMT English Approach and Table 2.9.5 Analysis of Key Language Patterns for AMT English Training.)

Figure 2.9.1 illustrates this downward flow of Workplace English customization – from key workplace factors at the top to job tasks, communication analysis, and finally language skills and systems at the bottom. Yes, the language patterns identified through this downward process will involve the essential elements of language: the four skills and four systems. But these are only addressed and integrated as they are relevant to the job task (see Table 2.9.4).

By contrast, it should be noted that many language texts, especially those for General English, are only organized around the skills and systems. Thus, General English tends to teach only to the bottom of this graphic.

In customized Workplace English, language skills and systems are still addressed, but they are only brought into the lesson in ways that support job tasks. Job tasks drive the Workplace English lesson; not skills and systems.

D. Sample analysis for an authentic AMT English approach

To provide a specific and authentic example of this analysis for AMT English, consider an exchange about work completed and work to be done between members of different teams during a shift turnover (Lomperis and Brauhn II, 2019). In Table 2.9.5, authentic AMT job language is analyzed for key patterns that a non-native English speaker will both have to comprehend

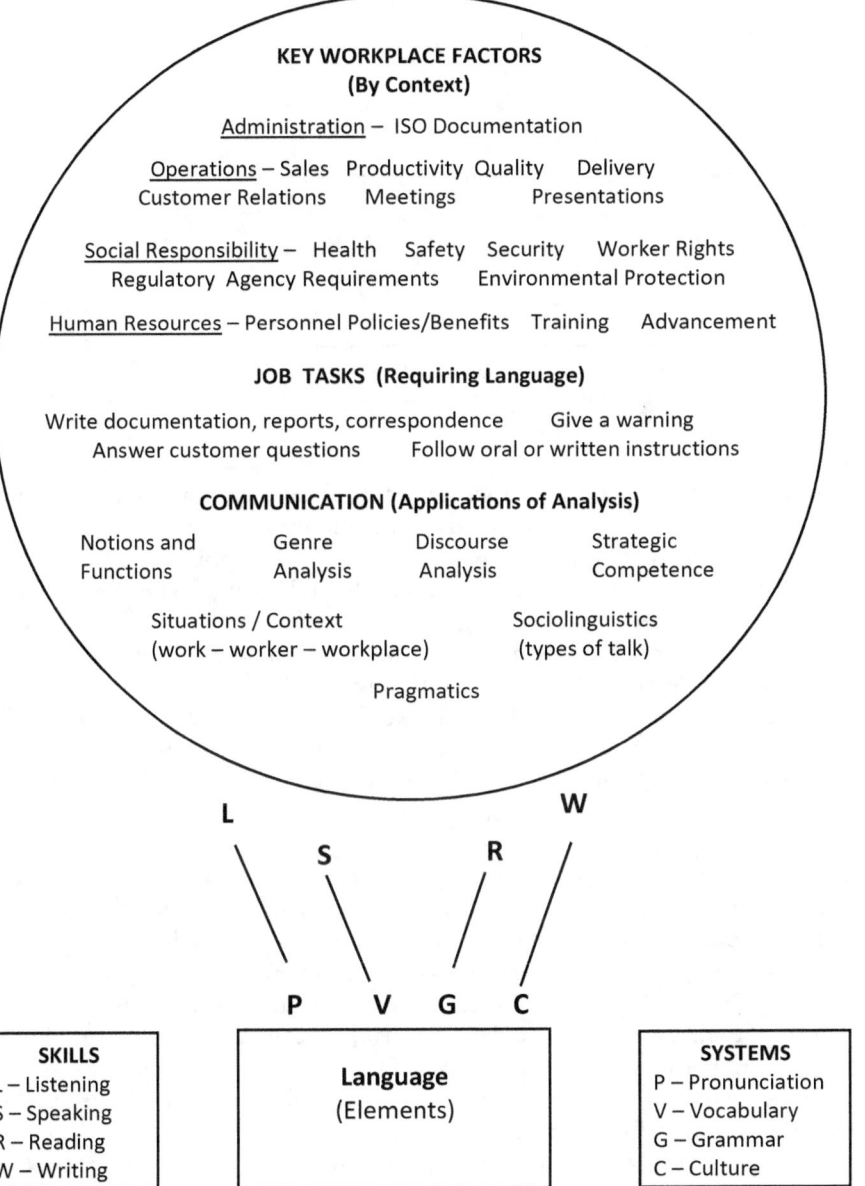

Figure 2.9.1 Language, communication, and the workplace.
Source: © Anne E. Lomperis: October 1998, 17 May 1999, 27 September 2002, 1 June 2019.

Table 2.9.4 Language skills and systems

Language Elements	Components	Notes
Language Skills	L - Listening	
	S - Speaking	
	R - Reading	In literate societies
	W - Writing	In literate societies
Language Systems	P - Pronunciation	Every language has a system of sounds.
	V - Vocabulary	Every language has a system of meaning.
	G - Grammar	Every language has a system of structure and word order.
	C - Culture	Every language has a system of cultural usage.

Language skills and systems are taught in Workplace English only as relevant and integrated into the job task. The lesson is not organized around them. Rather, the lesson is organized around the job task.
© Anne E. Lomperis, 7-28-19

and will have to use to respond. Under comprehension, there are high-frequency patterns to understand descriptions of work completed and instructions for work to be done. In terms of a response, there are high-frequency patterns to ask questions back about location, STEMP (Supplies-Tools-Equipment-Materials-Parts), and clarification/further instructions. There are also critical patterns for checking the method to verify a process and making judgment calls about the timing of this verification.

By analyzing the authentic job task exchange in Table 2.9.5, the workplace language trainer identifies key language patterns that are productive because they may be used again and again. That is, they have high frequency. Or a language pattern may be critical because it addresses verification and timing of a step in a process not to be skipped.

By contrast, the General English teacher may look at the same language usage above and follow a "knee-jerk" approach to create vocabulary lists of technical terms or identify grammar rules to form different kinds of questions. But this would completely miss the key language patterns relevant to the job task, which are also more directly motivating and engaging for the AMT trainee. Teach the job task and its key language patterns. Then provide the support of vocabulary and grammar. The job task leads with its relevant language patterns. Language skills and systems follow. (See above, C. The Hot Air Balloon of Customization.)

Compare the value of all this analysis that goes into the above customization with an excerpt from a typical General English lesson in Table 2.9.6 (Schoenberg and Maurer, 2012).

Note that this lesson states it has an explicit grammar focus: WHERE questions and answers; and the use of the verb [to] BE in the present tense.

Table 2.9.5 Analysis of key language patterns for AMT English training

Key Language Patterns	Authentic AMT Job Language
Patterns to Comprehend	*Shift 1, Native English Speaker*
High-Frequency Patterns	
1. Identification/description of work completed – a step in the process	I rigged the throttle system from the P.L. to the tele-flex in the pylon. (P.L. – Power Lever)
2. Instructions for work to be done – the next step in the process, including a <u>time sequence</u> ± action marker	You need to continue the procedure from the pylon to the fuel control, then start the fuel controller adjustment checks.
Patterns to Respond	**Shift 2, Non-Native English Speaker**
High-Frequency Patterns	
1. Location questions	*Where are the maintenance manuals?*
2. STEMP questions (about <u>S</u>upplies-<u>T</u>ools-<u>E</u>quipment-<u>M</u>aterials-<u>P</u>arts)	*Do I need the rig pin tools?*
3. Questions for clarification and further instructions	*What adjustments on the fuel controller do I need to make: acceleration, E.P.R., E.G.T? (E.P.R. – Engine Pressure Ratio) (E.G.T. – Exhaust Gas Temperature)*
Critical Patterns	
1. Checking method to verify a process	*Do I need to verify the rigging with an engine run …*
2. Querying judgment call/options about time	*… tonight or can it wait to first shift?*

Analyzing authentic job language for repetitive, productive patterns makes AMT English training more efficient than only addressing the grammar points out of context from the job task.
© Anne E. Lomperis and Richard D. Brauhn II, 1–26,27,29–19 and 7–28,30,31–19

There is not even any mention of embedding this language usage in the General English consumer task of identifying buildings, perhaps tourist attractions, by reading a street map. It also doesn't proceed to the next logical task of teaching how to ask for or give location directions to these establishments on the street map.

Instead, the very next question has nothing to do with the first. No context is preserved at all. There is an abrupt shift to identifying the country of origin of two (random) individuals. And not even a world map is provided to offer location information parallel to the earlier street map.

The only unifying principle to this lesson is grammar – and specifically, the verb [to] BE in present tense and the formation of questions about location. Short and long answers are also taught. But there is no treatment of the additional grammar features used in this lesson: pronouns, contractions,

Table 2.9.6 Grammar presentation from a General English textbook.

Grammar Points: Present Tense of Verb [To] BE; Questions with WHERE				
Questions with WHERE	Short Answers	Long Answers	Present Tense of Verb [To] BE	
Where is the art museum?	On First Avenue.	**It's** on First Avenue.	Third person singular: **is**	Contraction: **It's**
Where are Bruno and Elaine from?	Haiti.	**They're** from Haiti.	Third person plural: **are**	Contraction: **They're**
Diagram of a Street Map				
(Showing location of an art museum on the corner of two streets – First Avenue and Main Street - relative to a bank, post office, apartments, restaurant, and movie theater)				

This lesson only focuses strictly on grammar points. It does not explicitly set these points even in any General English task of finding locations on a street map or world map. It just teaches WHERE questions and answers in the present tense of the verb [to] BE.
Adapted by Anne E. Lomperis, 7-28-19, from Schoenberg, Irene E. and Maurer, Jay. 2012. *Focus on Grammar 1*, 3rd Edition. White Plains, NY: Pearson Education, Inc., p. 50.

prepositional phrases, and objects of the preposition (to stay true to a grammar approach).

It is this kind of evaluation of the limitations of General English and the higher-level analysis of job task language patterns that the Workplace English teacher brings to curriculum development. This analysis creates clear justification for the customization of Workplace English training. Customization is the "solution" for Workplace or AMT English. General English is not.

E. Testing

To remain consistent with the value of customization, it is important to make two points about testing for AMT English.

1. Placement testing for trainees to be assigned to AMT English support should be based on AMT technical content

This will allow appropriate placement into an AMT English curriculum (when such a curriculum can be developed and offered).

Some AMT training programs do no English placement testing at all. This can put AMT instructors and trainees in the untenable bind of trying to deal with trainees whose proficiency may be too low to grasp even minimal content. This does not serve the low proficient student at all. It wastes the time of higher proficient students. And it puts undue burden on the instructor.

Further, it can lead to unrelated tensions along other "fault lines" of race and religion, depending on the trainees' profiles. Academic integrity may also be compromised because of tendencies to cheat out of desperation to overcome the language hurdle with no other relief in sight. Such "sharing" may also be the norm for collaboration in some cultures. Shop safety may also be at risk, among several other issues (Brauhn II, personal email communication, March 11, 2019).

For those programs that do administer English placement testing, they may only use General English tests, which lead to placement of AMT trainees into General English programs. Such General English support is only relevant if the trainee truly needs to learn General English. This may be the case for a new arrival into an English-speaking country who needs to function as a local consumer. If not, a General English program can be a relative waste of time.

Granted, no AMT English test has yet been developed, as per all the discussion above. This need has already been identified as one of the four pillars in the agenda of building up the infrastructure of AMT English.

However, an interim measure might be to re-purpose old test questions from previous certification exams (Brauhn II, personal email communication, April 3, 2019). Other resourceful colleagues on the aviation or language training side may come up with additional, reasonable options.

2. Achievement testing of AMT English should be based on AMT job tasks

This will allow measurement of mastery of technical English relevant to the job tasks of AMT.

The current use with AMTs of the English test ("ICAO Level 4") for pilot and air traffic controller (ATC) job task language is a mismatch with AMT job task language. Pilot and ATC job task language primarily involves listening and speaking skills in communication between cockpit and tower. True, there is some overlap in job task language with AMTs, such as the listening and speaking skills needed in communication during shift turnover. However, the majority of AMT job task language requires reading and writing skills.

Reading of:

- FAA and manufacturer maintenance/service manuals for aircraft, engine, components
- Structural repair manuals
- Manufacturer service bulletin (SB) updates
- FAA Advisory directives (ADs)
- Wiring prints

(Lomperis and Brauhn II, 2019)

Writing of:

- Prescribed entries in maintenance/repair logs, which have legal and insurance implications, particularly in the event of an investigation (such as by the US National Transportation Safety Board [NTSB], or counterpart in other countries)

Since these AMT reading and writing skills are not addressed in the ICAO Level 4 test, a score on this test does not provide the information necessary to measure AMT English achievement for AMT job tasks. Hence, this mismatch only adds urgency to the need for AMT to develop its own AMT English test. As emphasized above, this is already on the outstanding agenda for the infrastructure of AMT English.

IV. Implications for advocacy, visibility, and wide audiences

This chapter has gone into considerable detail about the four pillars of infrastructure needed in Aviation English – and particularly for aviation maintenance English.

- Customized Aviation English teacher training
- Customized Aviation English curriculum development
- Customized Aviation English program design for implementation and delivery
- Customized Aviation English testing for aviation maintenance, in particular.

The goal has been to lay out the issues in ways that can be readily understood and carried forward to a wide audience of stakeholders. The rationale has been to show that customized Aviation English plays a critical role in unlocking access to technical aviation training. This is especially the case because so much of the growth and demand in the sector will be coming from world regions and countries where English training will be needed. Thus, English training is the first imperative in the sequence of language training that can enable technical training, which will increase graduates, who can mitigate the worldwide labor shortages in the aviation sector.

Thus, to engage the next generation of aviation professional is to provide for effective English training and remove this barrier to accessing training. English training thereby facilitates a full career in this sector.

To provide this effective, customized Aviation English training, the four pillars of Aviation English infrastructure must be built up (i.e., teacher training, curriculum development, program design, and AMT testing). This will take well-informed advocacy to create visibility and clarity of message to attract stakeholders across aviation, language training, and sources of funding and investment.

In the large scope of economic development, the compelling contribution of aviation to nations, regions, and the world overall is already documented and favorable to the argument. And almost every economic development policy and target population (See I. The Economic Context of NGAP) can be courted to address the labor shortage. This, of course, is the ultimate reason to engage the next generation of aviation professional.

A high-level initiative to propose is that every country establish an NGAP Plan and an NGAP Council with representative participation from all stakeholders. Aviation English must have a seat at this table to inform appropriate and sound planning and use of funds.

Grassroots mechanisms to begin this journey toward more collective efforts are to increase participation and networking through three language-related professional associations as listed in Table 2.9.7.

Table 2.9.7 Language-related professional associations and web addresses.

Professional Association	Web Address
1. International Civil Aviation English Association (ICAEA) Membership is free. Headquarters are in France.	www.icaea.aero
2. Teachers of English to Speakers of Other Languages, Inc. (TESOL) Headquarters are in the USA. Under the auspices of the English for Specific Interest Section (ESP IS) of TESOL, an Aviation English Industry Group was formed in March 2019. Contact the ESP IS through TESOL to join.	www.tesol.org
3. International Association of Teachers of English as a Foreign Language (IATEFL) Headquarters are in the UK. Contact their Business English Special Interest Group (BESIG) or their English for Specific Purposes Special Interest Group (ESP SIG).	www.iatefl.org

Finally, the aviation sector is part of the larger, overall transportation sector. Thus, outreach and sharing with those in the maritime industry and even in long-haul trucking will benefit all.

4. The International Maritime English Conference (IMEC) is a sub-committee of the International Maritime Lecturers' Association (IMLA). IMEC holds an annual conference.	www.imla.co/imec

Professional association membership facilitates visibility and networking about Aviation English.
© Anne E. Lomperis, 7-28-19

All are welcomed and encouraged to share their ideas and vision for addressing the demand and growth of the transportation sector overall – and particularly the aviation sector, as it seeks to engage the next generation aviation professional. Critical to this engagement in high-demand regions of the world is customized Aviation English training. By achieving English proficiency, the aviation sector can best unlock access to technical training, which generates certified graduates and an expanded, future labor force.

References

Friedenberg, J., Kennedy, D., Lomperis, A., Martin, W., and Westerfield, K. With contributions from van Naerssen, M. 2003. *Effective practices in workplace language training: Guidelines for providers of workplace English language training services*. Alexandria, VA: TESOL Publications. (Technology update, 2014.).

Friginal, E., Zhang, G., and Roberts, J. (2019, March). Understanding aircraft maintenance manuals in aviation: Training applications in TESOL. Poster session presented at the annual convention of TESOL, Inc., Atlanta, GA.

Lomperis, A.E. and Brauhn II, R.D. Slide 16, created 1-26,27,29-19, Webinar for ATEC (Aviation Technician Education Council), "My international AMT trainees don't have good enough English – now what do I do?" January 29, 2019. Re-formatted for book chapter, 7-28, 30, 31-19.

Martin, W.M. and Lomperis, A.E. 2002. Determining the cost benefit, the return on investment, and the intangible impacts of language programs for development. *TESOL Quarterly*, Vol. 36, No. 3, 399–429.

Schoenberg, I.E. and Maurer, J. 2012. *Focus on Grammar 1*, 3rd Ed. White Plains, NY: Pearson Education, p. 50.

2.10 Professional reflection – Evidence-Based Training: The story

Michael Varney and John Scully

Introduction

The purpose of this chapter is to explain the journey that we have been on for over 13 years; not to replicate or paraphrase Evidence-Based Training (EBT) documentation authored for the International Air Transport Association (IATA) and International Civil Aviation Organization (ICAO). But the truth is, the tenets of EBT have grown and grown as its actual practice has developed, and that growth has outstripped what was captured in regulatory documents and guidance material. To summarize very simply, the EBT concept can be described as defining what constitutes excellent performance in a safety critical field, while at the same time looking at how risks can be measured and mitigated through training in order to achieve that optimal performance. Today, there is a power in training that did not exist before EBT's birth. That power manifests itself in that major players in training now recognize that the old system needed to change. The evidence in the EBT story persuaded the authorities to allow approaches incorporated into training programs that we as experienced practitioners knew to be correct. This, then, is a story of that original idea, which started very simply but then grew in the minds of those closest to it, evolving into something bigger, better and much more relevant to pilot training. We will capture EBT's history because it is important to chart the genesis of an idea that is now enabling substantial improvements in pilot training today.

The chapter has been written by co-authors Michael Varney and John Scully. Mike's career began in the Royal Air Force flying the Buccaneer, followed by time as an airline pilot as commander on the Boeing 757/767. He spent eight years with the UK Civil Aviation Authority in operations and training oversight also flying the Airbus A319/320/321 and A330, before joining Boeing (Alteon) and then Airbus in Toulouse. Mike is an experienced instructor mainly on Airbus types, and in his Airbus role of Senior Director Training Development, Mike began the EBT Project. Mike worked for Etihad in a training management role and is currently President of the EBT Foundation, Director of the LOSA Collaborative and also works worldwide with his team EBT Solutions, helping airlines and authorities implement the program.

John's flying career began in 1965 and he has accumulated over 22,000 hours. He has flown with more than 25 airlines worldwide. He flew with Northwest Airlines for 25 years and was a flight instructor involved in the development of the airline's AQP Program. He moved to Airbus and held management positions in Flight Operations and Training, in addition to serving as the manufacturer's representative to the LOSA Collaborative. After retiring from Airbus, he led the large group analyzing data for the EBT project. He was the lead author of the Data Report for Evidence-Based Training, published by IATA in 2013 and is now a Vice President of the Evidence-Based Training Foundation, continuing the work he started all those years ago.

From the idea

Prior to joining Airbus, I was engaged in an airline with the implementation of Flight Data Analysis, sometimes called Flight Operations Quality Assurance (FOQA). During that time, I saw several dangers of the misuse for this highly popular and seductive new tool, the most obvious being individual monitoring of pilots in a judgmental, punitive culture. On joining Airbus in 2005, I saw another more positive side of the picture with experts in FOQA analyzing data to compare landings in the "long body" A340-600 versus the -200 and -300. Why? Because some A340-600 operators were experiencing an elevated rate of "hard" landings when compared to the shorter body variants.

The result was a detailed study with discussions with pilots and work in the simulator to understand issues, culminating in some recommendations for operations and training on the A340-600.

The aviation industry is awash with data, with many experts and organizations looking at safety trends on a regional and on a global scale. Results though always interesting, many times turn out to be underutilized in terms of where they lead. For me, working in the area of pilot training, I believed we needed takeaways; things we could do in training to fix the things that we are able to see from the data that we observe.

As an ex-regulator who was frequently involved in the certification of examiners, I got to watch line crews undergoing their regular checks in the simulator. My own experiences as a pilot had shown me that the pilot group, myself included, were extremely apprehensive about recurrent checks; I had experienced and observed a climate of fear that surrounded what were often 6-monthly recurrent survival exercises; trials by fire which were about getting the exercise done and getting back to the line unscathed by the stigma of repeats or retests; black marks in the execution of a V1 cut. *A V1 cut is a mandatory maneuver in any test or check to qualify or maintain a qualification as a commercial pilot, being the failure of a critical* engine at a point during take-off, where the take-off must be continued. On a twin-engine aircraft this means any engine, and on a four-engine aircraft it means one of the outboard engines, because this gives the greatest lateral control issue to the pilot.

Watching the development of CRM in the 1990s, I saw the very negative reactions of the more mature commanders who felt insulted to be taught what they believed was simply "airmanship". Why were they insulted? Perhaps because they were all of a sudden being bombarded by acronyms and psychological jargon from non-flying experts. There seemed to be very few practical takeaways. Looking back, why didn't we simply ask those experienced pilots for their views? Why did we assume that research and development should often exclude those who were most expert in the field of flying modern jet transports? CRM rightly acknowledged that operating an A320 or a B737 was not just about stick and rudder skills, but few answers and almost no tools for pilots to use came from early CRM training. Improvements occurred, perhaps because of the fact that CRM became a subject evoking some elements of self-correction by the pilot community. In short, we were just talking about it.

Like many of us, I knew intuitively that a relaxed flight deck and harmonious crew made life more pleasant and generally led to a good day even when things were difficult. This was CRM and it was truly important; as important as was our capability to execute the perfect V1 cut.

All of these issues were in mind when I approached Captain Jacques Drappier, then VP Flight Operations and Training at Airbus in Toulouse, with an idea. Shouldn't we work with the industry to look at our antiquated system and bring it up to date to effectively adapt the regulatory framework to train them on the new generations of aircraft we were now operating? Did we still need the V1 cut as a test of our prowess or were there other more important things? Could we combine "technical" with "non-technical" "skills" and use them in simulator training? Could we give pilots a better experience in training; one where systematically, they would have real learning opportunities, not just because on that particular day they got lucky with an instructor who really understood how to help them learn? Could we utilize $8–10 m simulators for something more than the same old maneuvers that we had been doing for the last 50 years? Could we simply look at the evidence and figure out which issues were the most important to fix in training? Could we draw distinctions between different aircraft generations to tailor recurrent training to be more helpful to the pilots that fly them?

Jacques was extremely supportive and in November 2007, I was invited to the IATA Training and Qualification Initiative (ITQI) brainstorming meeting in Montreal, having written a very simple paper called "Risk-Based Training."

Rightly or wrongly at this time the rules that governed training were really rules that governed checking that had been in place since the 1950s. The reason for these rules was simply the evidence of our history, the evidence of the 1950s and 1960s was often about unreliable engines which often failed at critical points in the flight, giving crews control issues. The results were often catastrophic and led to the development of rules for pilot licensing requiring pilots to undertake tests or checks at frequent intervals, to demonstrate their capability to execute certain prescribed and defined maneuvers. The V1 cut is a perfect example of this, being able to execute the take-off maneuver with the loss of one engine, and then return to land successfully flying a particular type of approach, e.g., using the Instrument Landing System (ILS) in poor weather. This generally included two maneuvers, the take-off and the approach, which could then be continued to a third maneuver, either a landing or a go-around with the failed engine.

My personal feeling for a long time was that completing a standard sequence of maneuvers for the revalidation of a license qualification was by no means effectively addressing any of the real issues being faced by crews in modern times and in modern aircraft.

Five years later when EBT was first published, looking back at that very simple paper, entitled "Development of Risk Based Airline Flight Crew Training" most of it had remained relevant to what we were then doing.

Interestingly enough, the first statement regarding the pilot shortage turned out to be premature.

This was immediately before the 2008 financial crisis that effectively postponed the problem but today, we can now say that in many regions of the world we really are in the grip of a pilot shortage. According to the latest information the industry faces a worldwide demand for more than 800,000 new pilots over the next 20 years, with demand for over 200,000 pilots in North America and 266,000 pilots in the Asia Pacific Region (Boeing, 2019).

Here are the other points made in the original paper regarding risk-based training:

- Regulatory prescriptions for crew training and checking are based on the apparent risks presented to first- and second-generation transport aircraft.
- Significant improvement in aircraft design and reliability render the likelihood of occurrence of many items mandated within training programs highly improbable.
- The crowding of recurrent training programs with outdated regulatory requirements plus a panoply of "sticking plaster" training "solutions" to meet post-accident public safety concerns now encroaches on the ability of operators to design effective programs within existing cost structures.
- All accident data indicates a substantial level of human interaction failure as primary cause.

- The majority of large transport aircraft accidents occur when aircraft are operating without technical malfunction.
- ICAO mandated the analysis of flight data in 2005. The availability of this data on a world fleet basis provides an opportunity to change the basis of airline pilot training to one based on risk of occurrence and to meet the real challenges in line operations.
- This purpose of the document was to outline the necessary steps to gather and analyze world fleet data, plus the outcome of activities such as LOSA, to provide a fleet and operation specific basis for the design of crew training and the safety standards for the regulation of training and checking.
- Do nothing and what happens? The perpetuation of increasingly anachronistic training and checking standards; the continuing fulfilment of erroneous mandatory requirements not indicative of the risks and challenges that pilots operating modern transport aircraft are liable to face.
- **Complacency that the continuous and repetitive training and checking of these items provides protection for crews facing quite different challenges in line operations.**
- The inability to focus on the non-technical and management skills to mitigate the real risks to aircraft as a result of, e.g., poorly executed normal approaches, badly managed go arounds, controlled flight into terrain (CFIT).
- The original mission statement of EBT was to assimilate, develop and deploy evidence-based best industry practice in airline initial and recurrent training and checking, to mitigate the real risks in a modern air transport operations.

We started with a plan to deliver the following:

- A methodology for the analysis of fleet and operation specific de-identified flight data, against a defined common standard.
- Gathering and analysis of evidence.
- Development of a global fleet specific risk matrix presenting the evidence for development of effective targeted risk-based training and checking solutions.
- Implementation of risk-based training and checking beta testing with nominated authorities and airlines.
- Global application of best practice through the availability of data and best practice.

First steps

My original idea had been to start working with the aircraft Original Equipment Manufacturers (OEMs) so we invited ATR, Boeing, Bombardier and Embraer and of course myself from Airbus to what was to become regular meetings in Montreal, at the IATA offices. The meetings were informal, really brainstorming sessions to define a collective view of the problem that we were all trying to address, then some first steps began to emerge along the path of fixing it. But we quickly realized that we needed to talk to pilots, so we invited the International Federation of Airline Pilots' Associations (IFALPA).

Meetings continued to try to define some steps and methodologies, and we devised a list of potential events that pilots were likely to face in operations. We wanted pilot opinion to lead the process, using expert opinion and then to look at data using the same events to verify our beliefs. We developed a questioning process called the "Intuitive Risk Matrix" which in a sense was a survey asking pilots on fleets of all aircraft generations to look at the likelihood and severity of a given set of events that we as a group felt to be relevant to risk mitigation by simulator training.

Even though the idea had merit, in practice, the matrix was anything but intuitive and was very cumbersome to complete, so we never really got a big enough sample of expert opinions to guide us; more of that later!

We began to work on combining the technical and non-technical skills. The term competency was not used at the time. We compared a number of CRM behavioral marker systems that were in use at the time, including the University of Texas Behavioral Markers, NOTECHS, a European researched system, and a system published in the UK CAA CRM guide (CAP 737 developed by Carey Edwards and his team at LMQ). It was this latter approach that was chosen; the language was accessible, and Communication was included, and we felt this was important. We wanted to start on solid ground with a system that had been developed and tested and then add to it the technical skills. The LMQ system had been validated in service and had some maturity.

The base data for the LMQ indicators was initially obtained from several hundred pilots during training courses in response to specific questions about their effective role models as pilots, and those who were ineffective. We continued to ask the same questions and the answers gave us a very high degree of consistency, providing confidence and again pointing very clearly to the use of our subject matter experts, the pilots, about who they wished to share the flight deck with and what it was that made an effective performer.

This was the beginning of what today is known as the Pilot Competencies (Figure 2.10.1). It was clear to the group that these competencies were a framework for measuring pilot performance, but at this stage we didn't fully understand how best to use it. Behind the headlines of the competencies, there are a series of Performance Indicators, which are used to link observed performance to a competency.

Pilot Competencies

Competency	Performance Indicators
Application of Procedures (APK)	a) Follows SOPs unless a higher degree of safety dictates otherwise b) Identifies and applies all operating instructions in a timely manner c) Correctly uses aircraft systems, controls and instruments d) Safely manages the aircraft to achieve best value for the operation, including fuel, the environment, passenger comfort and punctuality e) Identifies the source of operating instructions
Communication (COM)	a) Knows what, how, where, when, how much and with whom he or she needs to communicate b) Ensures the recipient is ready and able to receive the information c) Conveys messages and information clearly, accurately, timely and adequately d) Confirms that the recipient correctly understands important information e) Listens actively, patiently and demonstrates understanding when receiving information f) Asks relevant and effective questions, and offers suggestions g) Uses appropriate body language, eye contact and tone, and correctly interprets non-verbal communication of others h) Is receptive to other people's views and is willing to compromise
Flight Path Management – Automation (FPA)	a) Controls the aircraft using automation with accuracy and smoothness as appropriate to the situation b) Detects deviations from the desired aircraft trajectory and takes appropriate action c) Contains the aircraft within the normal flight envelope d) Manages the flight path to achieve optimum operational performance e) Maintains the desired flight path during flight using automation whilst managing other tasks and distractions f) Selects appropriate level and mode of automation in a timely manner considering phase of flight and workload g) Effectively monitors automation, including engagement and automatic mode transitions
Flight Path Management – Manual Control (FPM)	a) Controls the aircraft manually with accuracy and smoothness as appropriate to the situation b) Detects deviations from the desired aircraft trajectory and takes appropriate action c) Contains the aircraft within the normal flight envelope d) Controls the aircraft safely using only the relationship between aircraft attitude, speed and thrust e) Manages the flight path to achieve optimum operational performance f) Maintains the desired flight path during manual flight whilst managing other tasks and distractions g) Selects appropriate level and mode of flight guidance systems in a timely manner considering phase of flight and workload h) Effectively monitors flight guidance systems including engagement and automatic mode transitions
Knowledge (KNO)	a) Demonstrates practical and applicable knowledge of limitations and systems and their interaction b) Demonstrates required knowledge of published operating instructions c) Demonstrates knowledge of the physical environment, the air traffic environment including routings, weather, airports and the operational infrastructure d) Demonstrates appropriate knowledge of applicable legislation e) Knows where to source required information f) Demonstrates a positive interest in acquiring knowledge g) Is able to apply knowledge effectively

Figure 2.10.1 Pilot competencies and performance indicators.

Pilot Competencies

Competency	Performance Indicators
Leadership & Teamwork (LTW)	a) Understands and agrees with the crew's roles and objectives b) Is approachable, enthusiastic, motivating and considerate of others c) Uses initiative, gives direction and takes responsibility when required d) Anticipates other crew members' needs and carries out instructions when directed e) Is open and honest about thoughts, concerns and intentions f) Gives and receives both criticism and praises well, and admits mistakes g) Confidently says and does what is important for safety h) Demonstrates empathy, respect and tolerance for other people i) Involves others in planning and allocates activities fairly and appropriately to abilities
Problem Solving & Decision-Making (PSD)	a) Identifies and verifies why things have gone wrong and does not jump to conclusions or make uninformed assumptions b) Seeks accurate and adequate information from appropriate sources c) Perseveres in working through a problem without reducing safety d) Uses appropriate, agreed and timely decision-making processes e) Applies essential and desirable criteria and prioritizes f) Considers as many options as practicable g) Makes decisions when needed, reviews and changes them if required h) Considers risks but does not take unnecessary risks i) Improvises appropriately when faced with unforeseen circumstances to achieve the safest outcome
Situation Awareness (SAW)	a) Is aware of the state of the aircraft and its systems b) Is aware of where the aircraft is and its environment c) Keeps track of time and fuel d) Is aware of the condition of people involved in the operation including passengers e) Develops "what if" scenarios and plans for contingencies f) Identifies threats to the safety of the aircraft and people, and takes appropriate action
Workload Management (WLM)	a) Is calm, relaxed, careful and not impulsive b) Plans, Prepares, prioritizes and schedules tasks effectively c) Manages time efficiently when carrying out tasks d) Offers and accepts assistance, delegates when necessary and asks for help early e) Reviews, monitors and cross-checks actions conscientiously f) Ensures tasks are completed g) Manages interruptions, distractions, variations and failures effectively

Figure 2.10.1 (cont.)

Air Arabia	Flight Safety International
Air France	General Civil Aviation Authority - United Arab Emirates
Air Berlin	Griffith University
Airbus S.A.S.	Gulf Air
ATR	Gulf Aviation Academy
The Boeing Company	International Air Transport Association
Bombardier Inc.	International Civil Aviation Organization
British Airways Plc	International Federation of Airline Pilots Associations
CAE Inc.	LOSA Collaborative
Cathay Pacific Airways Ltd.	LMQ Ltd
Civil Aviation Authority – United Kingdom	Mechtronix Systems Inc.
Civil Aviation Department – Hong Kong, China	National Aerospace Laboratory (NLR) - Netherlands
Civil Aviation Safety Authority – Australia	Oxford Aviation Academy
Delta Airlines Inc.	Qantas Airways Ltd
Deutsche Lufthansa AG	Qatar Airways
Dragonair	Research Integrations Inc.
Directiongénérale de l'aviation civile – France	Royal Aeronautical Society (RAeS)
EasyJet	Royal Holloway, University of London
Embraer S.A.	Saudi Arabian Airlines
Emirates Airline	Thomsonfly Ltd
ETOPS S.A.S.	Transport Canada
Etihad Airways	Virgin Australia
European Aviation Safety Agency (EASA)	Wizz Air
European Cockpit Association (ECA)	
Federal Aviation Administration - United States of America	

Figure 2.10.2 EBT working group 2008–2012 participants.

At the same time, we set about trying to create a representative example of a typical 2-day training program with significantly reduced jeopardy and with much less focus on the traditional maneuvers.

As the idea became more visible, our working group was joined by a diverse range of experts and we began to hold bi-monthly meetings initially in Montreal, and then alternating between locations in Europe, North America and occasionally the Gulf Region. Organizations engaged in the development are listed in Figure 2.10.2.

As momentum increased, in June 2009 I received a letter from Nancy Graham, Director of the Air Navigation Bureau at ICAO, expressing interest in our work. The letter contained a challenge: if we could reach a truly international consensus, the result could be published by ICAO and recognition gained worldwide. For the first time we could have a worldwide standardized framework for recurrent training and checking based and better still, it would be based on the principles that were emerging from our work.

While all of this was happening and as the expert group was growing, we recognized that the work of data analysis would need specialists, and in early 2008 a parallel stream to the expert training group began. I asked an old friend, Captain John Scully, recently retired from Airbus if he would consider leading this initiative. John had a wealth of experience as an instructor and pilot in North America and Europe. Working for Northwest Airlines and Airbus, he also had a significant experience in the development of training programs. Prior to his retirement in 2007, he led Flight Data Analysis (FDA) at Airbus and helped customers to implement the program as well as other operational support. John had airline contacts all over the world, and he brought some great ideas to the table.

John assembled his team, many of whom gave their time as volunteers, around 60 people in total, and we remain extremely grateful for their diligent work which contributed significantly to the concept.

Data analysis – what we did

In writing this I spent some time with John to get his thoughts about what had been done and some of the lessons learned. Our intent is not to repeat information in the Data Report for Evidence-Based Training published by IATA in 2013, but more to discuss its objectives, its story, and what we had really learned from its process.

First of all, let's see how the data study stands up to its namesake, Evidence-Based Training? Or just how important really was the data analysis?

Perhaps we can look at this from a perspective of impact. The impact was significant in the influence it delivered to the regulatory community, as well as the rest of the airlines, which was certainly a primary goal. For things to happen, a paradigm shift was needed. The study changed minds, even though for the most part, the results were what we all expected; but having them quantified in a structured analysis sowed the seed for change.

Perhaps the most important result of the data study was that it did trigger a shift in thinking about the need to change training. After seeing the results, it was clear that we simply had to do something different. This fact allowed a door to be opened allowing major players not only to accept changes but actually demand them.

The results themselves were also compelling. We were surprised at the consistency of results from so many diverse sources of data, from LOSA, from FOQA, from surveys and accident-incident analyses to already other published and unpublished industry reports.

In the beginning we had some naive notions about how much insight the data would provide, but in fact the data provided in some cases more questions than answers.

However, the results did give us confidence, because they were always based on a very open and transparent analysis. Huge amounts of data were

International Civil Aviation Organization
Organisation de l'aviation civile internationale
Organización de Aviación Civil Internacional
Международная организация гражданской авиации
منظمة الطيران المدني الدولي
国际民用航空组织

Ref.: E4/2.15

18 June 2009

Captain Michael Varney
Senior Director, Flight Crew Development
AIRBUS S.A.S.
Internal PO Box B28 0A3
1 Rond-Point Maurice Bellonte
31707 Blagnac Cedex
France
Email: michael.varney@airbus.com

Dear Captain Varney,

        I wish to refer to the Evidence Based Training (EBT) initiative by the IATA Training and Qualification Initiative (ITQI) and to inform you that the development of a methodology to base training programmes on evidence collected through operational experience is of great interest to the International Civil Aviation Organization (ICAO).

        Training flight crews for the specific challenges identified in relation to aircraft types and operational environments represents an opportunity to improve safety at minimal cost. The concept of EBT has the potential to improve the efficacy of training, and will benefit from the implementation of Safety Management Systems by operators, that would identify risks associated with the aircraft type and the operations conducted, which can be mitigated by appropriate training. Training programmes, based on the evidence collected by aircraft manufacturers and the large operators, could be especially useful to small operators unable to elaborate training programmes targeted at those risks to which they are exposed.

        In citing our support of this initiative I would like to inform you that once the concept has reached sufficient maturity and has been validated, ICAO would consider developing provisions to enable the EBT methodology. Relevant material developed in this regard and adopted by the aviation industry could also be included in ICAO publications for wider reach.

        Please keep me informed of the ITQI activities in this regard.

Yours sincerely,

Nancy J. Graham
Director
Air Navigation Bureau

999 University Street
Montréal, Quebec
Canada H3C 5H7

Tel.: +1 514-954-8219
Fax: +1 514-954-6077

E-mail: icaohq@icao.int
www.icao.int

Figure 2.10.3 Letter from ICAO.

treated; some questions were not supported simply because the data became thin and unreliable, e.g., in the accident-incident analysis. We measured and compared results from many different sources albeit through the lens of subjectively determined training events, but by doing this, we achieved the relevance we sought.

There were some surprises, but in most cases, we already knew what the data was telling us, a great example of a surprise was an enhanced understanding of a well-known, but not well understood issue that we called the "Unstable Approach Paradox." Our mantra and teaching for so many years had simply been that a stable approach leads to an uneventful landing, and an unstable approach leads to an eventful and risky landing. This was in reality a gross oversimplification. What we learned from multiple studies is that pilots (for various reasons) did not want to execute go-arounds, and when they did, there were associated risks that in many cases exacerbated the situation. The data told us clearly that we needed to practice go arounds, and not just from minima without visual reference with an engine out in the simulator, when the pilots were expecting it but from virtually any position and configuration during an approach. Pilots needed to practice the maneuver from all sorts of entry conditions, configurations and heights, because the go-around is such a dynamic maneuver and almost invariably a surprise. The crew has to manage energy using automation or flying manually in situations they almost never practice in training. Our rote, mandatory go-around in training in many instances actually aggravated the situation in terms of risk (Figure 2.10.4).

Interestingly, we discovered that an unstable approach was an interesting barometer for the entire flight, highlighting the need to deal with this thorny issue (Figure 2.10.5).

A very interesting result that we perhaps hadn't before realized but were aware of intuitively, is that our studies clearly showed that the more modern the aircraft, the greater the impact training has on reducing risk (Figure 2.10.6).

We were continually surprised at the consistency of the outcomes across the range of data sources. When we were able to correlate risk ranking of factors in various data sources, the story was almost always the same. This fact gave us more and more confidence as we worked.

One of the biggest lessons we learned from our work is that our greatest resources for good information are our pilots themselves and that best way to proceed in the future is to depend more on their expertise while cross checking it with the data where and when the data exists. This opens the research to almost any area that we might want to explore regardless of the inherent limitations that the data or the lack of data presents. This bodes well for the future of airline pilot training and is one of the greatest strengths of EBT.

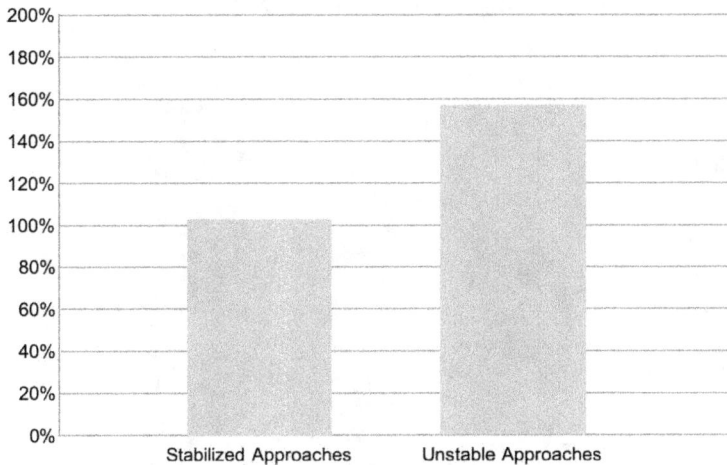

Figure 2.10.4 Go-around events per flights with go-around.

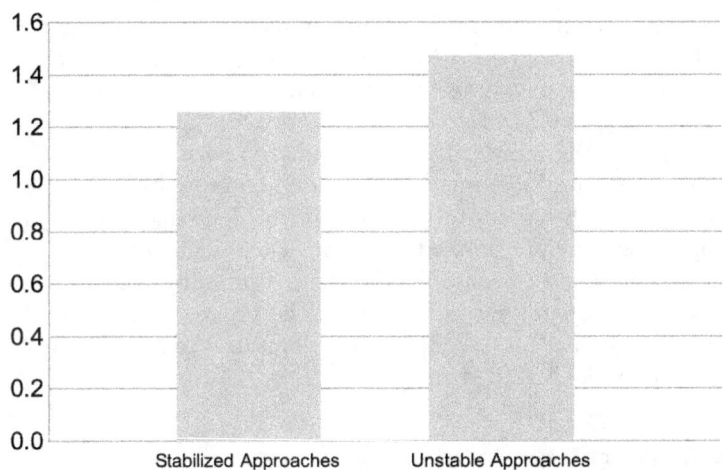

Figure 2.10.5 Events per flight (not related to approach and landing).

The data didn't give us answers necessarily about how to train, but more about where to train and the study itself highlighted the sorts of exposure that may be most useful in preparing pilots for the line, while helping them to further develop their capabilities throughout their careers.

When we began the study, there was a huge amount of available data and so it made a great deal of sense to access as much as we could about what

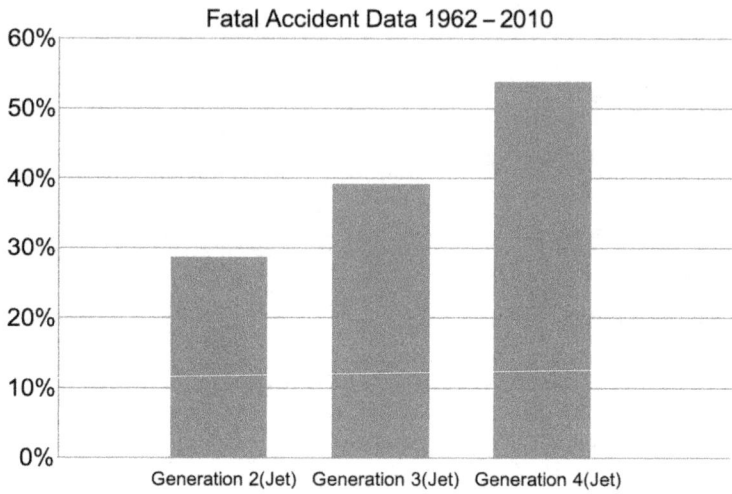

Figure 2.10.6 High training effect – Jet generations.

had already been done, adding it to our own research in an extensive meta-analysis. Our objective was to look as widely as possible capturing as many dimensions of the data as possible and then look for consistency across the data and convergence of the results. The greater number and diversity of sources consulted, the more balanced the outcome was.

The data study broke some new ground in terms of technique. This is particularly true with respect to the accident incident analysis. We tried to do something different. We looked at a huge number of accidents without dwelling on causation specifically, concentrating only on the presence of predetermined factors relevant to training. The process was rigorous, unbiased and gave us consistent results with logical variations across aircraft generations. (see IATA, 2014).

The LOSA story

One of the big questions in doing a very large study like the one we did is: "where do you start?" John considered that just about the most complete, detailed and relevant data that would also provide direction would come from that collected from Line Operations Safety Audits (LOSA). This was a program developed in the 1990s at the University of Texas under the supervision of Professor Robert (Bob) L. Helmrich, with Dr James Klinect and his team, now an independent collaborative; the LOSA Collaborative.

With the help of IATA, we asked the LOSA Collaborative to research the archive, which comprised detailed observations of around 10,000 flights.

What we wanted were the key areas in the archive that had a strong degree of training criticality. Training Criticality includes a measure of risk, while considering simulator training as a mitigator; in short, training criticality simply means the need for training.

First a brief overview of what LOSA is: A systematic process of peer to peer observations of normal operations, which result in a collection of narratives and Threat and Error Management data. It is anonymous and non-punitive by taking a "fly on the wall" look at normal operations. There are 10 characteristics of the process, all of which have to be present for it to an actual LOSA (Figure 2.10.7).

Since the original report that was done for the EBT data analysis, we have engaged much more closely with the LOSA Collaborative and the LOSA Archive (de-identified results of all LOSA's performed with airlines worldwide) (Figure 2.10.8).

The Collaborative produced two reports for us, which are published in the Data Report for EBT. The first is entitled LOSA Archive Report: 10 Target Areas for Evidence Based Training. The 10 areas included areas deemed by LOSA and the EBT data team to be rich in observational data that relate well to training as a risk mitigator. After the first report was well underway, LOSA suggested an obvious additional report that they had already done in house, which we all felt was extremely relevant: An Error Detection LOSA Archive Report providing insight into error types and levels of detection in the flight deck, intentional noncompliance and Threat and Error management countermeasures.

Both reports were very rich sources of data. This initial work in the data study gave us a clear sense about how and where we wanted to go and the results we obtained from LOSA gave us tremendous insight and context, and even at that early time we realized that so much more could be done with this particular data source.

At the time of the original study, there were details of around 10,000 flight observations in the archive. This number has now grown to in excess of 27,000. At the time of the first study, observers were trained to use the University of Texas Behavioral Markers. Since 2017, the Collaborative is using what is close to an industry standard system of competencies and performance indicators (Figure 2.10.3), and LOSA observers are trained in their use in an updated process. In short they are taught to consider whether a competency or competencies were observed in the management of a threat or error, specifically which competencies and associated performance indicators, and whether the observed performance helped or hindered the management of the threat or error; in other words how did the competencies underlie the processes for managing threats and errors. By doing this we are beginning to achieve the observation and measure of positive performance, which up until now has only been something many of us have wanted to do very much.

Jumpseat Observations
LOSA observations are limited to regularly scheduled non-training flights

Joint Management/Pilots' Association Sponsorship
The joint sponsorship ensures that change, as necessary, will be made as a result of LOSA data.

Voluntary Crew Participation
All LOSA observations are collected with voluntary crew participation. If the crew declines, the observer takes another flight with no questions asked.

De Identified, Confidential, and Non-Disciplinary Data Collection
LOSA observers do not record names, flight numbers, dates, or any other information that can identify a crew or individual. The purpose of LOSA is to collect safety data only.

Systematic Observation Tools
The LOSA observation form is normally predicated on the TEM framework. The observers need to describe the environmental conditions and events surrounding the pilots' behavior so that the crews' performance can be understood in full context.

Trained and Calibrated Observers
Observation teams will typically include line pilots, instructor pilots, safety pilots, management pilots, and representatives of the pilots' safety committee. Observers' training in the concepts and methodology of LOSA will ensure that the observations will be conducted in the most standardized manner

Trusted Data Repository
In order to maintain confidentiality, airlines should have a trusted data repository. The goal is that no individual observations will be misplaced or improperly disseminated through the airline.

Data Verification
Data-driven programs like LOSA require quality data management procedures and consistency checks. The end product is a database that is validated for consistency and accuracy before any statistical analysis is performed.

Targets for Enhancement
The final product of a LOSA is the data-derived targets for enhancement. It is then up to the airline to develop an action plan based on these targets.

Feedback Results to the Line Pilots
In order to ensure long-term success of LOSA, airlines should communicate the results back to the line pilots. Pilots need to see not only the results of the audit, but also management's plan for improvement.

Figure 2.10.7 LOSA – 10 characteristics.

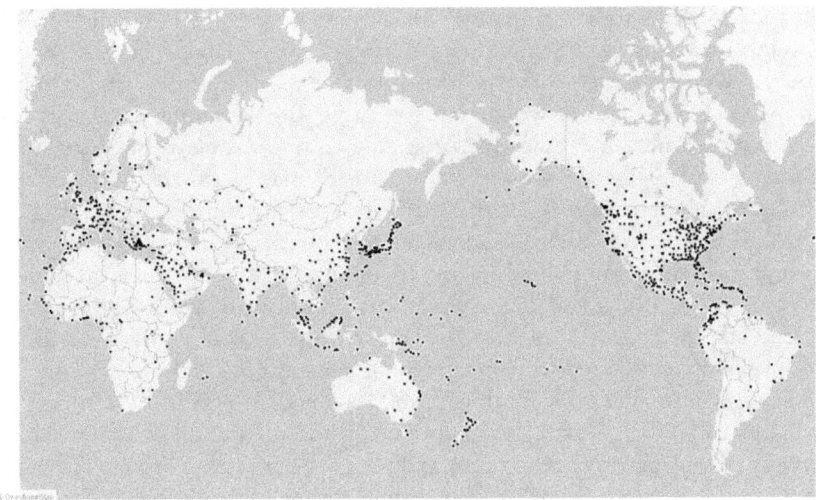

Figure 2.10.8 LOSA collaborative – destinations to January 2019.

Let's explore the background to this thinking. Historically safety efforts have been directed almost exclusively on the analysis of adverse events, or "what goes wrong". It remains important to understand and learn from adverse events, and this is a reason why we undertook and continue to update the accident and incident analysis to support EBT. But, if we only focus on what goes wrong, we are denying ourselves valuable lessons about how we actually operate, and why things go right.

People adapt their performance to manage variability, and maintain safe, effective operations. Without understanding how human performance contributes to maintaining safety and operational effectiveness, including in normal operations, it is not possible to know what these variations and adaptations are, and how people are making the system safe and effective.

During the original data analysis for EBT, we talked extensively about capturing positive performance, but it is only recently that we have begun to develop systematic methods for capturing this data.

The role data plays

Turning back to the analysis overall, it is important to know the limitations of the data and how to address them for the future and to really understand the importance of the role that the data plays.

Looking at the inherent limitations of the study brought us back to the greatest strength of the aviation system or the expertise of our practitioners and the capabilities that built the high degree of safety that exists in the aviation systems today. But now we have new tools and an open door to do the job in a much better manner and this occurred largely because of the data study. We attempted to tap our pilots' expertise using the cumbersome Intuitive Risk Matrix, which later became the Training Criticality Survey. We did not meet the objective originally to our standards but succeeded well enough to actually see the power of subject matter expert, pilot opinion and this gave us the resolve to harness this tool for the future.

John and I discussed the accident and incident analysis before we began and at this time John didn't want to do it; he was not convinced it would give us good results and there was a huge amount of work involved. He was eventually persuaded, and we set about looking at reported accidents and serious incidents across the spectrum of Generations 2,3,4 (Jet) and 2 and 3 (Turboprop) to the tune of almost 3000 events.

The analysis was a three-way approach, gathering published reports and asking type qualified pilots to read them and score the presence or absence of defined factors. There was no second guessing the report, just simple reading and scoring. The task was repeated by a second independent type-qualified pilot, and results were reconciled by John and his colleagues. The results were obviously type and therefore aircraft generation specific, and startling differences arose between older jet generation 2 aircraft and generation 3 and 4. There were also significant differences between the jets and turboprops. Once the data had been captured there was an elaborate second phase to the analysis, undertaken by John and an Airbus colleague, Dr Jari Nisula. In this phase, dimensions of risk and training criticality were examined and ranked, relative to the capabilities in today's flight simulators.

By this point we were starting to look at how the data could be used to drive the training program. Our original objective had been for the experts to develop a hypothesis through the Training Criticality study, and as mentioned, we did not meet that objective so instead we reversed the process and turned to the data itself for direction. We never completely abandoned our original objective based on our experts in the "Intuitive Risk Matrix" or the Training Criticality Survey, for in the end, we correlated its results with the accident incident analysis and were happy to see that they correlated nicely, which renewed our enthusiasm to make the process more user-friendly and do it better this next time around.

The recurrent training program

Now armed with the conclusions of the Data Study and without going into elaborate detail the expert training group was challenged to take results and develop a matrix over three years with prioritized training topics according to aircraft generations. We came up with three levels of priority; A – topics driven from the most significant data and highest training criticality, to be included every time a pilot undertakes recurrent training. B – exposure typically once a year from topics derived with a lessor training criticality, and C – exposure every three years to topics which also included those which were not necessarily driven by data but it was strongly felt by the expert working group that they should be maintained, e.g. TCAS maneuvers.

Within this structure, the old mandatory maneuver items of the traditional check were retained but in a new and shortened phase, which we called Maneuvers Training; the idea being to give pilots the opportunity to practice familiar checking items, but under training rather than as part of a check. The maneuvers were to be conducted in a much more intensive and focused manner utilizing repositioning of the simulator to avoid wasted time between each maneuver. This freed up 80 percent of a typical 8-hour recurrent training module over two days, to build relevant and realistic line-oriented training based on the data.

A look back: what we have learned

We were involved in the development of data analyses to support a new idea in training which captured the imagination of most all the people in the large working group. There are 2,000 pages of documents to support this at a regulatory level but reading the documents does not give a clear sense of the possibilities, possibilities we only began to realize when we actually began working with airlines in many continents of the world.

Expert pilots understand what makes an effective practitioner in the flight deck. Taking their consolidated opinions over several decades and continuing to listen to them has given us the competencies, and moreover they have given us language which is meaningful to pilots and instructors. We have developed a clear understanding of how to assess performance using these competencies, in a fair and objective way. It is all about a quality driven process of Observation, Recording, Classifying and Evaluating the competencies.

In 2011, my colleague at Airbus Captain Christian Norden, led a working group and consulted industry for the development of a competency-based grading system. The system has been designed to help support natural behavior in the training role and we developed it further to support EBT based on our in-service experience.

First of all, we defined to instructor the tasks in making an assessment (see Figure 2.10.9):

- **Observe** everything the crew do, including SOP actions, verbal and non-verbal communication, use of ops manual information, checklists, management Threats and Errors.
- **Record** anything of interest, i.e., when the crew do things well or things do go as planned.
- **Classify** what you have recorded against competencies, using performance indicators as a guide.

- **Evaluate** the overall performance in each competency using what we called the VENN methodology:

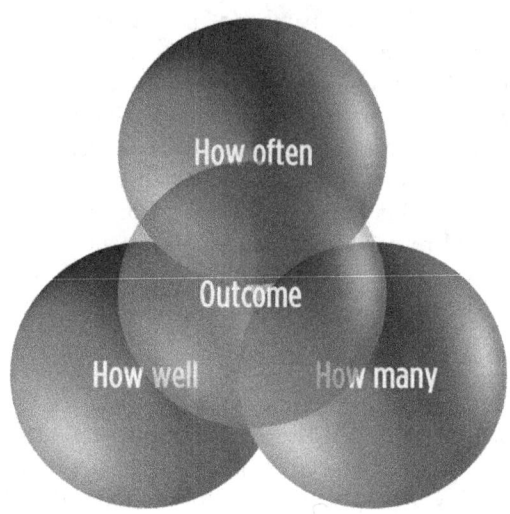

Figure 2.10.9 VENN system for pilot assessment.

HOW WELL (the pilot did not communicate effectively…)
HOW OFTEN (by rarely demonstrating…)
HOW MANY (of the performance indicators when required…)
OUTCOME (that resulted in an unsafe situation…)

Grades are assigned based on word pictures and associated observations of fact. This is crucially important to maintaining objectivity and fairness.

When it comes to competencies it is critical that we make assessments. We did not want a system of event-based training, because when assessing performance, we must be looking for underlying competencies in order to drive improvements. To do this we need to look at a bigger picture and focus on the process that the pilot and crews use to manage the events, rather than just their outcomes. To do this, we need quality data based on strong inter-rater reliability to build confidence in the observation system.

Instructors are taught to look for root causes of performance that merits enhancement, but this only speaks to low performance. EBT is more than simply the old way of eliminating poor performance. EBT at its best brings the potential to help even the most capable of pilots identify areas where they can improve. So rather than just look at the term root cause case of low performance, we identify the area, which will most help each individual pilot improve his or her performance.

This is a very different approach from that taken in programs like the Advanced Qualification Program, based on Instructional Systems Design and necessarily having a task and outcome basis, which does have some merit for initial training. We made a very conscious decision in EBT, that the first iteration of the program would be recurrent training of pilots already qualified and in operations. Our focus is to provide exposure under realistic line-oriented conditions, to the risks we see through data which could best be mitigated in simulator training. In doing this we need to focus the instructor and on the process the pilots employ to manage Threat Errors and Undesired States, rather than simply the outcomes of training events. *The reason for this is simple; build effective processes by exposing crews to challenging and variable but always realistic situations, and they will develop competencies and stretch their capability to manage almost any given situation including the unforeseen.* When threats are well managed and decisions and plans are well constructed with all possible contingencies considered, the execution of tasks included in executing an approach, diverting the aircraft etc. will be invariably done well, because the crew will understand their roles and the plans. The Pilot Flying (PF) will be backed up with very active monitoring of the flight path by a Pilot Monitoring (PM)

In coaching many instructors in their roles in EBT, we have seen experienced pilots, usually high performers in a training system with which they are familiar, experience unexpected conditions resulting in surprising and an exceptionally degraded performance. Taking opportunities in a non-jeopardy situation, we have seen very high performing pilots learning a great deal through this type of exposure.

The other aspect of the instructor task is something we did understand when writing the regulatory documents for EBT, but it is only through the practice of implementation that the power of it has been apparent, and that is the technique of Facilitation.

To support this, we believe the EBT concept must align with adult learning principles.

- **Concrete Experience** – (a new experience or situation is encountered, or a reinterpretation of existing experience).
- **Reflective Observation** of the New Experience – (of particular importance are any inconsistencies between experience and understanding).
- **Abstract Conceptualization** (reflection gives rise to a new idea, or a modification of an existing abstract concept the person has learned from their experience).
- **Active Experimentation** (the learner applies their idea(s) to the world around them to see what happens). (Kolb, 1984)

Overall, we have known where the focus of a new training program needed to be, and that is changing the mindset of the instructor population and getting them to understand the power of a safe learning environment is paramount. We have seen the greatest success in airlines that have understood the need to train the trainers and concentrate their efforts in this. Facilitation and coaching skills added to fair and objective assessments are critical to the credibility of the system. This simply requires discipline and rigor and regular training until results are consistently accurate.

When we look at implementation of the program, now with almost 40 states and over 50 airlines worldwide, it is hard to say where EBT has occasionally taken a wrong turn. We simply don't have the first-hand knowledge. What we can say is a lack of investment in time training instructors and assumptions that nothing much needs to be done would be greatest negative indicators, in addition to using the label of EBT to reduce training volume without consideration. There are those who claim EBT, because they have evidence and use it to inform training, but it is clearly not EBT because it lacks the true competency basis and structured focus based on first look through to tailored learning. There are those airlines who take what they want from EBT, but this is not EBT either. It can only be developed and delivered through the structured approach, itself very flexible to accommodate airline needs.

The true possibility of EBT is that in providing a relevant and useful experience to pilots, EBT enables the possibility of self-directed learning. This can only happen when the reflective process is supported by instructors who are able to create a learner-centered environment, hence the use of facilitation techniques to begin the journey of reflection and create what we call a safe space for learning. This is a place which many pilots will not recognize, for here they are treated as adult professionals who are motivated to improve their performance and supported by instructors in a system which does not judge them or slap their wrists for errors without providing the means for improvement. A facilitated debrief is a debrief where the instructor actively engages to support learning, by helping trainees to identify good performance, as well as areas which may merit improvement. The take-away for pilots is not in the form of everything that they have done wrong, but in areas for reflection aligned to competencies which provoke thought, conceptualization and experimentation.

We have been pleased to see some great indicators from a number of airlines we have worked with. Often, we ask airlines to survey their pilots to see how EBT is being received during the first semester. We recently received examples from Aer Lingus based in Dublin, Ireland. The survey is an indication about how the program is being received and the results are very encouraging. Figures 2.10.10–12 are three simple graphics which tell an important story.

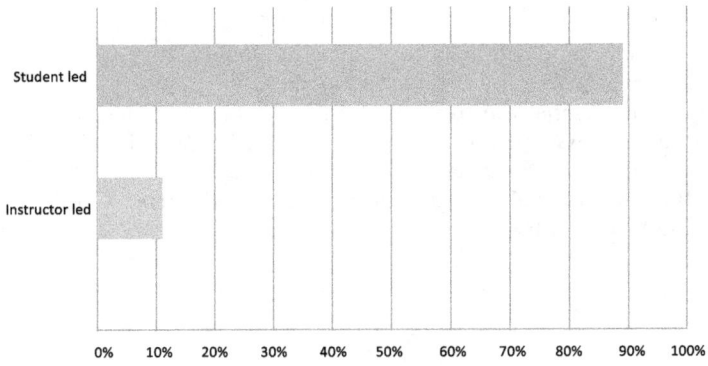

Figure 2.10.10 Was the debrief led by you or was it like a traditional debrief?

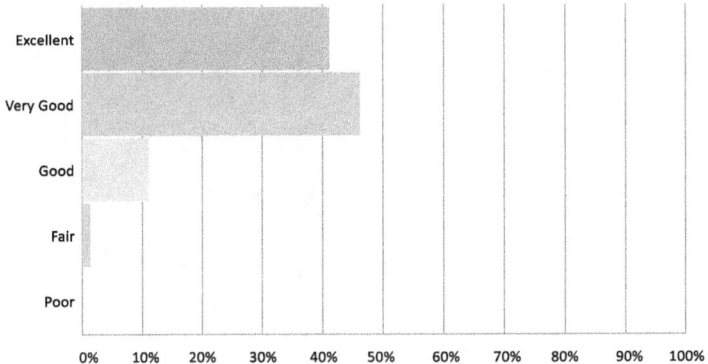

Figure 2.10.11 Overall, how would you rate the quality of the EBT sessions?

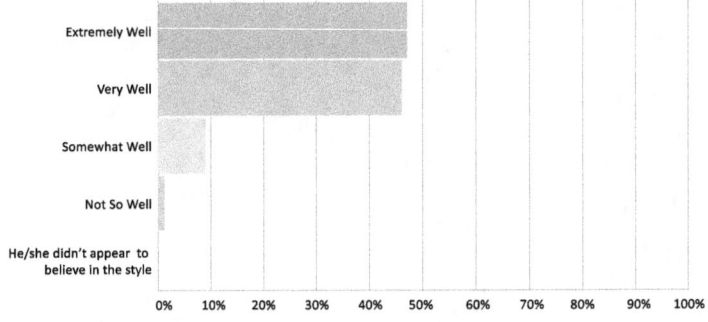

Figure 2.10.12 How well do you think your instructor embraced the facilitative style of instruction?

References

The Boeing Company (2019). Pilot & Technician Outlook 2019–2038. www.boeing.com/commercial/market/pilot-technician-outlook/

International Air Transport Association (IATA) (2014). Data Report for Evidence Based Training. www.iata.org/whatwedo/ops-infra/training-licensing/Documents/data-report-for-evidence-basted-training-ed%20one.pdf

Kolb, D. (1984). *Experiential learning*, Englewood Cliffs, NJ: Prentice-Hall.

Varney, M. (2007). Risk Based Training. Unpublished MS.

3 Retaining the next generation of aviation professionals

Section introduction

Suzanne K. Kearns

The retention of aviation professionals occurs throughout the entire pipeline of NGAP development. Consider a hypothetical journey of a young adult: he or she may be exposed to an aviation outreach activity (such as a visit to an aviation museum that sparks their curiosity about aviation). Perhaps they then explore other resources – books, webinars, air shows, or online forums. Most likely the young person will experience several "touch points" where they have been exposed to aviation outreach promoting various careers.

The culmination of this is when the young adult chooses to pursue vocational education (whether in a college, university, or trade school). Within a training program, they will have a variety of educational opportunities to grow and develop towards becoming a professional. Once their education has been completed, they begin looking for employment.

In the years past, many people at this point would choose to leave aviation to join a field with better entry-level working conditions. For example, in Canada it is common for entire classes of aviation maintenance technicians to be hired into the automobile sector where their skills are highly-transferable and valued. When this occurs, the investment of time and resources by the aviation sector in the outreach to and education of that individual are lost.

Therefore, retention must be considered at every link within this chain – during outreach programs, within educational offerings, and in developing working conditions and compensation packages within aviation organizations.

To promote retention, we must begin to view the entire air transport sector as a whole. The sector includes many professional groups – maintenance, airport operations, air traffic control, flight- and cabin-crew, regulators, and management among many others. If a passionate young adult is not successful in their first career choice (for example, as an air traffic controller) we should encourage them to consider a parallel career that is still within aviation (such as within airport operations) so that as a whole they are retained within the air transport sector.

Likewise, additional work in ensuring the international transferability of aviation credentials is required. Today, it is often challenging for experienced professionals who relocate to a new country to have their credentials recognized. To meet future demands for NGAP, we need to collaborate to support international mobility of credentials so parts of the world with greater training capacities can support regions with greater personnel needs.

Section 3 includes a variety of submissions that explore key aspects of the retention theme, including within educational programs, professional development/education, the regulatory impacts, and a discussion of how to maintain safety in a shortage situation:

3.1 **Chapter** – Collegiate flight programs: How student experiences impact student retention and successful completions *by Andrew Leonard and Elizabeth Bjerke*

   The chapter explores the Astin Input-Environment-Outcome model as a method to understand the various factors that impact aviation student retention and successful completion of academic programs.

3.2 **Chapter** – Executive education in aviation: Addressing the managerial aspects of the fastest growing industry *by Nadine Itani*

   This chapter explores the critical role of aviation executive education. It discusses the impact of the transforming training needs, changing learning preferences, the benefits of training technology, and value co-creation models.

3.3 **Chapter** – Entrepreneurial mindset development: A cog in the wheel of talent management in the aviation sector *by Raihan Taqui Syed, Manish Yadav, and Hesham Magd*

   This work explores the challenges of talent management and introduces entrepreneurial mindset development as a competency for aviation professionals. This work connects aspects of talent management within the management side of the aviation industry.

3.4 **Chapter** – The regulation of the airline industry: Why it matters to you *by P. Paul Fitzgerald*

   Regulation is a central theme throughout the global air transport sector, impacting operations, safety, security, and many other factors. This chapter explores the complex and fascinating world of aviation regulations and their role in shaping the aviation industry.

3.5 **Professional Reflection** – Managing the paradox: Asking for more qualified people in a shortage situation *by José Sánchez-Alarcos Ballesteros*

   As modern-day aviation is facing global shortages of professionals, the most common solution to increase ranks is decreasing qualifications. This is a dangerous choice that sacrifices safety. This chapter discusses the paradox of requiring more people in a shortage situation, and the maintenance of safety standards in the process. Automation, new design practices, and new recruitment practices are discussed.

3.1 Chapter – Collegiate flight programs

How student experiences impact student retention and successful completions

Andrew Leonard and Elizabeth Bjerke

Introduction

As the demand for air travel increases, so does the need for qualified pilots. According to The Boeing Company (2018), the commercial aviation industry will need 635,000 new airline pilots worldwide between 2018 and 2037, leaving collegiate flight programs scrambling to find ways to improve the success rate of students enrolled in their programs in order to increase the number of qualified pilots to meet this demand. Several studies have identified a concern regarding student retention within the first academic year; and have attempted to address the issues in early stages (Bjerke & Healy, 2010; Dillingham, 2014; Mekhail et al., 2010; Niemczyk & Ulrich, 2009). However, there continues to be a need to identify variables that may positively or negatively impact a student with regard to degree completion.

Collegiate aviation within the United States

Currently, there are more than 200 two- and four-year colleges offering non-engineering aviation degrees (University Aviation Association, 2017). These institutions offer a wide array of programs that include commercial flight, air traffic control, aviation management, unmanned aircraft systems and maintenance. These programs are also housed within varying colleges and departments at each institution. While some larger programs do fall within their own department or college, it is more common to see them housed within engineering, education, technology or business (Bjerke, 2009). Another major variability is the size of aviation programs. According to the University Aviation Association (2017), student numbers can be as high as 1,500 at some of the largest aviation institutions and as low as 50 in others. This variability among aviation education programs has left a gap regarding studies involving retention and graduation predictors of collegiate aviation students.

While variability does exist among these programs, there is commonality among certain areas of study regardless of institution. Over the last several years, there has been an increase in accredited aviation programs available to students in the United States and across the globe. Currently, there are 93 accredited aviation programs at 38 colleges and universities, with an additional 18 programs at six institutions waiting for final approval by the US-based Aviation Accreditation Board International (AABI, 2019). While receiving accreditation does not mean that each institution is identical, it does increase the commonality as they are required to follow the same guidelines and meet the same criteria that is then validated by an external review team.

Additionally, if we look specifically at flight (pilot-training) majors where students are receiving federal certificates and ratings, there are numerous Federal Aviation Administration (FAA) requirements that must be part of each institutions' program and achieved by each student in order to receive specific certificates and ratings. These requirements include the number of flight hours required, standardized written tests, and standardized practical tests, all of which must be completed by students regardless of the institutions they are attending (FAA, 2017). These FAA standards, along with the increasing number of aviation programs seeking accreditation, provide academic similarities among flight programs regardless of the number of students enrolled or the college in which the flight program is housed.

Higher education research on student success

Given that more students depart from their initial institution of higher education than graduate (Tinto, 1993), the study of student persistence has been popular in higher education literature for over a half of century (Astin, 1984; Metz, 2004–2005; Pantages & Creedon, 1978). Despite the vast amount of research and attention placed on the issue of student persistence, still more than a quarter of the students who enter four-year institutions leave after their first year. In addition, it is common to see around half of the flight students quit training before completion, usually because of financial difficulties (Kearns, 2018). Due to the fact that the aviation industry is facing a critical pilot shortage, it is imperative that institutions training the next generation of aviation professionals are well versed in ensuring success of its students. One such model to apply to collegiate aviation programs is the Input-Environment-Outcome (I-E-O model) developed by Alexander Astin (1993).

Over the last four decades, many student retention studies have been conducted and theories developed which strive to conceptualize the framework of retention and success in higher education. During this time many theoretical models developed such as Tinto's Institutional Departure Model, Bean's Student Attrition Model, the Student–Faculty Informal Contact Model by Pascarella, Astin's Student Involvement Model, the Non-Traditional Student Attrition

Model by Bean and Metzner, and the Student Retention Integrated Model by Cabrera, Nora, and Castaneda (Aljohani, 2016). While some theories focus on the individual student's personal attributes and shortcomings, Astin's theory recognizes the importance the environment plays along with individual preferences.

Astin (1984) started with his theory of Student Involvement that describes how desirable outcomes for institutions of higher education are viewed in relation to how students develop due to being involved in multiple aspects of the college environment. Astin defined engagement as "the amount of physical and psychological energy that the student devotes to the academic experience" (Astin, 1984, p. 297). While we often think of academic experience as things that occur in the classroom, Astin's theory encompasses all parts of the college experience. It also indicates that when looking at engagement both the amount of energy, and the quality of energy a student is putting in must be considered (Astin, 1984). A student could put in a significant amount of energy, but the outcome could be different depending on the quality of energy the student put forth.

Astin developed five basic assumptions about involvement. First, he argued that involvement requires an investment of psychosocial and physical energy. Second, involvement is continuous and the amount of energy invested varies from student to student. Third, aspects of involvement may be qualitative and quantitative. Next, what students gain from being involved (or their development) is directly proportional to the extent to which they were involved (in both aspects of quality and quantity). Last, academic performance is correlated with student involvement (Astin, 1984). This theory has many applications in the world of higher education and is one of the strongest pieces of evidence for co-curricular student involvement.

Furthering his theory, the I-E-O model was developed by Astin (1993) as a framework for research in higher education. The premise of this model is that educational assessments are not complete unless the evaluation includes information on student inputs, the educational environment and student outcomes (Astin, 1993). The main concepts of the theory are made up of three elements. The first is a student's "inputs" such as their demographics, socioeconomic status, previous education, and any other experiences leading up to their enrolment in a college or university. The second is the student's "environment", which involves any and all experiences a student has while enrolled at an institution. The last concept is "outcomes", which looks at a student's characteristics, knowledge, attitudes, beliefs, and values that exist after a student has graduated a college or university (Astin, 1993). One of the primary purposes of the model is to control for input differences, resulting in a more accurate estimate of how environmental variables affect student outcomes. The use of the model forces researchers to address not only the outcomes but also the inputs and environmental variables.

I-E-O model in collegiate aviation

A study was done to better understand and apply the I-E-O model as it specifically relates to collegiate aviation education (Leonard, 2018). Multiple variables were chosen based on previous research applying the I-E-O model in higher education. A summary of the findings is included below, along with a more in-depth application for collegiate aviation programs to utilize in the education of the next generation of aviation professionals.

When looking at input variables, or those variables students brought with them to college, it was found that high school grade point average, standardized entrance exam scores like composite ACT, family gross income, and father's education level had a significant impact. These findings would suggest that admissions policies for collegiate flight programs should favor high school grade point average and cumulative ACT score because they both were significant indicators of successful degree attainment and had a large effect on cumulative GPA at graduation. However, high school grade point average had the highest effect among all of the input variables. These findings are in line with previous research that suggested high school grade point average is a strong indicator of a student's overall intelligence and motivation.

Father's education level and family gross income were also found to have a significant relationship with degree completion, indicating as expected that those students whose fathers have a higher education and those students who come from a family with a higher gross income are more likely to be successful. While this variable may not necessarily be useful as part of an admissions policy, it could be useful in determining which students may benefit from additional support and scholarships once they have entered a collegiate aviation program.

When looking at the impact of environmental variables, or variables a student experiences once they are in college, the study found results in two differing categories which were identified as academic intensity and socialization of the discipline. In the area of academic intensity it was found that the number of credits a student enrolled in had a significant relationship to student success. This follows previous research that has shown that students who consistently take higher numbers of credits are more likely to graduate on time than those students who take on average fewer credits each year. Additionally, it was found that students who took credits during the summer semesters, specifically during their second and third years, were more likely to graduate in four years compared to students who took a lower number of credits or no credits during the summer semesters. While most institutions do offer summer courses, traditional flight programs in the United States are designed and advertised as being achievable in eight semesters over four years. Furthermore, when looking specifically at flight training, it was also found that students who complete their commercial flight training in a shorter amount of time with fewer flight hours are more likely to be successful with degree completion.

Other environmental variables, associated with the socialization of the discipline, found to have a significant impact on success of degree completion were whether a student was working on campus, working in an aviation-related position and working as a flight instructor. These results follow past research which indicates that students who work on campus and work in jobs that are connected to their degree of study are more likely to graduate than those students who work off campus or in positions not related to their areas of study (Astin, 1975). Furthermore, these findings are supported by the significant relationship between success of degree attainment and whether a student works as a CFI while enrolled as a student.

It was also found that both the number of days and the number of flight hours required to complete commercial training had a significant negative relationship with a student's success of graduating in four years. This would indicate that students are more likely to be successful graduating if they can complete their commercial flight training in the shortest number of days and flight hours possible.

Using the I-E-O model to improve practice

Using the I-E-O model, Astin (1991) believed that accurate assessment required correctly parsing students' inputs and the educational environments they experienced. The results of this study appear to support Astin's theory and suggest that collegiate aviation is following similar trends. Both a student's input variables and environmental variables can influence a student's success with regard to degree attainment. The end goal is to understand how to apply this model in order to improve the success of aspiring aviation students.

Input factors for consideration

In order to educate the next generation of aviation professionals for careers in the aerospace industry, we must first attract them into the exciting field of study. This needs to occur during the formative years of their lives. Many aviation organizations around the world have started initiatives to expose young people to aviation at an early age. These programs have grown in size and scope over the last few years as the pilot shortage has become more acute. It is vitally important for colleges and universities to partner with the aviation organizations conducting the outreach events in order to expose the children to the collegiate aviation path towards being an aviation professional.

Currently, although not always the case, collegiate flight programs are receiving high numbers of applications from individuals interested in pursuing a flight degree. While this would appear to help with the current pilot shortage, institutions do not have the necessary resources to be able to train all of the incoming students. It is necessary that collegiate flight programs utilize variables in the recruitment and admissions process that will help them to select students who are likely to succeed (Leonard, 2018). Research suggests that high school grade point average should be one of the primary variables utilized in the admissions process, with ACT scores being used as a supplement.

Collegiate flight programs need to be mindful of the negative impact the cost of flight training can have on student success. Research shows that the lack of funding is one of the main reasons students choose to stop training, limiting many high achieving students from being able to graduate from flight programs. Not only should universities be mindful of this during the decision making process with regards to tuition and flight costs, but financial help should be provided to students who come from families with a lower gross income to ensure the necessary funding is available to the students in a timely fashion. Furthermore, collegiate flight programs should increase the amount of funding available to students through scholarships and grants to insure that this variable doesn't limit high potential students from being able to complete their degree.

Environmental factors for consideration

Once enrolled in a collegiate aviation program, there are a number of environmental factors that come into play that can either enhance or hinder a student's experience and thus their likelihood of success in the program. These environmental factors are broken down into two areas: academic intensity and socialization of the discipline. Academic intensity focuses on the educational constructs related to completing a degree, whereas the socialization in the discipline relates to how an individual acclimates into their chosen field of study. Both factors are equally important in considering the successful completion of an academic degree, but can be discussed individually for impact.

Academic intensity

There are many ways in which a collegiate aviation program can impact the academic intensity in which its students pursue and succeed in their education and training. However, first and foremost, there needs to be effective advising process in place so that the student is well-informed and has an individual plan in place for a successful completion of their degree program.

Collegiate aviation programs need to encourage students to consistently take 30 credits or more each year, with a higher number of credits during a student's second and third year. This equates to approximately 10 courses each meeting 3 hours per week for 12 to 15 weeks. Leonard, 2018 indicates that taking a higher number of credits during the middle of a student's educational experience as compared to either end may result in a higher cumulative GPA. Furthermore, while some research has shown that taking a higher number of credits during a student's first year can increase the chances of degree completion, it has also been found that taking too many credits during the first year can have a negative effect on degree completion. When looking at the results of past research, it appears that four-year collegiate flight programs should advise students to take between 15 and 18 course hours per week during year one and higher credit loads during year two and year three. If a student needs to have a semester with a below average number of credits, it appears year four would be the best time for that to occur.

Collegiate flight programs need to ensure that students can complete their flight training in the shortest number of flight hours and days possible (Leonard, 2018). This not only cuts down on time to graduate, but also saves a student a considerable amount of money. Research has found that shorter time frames result in greater success of graduation. To do this, programs need to offer flight courses on a regular bases, and increase availability for training during the summer months. Furthermore, programs need to encourage all students to participate in these summer courses, and advise them of the benefits. While all students could benefit from maintaining increased academic intensity, students with lower input variables such as high school grade point average may benefit the most, and therefore institutions should consider giving them priority.

Collegiate flight programs should offer as many courses as possible during the summer semester and encourage students to participate in these classes. At many institutions, the summer semesters consistently see the lowest number of enrollments. By allowing students to train and take classes year round, not only do they stay proficient in their flight skills, but they can significantly decrease the amount of time to degree completion. If institutions can offer a larger number of courses during the summer terms, and encourage students to participate in these courses, graduation rates for those institutions are likely to increase. Furthermore, by increasing enrollment in the summer terms, additional space will become available in both the fall and spring semesters.

Socialization in discipline

Equally as important as academic intensity, is the concept of being socialized in the discipline of study, in this case aviation. Many students chose to pursue a degree in aviation without having a lot of background knowledge or exposure to the discipline. To ensure success and motivation, it is important to acquaint students early on in this exciting field of study so that they feel part of the aviation community. Some of this socialization happens almost immediately when they start their studies, other aspects need to be coordinated and encouraged.

Due to the nature of aviation education and training, students will most often begin their flight training within the first year of study. The first step in becoming a professional pilot would be to acquire the private pilot certificate. This is the most intense and meaningful way in which to become socialized in the discipline, as one is joining the ranks of being a certified pilot. The fact that this training occurs early in their collegiate career, it must be noted that this is often one of the most difficult courses for an aspiring aviator. Universities need to have defined mechanisms in place to track student progress in this challenging course in order to provide additional resources to help students succeed who may be struggling.

Another means of socializing in the discipline comes through involvement with aviation student organizations. Universities need to encourage and support the participation in aviation organizations. Many of the large aviation organizations support university student chapters. Involvement in these groups corresponds to numerous opportunities and ways in which students can accelerate their sense of belonging in the aviation community.

There also needs to be a concentrated effort in establishing and maintaining strong aviation industry connections. Universities need to partner with aviation industry leaders in order to provide opportunities for students to also engage with aviation professionals. These partnerships may take the form of career pathway programs for students, speaking engagements on campus and offering mentoring opportunities. The most impactful way to educate the next generation of aviation professionals is to connect them in a meaningful way with our current aviation professionals.

Leonard (2018) has indicated that students who worked on campus and in aviation related jobs were more successful with graduation than those who worked off campus or in non-aviation jobs. These findings suggest that programs need to provide opportunities for students to be active in their disciplines. One way this can be achieved is by offering more employment opportunities for students within the program. This can be particularly important to students who come from families with a lower gross income who may need to work in order to remain in school. Along with offering more aviation related jobs, flight programs should specifically advise students to work as a flight instructor while they are enrolled as a student. This will increase students' success with graduation and also help programs fill the need for flight instructors.

Conclusion

There is a direct influence on a student's success of graduation in a collegiate aviation program from both the input variables a student arrives at college with as well as the environmental factors the student experiences once enrolled. Collegiate aviation programs are currently facing high enrollment, limited resources, and a demand from industry to train pilots as quickly and efficiently as possible (UAA, 2017). Similar to previous research looking at traditional education programs, this chapter shows that Astin's model can be utilized to improve student success within collegiate flight programs and help these programs overcome current challenges.

As previously mentioned, collegiate flight programs are receiving high numbers of applications from individuals interested in pursuing a flight degree. While this would appear to help with the current pilot shortage, institutions do not have the necessary resources to be able to train all of the incoming students. As discussed earlier, it is necessary that collegiate flight programs identify variables that will help them to select students who are likely to succeed. The results of this study indicated that high school grade point average should be one of the primary variables utilized in the admissions process. Furthermore, ACT scores could be used in conjunction with high school grade point average, but is less reliable on its own.

The other input variable programs will want to consider is family gross income. While this variable was found to influence success of graduation, it should not be used as a variable to determine admittance to a program. However, recognizing the high cost of aviation training, help should be provided to students who come from families with a lower gross income to ensure the necessary funding is available to the students in a timely fashion. Furthermore, collegiate flight programs should increase the amount of funding available to students through scholarships and grants to insure that this variable doesn't limit high potential students from being able to complete their degree. Once a student has been selected for training and enrolled in a flight program, institutions need to ensure that students maintain a high level of academic intensity. One of the primary ways this can occur is through increased credit offerings. Students who on average take a higher number of credits each semester are more likely to be successful with degree attainment. While this increase in credit offering can be beneficial in all semesters, one area that institutions should focus is summer. Increasing the number of credits available in the summer semesters would not only benefit students in their training, but it would also help programs by increasing course availability during the fall and spring terms.

Collegiate flight programs also need to ensure that students can complete their flight training in the shortest number of flight hours and days possible. Shorter time frames result in greater success of graduation. To do this, programs need to offer flight courses on a regular bases, and increase availability for training during the summer months. Furthermore, programs need to encourage all students to participate in these summer courses, and advise them of the benefits.

While all students could benefit from maintaining increased academic intensity, students with lower input variables such as high school grade point average may benefit the most, and therefore institutions should consider giving them priority.

The other area of focus for collegiate flight programs is a student's socialization in aviation. This study indicated that students who worked on campus and in aviation related jobs were more successful with graduation than those who worked off campus or in non-aviation jobs. These findings suggest that programs need to provide opportunities for students to be active in their disciplines. One way this can be achieved is by offering more employment opportunities for students within the program. This can be particularly important to students who come from families with a lower gross income who may need to work in order to remain in school. Along with offering more aviation related jobs, flight programs should specifically advise students to work as a flight instructor while they are enrolled as a students. This will increase student's success with graduation and also help programs fill the need for flight instructors.

While much of the research and discussion in this chapter has focused on collegiate institutions in the United States, it is important to recognize the international impact this pilot shortage will have. Flight schools and training facilities around the world are faced with the important tasks of training pilots in order meet this global demand.

Collegiate flight programs in the United States share some similarities with international programs, but also have many differences. Things such as semester break down, course load requirements, student age all can be different. Furthermore, different cultures all have their own traditions, history, and ideals which create students with a wide variety of experiences. Because of this, we cannot expect that the findings in this research will always relate to every institution around the world. However, there are some key items that must be considered in order to increase the likelihood of a student's success.

First, a student's previous experiences matter. While students can have a wide range of experiences and background, making sure to consider these past experiences versus ignoring them will result in a better outcome. Second, academic intensity increases the likelihood of success. While intuitions can vary in their structure and design, increasing academic intensity can yield better results. Finally, the more time a student spends gaining experiences which relate to flight training, the more likely they are to be successful. While the specific approach to these three areas may look different depending on where in the world it is located, the general ideals are the same. If considered, these ideals should increase the efficiency and success of an institution's flight training program.

As the industry grapples with continued shortages of aviation professionals, it is imperative that universities and colleges with aviation programs look for effective and innovative ways to ensure success of their students. This begins with recruiting quality students in high school, supporting their education with scholarships and providing meaningful experiences for them within the collegiate aviation programs themselves.

References

Aljohani, O. (2016). Acomprehensive review of the major studies and theoretical models of student retention in higher education. *Higher Education Studies*. 6, 1–18. 10.5539/hes.v6n2p1.

Astin, A. W. (1991). The changing american college student: Implications for educational policy and practice. *Higher Education*, 22(2): 129–143.

Astin, A. W. (1975). *Preventing students from dropping out*. San Francisco: Jossey-Bass.

Astin, A. W. (1984). Student involvement: A developmental theory for higher education. *Journal of College Student Personnel*, 25(4), 297–308.

Astin, A. W. (1993). *What matters in college: Four critical years revisited*. San Francisco: Jossey-Bass.

Aviation Accreditation Board International. (2019). *AABI member institution accreditation status*. (AABI Form 217). Auburn, AL: AABI.

Bjerke, E. (2009). Utilizing pre-entry attributes and academic integration to predict student academic success and persistence to the second year for students in a collegiate aviation program. Available from Dissertations & Theses @ University of North Dakota. Retrieved from https://search.proquest.com/docview/304966253

Bjerke, E, & Healy, M. (2010). Predicting student persistence: Pre-entry attributes that lead to success in a collegiate flight program. *Collegiate Aviation Review*, 28(1), 25.

Dillingham, G. L. (2014). Aviation Workforce: Current and Future Availability of Airline Pilots. In: Office, U. S. G. A. (ed.). Washington, DC.

Federal Aviation Administration. (2017). *FAA Aerospace Forecast: Fiscal year 2017–2037* (forecast and performance analysis division APO-100). Washington, DC: U.S. Government Printing Office.

Kearns, S. (2018). Canada's aviation industry faces existential headwind – and that affects you. Retrieved from www.macleans.ca/opinion/canadas-aviation-industry-faces-existential-headwinds-and-that-affects-you/

Leonard, A. (2018). The impact of pre-entry attributes and college experiences on degree attainment for students in a collegiate flight program. Available from Dissertations & Theses @ University of North Dakota. Retrieved from https://search.proquest.com/openview/ae822d9a0b8d8549ce1934a9df885dc2/1?pq-origsite=gscholar&cbl=18750&diss=y

Mekhail, A., Niemczyk, M., Ulrich, J. W., & Karp, M. (2010). Using the table reading test as an indicator for success in pilot training. *Collegiate Aviation Review*, 28(1), 101–114.

Metz, G. (2004–2005). Challenges and changes to Tinto's persistence theory: A historical review. *Journal of College Student Retention*, 6(2), 191–207.

Niemczyk, M., & Ulrich, J. W. (2009). Workplace preferences of Millennials in the aviation industry. *International Journal of Applied Aviation Studies*, 9(2), 207–219.

Pantages, T., & Creedon, C. (1978). Studies of college attrition: 1950–1975. *Review of Educational Research*, 48(1), 49–101.

Boeing Global Services. (2018). *2018 pilot & technician outlook*. Chicago, IL.
Tinto, V. (1993). *Leaving college: Rethinking the causes and cures of student attrition*. Chicago, IL: University of Chicago Press.
University Aviation Association. (2017). *UAA institutional member list*. Memphis, TN: University Aviation Association.

3.2 Chapter – Executive education in aviation

Addressing the managerial aspects of the fastest growing industry

Nadine Itani

Introduction

The environment conditions surrounding the air transport industry are changing rapidly and unpredictably, making it far from being described a steady industry.

Global aviation agencies, states, industry enterprises and academia have been actively contributing to face the volatile, uncertain, complex and ambiguous surroundings that wrap the industry. One of the biggest concerns that have been haunting aviation organizations is the shortage of aviation professionals. The anticipated response to this ever-changing situation is through trying to predict the future by addressing early-warning pointers and identifying market and technology trends.

Over the past two decades, air transport has evolved massively as a technology dependent industry that has always relied on highly qualified professionals for its continuous development. With air traffic anticipated to double by 2035, a persistent challenge to aviation businesses is the talent gap. Related impediments are found in recruiting, engaging and retaining the talent needed to sustain the operations.

To address this talent gap, global aviation agencies are focusing on helping the industry attract and develop a massive workforce to support the growth in air traffic. The International Civil Aviation Organization (ICAO), the International Air Transport Association (IATA) and the Airport Council International (ACI) continue to engage with states, industry and academia on global training initiatives to cater for the growing demand for aviation professionals. The main objectives of such initiatives are to facilitate the effective implementation of training, to reduce costs, to upgrade quality, to increase efficiency and to generate synergies between un-harmonized world countries. However, many obstacles surface during the implementation phase of civil aviation training policies. Among the challenges are insufficient funds, shortage of experts and qualified instructors, poor specialized equipment, non-recognition of certificates between countries and a lack of harmonization of licensing requirements (Martinez and McEachern, 2018).

Adding more to the obstacles is the issue of the changing nature of training needs. Training needs are shifting and the inability to keep up with the pace of transformation will put specific skills and competence at risk of being obsolete. Consequently, the training models that are used to create and support those skills will become irrelevant.

The complexity of the situation highlights the need for a more inclusive approach towards the management side of the industry to address the leadership capacity building and the managerial competence needed for upgrading the performance of the air transport system.

The evolution of executive education

Since the nineteenth century, many universities and other higher education institutions hosted executive education programs. These programs have been appealing to participants from almost all sectors and roles and for different reasons. Farris et al. (2003) state the motivating reasons for enrollment in executive education programs that range from personal to professional. Among which we mention individual ambition, industry specialization, continuous professional development and a pathway to promotion or a career change.

Harvard and MIT were the early pioneers for hosting non-credit short courses focusing on war production competencies during World War II. During that period, non-credit executive education has evolved around special interest topics through programs that aim to supplement company-sponsored, technical education. The growing need for specific, functional training to individuals leaving the military and to dismissed veterans contributed significantly in the evolution of executive education in the fifties. GE, IBM, and Motorola were among the first companies in the United States to sponsor executive education programs which were designed by university faculty (Crotty and Soule, 1997).

The market of executive education continues to grow as more open-enrollment and specialized programs are being delivered worldwide. In today's challenging business environment, the topic of leadership retention is considered as one of the most critical topics in human resource management. Every ten high-level professionals leaving the company might cause up to one million dollars' loss per year (Solomon, 1997). Companies started acknowledging the value of executive development in retention planning which is evident through the increasing expenditure by corporations on executive training (Schneider, 2001).

In-company professional education has proven successful in meeting basic management up-skilling needs. However, such in-house programs fell short in providing skills for managers to grow their organizations and to drive organizational change. These targets are available through the learning opportunities provided by university-sponsored executive education programs (Hurra, 2013).

In their research on the role of executive education in strategic change, Prince and Stewart (2000) concluded that the strategic requirements of competitiveness, growth, reinvention and continuous change have driven the demand for securing effective leadership development from outside the organization. Being exposed to external industry experts as well as having the ability to network with peer executives have a significant impact on the professional development process.

Goodwin and Fulmer (1995) listed the attributes that guide a company in its selection for the university program. Among the characteristics are the learning provider's reliability, the attractiveness of the program, track record, cost, the customization flexibility, the contemporaneous of content, and the company relationships with the university's executive education department. Lippert (2001) considered that it is essential for the company to pick a program that allows the learning experience to be utilized internally by the executives through action learning, real case studies, role-playing, reinvention, simulations and pilot projects.

Aviation executive education: addressing the managerial aspects of the air transport system

Based on a 3.5 per cent compound annual growth rate for the air transport industry, forecasts indicate that the number of passengers transported by airlines will reach 8.2 billion in 2037 (IATA, 2018).

Acknowledging that the growth is now upon us, industry leaders concur that this growth will provide outstanding opportunities. Airlines are ramping up to serve more passengers by modernizing their fleets, adding new generation aircraft, and by becoming more sophisticated retailers to sustain competitive position while maintaining healthy profits. Additionally, the outlook is promising for green-field airport projects and infrastructure upgrades. However, the anticipated growth will also bring human capital-related challenges for the industry and for the educational institutions and training organizations that are catering for it.

This talent and staffing gap is easier to defeat the more prepared educational and training organizations are to train and retain the incoming stream of learners who will meet the emerging market needs. Maintaining quality education is critical while catering for the influx of the new recruits. Impediments to quality are directly linked to the quick increase in the number of both the learners and the programs. Bates (2018) considers university co-designed aviation programs more reliable by offering a foundation level for graduate skills in the aviation industry. Industry partnerships are the shortest way to reach effective and quality aviation education programs. Industry and academia are cooperating in the creation of a professional development and mentoring scheme which teaches, demonstrates, practices and assesses the non-technical skills required to work in the aviation industry.

ICAO's Manual of Evidence-Based Training lists the non-technical skills for a pilot among which are resource management, leadership and teamwork, communication, situation awareness, workload and stress management, problem-solving and decision making. With more aviation university programs spotted on the global radar, more attention to non-technical skills development is being a key output area that universities are keen to develop in their students. It is a reasonable approach for enhancing the outputs from the aviation education system through equipping the participants with the required skills and competence to assume their roles and to lead aviation projects.

Pierre Coutu, Lead Executive for the Global ACI-ICAO Airport Management Program states that there is an imbalance in the industry's approach to aviation professionals' competency building. He adds that the industry is probably not sufficiently addressing the managerial aspects of the air transport system. Technical matters no doubt need continuous attention to minimize the risk of suffering from major adverse consequences. However, the fact is no matter what the financial scope of investments in infrastructure, technology, systems and other assets, wise decisions about the system must be guided by expert professional management (Coutu, 2018).

The complexity of the business of aviation management (whether regulatory or operational) makes specific knowledge and expertise inevitable requirements. In addition to the business acumen, the management competencies that are commonly needed are leadership, administrative know-how, governance and foresight.

The above-mentioned management skills are adding to the reasons behind the choice of companies and their employees to enroll in executive education programs (Goodwin and Fulmer, 1995). Other reasons are to maintain regulatory compliance and to acquire new skills that can be implemented while on-the-job. ICAO has been very active in partnering with universities to provide aviation management programs. Current active university-based programs are: (a) ICAO – Ecole Nationale de L'aviation Civile (France) offering "Advanced Master's Program in Aviation Safety Management (ASM)", (b) ICAO – University of Waterloo offering the "Fundamentals of the Air Transport System" Course (online), (c) ICAO – Nanyang Technological Institute (Singapore) offering "Aviation and Air Transport Advanced Management Program", (d) ICAO – Concordia University (Canada) offering "Management Certificate in Civil Aviation".

Executive education can have a direct impact on real-world decision makers, presently and not sometime in the future. Universities, continuing education centers and other training organizations have designed programs to improve the management acumen of existing industry professionals through the offering of real-world management practices, recent policy innovations and evidence-based approaches to policy formation and impact analysis. By creating a collaboration with universities, organizations are able to free up much needed internal resources while still providing the mandatory upper-level training that is required for its employees. Another example of aviation university-based executive programs is the Advanced Certificate in Aviation and Aerospace (ACAA) offered by John Molson School of Business (Canada) in collaboration with HEC Paris (France). The certificate equips the participants with management tools and a global vision to enable them to drive change in the organizations they work at. The program is open to Executive MBA participants and other applicants with significant industry experience. By investing in executive education programs, organizations in the aviation industry would not only be preparing current industry employees for the management-level positions they will likely be required to assume in the coming years, but they will also be equipping them with relevant information pertaining to the newest technology, research, and innovative practices available.

Stakeholders and key design elements for executive education programs

To reach the desired learning outcomes and to ensure that the executive education program is attractive to industry, program directors are taking inclusive approaches to make sure that different industry stakeholders are contributing in the design phase of the program. The literature on executive education suggests that various elements of the program design should be influenced by a number of stakeholders including outside company executives as well as the university faculty itself (Myrsiades, 2001).

Collaboration with industry has led to the use of adjunct faculty and expert guest speakers. This approach keeps the content current and helps in making the program more attractive to the industry professionals in addition to giving it a hand-on appeal.

Since the participants in executive education programs come from various backgrounds, diversification in the selection process becomes relevant. Crotty and Soule (1997) and Filbeck and Webb (2000) describe the collaboration between universities and participants as more critical to a participant when it comes to the fit of the program to his/her needs.

However, in the design phase, there is a tendency to refer to two main stakeholders in collecting the training needs: the participants and the employers who are sponsoring the learners. The focus of attention is very much on the value delivered to the employee and the employer. Keeping the attention on the parties that are receiving the training and are sponsoring it financially may unintentionally exclude other significant stakeholders that would influence greatly the design of the programs (Shield and Coughlan, 2010). Other relevant stakeholders that should be consulted during the design phase of the executive education program are universities that are housing the program, faculty and lecturers, industry experts and highly experienced executives and academic partners that are collaborating either in the design or the delivery of the program.

Certain aspects of key design elements are observed as fundamental to the executive program design process. McCarthy et al. (2016) define the elements as shown in Table 3.2.1: "inputs" mainly related to staffing, industry collaboration and engagement and admission requirements; whereas "activities" are related to content delivery, assessment, faculty and adjunct recruitment; "outputs" related to learning outcomes, curriculum, accreditation and industry partnerships. Additionally, "impacts" address knowledge and skills, competencies, performance, organizational change and competitive advantage.

The stakeholders during the different phases of the executive program have different purposes and each interacts differently with each design element of the program. This will be especially significant when considering their role and contribution to the design of executive education programs. An example of stakeholders' engagement in program design is the aviation management program at the American University of Beirut in Lebanon. The program has been designed in a way where most of the stakeholders across the program design spectrum were consulted and have actively contributed in shaping the program's input. Air operators, airport executives, industry experts, academics and potential participants reflected their opinions and ideas of what an ideal aviation program shall look like and what top skills and competencies the participants should be acquiring. The program managed to attract participants from the local market and from the Gulf region where investments in aviation projects are growing.

4.1 Reinventing the pedagogic space through knowledge co-creation

There are plenty of challenges in the highly competitive world of executive education, among the challenges are the shifting training needs, the transformation of the traditional learning models, the need to be agile, the evolution of communities of practice, the changing regulatory requirements and the very limited time available for learning.

Introducing technology to learning is not simply through digitalizing the offering. New ways of passing on knowledge must be considered, including on-demand virtual lessons, co-development, post-program support and

Table 3.2.1 Key design elements for executive education programs

Element	Definition
1 Inputs	Staffing, industry collaboration, admission requirements.
2 Activities	Content delivery, assessment, faculty and adjunct recruitment.
3 Outputs	Learning outcomes, curriculum, accreditation, industry partnerships.
4 Impacts	Knowledge transfer, skill building, competencies, better performance, organizational change, competitive advantage.

Source: McCarthy et al. (2016).

follow-up. These changes have transformed the business practice along with all the phases of the learning and development supply chain.

Despite the digital revolution in learning, education has always required interaction between the learner and the teacher. Massive Open Online Courses (MOOC), blended learning, micro-learning and new training formats have found their way fast to the corporate world. However, to be effective and to be as efficient as classroom learning the new and emerging learning initiatives must overcome significant barriers. These new offerings must (a) provide the users with experience by creating a strong bond among participant, teacher and institution, (b) foster a collaborative and participatory approach through peer networks, and (c) provide complementary and engaging solutions.

This raises the importance of reconsidering the pedagogic space where the different stakeholders interact. According to Bertrand and Houssaye (1999), the pedagogical space is framed by three basic elements: the knowledge, the tutor and the learner (Figure 3.2.1).

What is more important than the existence of those three aspects is the dynamic relationship and the interactive rapport that exist among them. In

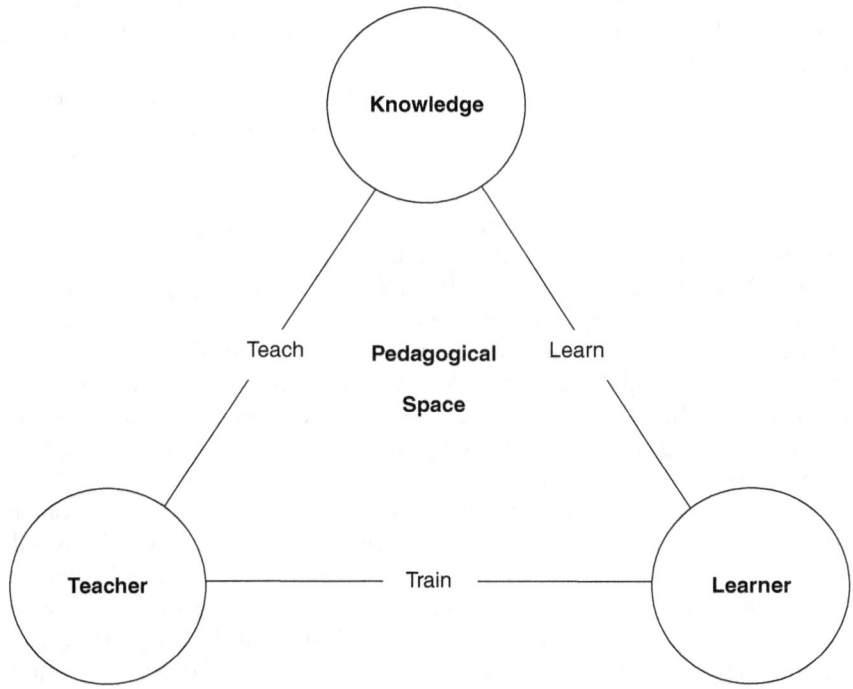

Figure 3.2.1 The pedagogical triangle
Source: Bertrand and Houssaye (1999)

other words, the active emotional and cognitive pedagogical space. This is where technology might play an integral part to recreate this space in a way to ensure that the experience of each stakeholder is being enhanced throughout the different phases of the education program from design to delivery and management. If the needs and the contributions of all the stakeholders are not well incorporated, the challenge of designing an inclusive and efficient executive education program, which will appreciate the needs of all stakeholders, remains.

One way to revive this pedagogical space is through breaking down the traditional teacher-learner relationship into a value creation process. Learners are being transformed from being consumers to being "prosumers" that means both producers and consumers at the same time. This is where the benefits of knowledge co-creation kick in.

Prahalad and Ramaswamy (2004) are considered to be the main promoters of the concept of co-creation a contemporary concept in the field of marketing. Value co-creation is generally known as a marketing and management strategy that emerges from the breakdown of the traditional producer-consumer exchange, whereby the producer creates value and the consumer consumes it (Vargo and Lusch, 2011). The popularity of co-creation has been growing along with the increasing dynamics of change and volatility of the business environment which forces companies to take more organizationally difficult adjustment measures to be implemented in a pretty short period of time.

Lufthansa has been using value co-creation concepts to better understand the customers. Lufthansa has deployed Bluetooth beacons and sensors in selected terminals, to be able to send out real-time messages to their customers. When a targeted customer goes through security and has Bluetooth enabled on their phone, the personalization process starts. The "Big Data Engine" program checks a traveler's mobile boarding pass and calculates how much time the traveler has left before departure. Time and the traveler's profile are cross checked in order to determine whether the customer is a potential candidate to subscribe in a loyalty program or to purchase a discounted pass. This information is combined with the data from the sensors in the lounge that calculate occupancy rates in real time. The company's value propositions are being shaped by the passenger's experience, his/her profile, personal preferences and consuming behavior.

Value co-creation has also made its way to the field of education and learning. Although there are now many tools that make knowledge acquisition more interactive, real-life contact remains necessary, whether with the teacher or the peers. Too many cases prove that learners can assume self-learning provided they are given the right tools needed. Learners have started adopting active and participatory roles that allow them to interact dynamically with educators (Dollinger et al., 2018). Through value co-creation learners become partners and the trainer becomes more a mentor and a facilitator providing individual support.

Additionally, this process allows for institutions and learners to work together to improve the learning experience and enhance participants' ability to act as partners. Díaz-Méndez and Gummesson (2012) confirmed that value co-creation can be used to trigger organizational innovation and creativity by tying the learners' resources with organizational resources to create a better experience. Whereas the learners' resources do not only comprise their opinions on the learning experience, it also includes their intellectual abilities, study habits, sense of responsibility and personality.

Among the benefits of knowledge co-creation is that it combines academic, technical and professional skills so that the course design is object-oriented (Douglas et al., 2008). Executive participants are mostly looking for solutions to their recurrent problems rather than theoretical and conceptual information. They want information that can be transformed into knowledge and they require tools to be able to bend this knowledge in order to fit it in their organizational context. Having said that, the learning courses are becoming more autonomous, reusable and modular, allowing the training supplier to respond to a significant change in the participant preferences and inputs.

The changing face of aviation learning and development

The business environment is continuously changing, and research on strategic orientation and scenario planning describes the future as volatile, uncertain, complex and ambiguous (Bennett and Lemoine, 2014). This puts lots of pressure on corporate leaders as they try to tackle the tide of change and detect market trends. Expectedly, executive education is also changing, and the challenge is how to attain result-oriented learning while catering to the executives' need for speed and immediacy. Today's executives can barely find time to learn. It is rare to find professionals that are willing to engage in a six- to eight-week management program. Nowadays, training is seen as a bonus where shorter and more intensive sessions are in high demand, especially considering the desire for immediate and measurable impact. ACI's and ICAO's leadership and air transport management courses range in duration between three to five days respectively.

What worked yesterday, simply won't work tomorrow

Corporate training has evolved over the years from classroom to personal computers to e-learning and to digital. Each evolution has been triggered by technology and economic change. As calls for re-thinking the competencies of the future get louder, little is being heard on the learning philosophy and the design paradigms that constitute the mental-model behind the whole learning process.

Research performed by O'Reilly Learning (2014) and Linkedin Learning (2018) on +4000 companies revealed that today's primary challenge for high performing organizations is that employees do not have time for learning. More than 50 per cent of the employees of the studied organizations want to learn at work, at their own pace and upon need. Additionally, the Center for Creative Leadership (2018) through its research on experiences that impact executive development, found that 70 per cent of workplace learning comes from real, on-the-job experiences. Compared to only about 10 per cent coming from formal, structured training programs. This has changed the learning game for corporations, making them think hard on how to make learning continuous in order to retain their best talent.

Traditional rules of pedagogy are no longer helpful in achieving learning objectives for the professionals in fast-paced industries. While the existing learning formats and Learning Management Systems (LMS) make sense, what is needed is to inventively incorporate it into the changing context. It is useful to introduce an innovative design thinking, learning philosophy which focuses on the learning experience and aims at embedding learning into the platforms used by the organizations. As per Bersin (2018) in "Learning in the Flow of Work", this is where all the digital learning is likely to go. Systems can coach and train employees to be better on the job.

A new age of digital learning

The digital world changed the dynamics of education and changed the way learners consume training. A new age of digital learning is finding its way fast to highly regulated industries such as the aviation industry. Taking advantage of the benefits of digital learning platforms is extremely important when considering attracting and retaining the up and coming millennial workforce.

Airlines, airports and other air transport related businesses have to train high numbers of employees and have to make sure that the employees complete a long list of compulsory and compliance training. And that is not all. The completed training shall be effective (Arthur et al., 2003). That means employees should be able to apply the knowledge and skills acquired on-the-job and are expected to deliver results. In the application of safety and operational training, as an example, there are now adaptive learning solutions that deliver small two–three-minute videos each day when an operator checks into work. The learning is carefully curated, spaced, and designed to deliver an outcome – and the employee answers questions to give the system enough information to decide what learning should come next.

Forward-looking airline companies are fetching training solutions that are scalable and cost-effective. With the anticipated large-scale wave of pilot retirement, it becomes a priority to fill those vacancies as efficiently as possible and to avoid any bottle-neck and to cut-off on the high training and education costs.

To keep pace with tide of change, airline learning and development professionals are drifting away from conventional training programs and they are teaming up with innovative learning companies instead. The latter are taking advantage of the 20 years of technology infrastructure built and also adding the principles of spaced learning, designed repetition, practice, and competency-driven recommendations right into an employee's work environment. Custom-created digital learning programs are diverse and cover different corporate training areas such as flight simulators, mechanics, stations, dispatch and collaboration management systems.

In the context of digital learning, IATA acknowledges the changing face of training and strives to keep ahead of this change. IATA has been working on developing innovative training solutions to help aviation learning and development decision makers meet the new demands. The new learning solutions integrate technology-enabled interactive platforms into the training portfolio to make learning more intuitive and engaging. IATA's new era of aviation digital training features e-learning products, gamification programs (Airline Manager 2 app), simulation software and virtual reality ground operations training (RampVR).

Conclusion

As the business environment becomes more complex by the day, the evolution of executive education gains momentum. The expected growth in the demand for air travel will bring along to the aviation training organizations more challenges in leading human resource learning and development strategies. While most learning and development experts agree that innovation in aviation learning will continue to be driven by an urge to improve the impact of the learning experience for less cost, they anticipate that this (r)evolution will be focused on two aspects: the nature of the content and how it is delivered.

However, the field of content is not where the next significant breakthroughs in aviation executive development will happen. Instead, it is expected to see innovation in the use of technology and the co-creation of sustainable on-the-job learning experiences. Those experiences are anticipated to be both organization and learner-centered and delivered in a way and in an environment where all parties in the learning supply chain take an active role.

Bibliography

Arthur, W., Jr., Bennett Jr., W., Edens, P. S., & Bell, S. T. (2003). Effectiveness of training in organizations: a meta-analysis of design and evaluation features. *Journal of Applied Psychology*, 88 (2), 234–245.

Bates, P. (2018). Enhancing aviation education. *ICAO Training Report*, 23–25.

Bennett, N., and Lemoine, J. (2014). What VUCA really means for you. *Harvard Business Review*, January–February.

Bersin, J. (2018). Learning in the flow of work. *Chief Learning Officer*, 17 (3), 12. Retrieved from http://search.ebscohost.com/login.aspx?direct=true&db=bth&AN=128444328&site=ehost-live.

Bertrand, Y., & Houssaye, J. (1999). "Pedagogie" and "Didactique": an incestuous relationship. *Instructional Science*, 27 (1), 33–51. Retrieved from http://search.ebscohost.com/login.aspx?direct=true&db=eric&AN=EJ584257&site=ehost-live.

Center for Creative Leadership. (2018). The 70-20-10 rule for leadership development.

Coutu, P. (2018). Redesigning aviation education: a collective effort. *ICAO Training Report*, 8 (2), 32–34.

Crotty, P. T., & Soule, A. J. (1997). Executive education: yesterday and today, with a look at tomorrow. *Journal of Management Development*, 16 (1), 4–21. doi: https://doi.org/10.1108/02621719710155445.

Díaz-Méndez, M., & Gummesson, E. (2012). Value co-creation and university teaching quality: consequences for the European higher education area (EHEA). *Journal of Service Management*, 23 (4), 571–592. Retrieved from http://10.0.4.84/09564231211260422.

Dollinger, M., Lodge, J., & Coates, H. (2018). Co-creation in higher education: towards a conceptual model. *Journal of Marketing for Higher Education*, 28 (2), 210–231. Retrieved from http://10.0.4.56/08841241.2018.1466756.

Douglas, J., McClelland, R., & Davies, J. (2008). The development of a conceptual model of student satisfaction with their experience in higher education. *Quality Assurance in Education: An International Perspective*, 16 (1), 19–35. Retrieved from http://search.ebscohost.com/login.aspx?direct=true&db=eric&AN=EJ800586&site=ehost-live.

Farris, P. W., Haskins, M. E., & Yemen, G. (2003). Executive education programs go back to school. *Journal of Management Development*, 22 (9), 784–795. doi: https://doi.org/10.1108/02621710310495775.

Filbeck, G., & Webb, S. (2000). Executive MBA education: using learning styles for successful teaching strategies. *Financial Practice & Education*, 10 (1), 205–215. Retrieved from http://search.ebscohost.com/login.aspx?direct=true&db=bth&AN=6364733&site=ehost-live.

Goodwin, J., & Fulmer, R. M. (1995). The systems dynamics of executive education. *Executive Development*, 8 (4), 9–14. doi: https://doi.org/10.1108/09533239510089508.

Hurra, G. (2013). A new model for executive education. *Journal of Executive Education*, 2 (2). Retrieved from https://digitalcommons.kennesaw.edu/jee/vol2/iss2/1.

IATA.(2018). Twenty year air passenger forecast, press release no. 62.

Linkedin Learning (2018). Workplace learning and development report: the rise and responsibility of talent development in the new labor market. Retrieved from: https://learning.linkedin.com/content/dam/me/learning/en-us/pdfs/linkedin-learning-workplace-learning-report-2018.pdf

Lippert, R. L. (2001). Whither executive education??? *Business and Economic Review*, 47 (3), 3–7.

Martinez, D., McEachern, B. (2018). Aviation training intelligence. *ICAO Training Report*, 8 (1).

McCarthy, P., Sammon, D., & O'Raghallaigh, P. (2016). Designing an executive education programme: towards a programme design matrix. *Journal of Decision Systems*, 25 (sup1), 566–571. doi: https://doi.org/10.1080/12460125.2016.1189640.

Myrsiades, L. (2001). Looking to lead: a case in designing executive education from the inside. *Journal of Management Development*, 20 (9), 795–812. doi: https://doi.org/10.1108/EUM0000000006161.

O'Reilly Learning (2014). High performance organizations report. Retrieved from: www.oreilly.com/business/free/high-performance-organizations.csp

Prahalad, C. K., & Ramaswamy, V. (2004). Co-creation experiences: the next practice in value creation. *Journal of Interactive Marketing*, 18 (3), 5–14. Retrieved from http://10.0.3.234/dir.20015.

Prince, C., & Stewart, J. (2000). The dynamics of the corporate education market and the role of business schools. *Journal of Management Development*, 19 (3), 207–219. doi: https://doi.org/10.1108/02621710010318783.

Schneider, M. (2001). Rating the management gurus. Retrieved June 1, 2019, from: www.bloomberg.com/news/articles/2001-10-14/rating-the-management-gurus

Shield, S., & Coughlan, R. (2010). Designing the MBA of tomorrow. *Design Management Review, 18* (3), 55–62. doi: https://doi.org/10.1111/j.1948-7169.2007.tb00214.x.

Solomon, C. M. (1997). Keep them! Don't let your best people get away. *Workforce*, 46–52.

Vargo, S. L., & Lusch, R. F. (2011). Stepping aside and moving on: a rejoinder to a rejoinder. *European Journal of Marketing, 45* (7/8), 1319–1321. Retrieved from http://10.0.4.84/03090561111137741.

3.3 Chapter – Entrepreneurial mindset development
A cog in the wheel of talent management in the aviation sector

Raihan Taqui Syed, Manish Yadav and Hesham Magd

Introduction

There is a distinct implication regarding lack of competent employees in various profiles within the regulatory environment and aviation industry as air transport activities in the next fifteen years are forecast to increase twofold (ICAO, 2018). The recently released Boeing forecasting report shares that more than 2 million aviation professionals must be hired by the global aviation industry. The projected requirements are – over 600,000 commercial pilots, nearly 700,000 maintenance engineers and over 800,000 cabin crew (ACI, 2019). The International Civil Aviation Organization (ICAO) has developed a capacity-building and aviation training roadmap which aids ICAO's members in developing strategies to ensure the availability of competent aviation professionals, technological capabilities and the required operational environment to carry out all aviation activities in compliance with the provisions laid out by ICAO and required performance specified in ICAO Standards and Recommended Practices (SARPs) (PACA, 2017).

Talent management in the aviation sector aids business managers in not only recruiting and developing aviation professionals but also retaining competent staff (ICAO, 2018). The competency model is a graphic representation which summarizes the list of competencies someone would need to do a job well (Dessler, 2013). Such a model forms a basis not only for mapping of competencies, but also to develop and assess them. Noe et al. (2017) propose that the competency model helps to identify appropriate employees to fill vacancies in organizations and also acts as a foundation for future development plans. On these lines, a competency mapping framework was proposed by Lin et al. (2018) for the Federal Aviation Agency's Flight Standards Training Division. The framework was based on comprehensive research of current procedures and approaches and incorporated new analysis methods and tools which enable concrete mapping; thus providing meaningful and effective guidance for all talent management functions. ICAO Document 9868 illustrates a competency-based assessment and training framework for aviation personnel. However, developing the list of competencies and associated training programs is a laborious and complex job

(Service for NAA, 2019). In this regard, the IATA Training and Qualification Initiative (ITQI) in collaboration with ICAO initiated the mapping of competencies for flight operation, engineering and maintenance personnel (ICAO, 2018).

Competency management is the process which links vision and strategy of the organization with people who are already part of it or intend to be and is followed by other supporting phases. This involves collecting and analyzing huge amounts of data regarding present and potential employees, in order to take correct decisions at departmental as well as organizational level. At business level, analytics is categorized into 3 levels – descriptive analytics, predictive analytics and perspective analysis (IBM Thought Leadership White Paper, 2013). Descriptive analytics utilizes data aggregation and mining techniques which provide insight into the past. Predictive analytics employs statistical tools along with forecasting techniques so as to gauge the future. Perspective analytics relies on optimization and simulation algorithms, in order to suggest possible options. The terminology with respect to analytics of employee data in organizations has seen a steady evolution. It is observed in books, journals and company websites that people analytics, HR analytics, human capital analytics, talent analytics and workforce analytics have been used. However, People Analytics as a term investigates analytics of employees from the organization point of view and not limited to the Human Resource (HR) department. Furthermore, People Analytics as a subcategory of organization analytics is more appropriate than HR Analytics.

As per Mr. Martin R. Kuehn, Seabury Human Capital President and Chief Executive Officer

> In the face of organizational change, effective talent assessment can empower leaders to better manage their talent by addressing newly identified development opportunities and implementing targeted training programs. Assessing and managing talent should be a continuous and integral part of managing an airline.

To overcome the talent gap challenge, competency management in the aviation sector requires a well-defined competency model which enables validity and measurability of the employee competencies over a defined period of time (Fewster, 2003). Also, traditional approaches for modeling have not fully leveraged the latest technology and analysis techniques to generate and analyze data. A new comprehensive model which takes into consideration all aspects of competencies to be possessed by NGAP is the requirement of the aviation industry (ACI, 2019).

It is observed that various international aviation agencies have been consistently investing time and resources in building effective competency development frameworks to enhance competency levels of aviation professionals on the technical side. However, more focus is required on the business and management side as well. The following sections focus on

Talent and Employee Competency Life Cycle Management, as well as on the significance of developing entrepreneurial mindset among the NGAP working on the business/management side within the globally expanding aviation sector.

Employee competency life cycle management

Talent Management as a system has been striving to achieve a dynamic equilibrium between people – as assets of strategic importance and the organization (Lewis & Heckman, 2006). Moreover, due to demographical changes within the aviation workforce, global expansion of the aviation sector, increased range of employees' age and multicultural workplaces, strategic management of talent in this sector is of paramount importance. Extensive studies are being conducted to build innovative models to enable organizations to bring the best out of their talent. TM practices impact an individual's career mainly at three levels – recruitment, development and retention (Behrstock, 2010) and are directly linked to employee competency. Competencies are sets of knowledge, skills, abilities and personal attributes which enable employees to successfully perform their jobs (Ruggerberg et al., 2011). These vary across different jobs in the same and different organizations due to the difference in organizational goals and strategies and individual job requirements. In this context, Employee Competency Life Cycle (ECLC) management (Draganidis & Mentzas, 2006) assumes significance as it plays a vital role in linking TM process to organizational strategy by comparing two sets of data – one which is based on organizational workflow analysis, and the other based on individual competency level (Sanghi, 2007). More importantly, ECLC management acts as a vital tool in linking TM process to organizational strategy. According to Draganidis & Mentzas (2006), ECLC consists of four inter-dependent phases – Competency Mapping, Competency Diagnosis, Competency Development and Competency Monitoring as illustrated in Figure 3.3.1. Effective management of this cycle would result in continuous improvement and development of individual and organizational competencies.

Yuvaraj (2011) defines *Competency Mapping* as a process of recognizing key competencies required to carry out designated jobs and associated tasks in an organization. Designing a TM plan and preparing inventory of the organization's employees which details the sum and degree of competencies possessed by employees is the primary step to be undertaken. *Competency Diagnosis* involves 'competency gap analysis' that allows employees to ascertain enhancements needed not only to contribute more efficiently to the organization, but also to advance in their career paths (Antonucci & d'Ovidio, 2012). *Competency Development* comprises of planning and conducting activities to enhance the number and proficiency of competencies possessed by employees so as to bridge the competency gap (Ruggerberg et al., 2011). The organizational policies drafted, practices followed, and

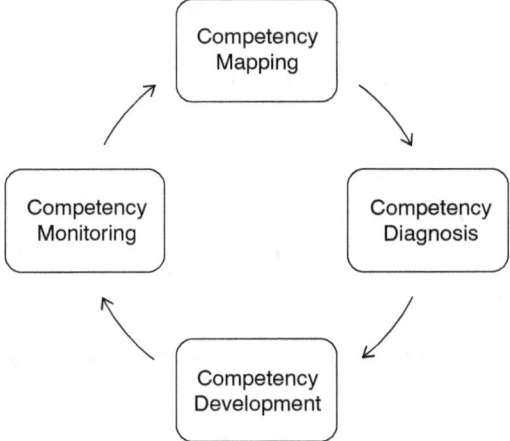

Figure 3.3.1 Employee competency life cycle (ECLC).

systems implemented strongly influence the competency development of employees. *Competency Monitoring* involves assessing and evaluating the results achieved in the previous phase (Draganidis & Mentzas, 2006). Continuous monitoring of employee competencies assists in effective realignment of employees as per the changing business needs of an organization.

Entrepreneurial mindset: vital competency to possess

Entrepreneurial mindset not only results in creation of new products and services, but also provides innovative solutions to existing organizational problems (Cha & Bae, 2010). As described by Kuratko (2005), five key characteristics are associated with entrepreneurial mindset – willingness to take calculated risks personally and professionally, capability to form a venture team and lead it efficiently, management skills to organize needed resources effectively, professional skill of drafting a business project meticulously and finally the vision to recognize opportunity swiftly. Such a perspective can be developed in individuals with appropriate resources and time. The two vital elements of entrepreneurial mindset – creativity and innovation (Shalley et al., 2009; Gundry et al., 2014), are considered to be the core factors enabling establishment and growth of organizations. Furthermore, Dromereschi (2018) emphasizes that creativity and innovation assist organizations to achieve 'competitive advantage'. On the other hand, it is also contended that entrepreneurial mindset has a strong, positive impact on the decision-making process (Audretsch & Belitski, 2017). This will be vital in coming years, with the expansion of the aviation sector and changing nature of the consumer market demands. Figure 3.3.2 encapsulates the

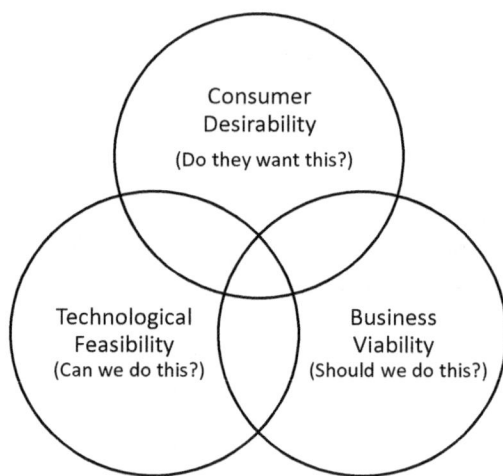

Figure 3.3.2 Decision-making sub-processes of an entrepreneurial mind.

significance of entrepreneurial mindset among aviation professional/managers within the organizational context.

It is critical that organizations realize that creating organizational entrepreneurial mindset is correlated with effective leadership and support (Arham, 2014). Organizational leadership is needed to support entrepreneurial mindset development by providing employee rewards (Twomey & Harris, 2000; Hornsby et al., 2002); resources (Hornsby et al., 2002); organic organizational structure (Horsby et al., 2002; Morris & Kuratko, 2002); and employee empowerment (Ngo & Lau, 2004; Drucker, 2007). It is fair to highlight that commitment and personal involvement are required from top management in creating and deploying clear values and goals consistent with the objectives of the organization, and in creating and deploying well defined systems, processes, methods and performance measures for achieving these goals. Cultivating and nurturing entrepreneurial mindset in organizations is recognized for its positive correlation with achieving organizational competitive advantage (Dalvi & Ahangaran, 2014), and this can be demonstrated through the achievement of reduction in costs or differentiating products/services through the combinations of resources and enhancement in productivity (Barringer & Ireland, 2013).

Recommendation

The findings of the latest IATA Human Resources Report (2018) divulges that retention is the greatest challenge along with training and development. Furthermore, candidates with technical skills in dynamic industry remain a priority for hiring managers across the aviation industry as technology is key driver for the customer relationship management and customer service aspects in terms of business sustainability and safety (IATA, 2014). However, in a dynamic aviation industry, to sustain and stay competitive, the most critical success factor is to develop and nurture the multifaceted professionals equipped with the right skillset and critical decision-making capabilities in challenging situations. These issues could be resolved with a proactive approach of implementing ECLC management effectively and incorporating entrepreneurial mindset development as a core non-technical competency for aviation professionals. While the former would ensure a steady enhancement of employee competencies through effective implementation of the four stages, the latter would ensure transformation of aviation professionals from followers to leaders. This would not only result in effective retention of employees as they would be motivated with their career growth, but also enable organizational sustainable growth. To ensure successful implementation of entrepreneurial mindset, it is recommended that organizations should focus on the use of transformational leadership style as it is more suitable for setting up and developing the entrepreneurial mindset in organizations, as transformational leadership focuses on motivating employees to work for goals instead of short-term self-interest and for achievement and self-actualization instead of security (Yang, 2008; Sudrajat, 2015). Transformational leadership is positively correlated to creativity and innovation which are components of developing entrepreneurial mindset (Agbor, 2008). Figure 3.3.3 illustrates the dynamic relationship between the different concepts discussed in this chapter with regard to aviation sector on a whole.

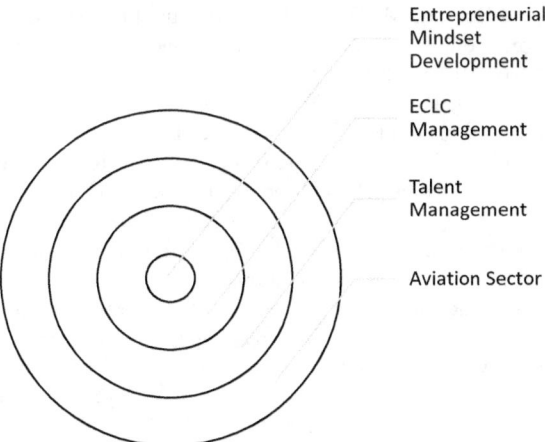

Figure 3.3.3 Conceptual illustration developed by the authors.

Conclusion

The aviation sector is a highly competitive and dynamic zone where competition is fierce. Organizations must adapt to changing their current work practices and focus more on developing and nurturing their employees through the development of entrepreneurial mindset. This would not only enable them to utilize non-human resources efficiently, but also cope with the present staff shortage. Entrepreneurial thinking and working are becoming crucial for the success of organizations in today's business environment. It is becoming now a matter of survival where entrepreneurial mindset must be introduced within the workforce and the entrepreneurial culture within an organization must be developed. While organizations such as Oman Airport Management Company (OAMC) are seeking graduates with entrepreneurial skills, it is highly recommended that the aviation sector as a whole incorporates EMD as part of non-technical competency management. This involves support of the organizational leadership and execution by talent managers.

References

ACI, I. I. (2019, 07 20) Article: International Airport Review. Retrieved from International Airport Review: www.internationalairportreview.com/article/26445

Agbor, E. (2008) 'Creativity and innovation: The leadership dynamics', *Journal of Strategic Leadership*, 1(1), pp. 39–45.

Antonucci, L. and d'Ovidio, F. D. (2012) 'An Informative System Based on the Skill Gap Analysis to Planning Training Courses', *Applied Mathematics*, 3(11), pp. 1619–1626. doi: 10.4236/am.2012.311224.

Arham, A. F. (2014) The relationship leadership behavior, entrepreneurial orientation and organizational performance in Malaysian small and medium enterprises, PhD thesis, RMIT university.

Audretsch, D. B. and Belitski, M. (2017) 'Entrepreneurial ecosystems in cities: Establishing the framework conditions', *Journal of Technology Transfer*, 42(5), pp. 1030–1051. doi: 10.1007/s10961-016-9473-8.

Barringer, B. R., Ireland, R. D. (2013) *Entrepreneurship: Successfully launching new ventures*. Fourth Edition, Pearson Education Limited, England.

Behrstock, E. (2010) 'Talent Management in the Private and Education Sectors: A Literature Review', *Learning Point Associates*, January, pp. 1–14.

Cha, M. S. and Bae, Z. T. (2010) 'The entrepreneurial journey: From entrepreneurial intent to opportunity realization', *Journal of High Technology Management Research*, 21(1), pp. 31–42. doi: 10.1016/j.hitech.2010.02.005.

Dalvi, M. R. and and and Ahangaran, A. G. (2014) 'Investigating the effects of entrepreneurship and sustainable competitive advantage by considering the merits of marketing and innovation capability: Case study – Isfahan province appliances companies', *International Journal of Academic Research in Business and Social Sciences*, 4(3), pp. 75–93.

Dessler, G. (2013) *Fundamentals of Human Resource Management*. Essex, England: Pearson Education Limited.

Draganidis, F. and Mentzas, G. (2006) 'Competency based management: A review of systems and approaches', *Information Management and Computer Security*, 14(1), pp. 51–64. doi: 10.1108/09685220610648373.

Dromereschi, M. I. (2018) 'The Role of Creativity in Entrepreneurship', *Studies and Scientific Researches. Economics Edition*, 18(20), pp. 49–81. doi: 10.29358/sceco.v0i20.278.

Drucker, P. F. (2007), *The Definitive Drucker: The Final Word from the Father of Modern Management*, New York: McGraw Hill.

Fewster, S. H. (2003). Global aviation human resource management: Contemporary compensation and benefits practices. *Management Research News*, 59–71.

Gundry, L. K., Ofstein, L. F. and Kickul, J. R. (2014) 'Seeing around corners: How creativity skills in entrepreneurship education influence innovation in business', *International Journal of Management Education*, 12(3), pp. 529–538. doi: 10.1016/j.ijme.2014.03.002.

Hornsby, Jeffrey S., Donald F. Kuratko and Shaker A. Zahra. (2002) 'Middle managers' perception of the internal environment for corporate entrepreneurship: assessing a measurement scale', *Journal of Business Venturing*, 17, pp. 253–273.

IATA (2014). www.peoplemattersglobal.com/news/hiring/finding-new-talent-in-aviation-is-the-greatest-challenge-iata-report-19043. Retrieved 05 13, 2019.

ICAO, I. C. (2018, July 17). Training Documents/ICAO. Retrieved from ICAO Website: www.icao.int/training/Documents/ICAO%20Aviation%20CapacityBuilding%20Roadmap.pdf

Kuratko, D. F. (2005) 'The emergence of entrepreneurship education: Development, trends, and challenges', *Entrepreneurship: Theory and Practice*, 29(5), pp. 577–597. doi: 10.1111/j.1540-6520.2005.00099.x.

Lewis, R. E. and Heckman, R. J. (2006) 'Talent management: A critical review', *Human Resource Management Review*, 16(2), pp. 139–154. doi: 10.1016/j.hrmr.2006.03.001.

Lin, D. Y., Shahhosseini, D. A., & Janke, P. C. (2018). Concept map-based aviation competency mapping and training. *ASEE Annual Conference*. ASEE.

Morris, M. H. and Kuratko, D. F. (2002), *Corporate Entrepreneurship*. Orlando, FL: Harcourt.

Ngo, H. Y. and Lau, C. M. (2004) 'The HR system, organizational culture and product innovation', *International Business Review*, 13(6), pp. 685–703.

Noe, R. A., Hollenbeck, J. R., Gerhart, B. and Wright, P. M. (2017) *Human Resource Management: Gaining a Competitive Advantage*. Berkshire, England: McGraw-Hill.

PACA, P. A. (2017, 10 17). MID Documents: ICAO. Retrieved from ICAO: www.icao.int/MID/Documents/2017/DGCA-MID4/IP4.pdf

Ruggerberg, B. J. et al. (2011) 'Doing competencies well: Best practices in competency modeling', *Personnel Psychology*, 64(1), pp. 225–262. doi: 10.1111/j.1744-6570.2010.01207.x.

Sanghi, S. (2007) *The Handbook of Competency Mapping: Understanding, Designing and Implementing Competency Models in Organizations*, 2nd Ed., New Delhi: Sage.

Service for NAA. (2019, 7 20) Retrieved from McKechnie Aviation Website: https://mckechnie-aviation.com/services/services-for-naa/competency-framework-for-aviation-authorities/

Shalley, C., Gilson, L. and Blum, T. (2009) 'Interactive effects of growth need strength, work context, and job complexity on self-reported creative performance', *Academy of Management Journal*, 52(3), pp. 489–505. doi: 10.5465/AMJ.2009.41330806.

Sudrajat, D. (2015) 'The relationships among leadership, entrepreneurial mindset, innovation and competitive advantage: A conceptual model of logistics service industry', *Binus Business Review*, 6(3), pp. 477–485.

Thought Leadership White Paper. (2013) Descriptive, predictive, prescriptive: Transforming Asset and Facilities Management with Analytics. IBM Corporation, USA. 1–6.

Twomey, D. F. and D. L. Harris. (2000) 'From strategy to corporate outcomes: Aligning human resource management systems with entrepreneurial intent', *International Journal of Commerce and Management*, 10, pp. 43–55.

Yang, C. W. (2008) 'The relationship among leadership styles, entrepreneurial orientation and business performance', *Managing Global Transitions*, 6(3), pp. 257–275.

Yuvaraj, R. (2011) 'Competency Mapping – A drive for Indian industries', *International Journal of Scientific & Engineering Research*, 2(8), pp. 1–7. Available at: www.ijser.org.

3.4 Chapter – The regulation of the airline industry

Why it matters to you

P. Paul Fitzgerald

Introduction[1]

Aviation is one of the most heavily regulated industries in the world. There is almost no aspect of the industry that is not subject to regulation in one jurisdiction or another. Issues as diverse as the carriage of emotional support animals, the language of onboard service, lavatories only for staff, onboard gambling and seat size have been adopted or considered by regulators in different countries and Table 3.4.1 in the Appendix lists the 57 different topics currently addressed by those regulating the international airline industry.

In addition to being comprehensive, the regulation of the airline industry is also intense. In 1969 when Boeing wanted to certify the prototype Boeing 747, the paperwork needed to bring the aircraft to US and international certification for airworthiness weighed almost as much as the prototype itself.[2]

The regulation of the airline industry is in constant evolution; at any given moment various jurisdictions are considering new initiatives to regulate the industry or whole new area of currently unregulated activity to target. Rather than making the reader an expert in aviation regulation, this chapter aims at making the reader aware of the impact and breadth of regulation and the need to keep it in mind when working in the airline industry.

History and basis of regulation

Since the early days of aviation, airlines have been seen as form of infrastructure in that they provide connectivity between two points. More importantly they can serve remote communities not linked to the rail or highway network because they need relatively little infrastructure. From the start, regulators have seen the potential of aviation to provide a variety of public goods, whether this be service to regional points, linking the capital with colonial outposts, fostering diplomatic ties or supporting the local aircraft industry.[3]

In recent years former state-owned airlines around the world have been privatized.[4] In almost every case, privatization came with increased government intervention, as regulators sought to achieve many of the public goods that had been achieved through state ownership.[5] In some cases regulators use subsidies to induce airline to provide cargo lift to the military in times of national emergency,[6] or provide service to rural destinations.[7] More often government intervention takes the form of regulation.

Safety regulation

All states, regardless of economic, political, social or geographic factors, regulate the safety of the airline industry. The basis for these regulations comes from the Chicago Convention[8] and its Annexes. States provide an aircraft's certificate of airworthiness[9] and consequently oversee the safety of aircraft. They are also responsible for the licensing of personnel[10] and, by extension, human factor issues.[11] Other responsibilities include the regulation of aircraft communications systems[12] and the investigation of accidents.[13] In addition, regulators in states where aircraft are manufactured will issue a type certificate to confirm the airworthiness of a type of aircraft, such as the Airbus A340[14] or the Boeing 777,[15] which are manufactured in their state.

Most new safety regulation is a result of the recommendations of accident investigation reports.[16] By way of example, the accident reports into the crashes of Lion Air 610[17] and Ethiopian Airlines 302[18] will undoubtedly provoke new safety regulations.

Global standard

In general, States must uniformly adhere to safety standards laid down in the Chicago Convention and its 18 Annexes.[19] This allows a Canadian pilot to fly for Emirates, or an Australian mechanic to work in Singapore. It lets Qatar Airways buy a Boeing 777 without requiring type certification by Qatari officials. The homogeneity of international standards is so important that if a State intends to deviate from them it must inform the Council of the International Civil Aviation Organization (ICAO).[20]

National differences

Nonetheless, there are minor difference in regulations but as long as they achieve the goals of the international standards, no action needs to be taken. Often these differences are explained by political factors as the next two examples will illustrate.

1) Required number of flight attendants

There are two ways of determining the number of flight attendants required for a flight. The de facto international standard is one flight attendant for every 50 seats,[21] while others, notably Canada and Australia, have long required one flight attendant for a predetermined number of passengers, 40 for Canada and 36 for Australia. In 2015, Canada adopted the international standard after a nearly two-decade-long fight between airlines and the flight attendants union,[22] and as of 2019, Australia was still consulting on a similar initiative.[23] If safety is the real issue, the de facto international standard should govern, nonetheless unions believe the two passenger-based standards result in more flight attendants per aircraft and this explains the protracted debates in both Canada and Australia.

2) Pilot retirement age

The retirement age for pilots is another issue where there are minor variations from one State to another. ICAO has recently set the retirement age at 65, where the co-pilot is less than 60,[24] and both the US and India have followed suit.[25] However, both China and Japan are raising pilot retirement ages in response to a looming pilot shortage.[26] In other countries, it is not the regulator, but the airline that sets the retirement age of their pilots,[27] either directly or through a collective agreement.[28]

These minor differences are possible, because the ICAO Annexes are meant to set minimum standards, and thus States are always free to choose to adopt a higher regulatory standard.

Security regulation

It is undisputed that a global regime of aviation security is essential "in order that international civil aviation may be developed in a safe and orderly manner,"[29] ICAO has led the development of current worldwide aviation security standards. It has added three Annexes to the Chicago Convention dealing fully or in part with aviation security: Annex 17 on Safeguarding International Civil Aviation Against Acts of Unlawful Interference,[30] Annex 9 on Facilitation[31] and Annex 14 on Aerodromes.[32]

In order to facilitate State compliance with these standards, ICAO has prepared a 5-volume Security Manual (Doc 8973)[33] to give in-depth guidance to law enforcement authorities. It then conducts regular audits of the aviation security practices of States[34] and offers technical assistance to States that need it.[35]

As with safety, States may adopt higher security standards as long as they comply with ICAO's Annexes. For example, the security standards applied at Israel's Ben Gurion Airport in Tel Aviv and to its flag carrier, El Al, are among the most stringent in the world,[36] but no other States have copied these standards.

At the same time, shortly after September 11th, the US passed legislation demanding that foreign airlines submit to the US government, the passenger name record (PNR) and advance passenger information system (APIS) data of all passengers on all flights serving or overflying the United States[37] and they also required air marshals on foreign flights serving the United States.[38]

These requirements may result in the potential extra-territorial application of American law to foreign carriers, in that a flight between Canada and Qatar would have to submit passenger's APIS/PNR information to American authorities[39] and Air New Zealand may be required to carry air marshals on its Auckland–London service, which is routed via Los Angeles.

Economic regulation

In years past, regulators determined the routes airlines could fly, the aircraft they could use, the frequency of flights and even stopover points.[40] Today the airline's financial viability is the regulator's concern and thus jurisdictions, such as the United States, impose a 90-day "zero revenue test" on new carriers, to ensure they have enough capital to fund three months of operations without receiving revenue.[41]

1) Ownership requirements

The question of who can own an airline is very political and different States have very different policies on this issue.[42] Foreign ownership limits range from the United States, which limits to 25 percent, the number of shares in an airline that may be owned by foreigners,[43] to Australia which has no limit with respect to the shares of a purely domestic Australian airline, and which allows up to 49 percent foreign ownership in an Australian international airline.[44]

There is a distinction between ownership and control, in that a party that owns 25 percent of the shares of an airline whose shares are otherwise widely held, might be in a position to nominate members of the board of directors or otherwise exercise control.[45] Thus, when an airline is considering an investment in a foreign carrier, regulatory authorities in the jurisdiction where the carrier to be acquired is based, will typically focus on the control, even if the share ownership criteria are met.[46]

2) Merger and Anti-Trust Immunity

Merger and Anti-Trust Immunity (ATI) are governed by the laws of the country in which the airlines are based, and the regulator that approves them varies by jurisdiction. In Australia, Canada, the European Union and New Zealand, competition regulators have jurisdiction over the airline industry,[47] whereas in the United States jurisdiction is shared between the Department of Transport, which approve various types of alliances, and the Department of Justice, which approves mergers.[48]

The approval of mergers is very complex and often becomes political, as opponents try to block the merger and proponents argue in favour. The United/Continental merger was opposed by concerned citizens[49] and the American Airlines merger with US Air was opposed by the US Department of Justice, the States of Arizona, Florida, Pennsylvania, Tennessee and Texas as well as the District of Columbia.[50] Due to the restrictions in foreign ownership in most jurisdictions, the merger of two airlines based in different countries is impossible. The sole exception to this rule is the European Union. There authorities may approve the merger of airlines based in two different EU Member states, such as that between Dutch-based KLM and Air France.[51]

The Metal Neutral Joint Venture (MNJV), is essentially an unincorporated merger of international airlines based different jurisdictions.[52] The airline partners of an MNJV share revenues and expenses and thus become indifferent as to which partner's aircraft operates a particular flight. Because the MNJV includes partner airlines based in different jurisdictions, each jurisdiction must grant ATI to the airline based in its territory. So the A++ MNVJ between Air Canada, Lufthansa (and partners) and United, required ATI approval from Canada,[53] the European Union[54] and the United States.[55]

Environmental regulations

In a world increasingly concerned about climate change, various initiatives have targeted a reduction of greenhouse gas emissions from the airline industry. The more notable are the European Union's Emissions Trading System[56] and ICAO's Carbon Offsetting and Reduction Scheme for International Aviation (CORSIA).[57] Unfortunately, the former has provoked international disputes and is arguably of extraterritorial application[58] and the latter, as an ICAO resolution does not have binding force.[59] Given the increasing profile of climate change and the realization that increased fuel efficiency and alternate fuels are not sufficient to dramatically curb GHG emissions from international civil aviation, it is inevitable that binding international regulations will emerge within the next few years.

Passenger-focused regulation

The fastest set of evolving and expanding regulations are those dealing with the interactions between airlines and passengers. An ICAO report states:

> Travel by air is commonly accepted as a commodity and no longer considered a luxury. Nevertheless, and despite a general reduction in airfares, passenger expectations remain high with respect to facilitation, comfort and timeliness of flights and, according to studies, the overall

air travel experience today is often perceived as not meeting expectations.[60]

Here ICAO diplomatically notices a growing gulf between the fare paid and passengers' expectations. This extent to which this is true does not matter; passengers have more votes than do airline executives and thus the number, variety and force of passenger-focused regulations are increasing.

1) Passenger rights

The first comprehensive passenger rights regime was European regulation EC 261/2004,[61] which deals with denied boarding, flight cancellation and flight delay. It sets different compensation levels depending on the length of the flight and other circumstances such as whether the passenger was given advance notice, or was re-routed to his/her destination with a minor delay as compared with the arrival time listed on the passenger's ticket.

The United States also has a passenger rights regime and it focuses on "Tarmac Delay"[62] and "oversales."[63] More recently, Canada has just adopted "Air Passenger Protection Regulations"[64] which embraces all of the topics of the European and American regimes.

The EU regime applies to all flights departing from all airports within the EU and to all flights operated by carriers based in the EU[65] but it does not cover connecting flights by non-EU carriers.[66] The US regime applies to all American carriers and to non-stop flights operated by foreign carriers from US Airports[67] and the Canadian regime applies to "all flights to, from and within Canada, including connecting flights."[68]

While the EU regime excludes compensation where the passengers have "received benefits or compensation and were given assistance [under a foreign regime],"[69] the others do not and consequently, it is possible to imagine situations where passengers might be eligible to claim under more than one applicable regime.

In 2012, ICAO identified passenger rights regimes in China, the EU, Israel, Latin America, Saudi Arabia, Singapore and the US.[70] Since then New Zealand,[71] Indonesia[72] and Thailand[73] have also adopted regimes.

A decade earlier, in 2003, ICAO argued that "States should minimize differences in the content and application of regulations, with a view to avoiding legal uncertainty that could arise from the extra-territorial application of national laws."[74] Unfortunately this advice does not appear to have been followed and thus it is likely that many new Passenger Rights regimes will emerge in the years to come; Australia is under pressure to regulate air passenger rights.[75]

As if to underscore the pace of evolution of passenger rights themes, a new American law, which became effective in October 2018, is calling on the

Federal Aviation Administration to "within one year ... establish minimum dimensions for passengers seats ... including minimums for seat pitch, width and length ..."[76] This would be the world's first seat-size definition.[77]

2) Disabled passengers

Most industrial nations also have legislation enshrining rights for disabled passengers.[78] For example, the US,[79] Canada[80] and the European Union,[81] have detailed regulations with respect to the transport of persons with mobility challenges. They regulate the carriage of wheelchairs[82] and medically-required oxygen,[83] and even the division of labour between airport authorities and airlines.[84] Some jurisdictions also require airlines to provide a seat for a medically-required attendant and two of these jurisdictions are Canada[85] and the United States.[86]

3) Service animals

Most developed jurisdictions recognize trained service animals as providing legitimate assistance to disabled persons. To this end, disabled persons are allowed to travel with their service animals[87] and regulations may require airlines to provide space for the service animal.[88] In general these service animals are trained, both in terms of behaviour and their ability to offer support to their disabled owners. For the most part, these service animals are dogs and their carriage is largely without incident.

4) Emotional support animals

In the autumn of 2002, Charlotte, a 300-pound Vietnamese pot-bellied pig, acting as a "stress reliever" animal, ran havoc on a US Air flight from Philadelphia to Seattle.[89] Shortly afterwards, the US Department of Transportation (DOT) provided advice on how to distinguish emotional support animals from pets.[90]

In May, 2008, the DOT published its final rule on emotional support and psychiatric service animals[91] and acknowledged the potential for abuse. As if to underscore that point, the National Service Animal Registry, claimed, "It's Easy to Register Your Pet as an Emotional Support Animal"[92] and offered advice on "mak[ing] your dog a service dog."[93]

The emotional support animals were carried on US domestic flights, on some international flight and on some domestic flights in Canada, that were operated by Air Canada but which also carried flight number and connecting passenger from United Airlines. In at least one instance, the presence of these animals provoked an allergic reaction in another passenger and legal actions followed.[94] A few years later, within the span of eight months, two passenger on two different airlines were bitten by emotional support animals,[95] and one of the victims sued the airline.[96]

Shortly afterwards, Delta reported an 84 percent jump since 2016 in incidents involving emotional support animals.[97] It consequently banned all puppies and kittens under 4 months of age as emotional support animals and banned all emotional support animals on flights longer than eight hours.[98] The airline is also requiring more detailed documentation with respect to the passenger needs and the animal's training and abilities.[99]

In 2016, the US DOT attempted to negotiate a change to the rules[100] noting a "concern that a growing number of passengers are presenting untrained animals that are essentially just pets and demanding the right to bring them onboard as service animals."[101] In May 2018, the DOT issued an advance notice of proposed rulemaking and set a 45-day comment period.[102] Over 4,500 comments were received and the Proposed Rule has not yet emerged.[103] This file is still evolving.

Training implications

Obviously, young aviation professions cannot be expected to make themselves experts in the international and domestic regulation of air transport overnight. In most cases, they will be able to consult with other persons at their place of employment or elsewhere, who have the requisite subject matter expertise.

In addition, the International Air Transport Association (IATA) offers training in various subjects and some of this is available on line and in foreign languages.[104] The International Civil Aviation Organization (ICAO) also offers training in various aviation subjects regulated by ICAO and these courses are offered in various locations around the world.[105] For airline professions with a few years of experience, McGill University's Institute of Air & Space Law, offers a "Graduate Certificate in Air and Space Law"[106] and applicants do not need to have a law degree.[107] Within the certificate program, aviation professionals may choose the course, *ASPL 613, Government Regulation of Air Transport*, which is one of the very few courses at any institute of higher learning in the world to focus on all of the issues discussed in this chapter.

It is also recommended to read publications like *Air Transport World*, and *Aviation Week & Space Technology* and to visit websites such as the *Aviation Herald* (www.avherald.com) and the *Aviation Safety Network* (https://aviation-safety.net) because these are very useful in highlighting those incidents that are likely to attract regulatory attention. The Aviation Safety Network website often contains links to the official reports of ICAO-approved accident investigation bodies and these are important, because the recommendations of an accident investigation body in one country, often influences worldwide standards.

Young aviation professionals should also consider joining professional associations where they can interact socially with more experienced aviation professionals and see presentation on various leading-edge topics and thereby keep on top of their game. One such organization is the Royal Aeronautical Society (www.aerosociety.com/), of which this author is a fellow, and which has a chapter in Montreal.

Conclusion

The regulation of the airline industry is both comprehensive and deep. Few, if any other industries, are as heavily regulated, and aviation regulations continue to evolve. Among those regulations that are immediately foreseeable, are new safety regulations as a consequence of two fatal crashes of the Boeing 737 MAX 8,[108] new passenger rights regulations in Canada,[109] and possibly Australia,[110] a review of Metal Neutral Joint Ventures by Canada,[111] and new regulations with respect to the carriage of emotional support animals.[112]

Also emerging are new environmental regulations as States begin implement their Greenhouse Gas reduction commitments pursuant to CORSIA.[113] Finally, the world's first seat-size regulation[114] is about to make its debut.

Many of these regulations will, at least initially, be of "national" application. However some will be of explicit international application, and others, such as America's seat-size regulation, may inevitably set a world-wide standard. For example, the 1990 American smoking ban on flights of six hours or less,[115] applied to flights serving or overflying the US in 2000[116] and within three years virtually every route of every airline worldwide was smoke-free.[117]

Moreover, in a global industry where international alliances and Metal Neutral Joint Ventures are major players, the de facto, if not de jure application of these new regulations to airline routes world-wide will not be long in coming.

Of course, in the five-year period, following the implementing of those regulations that are foreseeable today, other regulations, not yet visible on the horizon, will emerge. It is too early to tell what shape or impact they may have, but it is almost certain, based on past experience, that future regulations will be proclaimed in one jurisdiction or another, that will target domestic carriers and eventually affect international routes.

The breadth, depth and constant evolution of aviation regulation is fascinating as an academic pursuit; there is always something new! However, for airline managers, an awareness of the importance and role of regulation is important to ensure effective compliance and to be able to play a role in shaping future regulations.

Appendix

Table 3.4.1 The various topics covered by domestic and/or international regulation

1. Airfare advertising	20. Emergency Exits	39. Mergers
2. Air marshals	21. Engine; bird ingestion	40. Noise regulations
3. Airport curfews	22. Evacuation procedures	41. No-Fly List
4. Airport Security	23. Financial stability	42. Obese pax
5. Airport slots	24. Flight Attendant/Pax ratio	43. Oxygen carriage
6. Airworthiness	25. Flight crew laws & pods	44. Passenger Rights
7. Allergies	26. Foreign Ownership	45. Pax/bags match
8. APIS/PNR	27. Gambling on board	46. Personal assistant
9. Bankruptcy	28. GHG Emissions	47. Person w disability
10. Competition & ATI	29. HQ Location	48. Pilot Retirement Age
11. Code-share agreements	30. Hijacking	49. Regional service
12. Comfort animals	31. Immigration Liability	50. Rules of the Air
13. Cockpit Doors	32. In-Flight Entertainment	51. Screening Regulations
14. Customs & Duties	33. Insurance Regs	52. Seat pitch
15. Crew medical & drug	34. Labour	53. Security on board
16. Crew qualifications	35. Language of Service	54. Service animals
17. Crew rest	36. Liquids & Gels	55. Smoking
18. Dangerous airports	37. Liquor consumption	56. Tarmac delays
19. Disruptive passengers	38. Metal Neutral Joint Ventures	57. Traffic rights

Notes

1. P. Paul Fitzgerald, MBA, DCL, FRAeS, FCILT, is Adjunct Professor at the Institute of Air & Space Law, McGill University, Canada.
2. P. Paul Fitzgerald, "Freedom to Fly: Route Deregulation in the Canadian Airline Industry" (1989) 14 Ann Air & Sp L 47 at 49. By the way the prototype weighed 370,100 lbs or 167,874 kg.
3. See P. Paul Fitzgerald, *A Level Playing Field for "Open Skies": the Need for Consistent and Harmonized Regulation of Aviation* (The Hague: Eleven International Publishing, 2016) at 22–24 and 34.
4. Martin Staniland, *Government birds: air transport and the state in Western Europe* (Lanham, Md: Rowman & Littlefield Publishers, 2003) at 68.
5. Lester M. Salamon, "Economic Regulation" in Lester M. Salamon & Odus V. Elliott, eds, *The tools of government: a guide to the new governance* (New York: Oxford University Press, 2002) 117 at 120–124.
6. See U.S. Civil Reserve Air Fleet, 49 USC §§ 41,731–41,748.
7. See U.S. Essential Air Service (EAS) Plan, 49 USC § 41,742 (2011). Airlines bid for the route and winning carrier must offer a minimum number of daily flights over a designated route. This subsidy does not distort competition.
8. Convention on International Civil Aviation, 7 December 1944, TIAS 1591, 15 UNTS 295, ICAO Doc 7300 [Chicago Convention].
9. Article 31 and Annex 8 of the Chicago Convention.
10. Article 32 and Annex 1 of the Chicago Convention.
11. These include flight crew hours of service and Crew Resource Management. See John J. Coyle et al, *Transportation: A Supply Chain Perspective* (Mason: Cengage Learning, 2010) at 241 and Barbara G. Kanki, Robert L. Helmreich & José Anca, *Crew Resource Management* (Boston: Elsevier/Academic Press, 2010).
12. Article 30 and Annex 10 of the Chicago Convention.
13. Articles 26 and 37(k) and Annex 13 of the Chicago Convention.
14. See Eur. Aviation Safety Agency, EASA Type-Certificate Data Sheet, TCDS No. A.015, Airbus A340, at 23, online: www.easa.europa.eu/system/files/dfu/TCDS_EASA.A.015_%20Airbus_A340_%20Iss_22_14122015.pdf.
15. See also FAA, Type Certificate Data Sheet No. T0001SE, Boeing 777 (Jul. 6, 2016), online: http://rgl.faa.gov/Regulatory_and_Guidance_Library/rgMakeModel.nsf/0/322587e87743544386257fe90054398b/$FILE/T00001SE_Rev39.pdf.
16. See P. Paul Fitzgerald, "Questioning the Regulation of Aviation Safety" (2012) 37 Ann Air & Sp L 1 at 6–9.
17. On October 29, 2018, Lion Air Flight 610 crashed shortly after taking off from Jakarta. Online: Accident description, Database, Aviation Safety Network https://aviation-safety.net/database/record.php?id=20181029-0. This site will contain a link to the official accident report.
18. On May 10, 2019, Ethiopian Airlines Flight 302 crashed shortly after taking off from Addis Ababa. Online: Accident description, Database, Aviation Safety Network https://aviation-safety.net/database/record.php?id=20190310-0. This site will contain a link to the official accident report.
19. The 18 Annexes are Standards and Recommended Practices (SARPS) and once they are adopted they become international law. A list of the Annexes and a brief description of each is on the ICAO web-site www.icao.int/safety/airnavigation/NationalityMarks/annexes_booklet_en.pdf.
20. Article 38 of the Chicago Convention.
21. For EU, see Paragraph ORO.CC.100(b) of *Commission Regulation (EC) No 965/2012 of 5 October 2012 laying down technical requirements and administrative procedures related to air operations pursuant to Regulation (EC) No 216/2008 of the*

European Parliament and of the Council, [2012] OJ, L 296/1 at 53. For U.S. see 14 CFR § 121. 391(a)(1).
22 See Canadian Union of Public Employees v. Canada (Attorney General) et al, 2018 FC 518. Paras 5–18 of the Decision give the history of the campaign from 2000 to 2015.
23 See Australia Civil Aviation Safety Authority, "Project OS 09/01 – Review of Cabin Crew Ratios set out in CAO 20.16.3". See online www.casa.gov.au/standard-page/project-os-0901-review-cabin-crew-ratios-set-out-cao-20163.
24 See ICAO, (2006) 10 International Standards and Recommended Practices: Annex 1 to the Convention on International Civil Aviation: Personnel Licensing, art 2.1.10, "Limitation of privileges of pilots who have attained their 60th birthday and curtailment of privileges of pilots who have attained their 65th birthday."
25 See 14 CFR § 121.383 (2014); Fair Treatment for Experienced Pilots Act, Pub L No 110–135, 121 Stat 1450 (2007) (codified as amended at 49 USC § 44,729). India has the same standard, see Nicholas Ionides, "India forced to raise pilot retirement age again", Flight International 168:5014 (6–12 December 2005) 10.
26 William Dennis, "China To Raise Mandatory Retirement Age for Pilots", AIN Online (30 May 2017) online: AIN online www.ainonline.com/aviation-news/air-transport/2017-05-30/china-raise-mandatory-retirement-age-pilots. Japan raised the age from 62 to 64 in 2004 and to 67 in 2015. China is currently working to raise the age from 60.
27 Malaysia and Singapore are two countries where the airlines set the retirement age. See ibid.
28 Adamson v. Canadian Human Rights Commission, 2015 FCA 153.
29 Chicago Convention, Preamble.
30 ICAO, (2011) 9 International Standards and Recommended Practices: Annex 17 to the Convention on International Civil Aviation: Security.
31 ICAO, (2011) 13 International Standards and Recommended Practices: Annex 9 to the Convention on International Civil Aviation: Facilitation.
32 ICAO, (2004) 5 International Standards and Recommended Practices: Annex 14 to the Convention on International Civil Aviation: Volume I, Aerodrome Design and Operations.
33 ICAO, Security Manual for Safeguarding Civil Aviation Against Acts of Unlawful Interference, ICAO Doc 8973 – Restricted, 7th ed (Montreal: ICAO, 2010). This manual is only available to law-enforcement agencies.
34 See ICAO, The Universal Security Audit Programme (USAP), online: ICAO www2.icao.int/en/AVSEC/USAP/Documents/USAP_Overview.pdf.
35 See ICAO, "Implementation Support and Development (ISD)", online: ICAO www.icao.int/Security/isd/Pages/default.aspx.
36 See Ami Pedahzur, The Israeli Secret Services and the Struggle Against Terrorism (New York: Columbia University Press, 2009) at 36. See also John Harrison, International Aviation and Terrorism, Evolving Threats, Evolving Security (New York: Routledge, 2009) at 58–59.
37 Aviation and Transportation Security Act, Pub L No 107–71, 115 Stat 597 (2001) (codified as amended in scattered sections of 49 USC), s. 115.
38 See US, Department of Homeland Security, Transportation Security Administration, Aviation Emergency Amendment: Law Enforcement Officers on Flights To, From, or Overflying the United States (EA 1546-03-10) (28 December 2003).
39 See Application by Muhammad Aqif Chaudhry against Qatar Airways (Q.C.S.C.) carrying on business as Qatar Airways and as Qatar Airways Cargo (Qatar) (13 September 2013), 89-C-A-2017, online: Canadian Transportation Agency https://otc-cta.gc.ca/eng/ruling/89-c-a-2017, which allowed Qatar Airways to deny passage to a Montreal-Doha passenger because his name was flagged by American authorities.

40 See *Freedom to Fly, supra* note 1 at 81–87. See also *Agreement between the Government of Canada and the Government of the Hellenic Republic on Air Transport*, 20 August 1984, Can TS 1987 No 11 (entered into force 24 June 1987).
41 US, Department of Transportation, *How to Become a Certificated Air Carrier* (September 2012) at 17. The current wording is "In determining available resources [over the 3-month period], projected revenues cannot be included."
42 See Government of Canada, Competition Policy Review Panel, *Compete to Win: Final Report – June 2008*, online: Industry Canada www.ic.gc.ca/eic/site/cprp-gepmc.nsf/vwapj/Compete_to_Win.pdf/$FILE/Compete_to_Win.pdf.
43 See 49 USC § 40,102(a)(15).
44 *Air Navigation Act 1920*, Act No. 50 of 1920 as amended, s. 11A. The 49% limit is probably to ensure that Australian international carriers do no face ownership questions from States which the airline serves.
45 See, *In the matter of the acquisition of Northwest Airlines, Inc by Wings Holding Inc.* DOT Order 91-1-41 (1991). See Michael Carney &Isabelle Dostaler, "Airline ownership and control: A corporate governance perspective" (2006) 12 Journal of Air Transport Management 63.
46 See, CAPA, Center for Aviation, "Airline ownership and control rules: at once both irrelevant and enduring" (4 June 2017) https://centreforaviation.com/analysis/reports/airline-ownership-and-control-rules-at-once-both-irrelevant-and-enduring-345816.
47 The Australian Competition and Consumer Commission, Canada's Competition Bureau, the European Commission and the Commerce Commission of New Zealand all handle competition files for all industries, not just aviation.
48 See US, Government Accountability Office, *Airline Competition* (GAO-14-515) (2014), especially at 8–9.
49 See, *Malaney v. UAL Corp.*, No. 12–15,182 (9th Cir. 2014).
50 *U.S. v. US Airways Group Inc.*, 13-cv-01236, U.S. District Court, District of Columbia (Washington), online: www.justice.gov/atr/case/us-et-al-v-us-airways-group-inc-and-amr-corporation.
51 EC, *Commission Decision of 11.02.2004, Case No COMP/M.3280 – Air France/KLM*, online: European Commission http://ec.europa.eu/competition/mergers/cases/decisions/m3280_en.pdf.
52 See P. Paul Fitzgerald and Marion Hiriart, "Metal Neutral Joint Ventures – The Biggest International Airlines You have Never Heard of" (2018) 67 ZLW 447 at 449–451.
53 Canada has new powers to review MNJVs. See *Canada Transportation Act*, SC 1996, c 10, section 53.71 to 53.85.
54 EC, *Commission Decision of 23.5.2013 addressed to: – Air Canada – United Airlines, Inc. – Deutsche Lufthansa AG relating to proceedings under Article 101 of the Treaty on the Functioning of the European Union in Case AT.39595*, C(2013) 2836 final (2013), online: European Commission ec.europa.eu/competition/antitrust/cases/dec_docs/39,595/39,595_3012_4.pdf.
55 See US, Department of Transportation, Order 2009-7-10 (2009).
56 See EC, *Directive 2008/101/EC of the European Parliament and of the Council of 19 November 2008 amending Directive 2003/87/EC so as to include aviation activities in the scheme for greenhouse gas emission allowance trading within the Community*, [2009] OJ, L 8/3.
57 See ICAO, "Consolidated statement of continuing ICAO policies and practices related to environmental protection – Global Market-based Measure (MBM) scheme," Res A39-3, ICAO Doc 10,075 (2017), I-80.
58 See *A Level Playing Field, supra* note 2 at 248–250.

59 See Md Tanveer Ahmad, "Global Civil Aviation Emissions Standards – From Noise to Greener Fuels" in Armand de Mestral, P. Paul Fitzgerald & Md Tanveer Ahmad, eds, *Sustainable Development, International Aviation, and Treaty Implementation* (New York: Cambridge University Press, 2018) 32 at 42.
60 ICAO Secretariat, *Consumer Protection and Defination of Passenger Rights in Different Contexts*, ICAO Worldwide Air Transport Conference, 6th Meeting, Agenda Items 2, 2.2, Working Paper No 5, ICAO Doc ATConf/6-WP/5 (7 December 2012) at 1, online: ICAO www.icao.int/Meetings/atconf6/Documents/WorkingPapers/ATConf6-wp005_en.pdf.
61 It is formally called Regulation (EC) No 261/2004 of the European Parliament and of the Council of 11 February 2004 establishing common rules on compensation and assistance to passengers in the event of denied boarding and of cancellation or long delay of flights, and repealing Regulation (EEC) No 295/91.
62 See 14 CFR § 259 – Enhanced Protection for Airline Passengers. See, in particular 14 CFR § 259.5 which deals with Customer Service Plans.
63 See 14 CFR § 250 – Oversales. See, in particular 14 CFR § 250.9 which sets compensation levels.
64 See *Air Passenger Protection Regulations*, SOR/2019-150.
65 Regulation (EC) No 261/2004, Article 3 (1).
66 Emirates Airlines v Dieter Schenkel CJEU Case C-173/07.
67 See 14 CFR § 250 – Oversales. See, in particular 14 CFR § 250.9 which sets compensation levels.
68 See *Air Passenger Protection Regulations*, SOR/2019-150.
69 Regulation (EC) No 261/2004, Article 3 (1)(b).
70 See *ICAO Secretariat*, supra note 59 at 2.
71 NZ, *Civil Aviation Amendment Act 2004* (2004 No 8). See online www.legislation.govt.nz/act/public/2004/0008/latest/DLM240052.html?search=sw_096be8ed817de8e0_delay_25_se&p=1.
72 See Ridha Aditya Nugraha and Lalin Kovudhikulrungsri, "Aviation Legal Issues in Indonesia and Thailand: Towards Better Passengers' Rights in ASEAN" (2017) 1 Indonesia Law Review 23 at 28–31.
73 *Ibid* at 31–36.
74 See *ICAO Secretariat*, supra note 59 at 3.
75 Jodi Bird, "Flight delays and cancellations; Australia lags behind other countries when it comes to compensating consumers for flights delays and cancellations" *Choice* (30 January 2019), online: Choice.com.au www.choice.com.au/travel/on-holidays/airlines/articles/flight-delays-and-cancellations-compensation.
76 See *FAA Reauthorization Act of 2018*, Pub L No 115–254, § 577, 132 Stat. 3358.
77 Claire Quigley et al, *Anthropometric study to update minimum aircraft seating standards* (Loughborough University Institutional Repository, 2001), online: https://dspace.lboro.ac.uk/2134/701. The UK Civil Aviation Authority Airworthiness Notice 64 (1989) used to set a minimum seat pitch of 26 inches. A 2001 study commissioned by the EU, was based on the UK law and recommended a minimum seat pitch of 28.8, "and a minimum separation between seats of 8.3." It was never adopted.
78 See generally, Yu-Chun Chang and Ching-Fu Chen, "Meeting the needs of disabled air passengers: Factors that facilitate help from airlines and airports" (2012) 33 Tourism Management 529.
79 49 USC § 41,705 (2011); 14 CFR Part 382.
80 *Canada Transportation Act*, supra note 52, ss 5(d), 170–172. See also *Personnel Training for the Assistance of Persons with Disabilities Regulations*, SOR/94-42.

81 EC, *Regulation (EC) 1107/2006 of the European Parliament and of the Council of 5 July 2006 concerning the rights of disabled persons and persons with reduced mobility when travelling by air,* [2006] OJ, L 204/1.
82 *Ibid* at 6, art 12.
83 See *Applications filed pursuant to subsections 172(1) and (3) of the Canada Transportation Act, S.C., 1996, c. 10, as amended by Louise Bartlett on behalf of the late Calvert Gibson, Elizabeth Fulton, Harold Gaynes on behalf of Eugene Gaynes, Josie Gould, Margaret Rafferty, and Cathleen Smith against Air Canada regarding the reliability of the oxygen service provided by Air Canada.* (26 June 2008) Canadian Transportation Agency, Decision No 336-AT-A-2008.
84 *Regulation 1107/2006*, supra note 80 at 5–6, arts 7–10.
85 See *In the matter of an application filed by the Estate of Eric Norman, Joanne Neubauer and the Council of Canadians with Disabilities pursuant to subsection 172(1) of the Canada Transportation Act, S.C., 1996, c. 10, as amended, against Air Canada, Jazz Air LP, as represented by its general partner, Jazz Air Holding GP Inc. carrying on business as Air Canada Jazz, WestJet, the Gander International Airport Authority and the Air Transport Association of Canada concerning the fares and charges to be paid by persons with disabilities who require additional seating to accommodate their disabilities to travel by air on domestic air services* (10 January 2008), Canadian Transportation Agency, Decision No 6-AT-A-2008. The same Decision also prohibited Canada's airlines from charging a fare for an extra seat for a passenger an obese passenger.
86 See 14 CFR 382.29 for limited situation under which a US carrier must provide seating for an attendant.
87 See generally, Susan D. Semmel, "When Pigs Fly, They Go First Class: Service Animals in the Twenty-First Century" (2002) 3 Barry L. Rev. 39.
88 The Canadian Transportation Agency has ordered Air Canada and Air Canada Jazz to ensure sufficient floor space is provided for certified service animals at the person with a disability's seat. See *In the matter of Decision No. LET-AT-A-30-2008 issued February 11, 2008 – Robin East against Air Canada and Jazz Air LP, as represented by its general partner, Jazz Air Holding GP Inc. carrying on business as Air Canada Jazz (Air Canada Jazz)* (20 June 2008), Canadian Transportation Agency, Decision No 327-AT-A-2008.
89 Semmel, *supra* note 86 at 39–40.
90 *Guidance Concerning Service Animals in Air Transportation*, 68 Fed Reg 24,874 (2003).
91 *Nondiscrimination on the Basis of Disability in Air Travel*, 73 Fed. Reg. 27,613 (2008) (codified at 14 C.F.R. pt. 382).
92 National Service Animal Registry (NSAR), online: www.nsarco.com/.
93 *Ibid.*
94 See *Application by Marley Greenglass against Air Canada* (2 August 2013), Canadian Transportation Agency, Decision No 303-AT-A-2013. See also *Air Canada v. Greenglass*, 2014 FCA 288.
95 See Yaron Stein, "Marine vet's support dog attacks passenger on Delta flight," *New York Post* (6 June 2017) and Associated Press, "Support dog reportedly bites girl as she boards flight," *New York Post* (23 February 2018).
96 See Kelly Yamanouchi, "Delta passenger bitten by emotional support dog couldn't escape, says attorney," *The Atlanta Journal-Constitution* (8 June 2017).
97 See Alyssa Newcomb, "Cute, but not cute enough: Delta bans emotional support puppies and kittens," *NBC News* (11 December 2018), online: The NBC News www.nbcnews.com/business/consumer/cute-not-allowed-you-can-no-longer-take-your-emotional-n946631.
98 *Ibid.*

99 See Delta Airlines, "Service and Support Animals", online: The NBC News www.nbcnews.com/business/consumer/cute-not-allowed-you-can-no-longer-take-your-emotional-n946631.
100 *Nondiscrimination on the Basis of Disability in Air Travel*, 83 Fed. Reg. 23,804 (2018).
101 *Ibid.*
102 *Traveling by Air With Service Animals*, 83 Fed. Reg. 23,832 (2018).
103 See US, Department of Transportation, *Traveling by Air with Service Animals Advance Notice of Proposed Rulemaking (ANPRM)*, Docket DOT-OST-2018-0068, online: www.regulations.gov/docket?D=DOT-OST-2018-0068.
104 See IATA, Training: Developing professionals for tomorrow's air transport industry, online: www.iata.org/training/Pages/index.aspx.
105 See ICAO, Global Aviation Training, online: www.icao.int/Training/Pages/default.aspx.
106 See. McGill, Institute of Air & Space Law, Academic Programmes and Scholarships, online: www.mcgill.ca/iasl/about/programmes. See Graduate Certificate in Air and Space Law.
107 McGill, Faculty of Law, Eligibility, online: https://mcgill.ca/law/grad-studies/admissions-guide/eligibility. See Graduate Certificate in Air and Space Law.
108 See Lion Air 610, *supra* note 16 and Ethiopian Airlines 302 *supra* note 17.
109 See *Canada's "Air Passenger Protection Regulations"*, *supra* note 63.
110 See *Australia behind other countries*, *supra* note 74.
111 See *Canada has new powers*, *supra* note 52.
112 See *Traveling by Air with Service Animals – ANPRM*, *supra* note 102.
113 See *CORSIA*, *supra* note 56.
114 See *FAA Reauthorization Act of 2018*, *supra* note 75.
115 See generally, Jocelyn Pan, Elizabeth M. Barbeau, et al, "Smoke-Free Airlines and the Role of Organized Labor: A Case Study" (2005) 95:3 American Journal of Public Health 398.
116 49 USC § 41,706 Prohibitions against smoking on passenger flights.
117 The 15 remaining airlines that allowed smoking were based in the third world. See Airline information: Smoking policies at a glance (15 July 2003), online: https://web.archive.org/web/20131019235317/http://hem.passagen.se/fungus/airlines.html.

3.5 Professional reflection – Managing the paradox

Asking for more qualified people in a shortage situation

José Sánchez-Alarcos Ballesteros

Introduction

When there is a shortage of people, the most common strategy to overcome it is a decrease in required qualifications. This can be overcome by automation or very structured procedures in the spirit of the Scientific Organization of Work as defined by Frederick W. Taylor, that is, dividing tasks into pieces till the point that meaning is lost for the operator.[1] The first time that the strategy of decreasing qualifications was applied in aviation was during World War II in the so-called Operation Bolero, a plan to cross the Atlantic Ocean with brand-new B17s and inexperienced pilots. They calculated a loss of 10 percent of the aircraft during the operation, while pilots were instructed to follow the aircraft in front of them. After that, still during World War II, the loss of life during bombing missions led to similar practices.

In peacetime, this practice was not acceptable while requirements for pilots increased. Therefore, pilots became collectively highly regarded – and highly paid – and different methods were tried to decrease the collective bargaining power of their unions and, at the same time, to manage an eventual shortage situation.

Two trajectories were defined, both levered by technology:

1. Intensive use of Electronic Flight Simulators to train ab-initio pilots, with specific licenses like multi-crew pilot license (MPL).
2. Automation, able to correct mistakes by the pilots and offering nice and clear interfaces and, apparently, simplified.

These solutions appeared to work but some accidents, like XL888T,[2] AF447,[3] Asiana 214,[4] Lion Air 620,[5] Ethiopian Airlines 302[6] and some others, made evident that this training model can work in expected situations, but it has serious flaws to manage unexpected events.

Then, we reach the present situation: There is a shortage of people while, at the same time, there is evidence of inadequate training, leading to confusion and major events in unexpected situations.[7]

To manage this situation, pushing in two apparently contradictory directions will be required.

A part of the solution could come from the Ecological Interface Design (EID[8]) concept or any other option that makes visible to the pilot how the system reaches a conclusion and not only a final outcome whose process remains hidden for the pilot. However, EID or any interface inspired by the same principles, despite better suited to manage unexpected events, will not be easier than the present model under common situations but, perhaps, the opposite. Things would be made simpler instead of hiding the real complexity with the risk inherent to that practice[9].

A second part of the solution will come from different recruiting practices, without shortcuts but trying to attract more people with the right profile to aviation: a recruitment process centered in an easy interface could allow less experienced people performing tasks that, in the past, required highly trained professionals. However, if people must be able to overcome failures and wrong assessments from the system, that means again highly trained professionals, able to understand what is inside the system well beyond the interface design.

It's the economy, stupid

This statement, used during Bill Clinton's election campaign, can summarize where many of the present problems are. In the past, cases like XL888T, AF447 and, at present, the events related to B737MAX were attributed to lack of training. Actually, every time there is a major accident, a "lack-of-training" wildcard is expected to go out. "Lack-of-training" is a very comfortable label, since designs and organizations remain unquestioned because, at the end of the day, the origin of the event was a poorly trained operator.

However, not many people are able to see that "lack-of-training" as a main piece of the system: more complex products are supposed to require more trained operators but, as Bainbridge[10] discovered long ago in "Ironies of Automation", that is far from being the common practice.

Complex systems remain hidden under attractive interfaces and pilots receive operative knowledge about them – the kind of knowledge about computers that an average Windows user has – making the task far easier while in foreseen conditions. Deeper questions, for instance with the file system and how it works, are carefully avoided or concealed because the metaphors are supposed to be enough for a basic management of the system. Cases like those mentioned before show that the pilot is informed about the expected behavior of the plane, as long as everything works as expected. However, pilots are not informed about many potential failures able to trigger unexpected automatic actions, like those that happened in XLT888T or AF447.

In these situations, the system disguises its own internal complexity and the pilot is taught neither the plane nor the system but the interface. The circle closes precisely on the economic side: the payback of technology investment comes in two different but closely related ways:

1. More complexity does not mean more training but less. Part of the complexity comes precisely from the effort in designing easier interfaces. Actually, an old design like the first-generation Boeing 747 (B747), has lost about two thirds of the elements in the cockpit while complexity has clearly increased.
2. Harder to fly airframes can be built since, despite less training, pilots will be protected from their own errors by the system. The system can even overrule the pilot if the controlling algorithm decides that the pilot is mistaken.

The cases related to the Boeing 737MAX show both: An airframe, originally certified in 1967, had problems being adapted to new, bigger and heavier engines. Boeing found a solution by installing the engines in an advanced position but, by doing that, the behavior of the plane made it prone to serious mistakes in some situations.

Instead of adopting a solution that would make the airframe harder to fly and different from the original 737, Boeing adopted – and the FAA certified – a technological protection intended to guarantee similar behavior of the plane to former 737 series planes. Furthermore, at the beginning, pilots did not even know about the existence of such a system. Why bother them with technicalities?

So all the elements are present in the 737MAX, although this case is only being used to illustrate a far wider situation, one not limited to a model or a manufacturer: A harder to fly airframe that, supposedly, did not require more training since it was technologically protected. The final test to show whether pilots are given "Windows knowledge" is the fact that they did not know about the existence of the system.

The situation could equally be called "user transparency", a very common and paradoxical concept used in the IT field, whose meaning is exactly the opposite to transparency: It's a way to tell the users that they should not be disturbed with details like knowing how the system really works.

Therefore, under-training is a major part of the system, not an accident or a mistake by training designers but a central part. Claiming lack of training when a major accident happens can be true but, even if true, it is very often useless.

Once a whole system has been designed to be managed by people with a low training level, serious changes would affect every part of that system, that is, people and technology. Then, instead of major changes, after an accident there is a standard behavior: Pointing to lack of training,[11] adding a patch to the training program to manage the last specific event, perhaps a minor design change and ... wait for the next unexpected event, repeating the cycle. Complaining about lack of training is a part of the process.

Avoiding major changes in design and training is another part of the same process.

It could be claimed that 2017 was the best year in aviation safety and, despite 2018 showing worse figures,[12] this should not be read as a trend. Then, if the results are so good, why would anyone be interested in major changes?

The answer is apparent: To maintain the good results. Safety is not a static but a dynamic situation. Everyone claims that safety levels are kept but, at the same time, organizations make another turn on the efficiency screw and, apparently endorsed by the former results, some of them start becoming adventurous.

Many improvements in aviation bring a downside. Some planes that could be harder to fly are software protected – the B737MAX issue provides a clear example – and increasing engine reliability drives a decrease in the number of engines,[13] even for very long flights. Altimetry precision can be enhanced but, at the same time, more planes are packed in the same airspace[14] or a plane can be filled with lithium batteries[15] while improving fire protection against them.

All these movements together with those related to high complexity/low training situation are focused in efficiency.[16] Supposedly, these efficiency improvements happen while the safety level is kept. So, nobody should expect a sudden wave of accidents related with any of them. If, instead of a wave, a single efficiency-driven accident happens, the answer is pre-programmed: Trying to keep the focus on the individual features of the event, denying the systemic side of it.[17] Lack of training[18] is one of the favorite wildcards to do so.

The Disaster Threshold[19]

The Disaster Threshold is an idea coined by the German sociologist Niklas Luhmann. Organizational development based in complex systems and poorly trained operators is common in many activities. An observation of places like hypermarkets, banks and many others will show that people are attached to Enterprise Resource Planning systems, having only user knowledge about their specific task. Furthermore, many years performing operative tasks without the functional knowledge related with them will not allow these workers to build new knowledge, beyond managing some bugs in the system.

The economic sense of this option is in a single fact: People are easy to train and replace. Therefore, they should not expect high salaries. That's one of the main paybacks of technology in its purest form. However, there is a major question about this common practice: Is that acceptable in high-risk environments?

The economic sense is easy to understand but there is an important side-effect: Unplanned or unforeseen activities should not be expected to be adequately managed. The system could become unresponsive to those situations and, as far as the stakes are low, there is not a serious outcome.

A system designed with these parameters can be defined as a perfect bureaucracy. Since it works with much more information than a traditional bureaucracy, it will have more resources available in more situations. The width of foreseen situations increases but the incapacity to manage unforeseen events remains or increases too.

At a first glance, that does not seem an acceptable situation in high-risk environments, especially if these environments don't have a "Pause" button and things happen very fast. Very often, aviation and nuclear environments are compared regarding safety levels and, usually, the nuclear field scores higher, simply because flying planes don't have a "Pause" button while nuclear plants do.[20]

Then, what should the right training be in an open environment where the stakes are high and the available time is short? Two answers can be found:

1. Operating knowledge or "Windows knowledge" model is not enough. The pilot needs a functional knowledge of the system, not only the rules to operate an interface. The training and the authority over the system must be enough to manage both foreseen and unforeseen situations.
2. If unforeseen situations are scarce enough to be pushed to a corner and hidden under some convenient labels like "lack-of-training", "complacency", "non-compliance" or some others, they can be discounted as a kind of expected loss while pilots are given operating knowledge, more centered in the interface than in the system.

That is the point where the Disaster Threshold[21] starts to work. Everyone is conscious that absolute safety does not exist. The ICAO itself recognizes this and the early editions of its Safety Management Manual[22] spoke openly about "maintain the appropriate balance between production and protection". That's common practice and the statement is fully correct as far as "safety risks are kept under an appropriate level of control" as the ICAO establishes in the same paragraph.

However, defining the position for the appropriate level of control is hard since this is a mobile target. Trade-offs are acceptable as far as the disaster itself is not a part of them and it's not previously discounted to calculate the return on investment.

The Disaster Threshold is the point where trade-offs are not admitted anymore, and people concerned with safety don't want to keep playing under the established rules. At a time when information travels at lightspeed, trespassing the Disaster Threshold is dangerous for any company or any activity.

The 737MAX events showed a new risk source: It's not only the accident and the casualties but the social reaction coming from that. That's hard to calculate in risk assessments. Claiming lack of training is a common resource but it does not work once the control of information flow is lost ... and it's lost by the main players. A virtually infinite number of communicators can air their own position, reaching any imaginable place. By the same token, defending an official position is hard to sustain – as Boeing did after the first major accident – simply because it will add fuel to the fire.

That's why the "Windows knowledge" option does not work. Under this option, unforeseen events can find pilots untrained to manage them and, even if trained, handcuffed by a system designed to protect pilots from their own errors. Naming the event afterwards is not credible anymore. Concerned people will accept an unforeseeable event, not a discounted one. That's the Disaster Threshold and that's why functional knowledge is required for all generations of pilots, including the most recent.

Real knowledge, not metaphors

If metaphors are not a valid option to show how a system works, some companies are confronting social risks by being attached to them as a training practice. They are a good solution in efficiency terms but no answer should be expected under unforeseen situations.

Building efficient systems designed to be managed through strictly procedural knowledge can be a valid solution in environments whose risks are calculated with the same criteria used by an insurance company. However, it, does not work in high-risk environments where the idea of "disaster threshold"[23] and the social risk related with it apply. The idea is far from new: The old Scientific Organization of Work, as established by Taylor[24] is precisely about that: Poorly trained people manufacturing complex products, while any required thinking is performed by others. The present trend is simply the old Taylor recipe updated.

George Soros[25] was one of the first authors using a concept that applies here: Market Fundamentalism. Life risk should not be managed with market criteria, at least, once we have trespassed the Disaster Threshold.

Criticism of the present situation has come from different sides. Perrow[26] spoke about "tightly coupled organizations" and how a minor event could provoke a snowball effect if there are not flexible links in the organization. In some way, it could be said that errors in efficient organizations are also efficient, since they use the same channels to spread their effects as within ordinary operations. That's why a minor mistake can produce big effects.

Another criticism of the fundamentals of the present system is the concept of Law of Requisite Variety,[27] explaining why a complex system cannot be properly managed by having controls whose complexity is lower than the system itself. Parts of the system are managed by the system itself while the pilot receives a Windows-style metaphor about how it works.

Finally, other authors like Leveson[28] focus on system effects, that is, the fact that there are situations where an event cannot be assigned to a single part of the system, since every part worked as expected in the design, but in the wrong context.

Then, claiming lack of training every time a new major event hits, adding a patch to manage the specific event does not work anymore. A new training model aimed at giving the pilot the required knowledge in the required moment and full authority to use that knowledge is a must.

That cannot be done by keeping pilots in the position of a passive observer, supervising and waiting for the Warning System to tell them they are required. Among the different initiatives to change the situation, an EID[29] concept has attracted the attention of designers. However, although the concept is well known and has existed for some time, and its structure seems appealing, nobody could say that this has been successful.

The secret is again in the economic side: The EID concept gives an option to manage unforeseen situations but, at the same time, ordinary operations can be more complex than operations performed under highly automated environments. Furthermore, EID implies functional knowledge and the relationship between the different layers of the system or, in other words, higher training needs.

Higher training means higher investment, initially, and every time a new rating is required. Therefore, longer time is required to get people operating planes and these people are harder to replace than those whose training process is lower and shorter. EID is clearly aligned with the safety side, not the economic side. That's why it has been difficult to gain acceptance of the approach.

Any change aimed to respect the Law of Requisite Variety, that is, the idea of having a number of states in the control mechanism greater than or equal to the number of states in the system being controlled is expected to find a hard opposition since it will go against efficiency. Right now, a good part of the external variety is managed by the system itself and pilots are fed with the information that the designers suppose they should know. The commonly used labels "Need-to-Know" and "Nice-to-Know" are self-explanatory. However, there are situations where "Nice-to-Know" or even "Why-do-you-need-to-know?" become an imperative "Need-to-Know".

What if US1549[30] pilots, before trying to land on the Hudson river, had not known that Ram Air Turbine does not keep all the systems active while Auxiliary Power Unit does? They would not have switched on the APU and the chances of a successful outcome would have decreased seriously. Since some A320 pilots ignore this detail, should this item qualify as Need-to-Know or Nice-to-Know?

What if AF447[31] pilots, while going down on the ocean with two engines working perfectly had known the rationale under the bizarre behavior of a stall warning that remained silent in the worst condition, because the speed was so low that the system interpreted it like being on ground, went out when the plane started to recover and the system read it as flying at a very low speed? Could the accident have been avoided?

What if QF32[32] pilots had not been critical about the system, when it gave information about failures in an engine placed very far from the one that exploded and had not detected wrong information? Perhaps they would have lost precious time by attending to false warnings instead of solving the situation.

What if the BA38[33] captain, when both engines stopped during the approach, had not shown airmanship enough to raise the flaps in the final approach phase, against any conventional wisdom? The plane could have crashed against a building instead of gliding almost to the runway threshold.

What if the U232[34] captain, after an explosion broke all the hydraulic systems and no conventional control was available, had accepted that, since control surfaces could not be managed, nothing could be done? Probably, no one could have survived the crash.

From a cynical point of view, these cases are scarce enough to become irrelevant. Heavy loss of life could have happened in all these cases – full loss in AF447 and fewer than expected in U232 – but a full loss could be justified in all of them. Lack of training or fully unforeseeable situations could be enough to justify them. Then, why be concerned?

The general public, including aviation users, see that in a different way: A real pilot, not a systems operator, can have some chances to avoid the disaster. A blind system or a blinded operator does not.

Managing qualified workforce scarcity

The system, as it is right now, is perfect to handle qualified workforce scarcity and it is intended to improve in the short term. In this case, improving means insisting on the successful solution, pressing for more efficiency.

Some trends and present practices show that in a very clear way:

1. Single pilot[35]: Some manufacturers, regulators and airlines are speaking openly about the possibility of having a single pilot in the plane, of course, supported by more advanced systems.
2. Cargo drones[36]: Planes without a pilot inside, that can fly dedicated tracks far from passenger traffic.
3. Limited licenses[37]: There is a kind of rat-race at this point. After MPL license, trained ab-initio in a simulator to fly planes designed for multi-crew, instead of going step by step flying bigger and faster aircrafts, many regulators have accepted pilots with very low experience. Jokes like saying that the most expensive seat in a plane is the one at the right side in the cockpit are already commonplace.

If these three options to overcome scarcity of pilots' are analyzed together, some paths will emerge: If an organization wants to get rid of something or someone, the first step would be making that something or someone useless.

Why are there two pilots in planes above 19 passengers? The most obvious answer is that, if one of them becomes incapacitated, the other pilot can fly the plane, a similar answer as to why a plane has more than one engine.

However, that is not the only answer. Some flight phases have a very heavy workload that can be shared; one of the pilots is flying the plane while the other is monitoring, that is, there is a crosscheck to avoid mistakes. If there is an uncommon situation, there is an opportunity for a discussion among experts trying to get a solution.

If second-class pilots are accepted, there will not be a discussion among experts since, at least one of them is far from being an expert. Capt. Sullenberger[38] addressed this point in this way:

> A cockpit crew must be a team of experts, not a captain and an apprentice. In extreme emergencies, when there is not time for discussion or for the captain to direct every action of the first officer, pilots must be able to intuitively know what to do to work together.

For identical reasons, monitoring performed by someone without the right experience will be questionable; the workload can be shared, but the most expert will keep an eye on the actions of the other pilot and that can be more exhausting than doing everything by oneself. Then, the only reason that would remain in that scenario – having second-class pilots – would be having a backup in case of incapacitation.

Now, if this point is analyzed together with the single pilot project, an interesting fact can be found: Some of the defenders of this option will allege that the first officer in a plane is perfectly dispensable, if the plane can be controlled from ground in case of an emergency.

However, if the first officer is perfectly dispensable, and the practices of some airlines endorsed by the regulators would suggest that, it is because of a conscious organizational design: Get inexperienced pilots, put them in the first officer seat and, after that, claim that the first officer is useless.

There is still another issue related with that. If the solution is a pilot that, from ground, can override the pilot in the plane, it should be interesting recalling the RQ-170 case[39]: A military drone – military means, usually, higher security standards[40] – was forced to land in Iran. The hijackings of 9/11 would not be the worst nightmare to come true if hacking flying planes from the ground becomes feasible. That's valid not only for the single pilot proposal but for cargo drones.

Of course, cargo drones, right now, are in an experimental phase. However, if drones start to deliver goods and the experiment works, that would be the first step to move that practice into the passenger transportation field. How to convince passengers into a pilotless plane? Telling them that it is as safe as the piloted plane – if not safer – and maybe the plane ticket is far cheaper. Again, the Disaster Threshold concept would be dismissed under this option. People can be willing to accept trade-offs but not if the disaster becomes a real and discounted option in the risk assessment.

Therefore, it could be said that the main recipe in aviation to overcome the present pilot shortage can be summarized in two words: Keep going. There are many reasons to advise changing the course but, while these reasons don't offer a solution to the scarcity problem, the "keep going" solution does not seem acceptable and safety could suffer in both the short and long term if this complacent attitude about efficiency improvement is kept.

Alternative solution

This section will start with an anecdote that can show some ways to manage a scarcity problem: Anyone going to a casino can be surprised by the activity of the croupiers, especially those working the roulette. Several people are there; the most intriguing of them is one placed at the extreme end of the table, seated on a high chair and whose eyes are constantly moving, "photographing" every corner of the table. Once the bets are set, the ball runs and the lucky number is told, frantic activity occurs: The lucky ones receive their money and the money of the others is removed from the table. That's all; a lot of people, different amounts, different numbers, not a single thing written and, usually, no complaints. How do they do that and where do they get these people? The answer, from a Human Resources manager, was surprisingly simple:

> Some traditional bars, with a waiter serving drinks on a desk, required a skill to know what every client wanted, what every client had, how much this client must pay and both, serving and charges, should be managed fast and accurately. When someone was discovered to have these specific skills and, additionally, had the adequate look, the chances of being invited to the croupiers' school increased exponentially.

If this model is applied to recruit future pilots, key skills should be identified, that is, skills hard to acquire that can become the foundations for other more complex skills. The most common approach implies buying already developed skills instead of planning the acquisition of them. Otherwise, it would be hard to explain why some positions are in high demand while some others requiring a very similar set of skills show a surplus, instead of having a flow from the least to the most in-demand position. Since developing skills is expensive and time-consuming, many potentially skilled professionals are lost along the way. So, an early detection of skills to be nurtured could be an alternative approach.

The aviation field has some innovative models to overcome skills scarcity, that were used in wartime. The best-known among them are, perhaps, Operation Bolero and the German prewar model.

Operation Bolero involved crossing the Atlantic Ocean with B17 bombers, recently manufactured in the United States and widely used in World War II, to reach the British Isles. Since there was a serious scarcity of trained pilots, many people with very limited experienced flew them, with instructions to following the preceding plane.

In some way, this it resembles the present model of downgrading licenses and accepting people with lower experience to overcome scarcity of pilots. However, some practices are acceptable in wartime but harder to justify in civil transportation.

German prewar practice was very different: Since, after World War I, Germany had limitations on the size and type of army troops, they decided, before breaking openly the prohibition on training war pilots, to train pilots-to-be. They started to attract youngsters to gliding schools and the most skilled among them would become the seeds of the new Luftwaffe. As a side effect, gliding remained a popular activity in Germany.

Before defining a model to manage the shortage of pilots, there is another question: Why the shortage? Why, from time to time, is there a surplus of pilots[41]? Why, sometimes, do both happen at the same time, depending on categories of aircraft?

Shortage-surplus cycles are not a new phenomenon. Shortage encourages people to become pilots but, once they finish, they find that many people shared the idea and there is a surplus. The surplus empties the flight schools driving to scarcity and the cycle is repeated once again. Certainly, the market is growing due to social changes in large countries but, since this is not a sudden phenomenon, training and manufacturing could be adapted to this situation if, instead of reacting to the present needs, there is a planning of requirements.

Building capacity to overcome new requirements is not new in aviation. Actually, when the first wide-body planes appeared, some European airlines assembled a group devoted to maintenance – the Atlas group – where every airline would be in charge of maintaining a specific model for all the partners. However, as the market evolved, some of the partners reached production of a number of wide-body planes that made it worthwhile for them to build their own installations, driving some partners to have their costly installations underutilized. Experiences like that and the cost of training installations, despite innovations like the application of virtual reality to training, deter some investors from building capacity without clear long-term agreements.

That would mean not only building training capacity adapted to the market requirements but being conscious of the evolution of the professional profiles in aviation, adapting the training processes to the required skills. Then, pilots need skills different from classic "stick-and-rudder" but, at the same time, giving up stick-and-rudder skills brings problems long known. Cases like the aforementioned Asiana 214 are clear in that point but, well before that (2004), a serious warning was published[42] by CAA-UK about the loss of piloting skills.

Maintenance engineers are confronted with similar changes in the required skills and, after a serious mistake, that change can be found in an official report[43] in these terms: "With the introduction of aircraft like the A320, A330, A340 and Boeing 777, it is no longer possible for maintenance staff to have enough information about the aircraft and its systems to understand adequately the consequences of any deviation". Actually, even trying to do their best, a misunderstood schema can lead to the deactivation of a basic system[44] and a major accident.

Ait traffic controllers confront similar challenges and getting the picture of flying planes is impossible in some crowded areas without heavy technological support. Then, understanding the system they operate can be almost as important as understanding air traffic rules and dynamics.

Therefore, the challenge is getting real professionals, not only system operators, skilled, properly trained and in the numbers required. This profile would require serious design changes, offering a clear functional knowledge instead of "Windows knowledge" or metaphors about how things are supposed to work.

The first step would be to start by promoting activity. It is possible to start flying gliders at 14 years old – earlier than driving – and, hence, gliding schools could become a first recruiting place. Good students with good flying skills could be offered scholarships to remain in the aviation field.

The second step is a serious assessment of what are the most critical skills and knowledge, that is, those skills and knowledge that are harder, more expensive and more time-consuming to acquire. Once identified, a good amount of effort should be devoted to specific training of prospective pilots instead of waiting for experience to build them.

An example that reflects this problem is the difference in the training processes for controllers and for pilots. Future controllers are placed in virtual environments that include pseudo-pilots, often behaving in bizarre ways to develop the skills of the future controller. On the other hand, professional flight simulators make excellent reproductions of the physical environment, internal and external, but they are usually centered on the plane and its systems, while the right behavior in airspace and its complexities must be learned through experience. Pseudo-controllers can be found in some videogames played in networks, but they are not common in professional flight simulators, where interaction in complex environments usually does not go beyond collision scenarios.

Asking for thousands of hours of flight experience instead of specific competencies is limiting access to the jobs where the shortage can be found and, at the same time, it does not guarantee having the right experience if that experience is repetitive or it is not relevant. Simulator checks, commonly used in the recruiting process, speak about skills and mastery at handling the plane in normal and abnormal – but foreseen – situations.

Learning how to handle interpersonal situations, related to crew, passengers, ATCs, dispatching and many others is supposed to come from experience; managing decisions affecting services or safety, navigating difficult and crowded airspaces, assessment of uncommon situations and many others are supposed to come from experience. Furthermore, a young pilot will be judged less "serious" in some cultural environments.

Then, perhaps the scarcity of pilots in some categories is "manufactured" in the sense that it does not come from a real scarcity but from the lack of communicating vessels among the different stocks of professional pilots. Encouraging people to start flying at an early age, getting the best people, defining clearly the skills and knowledge that can become a bottleneck and building capacity to overcome it ... that's the solution, not downgrading the requirements still further.

There is a principle, very often forgotten, that remains critical in situations where talent for an activity is urgently required: How the recruiting process is managed.

Many recruiters see themselves as filtering agents; they set different steps in the process, attending to the cost of every step. Then, when there are many candidates, they will use a cheap method to eliminate a large number of them, i.e., curriculum review.

As the process advances, they introduce other more expensive and more individual-centered methods. Then, the pilot can be called for an interview in the headquarters of the airline, simulator tests and so on, but the filtering principle remains. Then, under this principle, the recruiter whether they are relevant or not. At the end of this process, many good candidates can be rejected while there is not a guarantee that the chosen ones are the best and most desirable options. Simply, they are those that did not give the recruiter a good excuse to get rid of them.

There is an alternative option: Defining in advance which are the critical competencies, attending to the difficulty, time or cost to be acquired. Then, the first stage of the process should be aimed to eliminate those that don't show these specific competencies.

Once there is a pool of acceptable candidates, the filtering attitude should be lost in favor of a different and non-filtering question: What does this candidate bring that could prompt an offer? The answer does not need to be a higher performance in the features used as filters. Valuable features can be outside of the profiles and, once the recruiters have these features before them, they should be able to recognize their value.

Recruiting by filtering only drives the elimination of valid options. By keeping attached to a single profile, people from other professional paths are denied access to the jobs and, hence, the recruiter contributes to scarcity by accepting only photocopies of a single profile. Thus, the recruiter could try to keep safe from hiring the wrong person but, at the same time, this can drive to a different and serious mistake in scarcity times: Rejecting the good candidate.

An alternative option could involve analyzing the required competencies, identifying the critical ones and keeping an open mind, which will help to incorporate new and skilled people into the market, not simply downgraded options to overcome scarcity.

Of course, recovering a role different from systems operator should have an impact on design too. Functional knowledge instead of metaphors is a must and this requirement could lead to a requirement for new competencies.

current planes are filled with systems and that won't change nor should it be criticized. However, the behavior of these systems must be understood. That can mean working from two different directions: Designing understandable systems and recruiting people able to understand them.

It should not be forgotten that planes still in production like the Boeing-777 have systems powered by an Intel 80,486 processor.[45] The cost and time of the certification processes mean manufacturers optimize software, making it harder to understand, instead of installing updated hardware without requiring software optimization that can lead to bugs and difficulties in understanding its functions.

For the pilots, gaining functional knowledge implies getting familiar enough with IT technology to evaluate algorithms and anticipate the behavior of the plane in normal and abnormal situations.

Both approaches are required at the same time. One of them will be useless if the other is not present. On the other hand, downgrading the job of the pilots as a first step towards the elimination of the job through technology is the current practice but, certainly, that's not the wisest way to fight scarcity nor to maintain safety.

Conclusions

Complex technology and low qualifications do not appear to be an adequate mix. It is especially inadequate in high-risk environments where some situations can require an answer in a very short time.

With the present scarcity of pilots it can be tempting to insist this mix is the solution, but it is more likely that the problem lies in a different place: Some pilots are in high demand, while others are in a situation of unemployment or underemployment.

Designing training programs that can capture the essential competencies required instead of simply asking for hours flown is one way to ensure a flow between the different levels on which a professional pilot can be.

Enabling pilots to foresee what the plane will do instead of being surprised by it can require design changes and training changes and, apparently, these changes could increase the present scarcity. However, that would be the wrong conclusion. In the main part, scarcity comes from incorrect management rather than increases in air traffic. Changing that can result in increased safety and job satisfaction.

Notes

1. Air Accidents Investigation Branch (1995). *Report 2/95 report on the incident to Airbus A320-212, G-KMAM London Gatwick Airport on 26 August 1993.* www.gov.uk/aaib-reports/2-1995-airbus-a320-212-g-kmam-26-august–1993.
2. Bureau d'Enquêtes et d'Analyses pour la sécurité de l'aviation civile (2010). *Report on the accident on 27 November 2008 off the coast of Canet-Plage (66) to the Airbus A320-232 registered D-AXLA operated by XL Airways German.*
3. Bureau d'Enquêtes et d'Analyses pour la sécurité de l'aviation civile (2012). *Final report on the accident on 1st June 2009 to the Airbus A330-203 registered F-GZCP operated by Air France flight AF 447 Rio de Janeiro – Paris.*
4. National Transportation Safety Board (2014). *NTSB/AAR-14/01 Descent below visual glidepath and impact with seawall Asiana Airlines Flight 214 Boeing 777-200ER, HL7742.* San Francisco, CA July 6, 2013.
5. PRELIMINARY KNKT.18.10.35.04 Aircraft Accident Investigation Report PT. Lion Mentari Airlines Boeing 737-8 (MAX); PK-LQP Tanjung Karawang, West Java Republic of Indonesia 29 October 2018 https://reports.aviation-safety.net/2018/20181029-0_B38M_PK-LQP_PRELIMINARY.pdf.
6. Aircraft Accident Investigation Preliminary Report Ethiopian Airlines Group B737-8 (MAX) Registered ET-AVJ 28 NM South East of Addis Ababa, Bole International Airport March 10, 2019 https://flightsafety.org/wp-content/uploads/2019/04/Preliminary-Report-B737-800MAX-ET-AVJ.pdf.
7. CAA PAPER 2004/10 Flight Crew Reliance on Automation https://publicapps.caa.co.uk/docs/33/2004_10.PDF.
8. Burns, C. M., & Hajdukiewicz, J. (2017). *Ecological Interface Design.* Boca Ratón, FL: CRC Press.
9. Leveson, N. (2011). *Engineering a Safer World: Systems Thinking Applied to Safety.* Boca Ratón, FL: MIT Press.
10. Bainbridge, L. (1983). Ironies of automation*Automatica*, 19(6), 775–779.
11. Bureau d'Enquêtes et d'Analyses pour la sécurité de l'aviation civile (2012). *Final report on the accident on 1st June 2009 to the Airbus A330-203 registered F-GZCP operated by Air France Flight AF 447 Rio de Janeiro – Paris.* www.bea.aero/docspa/2009/f-cp090601.en/pdf/f-cp090601.en.pdf.
12. IATA (2019) IATA releases 2018 airline safety performance. www.iata.org/pressroom/pr/Pages/2019-02-21-01.aspx.
13. Airbus (2014): *EASA certifies A350XWB for up-to-370 minute ETOPS* www.airbus.com/newsroom/press-releases/en/2014/10/easa-certifies-a350-xwb-for-up-to-370-minute-etops.html.
14. FAA (2017) *Reduced vertical separation minimum* www.faa.gov/air_traffic/separation_standards/rvsm/.
15. Boeing (2013) *Batteries and advanced airplanes* https://787updates.newairplane.com/787-Electrical-Systems/Batteries-and-Advanced-Airplanes.
16. Airbus (2019) *Commonality* www.airbus.com/aircraft/passenger-aircraft/commonality.html.
17. Bolai, R. (2010) *An analysis of McDonnell Douglas's ethical responsibility in the crash of Turkish Airlines Flight 981* https://turkishdc10.files.wordpress.com/2008/01/an-analysis-of-mcdonnell-douglas-crash-74.pdf.
18. Gebrekidan, S. (2019). *Ethiopian airlines had a Max 8 simulator, but pilot on doomed flight didn't receive training on it* www-nytimes-com.cdn.ampproject.org/c/s/www.nytimes.com/2019/03/20/world/africa/ethiopian-airlines-boeing.amp.html.
19. Luhmann, N. (2017). *Risk: A Sociological Theory.* London: Routledge.
20. www.nuclear-power.net/nuclear-power/reactor-physics/reactor-dynamics/scram-reactor-trip/.
21. Luhmann, N. (2017). *Risk: A Sociological Theory.* London: Routledge.

22 Doc, I. C. A. O. (2013). *9859–Safety Management Manual* (SMM). International Civil Aviation Organization.
23 Luhmann, N. (2017). *Risk: A Sociological Theory*. London: Routledge.
24 Taylor, F. W. (2004). *Scientific Management*. Routledge.
25 Soros, G. (1998). The crisis of global capitalism open society endangered.
26 Perrow, C. (2011). *Normal Accidents: Living with High Risk Technologies*, Updated Edition. New Jersey: Princeton University Press.
27 Ashby, W. R. (1991). Requisite variety and its implications for the control of complex systems. In *Facets of Systems Science. International Federation for Systems Research International Series on Systems Science and Engineering* vol 7. (pp. 405–417) Boston, MA: Springer.
28 Leveson, N. (2011). *Engineering a Safer World: Systems Thinking Applied to Safety*. MIT Press.
29 Bennett, K. B., & Flach, J. M. (2011). *Display and Interface Design: Subtle Science, Exact Art*. Boca Ratón, FL: CRC Press.
30 National Transportation Safety Board (2010). *NTSB/AAR-10/03 loss of thrust in both engines after encountering a flock of birds and subsequent ditching on the Hudson River US Airways Flight 1549 Airbus A320-214, N106US Weehawken, New Jersey January 15, 2009* www.ntsb.gov/investigations/AccidentReports/Reports/AAR1003.pdf.
31 Bureau d'Enquêtes et d'Analyses pour la sécurité de l'aviation civile (2012). *Final Report on the accident on 1st June 2009 to the Airbus A330-203 registered F-GZCP operated by Air France Flight AF 447 Rio de Janeiro – Paris*. www.bea.aero/docspa/2009/f-cp090601.en/pdf/f-cp090601.en.pdf.
32 De Crespigny, R. (2012). *QF32: From the Author of Fly!: Life Lessons from the Cockpit of QF32*. Sydney: Macmillan.
33 Burkill, M., & Burkill, P. (2010). *Thirty Seconds to Impact*. AuthorHouse.
34 National Transportation Safety Board (1990). *NTSB/AAR-90/06 United Airlines Flight 232 McDonnell Douglas DC-I0-10 Sioux Gateway Airport Sioux City, Iowa July 19, 1989* www.ntsb.gov/investigations/AccidentReports/Reports/AAR-90-06.pdf.
35 Lim, Y., Bassien-Capsa, V., Ramasamy, S., Liu, J., & Sabatini, R. (2017). Commercial airline single-pilot operations: System design and pathways to certification. *IEEE Aerospace and Electronic Systems Magazine*, *32*(7), 4–21.
36 Schirmer, S., Torens, C., Nikodem, F., & Dauer, J. (2018, September). Considerations of artificial intelligence safety engineering for unmanned aircraft. In *International Conference on Computer Safety, Reliability, and Security* (pp. 465–472). Springer.
37 Schroeder, C., & Harms, D. (2007). MPL represents a state-of-the-art ab initio airline pilot training programme. *ICAO Journal*, *62*(3), 15–16.
38 Matyszczyk, C. (2019). *Capt. Sully Sullenberger just made chilling statements about the Boeing 737 MAX crash. other pilots disagree*. www.inc.com/chris-matyszczyk/sully-sullenberger-just-made-chilling-statements-about-boeing-737-max-crash-other-pilots-disagree.html.
39 Hartmann, K., & Steup, C. (2013, June). The vulnerability of UAVs to cyber attacks: An approach to the risk assessment. In *2013 5th International Conference on Cyber Conflict (CYCON 2013)* (pp. 1–23). IEEE.
40 Shane, S., & Sanger, D. E. (2011). Drone crash in Iran reveals secret US surveillance effort. *New York Times*, 7. December 7, 2011. www.warcosts.net/wp-content/uploads/drones/517K_2_2011_Drone_Crash_in_Iran_Reveals_Secret_U.S._Surveillance_Effort_Over_Iran_December_7_2011_NYTimes.pdf.
41 Learmount, D. (2008). *Pilot shortage moves to pilot surplus* www.flightglobal.com/news/articles/pilot-shortage-moves-to-pilot-surplus-314849/.

42 Civil Aviation Authority UK (2004). Flight crew reliance on automation https://publicapps.caa.co.uk/docs/33/2004_10.PDF.
43 Air Accidents Investigation Branch (1995). *Report 2/95 report on the incident to Airbus A320-212, G-KMAM London Gatwick Airport on 26 August 1993.*
44 Comisión de Investigación de Accidentes e Incidentes de Aviación Civil (2011). *A-032/2008 Accidente ocurrido a la aeronave McDonnell Douglas DC-9-82 (MD-82), matrícula EC-HFP, operada por la compañía Spanair, en el aeropuerto de Barajas el 20 de agosto de 2008.*
45 Yeh, B. (1998). *Design considerations in Boeing 777 fly-by-wire computers.* Proceedings Third IEEE International High-Assurance Systems Engineering Symposium (Cat. No.98EX231).

Index

ab initio training 89, 90–91, 277; language education 149–162; multi-crew 100–102, 107, 111–112, 114
Absant Group 86
academic intensity 232–233, 235–236
accident-incident analysis 210, 212, 214, 217, 218
accidents 204–205, 277–284, 288; Avianca Flight 052 151, 159–160; Colgan Air Flight 3407 109, 110; CRM 2; Lockheed L-188 Electra 43; safety regulation 262, 268–269
Acharya, A. 50
ACHIEVR 144
active learning, 4 As 119–131
adaptive learning 171
Advanced Aviation Training Devices (AATD) 112
Advanced Certificate in Aviation and Aerospace (ACAA) 243
Advanced Qualification Program (AQP) 102, 202
advance passenger information system (APIS) 263–264
Aer Lingus 224
Aerospace Career Education (ACE) Academy 32
aerospace clusters 7–8
Africa 11–14
African Union Commission, Agenda 84
Agbor, E. 257
Ahangaran, A. G. 256
Airbus Foundation Discovery Space 30
Air Carrier Enhanced Pilot Training (ACE) 113
Air Carrier Training Aviation Rulemaking Committee (ACTARC) 110, 113, 115

Aircraft Fleet Recycling Association (AFRA) 44
aircraft maintenance engineers (AME) 58
Aircraft Owners and Pilots Association (AOPA) 172; High School Initiative 26, 28–29; You Can Fly program 28
Air Line Pilots Association International (ALPA) 105
Airline Safety and Federal Aviation Administration Extension Act (2010) 109
airline transport pilot certification training program (ATP-CTP) 109, 110
airline transport pilot workgroup (ATP-WG) 110
Airman Certification Standards (ACS) 108–109
Airports Council International (ACI) 22, 31, 239, 242, 247, 252, 253
air traffic controllers 24, 106, 149, 150–151, 152, 184, 185, 189, 197, 288
Air Transport Action Group (ATAG) 44, 181
Akcayir, M. 166
Aktas, C. B. 40, 44, 45
Albrecht, U. 164
Albritton, A. 20–23, 154
Alderson, J. C. 151
ALICANTO 20–23
American Association of Applied Linguists (AAAL) 188
American University of Beirut 244
Anderson, E. 56
Anderson, J. R. 95, 122, 124, 125, 127
Anderson, L. 129, 169
animals 267–268
anticipation in learning, 4 As 119–131
Anti-Trust Immunity (ATI) 264–265

Approved Training Organizations
  (ATOs) 105, 106
Araujo, P. 59
ARFlora 166
Arham, A. F. 256
Arthur, W. Jr 248
Asian Development Bank (ADB) 50,
  52–53, 55
assessment feedback loop 169–170
association of learning, 4 As 119–131
Association of Southeast Asian Nations
  (ASEAN) 49–50, 52, 55; ASEAN
  Economic Community (AEC) 49;
  ASEAN Single Aviation Market
  (ASAM) 49
Astin, A. W. 228–229, 231, 235
Atak, A. 161
ATEC Pipeline Report 133
Atlas group 287
Audretsch, D. B. 255
augmented reality (AR) 133, 137–138,
  140, 142, 144–146, 163–164, 165–166,
  173–178
automation 277–280, 283–285
Avianca Flight 052 151, 159–160
Aviation Accreditation Board
  International (AABI) 112, 228
Aviation in Asia (AIA) 54–55
Aviation Australia 134
Aviation English 55, 149–161, 181–199
Aviation Exploring program 30
Aviation Industry Stakeholder Map 181
Aviation Maintenance Technician
  (AMT) schools 133–146
Aviation Maintenance Technology
  (AMT) 184–186, 189–198
Aviation Outreach Model 25–27, 33
Aviation Program Gap Analysis 26
Aviation Safety Network 268
Aviation Skills Manifesto 71, 72, 76–77
Aviation Skills Partnership (ASP) 70, 72,
  73, 75, 77–78
Aviation Skills Plan 70–79
Aviation and Space Education
  (AVSED) 28
Aviators Africa Academy (AAA) 12–13
awareness of learning, 4 As 119–131

Bae, Z. T. 255
Bainbridge, L. 278
Barringer, B. R. 256
Bates, P. 241
behavioural objectives theory 94

Behrstock, E. 254
Belitski, M. 255
Bellotti, B. 173
Beluce, A. C. 146
Bennett, N. 247
Bersin, J. 248
Bertrand, Y. 245
Bhagat, W. 164, 165, 166, 170
Bjerke, E. 102, 152, 153–154, 227–238
Bloom's Taxonomy 129–130, 169,
  172, 173
Boeing 1, 20, 24, 89, 182–183, 204, 227,
  252; adaptive learning 171; certification
  261; community engagement 30;
  Technician Outlook 133
Bombardier CRJ-200 aircraft 172–173
Borgvall, J. 94
Brauhn II, R. D. 194, 197
Brent, R. 168
Brown, L. J. 163–180
Burrows, A. 38
Bygate, M. 156

cabin crew: Cambodia 63; number
  required 262–263; situated learning
  93–99; virtual reality 165; world
  demand 1, 24
cadet programs 1, 89–90
Cambodia 49–68; Rectangular Strategy
  50, 51, 55
Cambodia Air Traffic Services (CATS) 57
Campbell-Laird, K. 154
Canada 225, 262–263, 264, 265,
  266–267, 269; pilot shortage 15–19
Canadian Aviation Maintenance Council
  (CAMC) 17
Carbon Offsetting and Reduction
  Scheme for International Aviation
  (CORSIA) 265, 269
Catchpole, D. 91
Center for Creative Leadership 248
Certified Flight Instructor (CFI)
  101–102
Chamberlain, J. 175
Cha, M. S. 255
change agents, sustainability 36–48
Chang, R. 166
Charter for Aviation Skills 71
Chbab Srey 56
Chicago Convention 262, 263
Chickering, A. 168
Childs, R. J. 100–118
Circelli, D. 152

Civil Aviation Authority (CAA) 71, 73, 74–75, 287
Civil Aviation Authority of Singapore (CAAS) 58–59
Civil Aviation Safety Authority (CASA) 134
Civil Aviation Training Center (CATC) 55–57, 60, 63
ClarK, P. 36–48
Clark, R. C. 134, 135, 136
Code of Federal Regulations (CFR) 107
cognitive overload 138
Cohen, L. 94
Colgan Air Flight 3407 accident 109, 110
collegiate flight programs 227–238
community partnerships 40–41, 44, 45–46
Community of Portuguese Speaking Countries (CPLP) 84, 85, 86
competency-based education (CBE) 94, 95, 100, 102, 106–107, 113–114
competency life cycle management 254–256
competency model 252–253
Content-Based Language Teaching (CBLT) 150, 155–156
continuous partial attention 122
controller-pilot data link communications (CPDLC) 150
Corporate Social Responsibility (CSR) 44
Costa, A. 18
Coughlan, R. 243
Coutu, P. 242
Creswell, J. W. 96
Crew Resource Management (CRM) 2, 100–101, 103, 108, 113, 159–160; EBT 203, 206; language 150
Crisp, G. T. 139
Crotty, P. T. 240, 243
Crouch, B. 120, 131
Cunningham, T. 94

Dahlstrom, N. 102, 105–106, 107
Dalvi, M. R. 256
Damos, D. L. 94
declarative knowledge 124
De Klerk, S. 178
Delise, L. A. 100
de Neufville, R. 18
Department of Transportation (DOT) 267, 268
descriptive analytics 253
Dessler, G. 252

Díaz-Méndez, M. 247
Dickson, S. 110
Dimock, M. 119, 120
disabled passengers 267
Disaster Threshold 280–282, 285–286
distributive practice techniques 126
Dollinger, M. 246
Douglas, J. 247
Draganidis, F. 255
Drappier, J. 203
Dreams Soar 33
Dresner, S. 15
Dromereschi, M. I. 255
drones 284, 285
Dunleavy, M. 138
Dusenbury, M. 152, 153–154

Eagleman, D. 119, 121, 122
Ecological Interface Design (EID) 278, 283
economy: Cambodia 50–52; economic regulation 264–265; NGAP context 181–184
education 81–83; 4 As of learning 119–132; learning strategies 121–122, 128–130; Portugal 84–88, *see also* learning
Edwards, C. 206
e-learning, technicians 133–147
Elliott, J. 146
Ellsberg, M. 56
El-Zein, A. 38
Embry-Riddle Aeronautical University (ERAU) 101, 187
Emery, H. 152, 154, 155, 156
emotional support animals 267–268
employee competency life cycle (ECLC) 254–256
Engle, M. 159–160
English for Academic Purposes (EAP) 152, 153, 186
English as the Medium of Instruction (EMI) 152
English for Occupational Purposes (EOP) *see* Workplace English
English for Specific Purposes (ESP) 150, 151, 186
Enhanced Qualification Program (EQP) 110, 111, 113, 115
Enterprise Resource Planning 280
entrepreneurial mindset development 252–260

environmental issues 37, 38
environmental regulations 265, 269
European Aviation Safety Agency (EASA) 134, 144
European Cockpit Association (ECA) 105, 106
European Commission 26
European Flight Academy 91
European Space Agency (ESA), Partnership for Global Sustainability 9–10
European Union: Emissions Trading System 265; passenger rights 266
Everything But Arms (EBA) scheme 51
evidence-based training (EBT) 106–107, 114, 201–224, 242
executive education 239–251
Experiential Education (ExpEd) 177
Experimental Aircraft Association (EAA) 28, 30; Young Eagles 26, 29

Farris, P. W. 240
Farrow, D. R. 101
Fayer, S. 26
fear of missing out (FOMO) 122
Federal Aviation Administration (FAA) 26, 28, 100, 102, 103, 106, 108–114, 197, 228, 252; Aviation Maintenance Technician (AMT) schools 133–146; FAA/Industry Training Standards (FITS) 108; WITC 175–176
Federal Aviation Regulations (FARs) 107–108
Felder, R. M. 168
Ferroff, C. V. 96
Fewster, S. H. 253
Filbeck, G. 243
Filgo, K. M. 137
Fitzgerald, P. P. 261–276
flight attendants *see* cabin crew
Flight Crew Licensing and Training Panel (FCLTP) 102
Flight Data Analysis (FDA) 202, 205, 210
Flight Officer Qualification Aviation Rulemaking Committee (FOQ ARC) 109
Flight Operations Quality Assurance (FOQA) 202, 210
Flight Safety Foundation 114
Flight Safety International 150
flight schools, Canada 17, 18
flight training academies 90

Flin, R. 101, 106–107
flow programs 89–90
Folse, K. S. 160
Ford, C. L. 25
Fraher, A. L. 101
Friginal, E. 154, 155, 156, 159, 187
Fuller, A. 95
Fulmer, R. M. 241, 242
Fulu, E. 56
Fundamentals of Air Transport course 31

gaming 163–164, 173, 178, 288
Gamson, Z. 168
Gannon, T. F. 36, 43
Gardner, M. 146
gender: African aviation 12–13; Cambodia 56–57; gap 17; outreach 31–33
generational differences 119–122
Gen Z 37, 45, 120–122, 124–131
German prewar model 286–287
Giddings, B. 16
Girls in Aviation Day (GIAD) 26, 31, 32
Girls Fly Programme in Africa (GFPA) Foundation 32–33
Gittens, A. 17
Gladwin, T. N. 15
Glass, G. V. 136
go-arounds 212
Goodwin, J. 241, 242
Grace, M. 120, 126, 128
Graham, N. 209, 211
green curriculum 42
Gummesson, E. 247
Gundry, L. K. 255

Hainey, T. 173
Harms, D. 102, 105
Harris, D. 101
Harry, C. V. 57
Hays, R. T. 137, 145
Heckman, R. J. 254
Hedemann, C. 38
Heidema, J. 18
Helmrich, R. L. 214
Hocking, N. S. 111
Hodge, S. 93–99
Hofstede, 159–160
Holder, B. 151
HoloLens 164, 167–168, 172, 173–174
Hopwood, B. 15, 16
Houssaye, J. 245

Huang, V. 24–35
Huby smartphone application 10
Hurra, G. 240
Hutchins, E. 151
hybrid delivery 133, 134–135, 137, 138, 140, 146

iFly Academy 12, 13–14
Input-Environment-Outcome (I-E-O) model 228–234
Instructional Needs Assessment (INA) 191–192
instructional systems design (ISD) 102–103
Instrument Landing System (ILS) 204
interactive learning 135
Interactive Qualifying Project (IQP) 44
interdisciplinary approach 40
International Air Transport Association (IATA) 11, 15, 24, 31, 54, 85, 89, 102; digital learning 249; EBT 201, 206, 210, 214; executive education 239; Human Resources Report 256–257; MPL 103, 105, 106, 107; passenger growth 241; regulation 268; Training and Qualification Initiative (ITQI) 203, 253
International Association of Aviation and Aerospace Education (ALICANTO) 20–23
International Civil Aviation Organization (ICAO) 11, 24, 55, 93, 252–253, 268; CORSIA 265, 269; EBT 201, 209, 211, 242; executive education 239, 242, 247; FCLTP 102; language 149, 150–151, 153, 154–155, 159, 160, 184–185, 197–198; MPL 100, 102–107, 111, 113–115; NGAP Index 10; NGAP initiative 2, 20–21, 31, 33, 58–59, 71; NGAP Summits 20, 22; passenger-focused regulation 265–266; pilot retirement age 263; Safety Management Manual 281; safety standards 262; safety training 94, 95; security regulation 263; SHELL Model 159
International Federation of Airline Pilots' Association (IFALPA) 22, 105, 106, 206
International Federation of Air Traffic Controllers' Associations (IFATCA) 22
International Language Testing Association (ILTA) 188

International Transport Association 84
International Women in Aviation Conference 31
International Women in Aviation Organization 11, 31
inter–transdisciplinary approach 40
InterVistas Consulting 85
Intuitive Risk Matrix 206, 218
Ireland, R. D. 256
ISEC Lisboa 86
Itani, N. 239–251

JetBlue, Pilot Gateway Program 111
Jetstar Airlines 145
JetXplore 164, 172
Johnson, B. 120, 121
Johnson, K. J. 133–148
Jones, M. 50

Katiluite, E. 41, 42
Kato, P. 178
Kay, M. 149, 157
Kearns, S. K. 1–4, 5–6, 15–19, 31, 81–83, 95, 102, 113–114, 225–226, 228
Kelly, G. 56
Kennelly, J. J. 15
Khek, N. 59
Khmer Rouge 62
Kikkawa, Y. 93–99
King, J. 175
Kingma, S. 161
Kishino, F. 167
Klinect, J. 214
Kluge, A. 164, 168
knowledge co-creation 244–247
knowledge, skills, and attitudes (KSAs) 100
Knowlton Foundation 30
Kourousis, K. I. 7
Krathwohl, D. 129, 169
Krause, T. S. 15
Kuehn, M. R. 253
Kukovec, A. 151
Kuratko, D. F. 255

Lambrechts, W. 37
language: ab initio training 149–162; Aviation English 55, 149–161, 181–199
Language Proficiency Requirements (LPRs) 150–151, 154
Lappas, I. 7
Larrea, M. F. 93–99

Latorella, K. 175
Lave, J. 93, 95
Law of Requisite Variety 282, 283
learning: curriculum 95; objectives 94, 124, 129–130, 156, 170–173, 248; preferences 121; strategies 121–125, 128–130
Learning Management System (LMS) 135–137, 140, 248
Ledwaba, R. 32–33
Lemoine, J. 247
Leonard, A. 227–238
Leveson, N. 282
Levy, S. 50
Lewis, R. E. 254
Lin, D. Y. 252
Line Operations Safety Audits (LOSA) 201–202, 205, 210, 214–217
line-oriented flight training (LOFT) 103
Lin, J. 156
Linkedin Learning 247–248
Lippert, R. L. 241
Lippincott, T. 111
LMQ system 206
local governments 7–10
Lockheed L-188 Electra accidents 43
Lockheed Martin 165
Lomperis, A. E. 181–200
long-term memory 123, 127
Lufthansa 111, 246
Lufthansa Aviation Training (LAT) 91
Luhmann, N. 280
Lundgren, D. 110
Lusch, R. F. 246
Lusófona University 86
Lutte, R. K. 24–35, 89–92
Ly, S. 51

McCarthy, P. 244
McEachern, B. 239
McGill University 268
McGovern, M. E. 51
McGrew, L. 57
McGunagle, D. 36–48
McManners, P. J. 37, 41
Madathil, K. C. 138
Magd, H. 252–260
Mahony, P. H. 94
Malott, D. 102
Manson, D. 133–148
market fundamentalism 282
Markhoff, S. 111
Martinez, A. 100–118

Martinez, D. 239
Martin-Gutierrez, J. 135
Martin, L. 107
Martin, W. M. 190
Mathews, E. 155, 157
Maurer, J. 194
Mavin, T. J. 93–99
Mayer, R. E. 125, 134, 135, 136
media involvement 61
Medina, J. 122, 125, 127, 128
Mell, J. 155
Mellor, M. 15
memorization 123, 124–125, 126, 127
memory system 122–123
Mentzas, G. 255
Mercer 7
mergers 264–265
Meszaros, J. A. 49–68
Metal Neutral Joint Venture (MNJV) 265, 269
Metrass-Mendes, A. 18
Milgram, P. 167
Millar, E. 38
Miller's Law of 7 123
Mills, R. W. 89–92
Ministry of Women's Affairs (MoWA) 55, 56
minority groups 17
Mislevy, R. J. 178
Mitchell, S. 120
mixed reality (MR) 163–180
Mohr, E. S. 37
Mohr, K. A. J. 37
Monat, J. P. 36, 43
Moreira, M. C. 7–10
Multi–Crew Pilot License (MPL) 100, 102–107, 110–111, 113–115, 277
multi–disciplinary approach 40
multi–piloted operations 100–118
Munakata, M. 44–45
Murphy, D. 173
Myrsiades, L. 243

National Aeronautics and Space Administration (NASA) 28; Partnership for Global Sustainability 9–10; workshop 2
National Apprenticeship Service 73
National Civil Aviation Authority (ANAC) 86

National Education Association (NEA) 26, 54
National Navigation Services (NAV Portugal) 86
National Transportation Safety Board (NTSB) 109, 198
Nawata, Y. 153
Nazir, S. 164, 165
Ngbako, S. G. 11–14
Niemczyk, M. 119–132
Nishikawa, M. 153
Nisula, J. 218
No-Country-Left-Behind (NCLB) 59
Noe, R. A. 252
Nomura, S. 151
non-destructive testing (NDT) 165
nongovernment organizations (NGOs) 50
non-native English speakers (NNES) 149–161
Noonoo, S. 121
Norden, C. 219
NOTECHS 206

O'Brien, G. 15, 16
Ohio State University Career Eagles Aviation Initiative 30
Okal, A. 15–19
Oklahoma State University (OSU) 113
Oliveira, K. L. D. 146
Oman Airport Management Company (OAMC) 258
Omann, I. 16
Operation Bolero 277, 286–287
O'Reilly Learning 247–248
Organizational Needs Assessment (ONA) 191
Organization of Black Aerospace Professionals (OBAP) 32
original equipment manufacturers (OEMs) 21, 137, 205–206
Orr, A. 149–162
Oster, C. 110
outreach 24–35; Aviation in Asia (AIA) 54–55; Cambodia 60
ownership requirements 264

Paneo, M. 7
Pantelidis, V. S. 138, 141, 142
Paramasivam, S. 156
passenger-focused regulation 265–267
passenger name record (PNR) 263–264
passenger rights 266–267

Passos, C. 146
pedagogic space 244–247
PEGASUS 21
people analytics 253
Peou, S. 50
Perrow, C. 282
perspective analysis 253
pilot in command (PIC) 101
Pilot Competencies 206–208
pilots: Canadian shortage 15–19; cockpit teamwork 100–101; gender gap 17; industry partnerships 89–92; limited licenses 284–285; minority groups 17; multi-piloted operations 100–118; retirement age 263; shortage paradox 277–293; single 284–285; students 1; world demand 1–2, 20, 24, 204, 227
Pilot Training Next (PTN) program 163, 171
Pol Pot 62
Ponte de Sor 8–10
Portugal: higher education 84–88; Ponte de Sor 8–10
Portugal Air Summit 9–10
positive disruption approach 70
poverty, Cambodia 50, 51
Prahalad, C. K. 246
predictive analytics 253
Present Situation Analysis (PSA) 192
Prince, C. 241
privatization 261–262
Project Aerospace 32

Quadros, R. C. e 84–88

Rachal, K. 121, 123
Ram, A. 15–19
Ramaswamy, V. 246
regulation of the airline industry 261–276
rehearsal strategies 123, 124–125, 126, 127
Reid, R. 20–23
Restricted-Airline Transport Pilot (R-ATP) 100, 109–112, 115
retention of aviation professionals 81, 225–293; collegiate flight programs 227–238; entrepreneurial mindset development 252–260; executive education 239–251
Revel, P. 20–23
Rhoden, S. 94
risk management 101

Roberts, J. 149–162, 187
role-play 94
Rosenkrans, W. 107
rote-learning 124
Royal Aeronautical Society 269
Ruggerberg, B. J. 254
Rupasinghe, T. D. 165
Rus, R. C. 38

safety 280–282; regulation 262–263, 268–269; training 94, 95
Sánchez-Alarcos Ballesteros, J. 277–293
Sasanelli, N. 7
Scheiter, K. 136
Schneider, M. 240
Schoenberg, I. E. 194
Schroeder, C. 102, 105
Schunk, D. H. 114
science, technology, engineering, and mathematics (STEM) 13, 14; aviation outreach 26, 28, 32, 33; sustainability 36–48
Scully, J. 201–224
seat-size regulation 267, 269
Sector Skills Councils 73
security regulation 263–264
Seemiller, C. 120, 126, 128
Segalas, J. 38, 42
Serious Games (SG) 173
service animals 267–268
Shalley, C. 255
SHELL Model 159
Shield, S. 243
shortage-surplus cycles 287
short-term memory 123
Shrock, S. A. 121
Sihanouk, N. 62
Silva, M. F. F. 8
simulators 94, 102, 109, 112, 202–203, 277, 288
Singapore 50, 58–59
Singapore Aviation Academy (SAA) 58
Sing, C. C. 49
Singer, M. J. 137, 145
Single African Air Transport Market (SAATM) 84, 87
situated learning, cabin crew 93–99
Sivhuoch, O. 50
Skehan, P. 156
SkillsFuture initiative 58
Sliney, A. 173
socialization in discipline 233–234, 236
social practice 93, 95

social sustainability 16
Solomon, C. M. 240
Soros, F. 282
Sosulski, K. 135, 136
Soule, A. J. 240, 243
South Africa, iFly Academy 12, 13–14
South Korea's International Cooperation Agency (KOICA) 55
Spangenberg, J. H. 16
Sreang, C. 50
Staniskis, J. K. 41, 42
Staples VR 144–145
State Secretariat of Civil Aviation (SSCA) 55, 57
stealth assessment 139
Stewart, J. 241
Stoller, F. L. 155
Strickler, M. K. Jr 28
Sullenberger, S. 285
sustainability: Canadian pilots 15–19; STEM 36–48
Sustainable Aviation Fuel Users Group (SAFUG) 44
Sustainable Aviation Guidance Alliance (SAGA) 44
Sustainable Development Goals 50
Sutliff, D. 100–118
Swain, M. 156
Syed, R. T. 252–260
systems thinking approach 38, 43

talent management 252–260
Tan, A. K. J. 49–50
Tanggaard, L. 41
Tan, M. 59
Target Situation Analysis (TSA) 192
Task-Based Language Teaching (TBLT) 150, 156
Taylor, F. W. 277, 282
technical and vocational training institutes (TVET) 52–53, 55
technicians: skills 288; training 133–148, 181–200; world demand 1, 20, 24
technology 290; digital learning 152, 163, 166, 248–249; digital natives 120; e-learning 133–147; executive education 244–245; Gen Z 120; mixed reality 163–180, *see also* augmented reality (AR); automation; mixed reality (MR); virtual reality (VR)
Tennant, M. 94
Test of English as a Foreign Language (TOEFL) 154

Thavry, T. 57
threat and error management (TEM) 101, 103, 105
Thurer, M. 38
Tinto, V. 228
Toomey, A. H. 40
transdisciplinary approach 40
transformational leadership 257
Transport Canada Civil Aviation 101
Travis, J. 168
Tullo, F. J. 100, 101
Turney, M. A. 56
twinning 134–135, 137, 138, 140, 146

Ulrich, J. 120
United Aviate program 90
United Nations 50
United States 269; multi-crew pilot training 107–115; passenger rights 266–267; security regulation 263–264
United States Air Force (USAF) 163, 171
University Aviation Association (UAA) 112, 113, 227, 235
university aviation programs 21–23, 30, 100, 111–115
University of Clemson 144
University of Nebraska at Omaha Aviation Institute (UNOAI) 30
Unstable Approach Paradox 212
user transparency 279

V1 cut 202–203, 204
Vaidya, A. 44–45
Vai, M. 135, 136
value co-creation 246–247
Van Dam, A. 17
Van Eck, R. N. 139
Vargo, S. L. 246
Varney, M. 107, 201–224
violence, Cambodia 56
virtual reality (VR) 133, 137–138, 140, 142, 144–146, 163–165, 173–174, 177
Vlasek, S. 30
vocational training, Cambodia 52–53
volunteer service 44
Vrasida, C. 136

Waiz, S. 33
weather 175–177
Weather Technology in the Cockpit (WTIC) 175–176
WeatherXplore 175–177
Webb, S. 243
Wenger, E. 93, 95
Western Michigan University (WMU) 164
Whitehurst, G. 175, 176, 177
Wikander, R. 102, 105–106, 107
Wilson, J. R. 146
Wilson, S. 120, 121
Wittrock, M. C. 125
Witts, S. 69–79
women see gender
Women in Aviation International (WAI) 31; Girls in Aviation Day (GIAD) 26, 31, 32
Worcester Polytechnic Institute 44
Workplace English 186, 189–199
World Bank 50, 51–52
World Commission on Environment and Development 15
World Economic Forum: Future of Jobs Report 26; Global Human Capital Report 52
World Tourism Organization 49

Yadav, M. 252–260
Yamoussoukro Decision 84–85
Yasin, R. M. 38
You Can Fly program 28
Young Aviation Professionals Program 31
Young Eagles program 26, 29

zero revenue test 264
Zimmerman, B. J. 114, 123, 125, 128, 129, 130
Zizka, L. 36–48
Zoller, U. 40
Zsoka, A. 38, 42

For Product Safety Concerns and Information please contact our EU
representative GPSR@taylorandfrancis.com
Taylor & Francis Verlag GmbH, Kaufingerstraße 24, 80331 München, Germany

www.ingramcontent.com/pod-product-compliance
Lightning Source LLC
Chambersburg PA
CBHW071802300426
44116CB00009B/1180